MAGILL'S
SURVEY
OF
AMERICAN
LITERATURE

MAGILL'S SURVEY OF AMERICAN LITERATURE

Volume 4

McCarthy–O'Hara

Edited by
FRANK N. MAGILL

Marshall Cavendish Corporation
New York • London • Toronto • Sydney • Singapore

Published By
Marshall Cavendish Corporation
2415 Jerusalem Avenue
P.O. Box 587
North Bellmore, New York 11710
United States of America

∞ The paper used in these volumes conforms to the American National Standard for Permanence of Paper for Printed Library Materials, Z39.48-1984.

Library of Congress Cataloging-in-Publication Data
Magill's survey of American literature. Edited by Frank N. Magill.
    p. cm.
  Includes bibliographical references and index.
    1. American literature—Dictionaries. 2. American literature—Bio-bibliography. 3. Authors, American—Biography—Dictionaries. I. Magill, Frank Northen, 1907.
PS21.M34 1991
810.9'0003—dc20
ISBN 1-85435-437-X (set)   91-28113
ISBN 1-85435-441-8 (volume 4)   CIP

CONTENTS

MAGILL'S
SURVEY
OF
AMERICAN
LITERATURE

CORMAC McCARTHY

Born: Providence, Rhode Island
July 20, 1933

Principal Literary Achievement

McCarthy, one of the most important contemporary American novelists, has consistently extended the boundaries of what can be done with the English language and the novel.

Biography

Cormac McCarthy, like many of the characters in his novels, has kept moving from place to place, responding keenly to the pulse of his new settings. McCarthy was born in Providence, Rhode Island, and at the age of four moved to Knoxville, Tennessee, with his parents, Charles Joseph and Gladys McGrail McCarthy. After being graduated from a Catholic high school in Knoxville, McCarthy attended the University of Tennessee in 1951-1952. The next year he spent wandering around the country and doing odd jobs. He finally returned to the university in 1957 after four years' service in the Air Force. In 1960, the English department recognized his talent by granting him an Ingram-Merrill Award for creative writing. This may have encouraged him to leave school and devote his attention completely to his writing, which he did the same year, without receiving a degree. Since then McCarthy has eschewed academic patronage, though he has been the beneficiary of a number of generous institutional grants.

McCarthy's first novel, *The Orchard Keeper* (1965), like his subsequent fiction up to *Blood Meridian: Or, The Evening Redness in the West* (1985), draws upon his intimate knowledge of eastern Tennessee, the area where he spent his childhood and early manhood. The novel, written in Sevier County, Tennessee; Asheville, North Carolina; and Chicago, won the William Faulkner Foundation Award for best first novel by an American writer. By the time the novel was published, McCarthy had been granted a fellowship by the American Academy of Arts and Letters for travel abroad. His European travels, supported further by a Rockefeller Foundation grant (1966-1968), took him to London, Paris, and the island of Ibiza, while he worked on his second novel, *Outer Dark* (1968).

McCarthy returned to the United States in 1967, now married and with a completed novel. He and his wife, Anne de Lisle, a singer from Hamble, England, whom he had met on his travels, settled on a small farm in Rockford, Tennessee. Yet an-

other grant, a Guggenheim Fellowship for writing fiction, came his way in 1969.

During his career, McCarthy has, on the average, produced a novel every five or six years. *Child of God* came out in 1974, followed by *Suttree* in 1979, a novel on which he had worked throughout the late 1960's and the 1970's. Between the publication of those two novels, McCarthy, collaborating with film director Richard Pearce, wrote the script of "The Gardener's Son," included in the Public Broadcasting Service's series *Visions*. The drama, based on an actual 1876 murder in Graniteville, South Carolina, embodies themes to which McCarthy has typically been drawn. Rob McEvoy, a crippled son of a laboring family, kills the son of a mill-owning family. The event, as portrayed by McCarthy, is fraught with moral ambiguity. Of McEvoy, the murderer, McCarthy has said, "The kid was a natural rebel, probably just a troublemaker in real life. But in our film he has a certain nobility. He stands up and says, 'No, this is intolerable and I want to do something about it.' "

In the early 1980's, McCarthy's work was supported by grants from the Lyndhurst Foundation and the John D. and Catherine T. MacArthur Foundation. Though not going to the lengths of his contemporary Thomas Pynchon, McCarthy has chosen to live a secluded life, preserving his privacy and avoiding publicity. For some time he has lived in West Texas, a region he drew upon in the writing of *Blood Meridian*.

McCarthy's works, while well received by reviewers and admired by writers including Robert Penn Warren, Saul Bellow, Ralph Ellison, and Guy Davenport, have not enjoyed wide popular appeal. Fortunately, however, through the Ecco Press and Random House's Vintage Contemporaries, most of his novels are now available to readers in paperback.

Analysis

An overview of Cormac McCarthy's work shows the sure and steady development of the writer's craft, a deepening of metaphysical content, and expansion of thematic interests. His first four novels are rooted in the geography and experience of East Tennessee, the region where McCarthy grew up, while his fifth, *Blood Meridian*, moves from Tennessee to the American Southwest and Mexico during the 1840's.

From early in his career, following the publication of *The Orchard Keeper*, comparisons have been drawn between the Tennessee writer and William Faulkner, his Mississippi predecessor. There is certainly ample ground for comparisons to be made. The fictional worlds of both writers are rooted in their Southern experiences. Like Faulkner, McCarthy has been an innovator in language, capturing regional idioms and imbuing his prose with a luminous verbal quality. The narrative designs, not to mention the naturalistic burdens, of *Outer Dark* and *Child of God* often remind one of Faulkner, especially *As I Lay Dying* (1930) and *Sanctuary* (1931). McCarthy's work, however, is not derivative, and any comparison must emphasize his uniqueness. The social fabric of Faulkner's world is generally much richer and more interlocking than that of McCarthy, with the possible exception of *Suttree*. Faulkner's modernistic narrative technique allows for the expression of more of his characters' thoughts and subjective reactions than do McCarthy's tightly controlled, omniscient storylines. With *Blood Meridian*, McCarthy's style and concerns become unquestionably his own, not only as a result of shifting the locus of dramatic action from the South, but also by concentrating more intently on the problematic natures of human violence and evil.

Often McCarthy's narratives are shaped by the journeys they inscribe. The condition of homelessness and wandering are themes which run through the writer's oeuvre. In *The Orchard Keeper* John Wesley Rattner's search seems in part to be for his father who, unbeknown to him, has been murdered. At the end of the novel he is paying homage to his mother's grave. The movement of Culla and Rinthy Holme, in *Outer Dark*, as they look for each other and the offspring of their incestuous union, is a relentless groping for familial bonds and for an elusive home. Lester Ballard, the central character in *Child of God*, is left an orphan after his mother deserts him and his father hangs himself. Ever the outcast, fleeing the law, Lester's necrophilia seems a grotesque parody of love, a doomed attempt to reconstitute the family he never had. In *Blood Meridian*, the Kid loses his mother at birth and runs away from his father when he is fourteen, initiating a story chronicling his vagrant travels in an amoral universe.

McCarthy forces one to see and contemplate things one would normally find repulsive and would rather turn away from. In writing on *Child of God*, critic Doris Grumbach asserts that McCarthy "has allowed us direct communion with his special kind of chaos; every sentence he writes illuminates, if only for a moment, the great dark of madness and violence and inevitable death that surrounds us all." Lester Ballard's necrophilia, Culla and Rinthy Holme's incestuous relationship in *Outer Dark*, and the gross violence in *Blood Meridian* are all rendered beautifully, with subdued values of a sympathetic human vision, producing for the reader that odd union of disgust and thrill often associated with the Gothic.

Cormac McCarthy's project is an exploration of what humanity is, and his investigations take him to the fringes, aberrations where something has gone slightly afoul. His naturalistic inclinations lead him unflinchingly to follow the course of deformed lives, suggesting what a delicate social and biological machine man is and in what close proximity humankind is to perversion and violence. Lester Ballard, the reader is told, is "a child of God much like yourself perhaps." A haunting ambivalence lurks in the positioning of that "perhaps."

Subterranean worlds exist concurrently with the world on the surface, a thin membrane separating the two. The cavern figures frequently throughout McCarthy's work as a metaphor for the submerged and primordial. In *The Orchard Keeper*, young boys explore caves and find "the inscriptions etched in the soft and curdcolored stone, hearts and names, archaic dates, crudely erotic hieroglyphs—the bulbed phallus and strange centipedal vulva of small boys' imaginations." In *Child of God*, Lester Ballard finally takes refuge in a cave, moving his collection of dead companions. In *Suttree*, one of Gene Harrogate's hare-brained plots is to cause the city's bank to collapse into the cavernous reaches beneath Knoxville. With Suttree he talks over his scheme:

I reckon once a feller got in under there he could go anywheres he took a notion right in under the ground there couldnt he?

I dont know, Gene. There's lots of cave under there. Suttree was pulling a wire minnowbucket from the bottom of the river by a long cord. He swung it dripping to the rail and opened the top and lifted out two beers and . . . handed one to Harrogate and leaned back against the houseboat wall.

That goddamned truck like to of fell plumb out of sight.

I saw it.

What if the whole goddamned building was to just up and sink?

What about two or three buildings?

What about a whole block? Harrogate was waving his bottle about. Goddamn, he said. What if the whole fuckin city was to cave in?

That's the spirit, said Suttree.

A salient feature of McCarthy's fiction is the rich linguistic texture of the prose itself. Opaque, concrete, deceptively realistic, the words turn in on themselves, creating a world of their own, cut from their referential moorings. Detailed descriptions of the physical landscape are juxtaposed with sparse dialogue. The end result is that man is given a place in the universe no more elevated or sacred than the natural world which surrounds his. McCarthy's characters are not loquacious. They say what they need to in order to get what they want, in a thoroughly natural diction. Rarely is access given to the consciousness of characters. One sees what they do and what they say, but seldom are motives explicitly displayed, leaving readers to form their own interpretations and moral judgements. Characters themselves, in fact, seem to lack any self-consciousness of their own actions. Detached from their egos, they perceive things "unshaped by the construction of a mind obsessed with form."

Underlying McCarthy's work lies the profound mystery of what incomprehensible, implacable force moves humankind. What keeps these characters going? McCarthy's vision may often seem to be nihilistic and cruelly Gothic, with a relentless rapacity, yet it is not without a slim possibility of grace and redemption.

THE ORCHARD KEEPER

First published: 1965
Type of work: Novel

The lives of three men, outlaws of different kinds and ages, and various animals crisscross in the hills of eastern Tennessee.

Upon the publication of *The Orchard Keeper*, granted the William Faulkner Foundation Award for the best first novel by an American writer, Cormac McCarthy's promising literary talents were recognized; the young writer was singled out as a force to be watched and reckoned with.

Like a number of his subsequent novels, *The Orchard Keeper* is set in eastern

Tennessee. Its topography is related intimately in stunning prose, creating a remarkable, richly textured linguistic surface to the novel. Setting, for McCarthy, is of paramount importance. In fact, geographic contours seem to precede and form the characters which act within its folds. This stands as a kind of philosophical principle for McCarthy, who places the human dimension of life in perspective, always vigilantly invoking the presence of larger, more powerful, mystical forces that drive and control people's lives. The hilly region east of Knoxville is perfect for supporting the thematic thrust of the novel. During the time the novel is set, in the 1930's and early 1940's, the area was yet outside the jurisdiction of law and beyond the reach of modern civilization. The land itself, and the connection of its tenants to it, represents a cultural value akin to that espoused by Southern Agrarian writers such as John Crowe Ransom, Robert Penn Warren, Allen Tate, and others.

Threatened is man's ability to live independent of society's conventions and inflexible legal dictates. The novel serves as an elegy to a heroic past in which man lived in harmony with nature and made, individually, his own moral determinations. As McCarthy says in the last lines of the novel, its characters are among the last of their kind:

> They are gone now. Fled, banished in death or exile, lost, undone. Over the land sun and wind still move to burn and sway the trees, the grasses. No avatar, no scion, no vestige of that people remains. On the lips of the strange race that now dwells there their names are myth, legend, dust.

Only gradually does the reader come to know about the three main characters whose lives the novel intertwines: Marion Sylder, a bootlegger, John Wesley Rattner, a young boy who traps illegally, and Arthur Ownsby, an old, single man who is the orchard keeper. Though these characters have no discernible relation to one another when the reader meets them, they are drawn to one another as the narrative unfolds. Sylder has killed John Wesley's father, partly in self defense, without even knowing who the man was. The body of the dead man is dumped by Sylder into an insecticide-spray tank on the old decaying orchard kept by Ownsby. Ownsby finds the body but keeps it a secret, making periodic ritualistic visits to the makeshift grave, watching the body decay. Ownsby knows Sylder only by the car he used to run whiskey past the orchard, and he has no inkling he is responsible for the murder. John Wesley, however, knows both of them. He develops a friendship with the old man and comes to know Sylder after rescuing him from a creek where Sylder lands after driving his car off the road.

All of this is gathered in bits and pieces throughout the novel, for the narrative of *The Orchard Keeper* is the most disjunctive of any of McCarthy's novels. The characters themselves are thrifty with their speech; they keep things to themselves. Scenes are short and episodic, with periodic flashbacks triggered by characters' memories. Because the focus continually shifts, abruptly, without any signs as to with whom and where one is, the reader must continually adjust to new orientations. Plots are arrogant impositions on disconnected events. What McCarthy seems intent on uplifting in this novel is the remarkable random rhythm of human experience.

A sense of defeat lies heavily over the novel's end. The law, standing in conflict with a harmony of natural and human values, prevails. The old orchard keeper is hunted down, finally arrested for shooting an "X" in a metal tank, which he takes is a gross intrusion in his life, and committed to an asylum. Sylder is picked up by the law, too, for transportation of illegal substances. The boy, John Wesley, leaves the area, returning some years later, in the last episode of the novel, to find his mother's grave.

OUTER DARK

First published: 1968
Type of work: Novel

A brother and sister search for each other and the child born of their incestuous union, abandoned by its father and found by a tinker.

McCarthy's second novel pursues thematic issues raised in *The Orchard Keeper*, though its narrative is channeled more rigorously. The novel is about union, its sundering, and the perpetual questing which ensues.

The narrative is set in motion by the birth of a son to Rinthy Holme, the product of a union with her brother, Culla, with whom she lives alone in an unspecified place (bearing resemblances to eastern Tennessee). No genealogical or social references guide or orient their lives. Living alone, cut off from any social contact with anyone, theirs is an order primordial, prior to civilizing influences. Despite the absence of underpinnings for a socially determined morality, their acts have consequences and the brother and sister are condemned to wander across the countryside, by foot, helplessly and ceaselessly.

After the birth, Culla, feeling the guilt associated with the unnatural union, takes the child into the woods to die. An old tinker, however, comes across the child and picks it up to carry along with his other illegitimate wares—dirty books and moonshine. Instinctively Rinthy knows that the tinker has taken her child and commences her search for him. Culla, in turn, leaves to find his sister when he finds that she is gone. The story then follows the respective journeys of the brother and sister, parallel yet separate and unique. The worlds of the brother and sister are kept distinctly apart in the metaphysical realm and in the narrative. Neither sees the other; neither path intersects the other, as close as they might get to each other. One knows little of what they think, or if they think at all.

The two seem to move through the landscape almost like apparitions, guided by some omnipotent force unknown to either. Rinthy is driven by her maternal instinct to find and care for her child. Her milk never dries up, a sign that the forces that move her are deep, impersonal, and universal. Though distinctly vulnerable, she seems only vaguely aware of possible dangers along the way. She is taken care of by those whose paths she crosses, as if they intuitively recognize her natural purity and innocence of the world's ways.

Culla, responsible for the child's conception and the abandonment which sent Rinthy off in its search, is driven by guilt. Indifferent to his fate, perhaps thinking his ill luck a fitting retribution for his acts, he takes what comes to him, moving "in a void, claustral to sound." His wandering itself, let alone his cowed attitude, marks him. As he passes through places of permanence, he is suspect, taken one time for a fleeing felon, another time for a grave robber; another time he is accused of causing a horde of hogs to march off a cliff to their death. Finally, after a dramatic scene in which he barely survives the overturning of a makeshift river ferry, Culla is driven into the company of three malevolent marauders who abuse him, take his shoes, and bend his will by threats. The unprincipled nihilism of the gang's leader, who follows a law of brute force, stealing and torturing as he pleases, foretells the lawlessness of Glanton, the judge, and the wandering band of Americans in *Blood Meridian*.

The journeys come to tragic ends. Rinthy finds the tinker, but he refuses to relinquish his hold on the child, saying that she is poor and has nothing to give him in return for his provisional care. His own relationship with the child is a thin bulkhead holding back the huge lurking darkness of his own loneliness. The child, meanwhile, passes from the hands of the tinker to the three night riders, who taunt Culla, trying unsuccessfully to get him to admit to his paternity. They finally cut the throat of the baby and leave the remains, which Rinthy discovers shortly thereafter in a glade, with the tinker hanging from a nearby tree, vultures pecking at his carcass.

Outer Dark provides some basis for the comparisons often made between Faulkner and McCarthy. The handling of narrative in the novel and the almost absurd journeys of its characters call to mind *As I Lay Dying*. The poor, wandering Rinthy Holme seems cut from the same pattern as *Light in August*'s (1932) Lena Grove. A Gothic atmosphere hangs heavily over the novel. Dead corpses hang from trees, characters trudge through the night followed by ominous sounds and small unidentified lights; cannibalism lurks on the edges, and darkness surrounds things.

With all its journeying and strident tone the novel, like John Bunyan's *The Pilgrim's Progress* (1678) or John Milton's *Paradise Lost* (1667), invites allegorical interpretations. What purpose do these roads and these wanderings have? If some meaning is to be distilled, it might be simply that lives by their very nature must take some path which, in the end, will add up to no more or no less than those lines that have been traced. The human condition itself is a condemnation to homelessness. "They's lots of people on the roads these days," Culla says to a blind man he meets toward the end of the novel. The blind man agrees: "I pass em ever day. People goin up and down in the world like dogs. As if they wasn't a home nowheres."

In *Outer Dark*, McCarthy explores what a human being is when stripped of all encumbrances, material and spiritual. Like the best of his other novels, it is a testimony to man's amazing endurance and survival in spite of himself. At one point the tinker says to Rinthy, "I've seen the meanness of humans till I don't know why God ain't put out the sun and gone away."

SUTTREE

First published: 1979
Type of work: Novel

Stalking death, Cornelius "Bud" Suttree comes and goes from his houseboat on the Tennessee River, associating with the wretched of the earth.

Much distinguishes *Suttree*, McCarthy's fourth novel, from his previous fiction. More expansive and ambitious than his earlier work, *Suttree* traces the life of one single central character, Cornelius Suttree, from October, 1950, to the spring of 1955. The world the novel displays is primarily urban, with most of the action taking place in McAnally Flats, a down-and-out district of Knoxville, Tennessee, whose grim landscape McCarthy describes with startling precision and beauty. The comic elements of the novel offset the continual presence of death and despair.

At the heart of the novel are Suttree and the river on which he lives on a houseboat at various intervals in the story. Rejecting the sober, comfortable middle-class values of his father, he chooses instead to explore the more essential, unseemly side of life on the edge in the underground world of McAnally Flats—home of drunks, derelicts, gamblers, whores, homosexuals, murderers, evangelists, and thieves. Suttree continuously returns to the river, where he sets up his fishing lines, until the end of the novel, when the Flats are threatened by demolition for the construction of a freeway. His is a search for living authentically with himself and his world.

Much of the heavily populated novel chronicles Suttree's intermittent interactions with a constellation of colorful characters: the ragpicker, J-Bone, Oceanfrog, an old former railway worker, a family of musselhunters, hulking black Ab Jones, an Indian fisherman, Blind Richard, a black sorceress, the gay Trippin Through the Dew, a whore he shacks up with for a spell, and, most memorable of all, Gene Harrogate, the infamous watermelon humper whom he first meets in the workhouse where both are serving time for their dubious wrongdoings. Anytime Harrogate appears, the reader is assured of some comic mishap. Suttree himself, a solitary creature whose main difficulties in life seem to be associated with living with himself, proves to be immensely tolerant and compassionate. He stands by his fellow outcasts, regardless of their race, creed, or felony, and lends a hand when they are in need—fleeing from the law, trying to get rid of a dead body, or engineering an illegitimate plot.

The omniscient narrative, centered on Suttree, moves fluidly from experience to experience. He is an American Ulysses; when Suttree bumps into people and forms attachments, things happen. Seldom does he take his fate into his own hands. Trouble tracks him down and he does not run from it. As in life, characters leave the scene, die, are abandoned or forgotten, and sometimes reappear unexpectedly, unpredictably, and inopportunely. Until the end, Suttree and the river remain. McCarthy rarely admits his reader to the workings of his characters' minds. From actions and speech one must form impressions about what motivates Suttree.

The world Suttree inhabits and internalizes is filled with loneliness and death. It is never clear whether death stalks him or he stalks death. Death hovers over his very birth, snatching the twin brother with whom he has shared his mother's womb. At one point in the novel he learns of his son's death and, in a rare assertion of will, leaves Knoxville to attend the funeral. Even there he watches from the side, cast out by his in-laws, who blame him for his treatment of their daughter, his estranged wife. Suttree also lives through the deaths of several friends, and toward the end of the novel, in a feverish bout with typhoid, he nearly crosses the threshold himself. As he is recovering, he shares his message from the other side with the nurse: "I have a thing to tell you. I know all souls are one and all souls lonely."

Suttree becomes attached to two women during the course of the novel, each of whom, for a time, lifts him out of his solitude. The nature of his problematic relationships with women, including his mother and his first wife, is a pressing theme throughout. With Wanda, the daughter of the man with whom he had become partners in a mussel shell-gathering operation, Suttree experiences a wholly innocent, idyllic sexual relationship, broken off first by his fear and eventually by her death in a rock slide. Not long afterward, Suttree takes up with Joyce, whose work as a prostitute brings in enough money for them to move into an apartment together and buy a roadster. This connection, too, must end, though not in death.

Suttree finds a kind of redemption that is rare in McCarthy's work. He confronts and transcends his own death, both in his battle with typhoid and in the form of a corpse he finds in his own bed on his houseboat when he gets out of the hospital. In another assertion of his own will, Suttree finally decides to leave McAnally Flats. The last the reader sees of him he has gotten into a car which has stopped for him, and he is heading for some destination unknown.

An outstanding feature of the writing in *Suttree* is the fine balance achieved between dialogue and lyric descriptions of landscapes. McCarthy's rendering of the unique, natural dialect of the region is unprecedented and unsurpassed. As in *The Orchard Keeper* and *Blood Meridian*, the geographical terrain itself is tangible and vibrant. The relation between description and dialogue is analogous to the dialectic between the natural and the human world in the novel. Each plays a part, as they interact with and shape each other.

BLOOD MERIDIAN

First published: 1985
Type of work: Novel

A band of American renegades indiscriminately murders, plunders, tortures, and scalps Indians, Mexicans, and others on their expedition through the Southwest and Mexico in the 1840's.

With *Blood Meridian: Or, The Evening Redness in the West*, a novel of epic proportions and startling originality, McCarthy shifts his eye from Tennessee to the
American Southwest and northern Mexico. The novel, set in the 1840's, when the
border between the United States and Mexico was under dispute, is an orgy of violence, vain striving, and desperate marauding. It gives form to the frontier theory,
the idea of manifest destiny, which inspired Americans to seek dominion over the
land and to expel, murder, or subjugate those peoples who stood in the way of their
mission. As the subtitle of the novel suggests, the book has elements of the Western,
though McCarthy rigorously subverts the convention and its values. There are indeed cowboys, Indians, and Mexicans, but the shoot-outs, massacres, and raids (all
shown in graphic detail) take place in a vacuum of values where there is no such
thing as a "good guy" or a "bad guy." Alan Cheuse is on track in calling *Blood
Meridian* "a Western that evokes the styles of both [film director] Sam Peckinpah
and [artist] Hieronymus Bosch."

The narrative loosely follows a young protagonist whom the reader knows only
as "the kid" (born a hundred years before his creator, in 1833) as he leaves his
Tennessee home at the age of fourteen, winds his way west to Texas, and is enlisted
in a vigilante army of Americans who, under the command of Captain Glanton,
march through the inhospitable plains, deserts, and mountains of Texas, Chihuahua,
Sonora, Arizona, and southern California terrorizing Indians, Mexicans, and one
another along their wrathful path. Hosts of colorful characters appear and vanish
through the journey's course. Most important among them is Judge Holden, who
first meets and observes the kid early in the novel and then picks up his trail later,
following him until their ultimate showdown near the novel's end.

Early in the novel, the kid meets a hermit who propounds his belief in evil and its
mysterious, self-generating nature. This is one of the first instances of the novel's
preoccupation with evil, and it serves as a reference for one's acquaintance with the
judge, an embodiment of evil as formidable as any found in American fiction, Herman Melville's Ahab included. Judge Holden propounds and elaborately defends his
Nietzschean world view in a long speech to his companions:

> Moral law is an invention of mankind for the disenfranchisement of the powerful in
> favor of the weak. Historical law subverts it at every turn. A moral view can never be
> proven right or wrong by any ultimate test. . . . Man's vanity may well approach the
> infinite in capacity but his knowledge remains imperfect and howevermuch he comes
> to value his judgements ultimately he must submit them before a higher court. Here
> there can be no special pleading. Here are considerations of equity and rectitude and
> moral right rendered void and without warrant and here are the views of the litigants
> despised. Decisions of life and death, of what shall be and what shall not, beggar all
> questions of right.

Knowledge, for the judge, is a weapon. To know things is to control them. His
imperialistic view of knowledge is an extension of eighteenth century European Enlightenment attitudes. "Whatever in creation exists without my knowledge exists

without my consent," he proclaims at one point. In this spirit, he carries with him a journal in which he scrupulously records the minute details of flora and fauna, preserving specimens of birds, catching and drawing butterflies. To what end? In order to gain mastery over things, people, and new territory.

If this novel is about the nature of tyranny and the violence it looses on everything around it, it is also about the unconquerable mystery of the world and its laws, omnipresent and omnipotent. The force of the natural world challenges an anthropomorphic view of the universe. The novel itself is a veritable catalog of plant and animal life, a verbal map of the territory. The landscape is described with the same scrupulous attention to detail that has characterized McCarthy's writing since his first novel, *The Orchard Keeper*.

What is amazing in this picture of things is that humans survive at all. Characters in this novel live far longer than either logic or luck would have it. That, too, is part of the mystery and awe. Figures trudge through the landscape, often freezing in snow or parched and hungry, dressed in tatters, covered in dust, and caked with blood from their last battle. The novel miraculously transforms such grotesque ghouls and hideous happenings into objects of aesthetic beauty.

In the end, in an unavoidable face-off, the judge—now in the garb of the authority that society has bestowed on him—overpowers the kid. Once again McCarthy prompts a critique of the moral underpinnings of society, opens to question the goodness of the man in the white hat, and ominously entertains the possibility of evil's triumph.

Summary

In a reckoning of those voices in contemporary American literature which have been most innovative and have spoken most powerfully about the human condition, a place will certainly be reserved for Cormac McCarthy. Like his predecessor, William Faulkner, McCarthy makes a regional experience accessible, displaying a version of reality that is unique and unforgettable. The issues arising so naturally from McCarthy's fiction are those which have always been at the center of American literature—an uneasy truce with the land, the conflict between the individual and society, the relation between technology and nature, and the struggle to come to terms with genealogical and historical precedents. All of this is made the more remarkable by McCarthy's distinctive literary style—his vibrant images, rugged language, and precise diction.

Bibliography

Bell, Vereen M. *The Achievement of Cormac McCarthy*. Baton Rouge: Louisiana State University Press, 1988.

_____. "The Ambiguous Nihilism of Cormac McCarthy." *Southern Literary Journal* 15 (Spring, 1983): 31-41.

Ditsky, John. "Further into Darkness: The Novels of Cormac McCarthy." *Hollins*

Critic 18 (April, 1981): 1-11.

Schaefer, William J. "Cormac McCarthy: The Hard Wages of Original Sin." *Appalachian Journal* 4 (1976-1977): 105-119.

Winchell, Mark Royden. "Inner Dark: Or, The Place of Cormac McCarthy." *The Southern Review* 26 (April, 1990): 293-309.

Young, Thomas Daniel. *Tennessee Writers.* Knoxville: University of Tennessee Press, 1981.

Allen Hibbard

MARY McCARTHY

Born: Seattle, Washington
June 21, 1912
Died: New York, New York
October 25, 1989

Principal Literary Achievement
Known predominantly for her adversarial literary stance, McCarthy enlarged the tradition of autobiographical fiction through her satirical analyses of societal weaknesses.

Biography
Novelist, short story writer, essayist, drama critic, and poet, Mary Therese McCarthy was born the first of four children to Therese Preston and Roy Winfield McCarthy on June 21, 1912, in Seattle, Washington. Although the first six years of her childhood were nurtured within her close-knit family, McCarthy's life altered abruptly when her parents died in the 1918 flu epidemic.

For the next five years, McCarthy and her brothers were forced as orphans to live in a deceit-filled, irrational, abusive Minneapolis house. This atmosphere, as well as the never-mentioned death of her parents, conditioned McCarthy to detach from her emotions, to distrust others, to see herself as an outsider, and to avoid intimacy. She also learned to depend upon her Roman Catholic religion and her mind in order to survive. At eight years old, she began writing poetry. Satire became her weapon against despair.

The children were rescued in 1923 by their grandfather Preston; the boys were separated from their sister, who joined the Protestant Preston household before attending a Catholic boarding school, Forest Ridge Convent. Again, McCarthy was isolated. This isolation continued throughout her college preparatory education as she struggled to discover the means to acceptance. Exploring options that ranged from joining a convent to committing suicide, the adolescent repeatedly reinforced her self-antagonism by trying to conform. During McCarthy's one year in a public high school, the academically gifted student's grades verged on failure, so her grandparents sent her to an Episcopal boarding school.

At Vassar College, she majored in Elizabethan literature, acted onstage, and founded an alternative literary magazine with three other students. Discovering that a literary career was more appealing to her than one onstage, McCarthy moved to New York

City following graduation as a Phi Beta Kappa and successively became a book reviewer, an editor, and a theater critic. She also spent three years (through 1948) as a college instructor. The Horizon award for *Oasis* (1949) and a Guggenheim Fellowship (1949-1950) enabled her to devote more energy to literary writing. Consequently, a collection of short stories, *Cast a Cold Eye* (1950), and the novel *The Groves of Academe* (1952) were published.

In 1957, McCarthy received a National Institute of Arts and Letters grant. *A Charmed Life* (1955), lauded for its caustic, provocative characterization, and a nonfictional pair, *Venice Observed* (1956) and *The Stones of Florence* (1959), praised for humanistic style, brilliant literary precision, and historical accuracy, were the three books that immediately preceded her second Guggenheim Fellowship (1959-1960). After having been intentionally delayed for almost two decades, *The Group*, a best-seller, was published in 1963. *Vietnam* (1967) and *Hanoi* (1968) are the results of her tour in Asia during the Vietnam War. In 1979, the author published *Cannibals and Missionaries*, a novel she described as her last. Collections of McCarthy's essay and reviews have also been published.

In 1984, McCarthy was awarded the National Medal of Literature and the Edward MacDowell Medal for her extraordinary contributions to the field of literature. She was accorded membership in two prestigious organizations, the National Institute of Arts and Letters and the American Academy of Arts and Letters.

McCarthy became infamous for transferring recognizable physical, emotional, and behavioral characteristics of acquaintances to the fictional page. Her husbands have been no exception; McCarthy fictionalized the players in each of her four marriages and three divorces. After twenty-eight years of marriage to James West, McCarthy died in 1989 from cancer.

Analysis

McCarthy's primary literary technique, direct and indirect satire, is uniquely suited to her personality and writing style. McCarthy mercilessly focuses upon issues of self-deception, ignorance of history, and lack of human emotional ties. Her dominant societal target, and the one with which she is most familiar, is the "privileged" class. Nevertheless, this familiarity, as some have suggested, does not prevent her from achieving the distance to maintain a compelling satirical stance. What is at times problematic is her lack of internal character development, which, in turn, dilutes the satirical impact of her writing. Greet in *Cannibals and Missionaries*, Libby in *The Group*, and Alma in *The Groves of Academe* are three characters whose more fully realized presentation could have maximized McCarthy's point of view.

As a social critic, McCarthy is least likely to tolerate that form of self-deception in which the individual opts to negate his or her own knowledge in favor of external conformity. Kay, *The Group*'s protagonist, who dies at twenty-nine, seeks out and adapts to external expectations rather than developing her own sense of self-worth. On the other hand, in *Cannibals and Missionaries*, the most conspicuous quarry by normal expectations for satirical focus is Jeroen, a character whom McCarthy instead respects for his integrity and commitment.

Characteristically, McCarthy writes about a human behavior that intrigues or baffles her, seeking the underlying causes for a socio-cultural pattern she perceives as destructive. As a result, the author inundates her writing with intricate detail. These details, both personal and environmental, help to define the incongruity with humor and give her work the precision for which it is justifiably renowned. McCarthy's intellectual humor, in the form of purposefully inept literary allusions voiced by a pretentious character (Harald in *The Group*), serves admirably as a device by which the character undermines himself or herself. The author also uses historical allusion to emphasize the critical condition she has targeted. *The Groves of Academe*, centered upon the adaptive and deviant behaviors of a college administration and faculty, is rife with both forms of allusion.

Four other forms of humor are employed by the author as reinforcing stylistic devices: antithesis, exaggeration, irony, and parody. In *The Group*, a classic example of antithesis is Pris and Norine's conversational skirmish regarding child-rearing practices. Pris, whose child is reared according to the discipline of a strict schedule, battles Norine, whose child is reared with complete freedom for experimentation. Exchanging verbal blow for verbal blow, Pris (who can be intimidated by any obstreperous voice of authority) predictably yields the victory to Norine.

Foreshadowing (most often in McCarthy's first chapters) and dramatic irony underscore the author's themes. Two examples of foreshadowing are the discomfort at Kay's wedding in *The Group* as a predictor of her untimely death and, in *Cannibals and Missionaries*, the cat's first escape from its cage on the Boeing 747 precipitating thoughts among the passengers of hijacking so that the actual hijacking is discounted as the cat's having again escaped. After the explosive conclusion to the hostage situation, McCarthy provides an epilogue chapter heavily underscored with dramatic irony. As the two relatively unscathed survivors aboard a plane to take them home review the journalist's diary written during their captivity, they note a passage in which she states that she would sacrifice an arm for Jeroen to achieve his end in style; she has.

THE GROVES OF ACADEME

First published: 1952
Type of work: Novel

The devious Professor Henry Mulcahy of Jocelyn College deceives his colleagues into pressuring the administration for a renewal of his teaching contract.

The Groves of Academe is McCarthy's satiric foray against the administrations and the faculties of liberal higher education. The title is derived from a Horatian quotation concerning the search for "truth" within the "groves" of academia. Clearly, from the opening of the first chapter, Henry Mulcahy and the other erudites who scheme to manipulate people and situations to their own ends do not have the search for truth first on their agenda. Even the most nobly portrayed professor, Domna Rejnev, places her own self-interest above truth and the safety of a colleague.

The plot of this scathing comedy of manners advances through the psychological machinations of Mulcahy, a pale, bulbous, tense, incompetent but intelligent instructor with a one-year contract, who fights for reinstatement on the basis of having previously been a member of the Communist Party and of his wife's devastatingly poor health. The ingenuity of his first claim is that no progressive college, such as Jocelyn College, in the age of Joseph McCarthy's anti-Communist witch hunts, would risk a public accusation of terminating a contract on the basis of political beliefs. Underlying his second claim is the idea that the news of his termination would seriously endanger the life of his wife Cathy because of the dangerous illness of which she has no knowledge. Neither basis is true; however, Mulcahy has a facility for convincing himself that a lie is truth and then for rallying others to believe. His perceptive reading of what motivates others to act, as well as of their subsequent predictable actions, illustrates his perverted brilliance.

He is also capable of manipulating the actual truth in his favor. At the end of the novel, when the president and involved faculty members in desperation conduct a covert interview with a visiting poet, who confirms that Mulcahy has never joined the Communist Party, Mulcahy uses the president's actions as blackmail to retain his position. In addition, he admits to the defeated college president that self-serving justice, not truth, is his preeminent issue. As such, Mulcahy functions as the entrenched antithesis of the utopian standards set by the progressive college.

In direct counterpoint, Domna Rejnev is the altruistic, nobly bred, well-intentioned, intelligent young professor of Russian and French who has dedicated her life to her students. She is both responsible and competent. She is also the "friend" whom Mulcahy beguiles into his most determined advocate. In concert with Alma Fortune, a more politically experienced but equally sincere faculty member, Rejnev and committee successfully present a case for the renewal of Mulcahy's contract.

Once Rejnev discovers the truth, her only recourse is to withdraw from contact with Mulcahy and to begin quietly documenting Mulcahy's reckless and incompetent behaviors. Nevertheless, when he later confronts her with the question of who was responsible for the departmental meeting in which he was forced to justify the guest list for his poetry conference, Rejnev tarnishes her idealistic passion for justice by misleading the villainous professor to blame Fortune, when Rejnev herself had reported her concerns. Thus, the contamination spreads.

McCarthy presents Jocelyn College as a progressive educational institution that, based upon a student's aptitudes, interests, and psychological profiles, ideally functions to maximize the student's self-actualization. The inevitable problem is the human equation. Individualized instruction, a tutorial course of study in the student's major field, suffers from both faculty and student abuse or neglect. In another program, the February field-period, consisting of one month of off-campus work in the student's chosen field, any number of complications sabotage the founder's intent. Nevertheless, every fall term the faculty, cognizant of the abuses, manage to retain their four free weeks by voting to maintain the field-period.

McCarthy's satiric thrust in this novel is against those colleges with utopian goals who lack concrete objectives and who do not take into account the human factor. In other words, blind trust in humanity's hunger to expand their minds and to share their knowledge freely is destructive without direction. The search for truth is withering on the vines of academe.

THE GROUP

First published: 1963
Type of work: Novel

The lives of nine Vassar College women, eight of whom make up "the group," are depicted in the seven years following graduation.

Popular acclaim for *The Group*, McCarthy's only best-seller, has not been reflected by critical reaction. The novel has been lambasted as being written on the level of pulp romance fiction and as containing stock, barely distinguishable characterizations and a strategic lack of focus. On the other hand, many Vassar graduates have been incensed at the apparently realistic characters portrayed without empathy. Both groups have overlooked the penetrating satire through which McCarthy so often expresses her themes.

Three interrelated themes are presented through each chapter's focus on one character at a time. The women, well-educated and not devastatingly affected by the Depression, are ill-prepared to cope with life in the real world. One crucial detriment, manifested repeatedly by the different characters, is that these aware women are incapable of putting their progressive philosophies into action. Instead, they become caught up in their own immediate needs or in surrounding circumstances.

Another recurrent McCarthy theme revolves around the inadequacies of living entirely for the present moment without a sense of history. Even as the women delight in Kay's nontraditional wedding celebration, they are also discomfited by the absence of any member of Kay's family and are superstitious about Kay's behaviors that are traditionally considered unlucky. Without the emotional and the spiritual foundations of a family heritage, a stable self-identity is difficult to realize.

Although McCarthy extensively employs in this novel a technique she has termed "ventriloquism" (allowing the actions, the words, and the intonations of each character to evolve as unique to that character without the controlling intervention of the novelist's voice), expression of her belief system was important enough to her that she set aside her writing of *The Group* for eighteen years to find the appropriate internal voice. In the early 1960's, her development of Kay as a dynamic, rather than a static, character became the voice she had long sought.

Kay Leiland Strong Petersen, whose marriage opens the novel and whose death concludes the novel, is the unifying thread among the other characters' stories. A shy, slightly overweight Westerner upon her arrival at Vassar, Kay outwardly transforms herself into the stereotypical ambitious, iconoclastic disbeliever in all but the material real. Inwardly, however, she remains the shy outsider, lacking self-awareness, seeking to identify herself by association with her friends and her husband. What her friends think of as snooping and confrontive behaviors are actually Kay's means of discovering an acceptable identity. Kay's marriage to Harald is another form of this destructive dependency. While she looks to him for love (in which she has externally professed not to believe), guidance, support, and identification, he is indolent, uncaring, self-involved, adulterous, deceitful, and abusive. Reputed to be modeled after McCarthy's first husband, Harald is, in fact, one of the most villainous male characters in the author's entire body of fiction.

Nevertheless, Kay maintains the façade of their marriage for her friends and her family in Salt Lake City because she does not believe that she has the ability to accomplish her dreams on her own. Only after her husband has hit her, locked her in their dressing room, and committed her to a mental institution, is she able to acknowledge her hatred of him. Within the year, she divorces Harald and dies in a mysterious fall out the window of her Vassar Club room.

In the first chapter, McCarthy caustically discloses a "modern" philosophy of relationships: "If you were going to use a person, then you had to make the best of them." In her succeeding chapters, the consequences of each character's life choices indicate that the opposite may instead be true. Three of the six married women have marital relationships about which no serious defects are revealed. Actually, little is known about Pokey's marriage other than that she has continued in the role of New Jersey wife. Libby has been married to a famous author-client for about a year. And empathetic Polly, a hospital technician, has married a good-hearted former psychiatrist now turned medical researcher.

The intelligent, aloof rationalist, Helena, appears comfortable with the persona she has achieved. Competent and single, she and her mother, Mrs. Davison, are largely responsible for Kay's funeral arrangements. Having returned from Europe three months earlier, the forthright Lakey brings her opening actions in the first chapter full circle by buying Kay the off-white designer dress she had always wanted. Unmarried, Lakey is fulfilled in a lesbian relationship.

Shy, stammering Pris has adjusted, with some reservations, to motherhood and marriage with a pediatrician who uses his family as guinea pigs for his child-rearing theories. Dottie, the only group member absent from Kay's funeral, has compromised her affectionate, sensual nature by settling for a pragmatic marriage to an Arizona widower rather than seeking a relationship with the man she says she loves. Norine, the morally corrupt outsider of the group, first marries an impotent man and engages in several adulterous affairs, including one with Kay's husband, then marries a Jewish banker even though she admits to still loving Harald.

One of the problems in *The Group* is the unevenness of its characterization. Although the novel is saturated with detail, some characters (Pokey, Helena, and Libby in particular) are not given as full a treatment as they deserve. Another difficulty may be that the author's ventriloquistic distance fosters ambiguity. Nevertheless, McCarthy's writing is most vital when she describes the attitudes and the interactions of a society trapped by its own conditioning. For example, each episode of Dottie's love affair, including her pre-wedding talk with her mother, scintillates with humor and pathos, and Helena's reactions to Norine and Norine's home are exquisitely drawn in an unexpectedly dramatic confrontation. *The Group* is considerably more than a venture into the pulp romance genre.

CANNIBALS AND MISSIONARIES

First published: 1979
Type of work: Novel

A handpicked group of liberals investigating allegations of the Shah of Iran's torture of political prisoners and a first-class tour of millionaire art collectors are hijacked by a multi-national terrorist group.

Cannibals and Missionaries, McCarthy's least autobiographical novel, is more a character study of human response to fear, deprivation, and imprisonment than a classic espionage tale. The title is derived from a riddle asking how, in a two-passenger boat, three cannibals and three missionaries can cross a river without ever having the missionaries outmanned. Even though the solution is supplied by the "friendliest" captor, Ahmed, the answer to the question of which group (terrorists, millionaires, or liberals) is the cannibals and which is the missionaries is left to the reader.

The investigative committee led by Senator Jim Carey and Dutch Parliamentary Deputy Henk Van Vliet de Jonge is the terrorists' primary target; the first-class tour group with Charles Tennant as self-appointed liaison is a secondary target. Jeroen, a surprisingly sympathetic figure, leads an international terrorist force that has secured a farmhouse stronghold in Flevoland on the polders of Holland by posing as a television crew filming a documentary.

The terrorists' demands are fivefold. For the helicopter that transported them to the polders and its crew, the ransom is more than one million dollars, half to the terrorists and half to the Surinam poor. For the liberation of the committee members, including a college president, two religious figures, an international journalist, a Middle East specialist who is an undercover agent, and a history professor, the stipulations are more complex: NATO's withdrawal from Holland, cessation of Dutch-Israeli relations, and the release of "class-war prisoners." For their wealthy captives, the terrorists have demanded a one-man helicopter to carry taped ransom demands to families of the prisoners.

Jeroen believes that murder should be the last avenue of action. Formerly an artist, he has conceived a plan by which his wealthy prisoners can ransom themselves and pay for their capitalistic crimes by relinquishing to his group specific art master-pieces from their collections. In this way, he lowers his captive count and holds instead as hostage paintings that the world might be even more reluctant to count as casualties. The first-class prisoners are eventually exchanged for their artworks; how-ever, the investigative committee remains hostage because the Dutch government cannot accede to the demand of NATO withdrawal. Consequently, Jeroen, who un-derstands action as his only remaining art form and who sees a primary aim of ter-rorism as retributory, taking from a corrupt society that which is irreplaceable, acts.

After ordering all prisoners and guards out of the house for an extended exercise period, he detonates the farmhouse, the paintings, and himself. Unfortunately, Greet, one of the terrorists, senses impending disaster and returns early. As a result, only the Episcopalian priest, Frank Barber, and the college president, Aileen Simmons, escape death or serious injury. Jeroen dies in the explosion, knowing that his precau-tions to avoid senseless slaughter have been futile.

Expected and unexpected character bonding, as well as the materialization of idiosyncratic behaviors, create a spell-binding effect. The most sympathetic terrorist characters are self-sacrificing Jeroen, dedicated to his cause, Ahmed, the young poet, and Greet, once a KLM hostess, now (out of love) committed to Jeroen. The most sympathetic among the captives include Henk Van Vliet de Jonge, the flawless poet-politician who understands Jeroen's commitment; Senator Jim Carey, an alcoholic widower poet-politician past his time of effectiveness; Sophie Weil, a brilliant and beautiful journalist uncomfortable with the spoken word; and Charles Tennant, the wealthy raconteur who cannot bear to be separated from the action. The author's characterization of these, as well as many of the other less sympathetic characters (such as the alcoholic, cat-carrying undercover agent Victor Lenz), is witty, percep-tive, and provocative.

Nevertheless, certain deficiencies detract from the potency of this novel. McCar-thy stated that *Cannibals and Missionaries* was her last novel because as one ages one's awareness is blunted. Although she had conducted detailed factual research for the book, her non-realistic, soft-edged portrayal of the terrorist force is disappoint-ing. Furthermore, her customary philosophical editorializing is conspicuously ab-sent except for discussions of art. Finally, whether intentionally or unintentionally, the author's pace distractingly falters.

MEMORIES OF A CATHOLIC GIRLHOOD

First published: 1957
Type of work: Autobiography

McCarthy subjectively relates her childhood experiences and her family mem-ories, with editorial comments on their verifiability.

Memories of a Catholic Girlhood, the most deeply passionate of McCarthy's published writings, is a moving chronicle of her early years, through her adolescence. Beginning her account with a careful, italicized address to the reader, the author sets the tone for the following eight chapters by philosophizing that "to care for the quarrels of the past . . . is to experience a kind of straining against reality, a rebellious nonconformity that, again, is rare in America." Although this was written within the context of discussing the merits of Catholic education, it is also a skillful summary of *Memories*, her other writings, and her life.

Discriminating between what she herself remembers but cannot be corroborated, what has been corroborated, and what is in conflict with her own memories, McCarthy painstakingly pieces together the fragments of her early history. Following each chapter except the last, she acknowledges, again in italicized print, the substantiations and the contradictions to her story. This technique imbues *Memories* with an almost indisputable credibility.

Although McCarthy's presentation is essentially chronological, as with all memories, there occurs an associational movement back and forth in time. Gradually the full picture emerges. Recollections of a favored beginning reveal a period of delightful surprises and unconditional love. Her father, at home because of a chronic heart problem, was an irrepressibly joyful companion. Both parents, deeply in love and married against their families' wishes, willingly shared that love with their children.

The flu epidemic in 1918 raged through her family when her father's parents withheld his monthly stipend and insisted that the family return from Seattle to their hometown of Minneapolis. Only dimly aware of her surroundings by the time the train reached its destination, McCarthy awoke some days later in a bleak, institutionalized sewing room of her wealthy grandparents' house.

Some weeks later, after waiting daily for her parents' return, she realized on her own (because no adults had spoken with her) that her mother and her father had died. Consequently, when her three brothers disappeared one day, she took for granted that they also were dead. The resulting emotional paralysis that McCarthy describes in herself as a child of six was exacerbated by the abusive five years she endured after being sent to join her brothers.

Unwilling to take on the rearing of four children, her grandparents had hired their great-aunt Margaret and her husband, "uncle Myers," to care for them in a dilapidated house two blocks away. Shabbily clothed, ill-fed, beaten regularly (with no apparent pattern other than if anyone younger "misbehaved," he and all his older siblings were whipped), McCarthy and her brothers learned that no one was to be trusted. No explanations were given for the adults' behaviors. Instead, their "role models" were erratic, irrational, manipulative, and self-involved.

Being rescued by their maternal grandfather Preston, apparently not because of the abuse McCarthy and her oldest brother had detailed but because McCarthy was not wearing her glasses (a punishment for falling and breaking them), was both a relief and a source of bewilderment to McCarthy. Another puzzle was the fact that she remained temporarily with her maternal grandparents while the boys were sent to boarding school (the youngest, Sheridan, later than the others).

Although satire is noticeably absent in *Memories*, irony is utilized most effectively in highlighting McCarthy's internal processes as she copes with different environments. For example, in order to gain positive attention at a Catholic all-girls boarding school, the author evaluates several plans and chooses to announce just before a retreat that she has "lost" her faith. In the process of her arguments with two priests, however, she realizes that what she thought was simply an attention-getting lie is actually the truth. To make the problem even more complex, she must now pretend for the rest of her stay at this school that she has found her lost faith so that she can receive Eucharist with the other girls.

The impact of her early dehumanizing experiences as well as of those school years when she could not overcome her "outsider" feelings was to color McCarthy's life in both her satiric writing style and her detachments from people. *Memories of a Catholic Girlhood* is a poignant chronicle of debasement, the search for meaning, and survival.

Summary

Mary McCarthy's literary career was fraught with controversy. Her novels with the greatest public acclaim received the worst critical response. Nevertheless, through satire, she continued to fictionalize the people and the events in her life out of her fascination with human motivation.

Writing primarily about the intelligentsia, she has nevertheless managed to capture the imagination of the American public and the attention of honored American literary institutions. Her attention to detail, her painstaking research, her rapier wit, and her understated use of humorous devices fuse into a literary style uniquely her own.

Bibliography

Gelderman, Carol. *Mary McCarthy: A Life.* New York: St. Martin's Press, 1988.
Goldman, Sherli Evens. *Mary McCarthy: A Bibliography.* New York: Harcourt, Brace & World, 1968.
Grumbach, Doris. *The Company She Kept.* New York: Coward-McCann, 1967.
McKenzie, Barbara. *Mary McCarthy.* New York: Twayne, 1966.
Stock, Irvin. *Mary McCarthy.* Minneapolis: University of Minnesota Press, 1968.

Kathleen Mills

CARSON McCULLERS

Born: Columbus, Georgia
February 19, 1917
Died: Nyack, New York
September 29, 1967

Principal Literary Achievement

For her haunting tales of love and loneliness told in her own evocative style, McCullers is considered one of America's exceptional writers.

Biography

Born Lula Carson Smith, McCullers was reared in a town near a big Army post in rural southwest Georgia by a successful jeweler and a remarkable mother who encouraged her genius. An aloof, precocious child, she longed to be rich and famous and live in the snowy North. By the age of eight years, she was producing little plays with neighbor children. At ten she took piano lessons and aspired to play concerts on stage. It is said that she read every worthwhile book in the local library. At fifteen, she came down with rheumatic fever, misdiagnosed at the time, which led to debilitating illnesses later.

After high school, her parents sold heirloom jewelry so she could sail to New York and study at the prestigious Juilliard School of Music. Unfortunately, the money was lost on the subway, and she was forced to work odd jobs to pay for courses in creative writing. During a summer vacation in Georgia, Carson was introduced to Reeves McCullers, a charming, handsome, and intelligent soldier who soon left the Army to join her at Columbia University. When she was taken ill, Reeves brought her home, where they were married on September 20, 1937. McCullers followed her husband to Charlotte, where he found work as a debt collector, and then to Fayetteville, an army town much like Columbus. There she finished her first novel, *The Heart Is a Lonely Hunter* (1940), and wrote her second, *Reflections in a Golden Eye* (1941), not for publication, she later said, but for fun.

The Heart Is a Lonely Hunter changed their lives forever. McCullers lived the rest of her life as a literary celebrity. They moved to New York and began to mingle with other artists and celebrities. At the Bread Loaf Writer's Conference, the Yaddo Artists' Colony, and elsewhere, McCullers befriended writers such as W. H. Auden, Eudora Welty, Louis Untermeyer, Tennessee Williams, Truman Capote, Klaus Mann, and Arthur Miller, as well as actress Marilyn Monroe, composer David Diamond,

and Swiss socialite Annemarie Clarac-Schwarzenbach, for whom Carson felt a special affinity. In September, 1940, McCullers left her husband to live with Auden, dancer Gypsy Rose Lee, and magazine editor George Davis in Brooklyn Heights.

On a trip to Georgia that winter, McCullers suffered strokes that impaired her vision. Seeking a reconciliation, Reeves brought her back to New York in April. There they embarked upon a complex triangular love affair with Diamond. After Reeves left her for him, McCullers sued for divorce, but continued to see both of them. Poor health kept her from living with Diamond in Mexico, so she returned to Yaddo and wrote *The Ballad of the Sad Café* (1951).

After the divorce, Reeves reenlisted in the Army, was wounded in the invasion of Normandy and decorated for bravery, and returned to the United States. On March 19, 1945, Carson and Reeves McCullers were remarried in a civil ceremony. They set sail for Europe after *The Member of the Wedding* was published in 1946 and the Guggenheim Foundation awarded her a second grant. She was enthusiastically received by major writers in Rome and Paris. In August and November, 1946, she was paralyzed on the left side by strokes. Recuperation was followed by another separation. In March, 1948, Carson attempted suicide and was briefly placed in a psychiatric clinic in Manhattan. Soon restored to her mother's care, she was reunited with Reeves by summer's end.

Convinced by Tennessee Williams to adapt *The Member of the Wedding* for the stage, McCullers found herself the toast of Broadway in 1950. Winner of the New York Drama Critics Circle Award, she sold the film rights for $75,000 and headed for Europe. Reeves stowed away on the ship. They bought a house near Paris, but the marriage could not be saved. When he proposed a double suicide, Carson fled for her life; Reeves killed himself on November 19, 1953.

McCullers continued writing and lecturing in the United States, but there were more setbacks. Devastated by her mother's death in 1955, she was further weakened by pleurisy, cancer, pneumonia, and several surgeries, including a radical mastectomy. Under the care of psychiatrist Mary Mercer, McCullers continued to write until pain prevented her from completing her signature. She lived to see the success of Edward Albee's adaptation of *The Ballad of the Sad Café* on Broadway and the beginning of film production of her first two novels. On August 15, 1967, she suffered a massive brain hemorrhage that left her comatose until her death several weeks later.

Analysis

Spiritual isolation is the abiding theme of Carson McCullers' fiction. At the core of modern life, she saw a tragic failure of individuals to connect with one another emotionally, to return love, or to commit themselves to a socially edifying pattern of shared values. Her characters struggle through agonies of psychic stress to realize the radical loneliness in their lives. Sexual deviation, violence, and sexual initiation in adolescence move them to their personal crises.

Typically, her characters live in perfectly normal surroundings, such as a small mill town or an Army post in peacetime, but her revelation of their inner lives is so penetrating and their psychic turmoil is so grotesque that they seem to inhabit a world of existential dread. Overwrought inward obsessions define characters such as Weldon Penderton, Mick Kelly, or Frankie Addams, though their predicaments may appear absurd to ordinary people. Perhaps no American writer since Edgar Allan Poe has painted the mental landscape as well as McCullers; she has deftly delineated the subtle nuances of psychic states lying along the continuum linking psychosis and neurosis with normalcy.

Her relation to the literary tradition of Southern Gothic fiction is easily misunderstood. It is true that her characters include deaf-mutes, lunatics, criminals, fanatics, a giant in love with a dwarf, eunuchs, perverts, and variously mutilated, disfigured, and misshapen people; yet, the grotesquery in this gallery was not designed merely for sensational effect or regional humor. McCullers uses her bizarre characters to demonstrate how intricately the usual and the unusual are entangled in human nature, and, as a result, how delicate is that balance of wildly divergent impulses called normality. To overemphasize the grotesquery in her fiction may obscure one of her most valuable insights: Spiritual isolation is a universal condition of modern humankind and not the result of individual eccentricity.

A radical inability to connect meaningfully with others traps McCullers' most memorable characters within themselves. Her best characters yearn to find meaning in life and to carve out a victorious place in the order of things. Mick Kelly aspires to master the cosmic harmonies of music and find fame on the concert stage. Doctor Copeland works to free blacks from the bondage of segregation. Others seek fulfillment in the rigid patterns of military life or the emotional concord of a good marriage. Instead, they become deracinated souls, isolated from one another and cut off from the meaning they seek from life. Mick Kelly winds up behind a counter at a ten-cent store. Doctor Copeland is beaten by the police and alienated by his own family. Although some characters and situations in McCullers' fiction reveal the glories of unselfish love, the warmth of domestic accord, and the capacity for courage in ordinary people, her plots tend to exacerbate rather than resolve antagonisms that divide people, and the prevailing mood is one of existential angst.

A critic once complained that *The Member of the Wedding* was without a beginning, middle, or end. McCullers' fiction does depend upon character revelation, a lyrical style, and narratorial bearing more than a story line. Far from being plot-ridden, her stories are musically structured. She once told her publisher that *The Heart Is a Lonely Hunter* was composed like a fugue, with theme and countertheme developed contrapuntally as characters interact in mingled harmony. The emotional pace and tone of *The Ballad of the Sad Café* and *The Member of the Wedding* are established by abrupt beginnings, long middles, and brief, haunting codas. The sound of music often sets the mood, reveals a character, or makes a point. For example, the rapture of a classical concerto transports Alison Langdon and her houseboy, Anacleto; a deaf-mute's radio plays unheard; and the harmony of a chain gang's song lifts each member's soul.

A distinctive lyrical quality pervades language as well as structure in her tales. Simple but intense, humorous yet sympathetic, elegant but never high-flown, McCullers' storytelling voice is capable of interweaving an utterly realistic narrative and wild descriptions and preposterous details. An uncanny instinct for colloquial idiom makes her tone ring perfectly clear and sweet, without a trace of sentimentality or judgmental dogma.

Some critics who admire her individual works have been disappointed with her career. They say that she limited her work to a narrow range, sociologically and intellectually, relying too much on characters like herself. Given that she worked within self-imposed limits and against odds beyond her control, however, McCullers achieved spectacular success. Her career was foreshortened by crippling pain and early death, but all the books she wrote in her twenties sold more than half a million copies each, and all were adapted to stage or screen or both. If she focused on the heart rather than the intellect, and on people rather than society, she succeeded nevertheless in illuminating the lonely depths of the souls of modern men and women made tragically incomplete by the failure of love.

THE HEART IS A LONELY HUNTER

First published: 1940
Type of work: Novel

In a small Southern town, four lonely people look to a deaf-mute for understanding and friendship.

The Heart Is a Lonely Hunter was the result of a strange creative process. Bedridden for weeks, McCullers wrote some character sketches. One day, in a flash of inspiration, she announced to her mother that the story would revolve around a deafmute named Singer to whom others pour out their hearts. The novel grew organically, without a controlling plot.

In part 1, the five main characters are introduced. Always polite, immaculately clean, and soberly attired, John Singer is oddly paired with Spiros Antonapoulos, a fat, retarded deaf-mute. After illness requires him to stop drinking wine, Antonapoulos develops antisocial habits. Singer offers excuses to the police, but his friend is committed to an insane asylum.

At an all-night café owned by Biff Brannon, Singer meets the radical drifter Jake Blount and the respected black doctor Benedict Copeland, men who hold Marxist views and aspire to revolution. Despite sharing similar views, their personalities are quite different. Blount is by turns a well-spoken fanatic and a swaggering, violent drunk. He accuses capitalists of liking pigs more than people, since people cannot be sold as sausage. People in the café, except for Singer and Brannon, dismiss such talk as drunken ranting. By contrast, Doctor Copeland is quite dignified and high-minded and is a well-read student of the philosopher Benedict de Spinoza. Single-mindedly devoted to the "strong, true purpose" of desegregation, he uses his brain rather than his heart, and thus alienates potential allies such as Blount and his own family. In their different ways, Blount and Copeland allow fanaticism to dry up their power of love.

Mick Kelly, a talented yet lonely girl of thirteen, is the most fully drawn character. Her family runs the shabby boardinghouse where Singer lives. To him she opens the "inside room" of her being, confiding in him her innermost feelings and aspirations.

In part 2, frustrations abound. Mick's experiences are tragically disappointing. To prove that she is like other girls, she throws a carefully orchestrated party, but then finds herself delighted when order breaks down and guests go running through the neighborhood. After her younger brother Bubber accidentally shoots Baby Wilson with a rifle and causes a superficial but bloody wound, Mick compounds Bubber's agony with talk of a child-sized electric chair awaiting him at Sing Sing. As a result, the boy is never his open, playful self again. Mick then has an embarrassing encounter with the boy next door. At the swimming hole, Mick dares him to strip naked, and he does. She does too, and they have sexual intercourse, only to feel guilt and shame afterwards.

Doctor Copeland's struggle reaches a grim crisis when his son is tortured in prison by being tied up for three days with his legs in the air. Both feet are frozen and must be amputated. Demanding to lodge a complaint, Doctor Copeland is himself arrested, beaten, and kicked in the groin by the sheriff's men. Blount distributes leaflets calling on workers to revolt, but he succeeds only in provoking a race riot that leaves two blacks dead.

Biff Brannon is freed from a loveless marriage by his wife's death. In a bedroom rearranged not to remind him of her, he smokes his cigars, rocks in his chair, and thumbs the pages of his twenty-year collection of newspapers. Wearing his mother's gold ring and his wife's perfume, he retreats from the world of manly assertiveness into passive self-sufficiency.

One by one these lonely hunters pour out their hearts to Singer, though he does not really understand them and wonders why they share inner secrets with him. The saddest scene occurs in his room when they visit him all at the same time. He hopes they will enjoy the radio he bought for their pleasure, but they stand around nervously, unable to connect emotionally with one another. Singer's only friend is Antonapoulos, whom he visits with gifts that go unappreciated. When he arrives at the asylum one summer day, he learns that his friend has died. Heartbroken, he returns to his room and shoots himself in the heart.

Part 3 briefly tells what happens after Singer's suicide. More baffled by his death than his life, Brannon recognizes his own failure to love. Blount leaves town in the aftermath of the riot with forty dollars given to him by Brannon. Doctor Copeland gives up the struggle and moves in with rural relatives he had earlier scorned. Mick changes her mind about the "inside room" so lavishly furnished with dreams. She decides not to buy a piano, drops out of school, and goes to work at the ten-cent store.

Critics have disliked the novel's shapeless plot and crushing pessimism, but the author explores deep personal problems against the backdrop of a realistically drawn social landscape.

REFLECTIONS IN A GOLDEN EYE

First published: 1941
Type of work: Novel

Frustrated by impotence, deviance, and his wife's adultery, an Army officer murders an enlisted man.

Written in a matter of weeks, *Reflections in a Golden Eye* demonstrates the range of McCullers' talent. Here she goes beyond the realism that made her first novel so endearing and delves into a surreal world of dark, psychic impulses. Passions seethe beneath the rigid but fragile surface of military life on an Army post in peacetime. Six characters figure in the story.

Captain Weldon Penderton, an impotent, middle-aged man with homosexual in-clinations, is married to the beautiful Leonora, daughter of the fort's former com-mander. Leonora is having an affair with a neighbor, Major Morris Langdon; Lang-don's wife, Alison, cut off her own nipples with garden shears while mourning the death of a deformed baby. Morris and Leonora pass the time riding horseback and making love in a blackberry patch while Alison, a virtual shut-in, spends her days listening to classical music with her Filipino houseboy, Anacleto.

Private Williams, a mysterious young man with an affinity for animals, becomes Leonora's favorite stable boy. He cares for her high-spirited stallion, Firebird. One afternoon while Williams is sunbathing nude on a rock in the woods, Weldon, a poor horseman, takes Firebird out for a ride. As Williams looks on, the stallion breaks into a gallop that Weldon cannot control. Losing his balance, he slides out of the saddle and is dragged some distance. When Firebird finally stops, Weldon whips him viciously with the branch of a tree. Leonora soon discovers what has happened to her horse; during a party that evening, she gives her husband a sound thrashing with her riding crop in full view of the guests.

Much of the following action occurs, symbolically, at night. In the grip of a strange attraction, Weldon finds himself following Williams about the fort, gazing in through barracks windows for a glimpse of the youth. One night, Alison sees a shadowy fig-ure entering the Pendertons' house. Thinking it is her husband, she investigates, only to discover that it is Williams on one of his visits to Leonora's bedroom, where he silently watches her sleep. Alison delivers her hysterical report to Weldon, who refuses to believe it. When Alison announces her intention to file for divorce, Morris hastily has her committed to an insane asylum, where she commits suicide shortly after arrival. The story moves swiftly to its bizarre conclusion when, several nights later, Weldon happens upon Williams in Leonora's bedroom and shoots him. Only too late does he realize that he has destroyed the object of his strange fascination.

The novel explores a nightmarish world in which moral values have been lost. The loutish Morris Langdon, Leonora, and Private Williams live on an animalistic level of insensitivity and stupidity. Even their more imaginative counterparts, Alison, Anacleto, and Weldon, are doomed to destruction by their intensely convoluted emotions, self-loathing, and warped perceptions.

Moral direction and rational thinking have no part in the mad game played by the characters in this black comedy, for their visions of life are too distorted by personal suffering or emotional incapacity. Imagery in the novel plays tricks with perception: mirrors, windows, multifaceted eyes, the blur of colors Weldon sees as he hangs onto Firebird, and the grotesque reflections in the golden eye of Anacleto's ghastly green peacock. The characters themselves are never developed into fully human creations, but remain abstract refractions of tragically incomplete psychic states.

THE MEMBER OF THE WEDDING

First published: 1946
Type of work: Novel

To escape the pains of adolescence, a lonely girl dreams of being united with her brother and his bride after the wedding.

In *The Member of the Wedding*, attention is concentrated on twelve-year-old Frankie Addams, her six-year-old cousin John Henry West, and Berenice Sadie Brown, a middle-aged black housekeeper. Their card playing, eating, and talking in the kitchen during the last weekend of August constitute most of the action. It has been a bad summer for Frankie. Her best friend has moved away, she is too big to curl up beside her father in bed, and she belongs to no group. A lonely heart, she searches for "the we of me." In part 1, she latches onto the notion that she can join her brother and his bride after their wedding.

In part 2, she changes her name to F. Jasmine Addams and begins to believe that she belongs. She senses a fellow feeling with everyone she meets in town, including a soldier who buys her a drink at the Blue Moon and makes a date with her for that night.

Back home in the kitchen that afternoon, Berenice argues against Frankie's plans for the wedding. To show how foolishly people are served by unrealistic ideas of love, she tells of her four marriages. The first had been blissful, but, widowed, she married a succession of no-good men simply because they reminded her of her first husband. The last husband gouged out one of her eyes in a fight. Berenice's deep voice draws sympathy if not understanding from Frankie. Sometimes they break into song together, with John Henry's high notes sailing overhead and Frankie's voice harmonizing in the range between. They take turns pretending to be God. John Henry would remake the world with chocolate dirt and lemonade rain. Berenice would rid the world of war, hunger, and racism. Frankie likes Berenice's world, but she would also eliminate summer, enable people to change sexes at will, and start a worldwide club with membership certificates.

The long conversation does not resolve Frankie's inner turmoil. Having kept her rendezvous with the soldier a secret, she meets him at the Blue Moon on Saturday night. He uses a double-talk that is difficult for her to understand, but she accepts his invitation to his hotel room. After he throws her onto the bed, she knocks him out cold with a water pitcher and crawls down the fire escape, wondering if she has killed him.

Early the next morning, Frankie attends her brother's wedding, but her plan fails, because she cannot find words to ask if she can tag along. Finally, she must be dragged from the car so that the couple can make their getaway. Feeling worse than ever, she runs away that night, making it as far as the Blue Moon before a policeman recognizes her and restores her to her father.

The novel closes with a brief glimpse of moving day, when Frankie and her father go to live with relatives. She has a new best friend, a girl who likes reading poetry and pasting pictures in an art book. Now calling herself Frances, she is unmoved by the hardship that their relocation brings to Berenice and insensitive to the terrible death of John Henry from meningitis. The novel's ending shows that the girl's isolation is an ongoing condition, not the result of a dreary summer, a wrecked wedding, or a traumatic first date. With or without a best friend, Frankie remains seriously out of touch with the deepest feelings of those closest to her.

THE BALLAD OF THE SAD CAFÉ

First published: 1951
Type of work: Novella

A jilted husband returns to ruin his former wife's love affair with a hunchbacked dwarf.

A weird love story, *The Ballad of the Sad Café* was dedicated to David Diamond, her husband's lover. The story elevates elements of their triangular relationship to archetypal significance. Once a dingy old building in the middle of a town where "there is absolutely nothing to do," the café itself becomes a symbol of the human heart. Like a magic lantern, it may be lit by love—in this case, the love of a tall, muscular woman, Miss Amelia, for an itinerant hunchbacked dwarf, Cousin Lymon.

Townsfolk are flabbergasted when Miss Amelia offers him room and board, for she has cared nothing for the love of men and seldom invited them inside except to trick them out of money. After three days, they suspect that she has killed him. When a delegation arrives to investigate, however, they are surprised to find Cousin Lymon strutting around as if he owned the place. Miss Amelia has been completely transformed. Once stingy and shrewd, she now treats them with hospitality and generosity. Love has converted the town from boredom to joy, as the café hums with merriment and fellowship.

Six years later, the lantern is shattered when Miss Amelia's jilted husband, Marvin Macy, returns from prison. Years ago, their bizarre marriage had scandalized the town. On their wedding night, the bride bolted from the bedroom within half an hour. Whenever the groom came within reach, she gave him a violent drubbing. On the tenth day, he left town, vowing revenge. Before this marriage, Macy had been a terrible character, known as a defiler of young women and a brawler guilty of many crimes. In his pocket Macy carried the salted ear of a man he killed in a razor fight. His love for Miss Amelia transformed him however, and he became religious and well-mannered. His heart has been hardened however, by his wife's rebuff.

When he returns, townsfolk expect trouble. To their surprise, Cousin Lymon falls madly in love with him. In fact, he makes a public spectacle of himself, following the handsome wastrel around and moaning when Macy snubs him. Miss Amelia bears this abuse with chagrin, until matters came to a head on Ground Hog Day. Miss Amelia squares off against Macy in a brutal fight. Physically an even match, they grapple destructively but indecisively until Cousin Lymon pounces on Miss Amelia and begins choking her. She is beaten before anyone realizes what has happened. Victorious, the two men wreck her moonshine still, ransack the café, and leave town together.

In humiliation, Miss Amelia's heart turns cold. She raises the price of everything to one dollar, and customers stop coming to the café. Brooding in solitude, she lets her hair grow ragged and her body become thin. Once again, the town reverts to empty dreariness in which "the soul rots with boredom."

In a noteworthy passage, the balladeer reflects upon love. At the heart of love's mystery, he finds a cruel paradox: Love is not a mutual experience, but very different for lover and beloved. The quality of love is determined solely by the lover, as odd pairings in the story show. Macy is reformed by love for a woman who rejects him. She is similarly tempered by an unreciprocal feeling for the dwarf, who is himself transmogrified by an unrequited homosexual infatuation. Love proves no cure for the radical loneliness of the soul, but rather intensifies its pain.

The story has a haunting, lyrical beauty. Characters are portrayed concretely, but not dramatically. There is almost no dialogue, and virtually all events are related in flashback. The story is bracketed by references to the lyrical song of the chain gang. Perhaps Miss Amelia is more imprisoned by loneliness than the convicts are by chains, for their voices rise above their suffering and despair to recognize their unity.

Summary

The Southern writer William Faulkner said the only thing worth writing about is "the human heart in conflict with itself." By that standard, few have surpassed Carson McCullers, for she probed the tormented recesses of inner emotions. Tracking problems of loneliness and love to their lair within the heart, she found joy mingled with suffering so intense that her characters may seem grotesque. Nevertheless, her readers gain insights into life as it actually is lived. Neither sentimental nor moralistic, McCullers' novels make a more solid impact on the imagination than does merely sensational or experimental fiction.

Bibliography

Carr, Virginia Spencer. *The Lonely Hunter: A Biography of Carson McCullers.* Garden City, N.Y.: Doubleday, 1975.

Cook, Richard M. *Carson McCullers.* New York: Frederick Ungar, 1975.

Evans, Oliver. *The Ballad of Carson McCullers: A Biography.* New York: Coward-McCann, 1966.

McDowell, Margaret B. *Carson McCullers.* Boston: Twayne, 1980.

Shapiro, Adrian M., Jackson R. Bryer, and Kathleen Field. *Carson McCullers: A Descriptive Listing and Annotated Bibliography of Criticism.* New York: Garland, 1980.

John L. McLean

ROSS MACDONALD

Born: Los Gatos, California
December 13, 1915
Died: Santa Barbara, California
July 11, 1983

Principal Literary Achievement

In a series of detective novels featuring private eye Lew Archer, Macdonald transcended the limitations of the genre, probing the enduring effects of crimes on both victims and their descendants.

Biography

Ross Macdonald was born Kenneth Millar in Los Gatos, California, on December 13, 1915, the son of John Macdonald Millar and Annie Moyer Millar. (He did not adopt the Macdonald pseudonym until 1956.) In 1919, the family moved to Vancouver, British Columbia, where his father (primarily a journalist) was a harbor pilot for a while. His parents separated the same year, and Macdonald (whose mother was a near invalid) lived with different Canadian relatives for about two years in 1928 and 1929 while attending St. John's, a boarding school in Winnipeg. From there he went to Medicine Hat, Alberta, for a year to stay with an aunt, and then moved to Kitchener, Ontario, where he lived with his mother and grandmother and studied at Kitchener-Waterloo Collegiate and Vocational School. While there (1930-1932), he met Margaret Ellis Sturm, whom he would marry years later. Both published for the first time in the same issue of the school magazine, *The Grumbler*; Macdonald's story, a parody of Arthur Conan Doyle, featured a detective called Herlock Sholmes.

The 1932 death of his father gave Macdonald a legacy which enabled him to enter the University of Western Ontario; when his mother died in 1935, however, he left school and spent much of 1936 and 1937 traveling in Europe. Finally, on June 1, 1938, he received his A.B. degree, and the next day married Margaret Sturm. After attending summer school at the University of Michigan, they returned to Toronto, where Macdonald did graduate work at the Ontario College of Education. A daughter, Linda Jane, was born to the couple in June, 1939, and for the next two years Macdonald taught English at his former secondary school while returning to Michigan in the summers for graduate work. After Margaret published her first mystery novel, *The Invisible Worm*, in 1941, Macdonald was able to become a full-time graduate student at the University of Michigan, but service in the U.S. Navy inter-

rupted his studies in 1944. Immediately prior to his induction, he had completed his first novel, *The Dark Tunnel* (1944), a spy story; while serving as communications officer on the escort carrier *Shipley Bay* in the Pacific, he wrote *Trouble Follows Me* (1946).

When he returned to civilian life in March, 1946, Macdonald and his family settled in Santa Barbara, California, where he wrote two novels in less than nine months: *Blue City* (1947) and *The Three Roads* (1948). (All these books were published under his real name, Kenneth Millar.) After an abortive attempt at autobiographical fiction, he produced his first Lew Archer novel, *The Moving Target* (1949), using the name John Macdonald (his father's given names) to avoid competing with his wife, who had already published eight mysteries. While writing his early detective fiction—by *The Drowning Pool* in 1950, he had become John Ross Macdonald to distinguish himself from John D. MacDonald, another crime-fiction author—he completed his graduate work at Michigan, receiving the Ph.D. in 1952. His dissertation was a study of the psychological criticism of Samuel Taylor Coleridge, the nineteenth century English romantic poet.

Between 1952 and 1956, Macdonald wrote a novel a year, with the name Ross Macdonald first appearing with *The Barbarous Coast* (1956). His seventeen-year-old daughter Linda's involvement in a vehicular homicide in 1956, for which she was sentenced to eight years of probation and ordered to undergo psychiatric care, led the Macdonalds to move to Menlo Park, near San Francisco, where he as well as Linda underwent psychotherapy for a year. In 1970, he recalled this as a period when "seismic disturbances occurred in [his] life." He wrote: "My half-suppressed Canadian years, my whole childhood and youth, rose like a corpse from the bottom of the sea to comfort me." Because of the problem with his daughter and its aftermath, he said, "I've taken a step towards becoming the writer [Alfred Knopf, the publisher] would like to see me be." After returning to Santa Barbara in the summer of 1957, Macdonald taught creative writing to adults and wrote book reviews for the *San Francisco Chronicle*. He also wrote *The Galton Case* (1959), the first of his books to develop variations on the Oedipus theme and the archetypal motif of the search for a father. Also in 1959, Linda Millar, then nineteen, disappeared for almost two weeks and was the object of a widespread and highly publicized search. Her difficult life (she died in 1970 at thirty-one) is reflected in a number of troubled girls who appear in the novels.

During the 1960's, Macdonald became involved in environmental issues, joining the Sierra Club and Audubon Society, cofounding Santa Barbara Citizens for Environmental Defense, and even picketing. These concerns are manifest in such novels as *The Underground Man* (1971) and *Sleeping Beauty* (1973). In terms of his career, the decade began with *The Ferguson Affair*, a non-Archer mystery that had three hardcover printings in 1960, his biggest success thus far. In 1966, a popular film version of *The Moving Target* was released; called *Harper*, it starred Paul Newman. The decade concluded with *The Goodbye Look* (1969), Macdonald's first genuine best-seller and his first novel to attract widespread critical attention.

The publication of *The Underground Man* in 1971 was the occasion for a front-page review by Eudora Welty in *The New York Times Book Review* and a *Newsweek* cover story. The book was adapted for a television film in 1974, the year in which the Mystery Writers of America gave Macdonald its Grand Master Award. Two years later, his twenty-fourth and last novel, *The Blue Hammer* (1976), was published, a best-seller in the United States and abroad. By the close of the decade, Macdonald had begun to suffer the first symptoms of Alzheimer's disease, of which he died on July 11, 1983.

Analysis

The traditional detective novel is a puzzle: It begins with a crime, proceeds through a search for a solution, and concludes with the culprit exposed. Characterization is minimal and often stereotypical, and there is little thematic development beyond the obvious: Crime does not pay, for the criminal never triumphs, and eventually normality is restored. Macdonald's work is atypical. By his fourth novel, he was writing complex studies of the human condition that had begun to move beyond genre fiction to the realm of mainstream literature. Though mysteries are central and a private detective is narrator and prime protagonist, Macdonald's multilayered narratives mainly examine the ways in which the past impinges upon the present and how people often are trapped by a heritage of which they are unaware.

Having begun as a spy novelist with *The Dark Tunnel* and *Trouble Follows Me*, Macdonald in 1947 published his first hard-boiled novel in the Raymond Chandler and Dashiell Hammett tradition: *Blue City*. Its exile theme and its inclusion of a search for a father foreshadow his later works, including his fourth book, *The Three Roads*. The title recalls Sophocles' *Oedipus Tyrannus*, and the plot focuses upon the attempts of its hero, Bret Taylor, to reestablish his identity by recalling his past after a wartime bout with amnesia. This is the first Macdonald book with California as the primary locale—a territory he would mine in his remaining twenty novels. A year later, in *The Moving Target*, he introduces his private eye and narrator Lew Archer, who is featured in seventeen more novels and two story collections. Archer's name comes from Miles Archer, Sam Spade's murdered partner in Dashiell Hammett's *The Maltese Falcon* (1930). According to Macdonald, though, Archer is "patterned on Raymond Chandler's Marlowe," also a "semi-outsider . . . fascinated but not completely taken in by the customs of the natives." Unlike Chandler, Macdonald does not consider his detective to be the character who provides the "quality of redemption"; instead, he says, that quality "belongs to the whole work and is not the private property of one. . . . The detective-as-redeemer is a backward step in the direction of sentimental romance, and an oversimplified world of good guys and bad guys."

In 1973, after having written about Archer cases for almost a quarter of a century, Macdonald commented, "My narrator Archer's wider and less rigidly stylized range of expression, at least in more recent novels, is related to a central difference between him and Marlowe. Marlowe's voice is limited by his role as the hard-boiled hero." Archer, in fact, is an unusual private eye in many ways. For example, money is incidental to him, important mainly to pay the rent; further, he invariably is drawn emotionally to one of his clients—not usually sexually, but rather from a feeling of kinship with fellow sufferers, for he thinks that he "sometimes served as a catalyst for trouble, not unwillingly." Though not obsessed with the past in the way his clients and suspects are, when he looked in a mirror, he once said that "all I could read was my own past, in the marks of erosion under my eyes." The past is a living presence that causes him to empathize with those who are its prisoners. Above all, Archer is a good listener who often solves cases because he learns so much from those who take him into their confidence and talk freely to him. Unlike most series detectives, Archer is neither static nor two-dimensional, for Macdonald expanded the persona over the years: Archer's moralizing and sermonizing tendencies increase in the later novels. While his ratiocinative instincts remain as sharp as ever, they are tempered by a greater sensitivity; he becomes more humane.

Macdonald's novels also developed as the years passed, with major thematic concerns surfacing. In *The Drowning Pool*, the themes of corporate greed and environmental destruction are central; they are motifs that figure prominently in such later books as *The Underground Man* and *Sleeping Beauty*. In *The Doomsters* (1958), Macdonald believed that he had made "a fairly clean break with the Chandler tradition, which it had taken some years to digest, and freed me to make my own approach to the crimes and sorrows of life." His most complex novel to that point, it has a plot (not simply a series of scenes in the Chandler manner) that presents a family saga as a means of dramatizing a theme. Furthermore, Archer for the first time becomes involved in the events and is not at all the detached private eye hired for a job. The novel leads directly to Macdonald's next one, *The Galton Case*, his thirteenth, by which time he, by his own account, had "learned what every novelist has to learn: to convert his own life as it grows into his fiction as he writes." In writing it, he delved into his own past while maintaining aesthetic distance and gave a new dimension to what had become his customary concerns: the identity quest, greed, alienation, and the "pastness of the present."

In the eight novels of the next decade (all but the first, *The Ferguson Case* of 1960, featuring Lew Archer), the growth of Macdonald's plotting skills continues, whereas his characters remain superficial; the length limitations to which mystery genre writers had to conform may have mitigated against attempting both complex plotting and in-depth character development. In each of the books, his standard mix of posturing and duplicitous people—young victims, troubled women, arrogant yet insecure and unhappy rich people—confront resurrected pasts. An observation by Archer about one such person is applicable to many: "The mind that looked at me through his eyes was like muddy water continually stirred by fears and fantasies and old greed." Macdonald's last novel of the decade, *The Goodbye Look*, was his first best-seller and the first of his books to be reviewed on the front page of *The New York Times Book Review*, unusual for a mystery writer. Written during the Vietnam War, it has an antiwar theme in addition to Macdonald commonplaces; by this twenty-first of his novels (and the sixteenth Lew Archer novel), Macdonald's surer hands juggle his most complex plot to date, encompassing six different families whose paths cross over a quarter of a century.

Before being incapacitated by Alzheimer's disease, Macdonald wrote three more novels: *The Underground Man*, *Sleeping Beauty*, and *The Blue Hammer*, the first of which is generally considered his masterpiece. In addition to the recurring presence of familiar Macdonald motifs, there is in it a major focus upon the environment and ecological matters, the latter through means of a forest fire that rages during most of the book. The multiple plots, dealing with past and present events, are unified not only by the tight organization and overlapping of characters but also by their exemplification of the thematic underpinning, again involving the pastness of the present.

Sleeping Beauty is something of a sequel to its predecessor, focusing as it does upon the environment by means of an oil spill that is its primary symbol. The fragile link between man and nature, with human greed upsetting the necessary balance, is always in the background of the plot, which progresses through three generations of a family's corruption and concludes with a metaphorical linking of the human and natural tragedies. Also of interest in the novel is the suggestion that Lew Archer is faltering: Becoming too involved emotionally with a young woman, the "sleeping beauty" of the title, he unwittingly permits a murderer to commit suicide.

Macdonald's last novel, *The Blue Hammer*, which had its genesis in notebook entries written fourteen years before he completed it, is a fully realized delineation of the double motif and the need for self-realization; it is his most complex treatment of these and other standard motifs since *The Goodbye Look*. Critics complained about his reliance upon timeworn formulas and his reworking of previously utilized plots and characters, amounting to little more than a variation on old themes. Along with the sameness, however, there are significant differences. The Cain-Abel motif is new, and Archer is more introspective. Further, though he had been the consummate loner in so many novels over twenty-five years, the changes suggested in *Sleeping Beauty* lead in this novel to his first love affair, which not only ends in disappointment ("when she dropped out of sight, I felt the loss of part of myself") but also distracts him from his proper pursuits.

In *The Underground Man*, a minister sends a letter to a character whose search for his father initiates most of the key events, including the son's murder. Reverend Riceyman's message, which Archer calls "good advice," can serve as a coda to most of the Macdonald canon: "The past can do very little for us—no more than it has already done, for good or ill—except in the end to release us. We must seek and accept release, and give release."

THE MOVING TARGET

First published: 1949
Type of work: Novel

Private detective Lew Archer's search for a kidnapped oilman leads to the exposure of an alien smuggling operation.

The Moving Target is a quickly paced mystery-adventure novel filled with chases, fights, and murders that Macdonald described as "a story clearly aspiring to be a movie," which it became: *Harper*, starring Paul Newman, in 1966. His fourth novel, it is a landmark in his career, marking as it does the debut of Lew Archer, a Los Angeles private detective patterned after Raymond Chandler's Philip Marlowe, with whom Archer shares a sense of righteousness; Archer, however, is more introspective and realistic. Being the narrator, he becomes the moral center of the book.

Linked as the book is to the "hard-boiled" detection fiction tradition, Archer is challenged by several dangerous physical encounters with adversaries. In one struggle: "I clubbed the gun and waited. The first two got bloody scalps. Then they swarmed over me, hung on my arms, kicked my legs from under me, kicked consciousness out of my head. . . . I came to fighting. My arms were pinned, my raw mouth kissing cement." In another encounter, "His fist struck the nape of my neck. Pain whistled through my body like splintered glass, and the night fell on me solidly again." A bit later he overcomes his captor, they fall into the water struggling, and Archer kills the man in self-defense. (In later novels, Archer's challenges become increasingly cerebral instead of physical, as he moves from thirty-five years old to middle age.)

With its Southern California setting and characters whom money, or the desire for it, corrupts, the novel anticipates the anti-acquisitiveness of later Macdonald books. At the very start, for example, Archer comes upon the oceanfront estates of Cabrillo Canyon and muses: "The light-blue haze . . . was like a thin smoke from slowly burning money. . . . Private property: color guaranteed fast; will not shrink egos. I had never seen the Pacific look so small." Though the plot is not as complex as those of later novels, it is multifaceted. The primary action, about the disappearance of Ralph Sampson, an oilman, is intertwined with a story line concerning an illegal Mexican alien smuggling operation that Archer happens upon while tracking the kidnappers. Sampson does not appear until the end, when Archer finally discovers his body, but his personality pervades and motivates the action. Miranda, his daughter, recalls that he "started out with nothing . . . his father was a tenant farmer who never had land of his own." She understands, therefore, why Ralph wanted to own so much land, but she laments that "you'd think he'd be more sympathetic to poor people . . . the strikers on the ranch, for instance."

Miranda is being courted by Alan Taggert, Sampson's pilot and surrogate son (replacing one killed in World War II), whose primary interest is her father's wealth, and this greed involves him in the ransom kidnapping of his employer. Ironically, Taggert is killed by a rival suitor, Sampson lawyer Albert Graves, a former district attorney who, having worked for millionaires so long, "saw his chance to be a millionaire himself" by marrying Miranda and killing his new father-in-law so he would not have to wait for access to his riches. Says Archer of his longtime friend and erstwhile colleague: "He wasn't looking down; he was looking up. Up to the houses in the hills where the big money lives. He was going to be big himself for a change, with a quarter of Sampson's millions."

THE GALTON CASE

First published: 1959
Type of work: Novel

An old woman's desire for reconciliation with her son and the appearance of a putative grandson involve Archer in a complex variation of the Oedipus theme.

According to Ross Macdonald, he and young John Galton in *The Galton Case* have much in common, including "a sense of displacement, a feeling that, no matter where we were, we were on the alien side of some border. . . . [L]ike dubious claimants to a lost inheritance." Among Macdonald's notebook jottings about the novel is the statement, "Oedipus angry vs. parents for sending him away into a foreign country," and he has written that the book "was shaped not in imitation exactly, but in awareness of . . . early Greek models."

The action begins twenty years after Anthony Galton has dropped out of sight with his pregnant wife, a young woman of dubious background whom his wealthy parents rejected. His elderly mother's attorney hires Lew Archer to solve the mystery, which the detective does easily, largely because of an extraordinary streak of good luck. Having ascertained that Galton became a poet with the name "John Brown," Archer locates the missing man's remains. This is only the beginning of the story, however, for Archer also happens upon a young man who may be Galton's son, a twenty-two-year-old calling himself John Brown, Jr., and bearing an uncanny resemblance to his supposed father. Archer suspects that he is an imposter, however, so with one case done, the private eye embarks on another—to establish the identity of John Brown, Jr. Thus begins an odyssey taking him throughout California as well as to Nevada, Michigan, and Canada. Along the way he uncovers a conspiracy to dupe old Mrs. Galton and gain control of her wealth, a plan involving not only assorted gangsters and former convicts but also her trusted attorney. In typical Macdonald fashion, its origins go back decades, so Archer must delve through a tangled morass of tormented lives, along the way suffering a broken jaw and other physical traumas. Peeling away layers of the past, he ascertains that though John Brown, Jr., was part of the original plot, having been hired to play his role because he resembled

Anthony Galton, he was not, after all, Theodore Fredericks of Pitt, Ontario: He really was John Galton.

Despite their many unusual twists and unexpected turns, the multiple plots are clearly linked, and they progress logically to their common conclusion. So much of Archer's success depends upon coincidence and sheer luck, however, that credibility sometimes is strained. This problem notwithstanding, *The Galton Case* is a compelling novel, for Macdonald maintains suspense throughout and paints memorable domestic scenes, not only in the Galton household but also between Gordon Sable (Mrs. Galton's attorney) and his alcoholic wife, and Mrs. Fredericks (John Galton's mother) and her alcoholic husband. The pair of tense meetings that Archer has with Marian Matheson (erstwhile maid of the fugitive young Galtons and their baby) advances his case and adds emotional power to the novel. Macdonald is at his best, however, in scenes with Sheila Howell (daughter of Mrs. Galton's physician) and John Galton, who have fallen in love. The girl has an epic confrontation with her father, who doubts Galton's veracity; later, Archer locates the pair after they have fled together. This latter scene is an unaffectedly tender portrayal of young love, and the incident recalls the flight of John's parents years earlier. Further, on this occasion Archer sees old scars of childhood abuse on John's back, which remind him of marks reportedly seen on his mother's body decades ago.

Many of the characters are familiar Macdonald types, but standing apart from others is the boy who turns out to be the Galton heir after all. Handsome and personable, he seems from the start to be too good to be true, and indeed, at the beginning he is an excellent deceiver. His acting ability and careful preparation notwithstanding, the real reason that he is so convincing is that, unknown even to himself, he actually is the person he pretends to be. The man he knew as his father had actually murdered his real father, and his mother, who witnessed the crime, had married her husband's killer and remained silent for sixteen years lest Nelson Fredericks kill her son. Pretender though he is at the start, the boy is motivated by a desire to escape from a stifling environment, and despite his talent to deceive, he is honest with wealthy Ada Reichler, whom he meets while a student at the University of Michigan (where he is known as John Lindsay), taking her to Pitt so that she can see the kind of background from which he comes. At the end, he even is able to say to Mrs. Fredericks, "I don't hate you. . . . I'm sorry for you, Mother. And I'm sorry for what I've said." Having completed his search, he is at peace with himself and everyone else.

While writing the book, Macdonald wrote to his publisher that he wanted it to be a transition work for him "out of the 'hard-boiled' realm. . . . [M]y ambition . . . is to write on serious themes." Despite the intent, much violence remains, but the thematic content is more fully developed than in earlier novels. One theme, already a standard in Macdonald, is the contrast between the haves and the have-nots, with Archer's disdain for the wealthy and greedy again in focus. This is subordinated to the identity theme, however, not only the son's search for his father (which would be Macdonald's concern in *The Underground Man*), but also the boy's quest to establish precisely who he is, which leads into still another common Macdonald theme, the intertwining of past and present. Near the close of *The Galton Case*, Marian Matheson asks Archer, "Is this trouble going to go on forever?" Finally, after twenty-three years, he can say, "We're coming to the end of it."

THE CHILL

First published: 1964
Type of work: Novel

A runaway bride and the murder of a woman professor lead to the reopening of old crimes and the discovery of changed identities.

The Chill, which won a British Crime Writers' Association Silver Dagger Award, begins with young Dolly Kincaid abandoning her husband the day after they are married. Alex Kincaid hires Lew Archer to find her, which he does effortlessly, but this turns out to be only the beginning of the story, involving a triple murder case extending back over many years. Young Alex, early in the story, remarks with awe to Archer: "It's almost as though history is repeating itself." Later, when someone says to him, "Anyway, it's all past history," Archer replies, "History is always connected with the present." On another occasion, he compares his present problem with earlier ones, "which opened up gradually like fissures in the firm ground of the present, cleaving far down through the strata of the past." The thematic and structural traits of *The Chill* place it in the Macdonald mainstream, a continuation of his contemporary Oedipal legend, but it is more complex than its predecessors, and it concludes with a stunning reversal that Archer happens upon only at the very end.

Dolly, the runaway bride, had witnessed the shooting of her mother years previously and testified against her father. Upon his release from San Quentin, he pleads his case to her, and she realizes that an unknown woman, not Thomas McGee, had committed the crime. Rent by guilt, she flees Alex and goes to a local college, supporting herself by assisting the dean's mother. Within a short time, Helen Haggerty, a French professor who serves as Dolly's adviser, is murdered, and the girl finds the body. An emotional wreck, Dolly is treated by a psychiatrist who had seen her as a child. Through his therapy, she sorts out the confusions of past and present, resolving her doubts about herself and others.

Meanwhile, Archer travels from California to Nevada and Missouri to do his own sorting and unraveling, and he finds that Haggerty also had witnessed a murder when she was a girl and was blackmailing Dean Bradshaw, an old beau. He also learns that Bradshaw had been leading at least two lives, hiding romantic liaisons from his elderly mother, with whom he lived. Haggerty's death leads Archer to delve into the long-ago death of Luke Deloney in Missouri, officially an accidental self-killing but actually a murder. As he peels away the layers of the past in an attempt to get at the truth about present events, Archer is confronted by new problems, with previously unknown people emerging and a bewildering sequence of events occurring. Roy Bradshaw becomes increasingly suspect, as the supposed facts of his life conflict: his excessive devotion to his mother, with whom he lives; his secret divorce from a woman called Letitia Macready; his similarly quiet marriage to his colleague Laura Sutherland; the summer tour of Europe that he never took, despite postcards home to Laura and his mother; and the many years of psychiatric care he underwent. In contrast, old Mrs. Bradshaw seems to be the epitome of stability, except for her obsessive attachment to her son.

At the very end, however, Archer sees that not even she is the matriarch he assumed she was. Signaling the startling revelation is Roy Bradshaw's cryptic statement, "I'm beginning to hate old women"; moments later, Archer sees a family picture and realizes that the Bradshaws are not mother and son but husband and wife. She had been Letitia Macready but pretended to have died in Europe to cover her murder of Deloney: she perpetrated the later charade to obscure her motive for murdering Helen McGree. It was she who killed Helen Haggerty out of fear that the younger woman was going to steal Roy. The ultimate irony is that she unintentionally kills Roy while going to murder his new wife.

After he has exposed the truth, Archer calls Letitia Osborne Macready Bradshaw an "old woman," and she snaps back, "You mustn't call me that. I'm not old. Don't look at my face, look into my eyes. You can see how young I am." He reflects: "She was still greedy for life." This senator's daughter also was greedy for love, money, and power; sustained by her fantasies, she permitted the obsessions to corrupt her and consequently ruin or destroy many lives. The morality tale, one of Macdonald's most successful books, concludes with Archer's "No more anything, Letitia." After decades, then, Archer has excised evil from society, and the survivors—particularly Dolly—can face the future confidently, secure in the knowledge that the past no longer holds secrets from them.

THE UNDERGROUND MAN

First published: 1971
Type of work: Novel

A son's attempts to learn the facts behind his father's long-ago disappearance dredge up the past and unleash a tragic sequence of events.

Like many other Macdonald novels, *The Underground Man* takes place primarily in the fictitious Santa Teresa, which bears more than a passing resemblance to Santa Barbara, where Macdonald lived for thirty-five years. Also typical is the fact that the action ranges widely throughout California.

Early in the book, Lew Archer becomes involved in the entangled affairs of a well-to-do Santa Teresa family split in marital disputes. Leo Broadhurst, scion of the clan, had vanished fifteen years earlier, leaving his wife for another woman, but then also seemingly deserting the second woman as well. His son, consumed for years by the desire to find his father, finally advertises for information in a newspaper, but his reward offer succeeds only in dredging up the past and does not locate Broadhurst. One reward seeker is Albert Sweetner, an escaped convict who had been a foster child of Edna Snow, onetime Broadhurst housekeeper. Sweetner's return revives a long-past scandal involving a teenage girl who is now a married woman. While the past closes in on these people and others, threatening their present lives, a raging forest fire also endangers them and their property and gives a sense of urgency to Archer's need to resolve the growing mystery—the flames are on the verge of destroying evidence.

During the few days that the action of the book covers, Archer learns that Broadhurst was a womanizer whose wife shot him; as he lay dying, Edna Snow finished him off with a knife—both exacting delayed revenge. By the end of the novel, events have moved full circle: The mystery of Leo Broadhurst's disappearance is solved, but his son dies in the process. Albert Sweetner also is killed, and another character commits suicide. There are positive futures for some others, but Lew Archer is the only one unchanged; he has not even made much money from his efforts. More than in any other Macdonald novel, the characters in *The Underground Man* have "all the years of their lives dragging behind them." Even Archer, nearing the close of the case, feels "shipwrecked on the shores of the past." At the end, Archer wishes for Leo Broadhurst's young grandson "a benign failure of memory."

Central to the novel are the quest and Oedipal motifs, which are most poignantly delineated in the character of Stanley, whose love-hate relationship with Leo is the motivating force of his life. As one character explains it, "he's angry at his father for abandoning him; at the same time he misses him and loves him." This omnipresence of the past is the primary theme of the work. The forest fire raging in the background of much of the action is a leitmotif serving as metaphor for man's alienation from his fellows, from himself, and from nature. It consumes everything in its path in the same wantonly destructive manner as the characters pursue their dreams or rebel against their nightmares. Archer's first reaction to the blaze invokes war, alienated man's ultimate destructive act: "Under and through the smoke I caught glimpses of fire like the flashes of guns too far away to be heard. The illusion of war was completed by an old two-engine bomber, which flew in low over the mountain's shoulder." Later, when he reaches the Broadhurst ranch, Archer notices that the darkening fruit "hung down from their branches like green hand grenades." (War imagery is common in Macdonald's novels, a lasting effect of his experience in the Pacific during World War II.)

Counterpointing the symbolic squabbling of the symbolic jays in the opening scene of the book and the forest fire throughout is the rain at the end. By quenching the life-threatening blaze, the storm offers a purging of the old and a renewal of life. "When I went outside," Archer says, "the rain was coming down harder than ever. Water was running in the street, washing the detritus of summer downhill toward the sea." Further, the title of the novel recalls Fyodor Dostoevski's *Zapiski iz podpolya*

(1864; *Notes from the Underground*, 1918); by calling attention to it, Macdonald leads the reader to see his themes of guilt and suffering in bolder relief.

With this twenty-second of his novels (the seventeenth with Lew Archer), Macdonald gained his long-sought recognition as successor to Chandler and Hammett in the hard-boiled school. At the same time, he was accepted as a serious novelist. *The Underground Man* is his major achievement, the work in which his worldview— including social commentary, mainly on environmental and ecological matters—is most fully and most memorably expressed. The several story lines in this novel are more skillfully developed and more unified than in any of his previous books, and the portrait of a corrupt society is especially memorable, with Archer's efforts revealing the venality behind the façade of propriety. Finally, despite echoes of earlier books, *The Underground Man* has its own voice and quality, and it perfectly combines timeless and timely themes.

Summary

Writing as Ross Macdonald, Kenneth Millar produced a series of detective novels with plots more complex than is typical of the genre and characters more fully realized than is the usual practice. More important, his narratives are vehicles for themes, primarily variations on how people corrupt the American Dream by their greed and lack of vision. Each of the novels is a tragedy, with the destruction, wrought from within the characters, unleashing avenging furies whose disastrous forces endure through generations. Through the efforts of Lew Archer, the moral center of almost all the tales, evil finally is purged, and the survivors can look forward to normal lives.

Bibliography

Bruccoli, Matthew J. *Kenneth Millar/Ross Macdonald: A Descriptive Bibliography.* Pittsburgh: University of Pittsburgh Press, 1983.
_____. *Ross Macdonald.* San Diego: Harcourt Brace Jovanovich, 1984.
Schopen, Bernard H. *Ross Macdonald.* Boston: Twayne, 1990.
South Dakota Review 24 (Spring, 1986). Special Macdonald issue.
Speir, Jerry. *Ross Macdonald.* New York, Frederick Ungar, 1978.
Wolfe, Peter. *Dreamers Who Live Their Dreams: The World of Ross Macdonald's Novels.* Bowling Green, Ohio: Bowling Green University Press, 1976.

Gerald H. Strauss

THOMAS McGUANE

Born: Wyandotte, Michigan
December 11, 1939

Principal Literary Achievement

Recognized as a prose stylist in the tradition of Ernest Hemingway and F. Scott Fitzgerald, McGuane has produced masculine fiction that focuses on the problems of finding an acceptable place and vocation in the latter half of the twentieth century.

Biography

Thomas Francis McGuane III was born in Wyandotte, Michigan, on December 11, 1939, to Thomas Francis II and Alice McGuane. His family contained some "fantastic storytellers," and McGuane inherited both the ability and the inclination to make storytelling his life. As a child, McGuane read nature books at his family's summer retreat, a fishing camp in northern Michigan that resembles the setting for his first novel, *The Sporting Club* (1969). His other passion, which he has also pursued since his childhood, is sport fishing, an activity that appears in most of his novels.

McGuane attended and was graduated from Cranbrook, an exclusive boarding school in Michigan. During those years he ran away to a Wyoming ranch owned by the father of a girlfriend and returned an avowed "sociopath." He later used this experience and the resulting attitude as the basis for his second novel, *The Bushwhacked Piano* (1971). His college career began on an unpromising note when he flunked out of the University of Michigan. He briefly attended Olivet College and then was graduated from Michigan State University with honors. In 1965, he received his M.F.A. in playwriting from Yale University and spent the following academic year at Stanford University on a Wallace Stegner Fellowship. McGuane has supported himself by writing screenplays, including *Rancho Deluxe* (1973), *Ninety-Two in the Shade* (1975), *The Missouri Breaks* (1975), and (with Bud Shrake) *Tom Horn* (1980), and by directing *Ninety-Two in the Shade*. Raising cutting horses brings in enough money to pay his ranch mortgage, and he has become an expert sport fisherman, sailor, and rodeo competitor.

Throughout his college career, McGuane avoided what have been considered the typical undergraduate excesses of alcohol and drugs to the point that he was called the "White Knight." In December of 1972, however, he lost control of his Porsche

on an icy road en route to the Florida Keys, an accident that barely damaged the car but left McGuane so shaken that he could not speak for hours afterward. This brush with death made him see that art was not as important as life, and he abandoned what had been his relentless pursuit of writing. The following years were filled with tales of wild behavior, excessive drinking and drug use, and hasty marriages, encouraged in part by McGuane's involvement in screenwriting and directing in Hollywood. He had affairs with actresses Elizabeth Ashley and Margot Kidder and was divorced by his wife, Becky, after thirteen years of marriage when she learned that Kidder was pregnant. After nine months of marriage, Kidder and McGuane also were divorced.

McGuane admits his years of excessive behavior, but he maintains that the stories are exaggerated. Indeed, the amount of work that he produced indicates that close to 80 percent of his waking hours were spent writing and directing. His marriage in 1977 to Laurie Buffett (sister of singer Jimmy Buffett) helped stabilize his life, and since then he has approached both life and his art with greater balance.

McGuane's third novel, *Ninety-Two in the Shade* (1973), draws on his experience sport fishing in the Keys. His fourth novel, *Panama* (1978), a departure from his first three, is a prolonged howl of despair from a washed-up rock star that reflects McGuane's own mixed feelings about his turbulent years in Hollywood. A more settled McGuane wrote three novels focusing on male restlessness in a country deteriorating into materialism and fads. *Nobody's Angel* (1982), *Something to Be Desired* (1984), and *Keep the Change* (1989) are set in the ranch country of Montana and feature protagonists who are looking for a way to live in a world that offers few satisfactory choices. In *Nobody's Angel*, Patrick Fitzpatrick, disoriented by the deaths of his father and sister (recent events in McGuane's own life) fails to find a suitable answer to his search. The relatively upbeat conclusions of *Something to Be Desired* and *Keep the Change* reflect McGuane's satisfaction with his more orderly and settled life. He approaches his writing with energy and seriousness, but he receives equal pleasure from raising and training horses and successfully competing in rodeos.

An Outside Chance: Essays on Sport (1980), shows a slightly different side of McGuane than is revealed in his fiction. He is intensely interested in sport, especially fishing, and writes about it with a perception that most sportsmen and sports writers do not possess. In 1986, McGuane published a collection of short stories, *To Skin a Cat*; the stories in this collection deal with the same concerns found in his novels, adapted to the more structured form of the short story.

Analysis

The novels of Thomas McGuane reflect his interest and experience in playwriting and screenwriting. He gives readers visual images of moods, emotions, and action, and he refrains from simply telling readers what his characters are thinking, feeling, and doing. His characters speak tersely and rarely say explicitly how they feel. This spareness and terseness can be confusing to first-time readers of McGuane, especially since his worldview and the antics of his characters are definitely not mainstream. Recognizing his themes and understanding his style and humor are necessary before readers can appreciate the richness of McGuane's craft.

A consistent theme in all McGuane's novels is father-son conflict. The father is a distant figure who, although respected and maybe even loved by his son, never had what one would call a warm relationship with his family. The son, the novel's protagonist, feels a sense of loss at not having a strong, concerned male as a guide and role model. In *Something to Be Desired*, the protagonist is himself a father, and he must work through his relationship with his son and try to avoid being the same kind of father that his had been. In three novels, surrogate fathers appear—C. J. Clovis in *The Bushwhacked Piano*, the grandfather in *Nobody's Angel*, and Otis Redwine in *Keep the Change*—but none of these older men has the strength of character that the real, but nonfunctioning, father has. This absence of the father leads in part to the unrest and aimless behavior of the protagonist as he searches for something to do and a way to act.

McGuane sees the twentieth century United States as a "declining snivelization." His protagonists search for the kind of America that young men used to grow up with, a lost primeval virtue that used to define American manhood. In *The Sporting Club*, one sees the vulgarity, weakness, and ineptness of wealthy Detroit businessmen as they pursue sport and "justice" at their hunting and fishing retreat. In *Ninety-Two in the Shade*, Key West is filled with inept, arrogant suburbanites who demand trophy fish from their guides. Good fishing lanes are ruined by the earsplitting roar of military jets, mobile homes crowd the water's edge, and political corruption simmers just below the surface of daily life. In *Panama*, Chet Pomeroy returns to Key West to find the changes that represent the general changes in the United States. A family jewelry store is now a moped rental shop, and a taco stand has replaced a small book store.

In the next three novels, the protagonists return to the ranch country of Montana to look for the values no longer sought by the schemers of Key West and Latin America. They discover that Montana and ranching have been invaded by the same forces that have ruined Key West. Patrick Fitzpatrick (*Nobody's Angel*) discovers that men with Oklahoma oil money play at ranching. Lucien Taylor in *Something to Be Desired* is successful only by turning his ranch into a hot springs spa for the wealthy and aimless who travel around to the fashionable watering holes. Although Joe Starling (*Keep the Change*) is successful with one season of ranching, his work comes to nothing because of the scams of his uncle in a town that attaches to Joe the sins of his father. The only moral courses for these protagonists are to discover what to do by the process of elimination or to opt for lunacy.

Those same three protagonists are unable to be content with the lives they live, feeling that some romance is missing from their lives. This dissatisfaction leads to aimless behavior and antics that are both bizarre and self-destructive. Patrick gives up, but Lucien and Joe find something that gives them a degree of satisfaction.

McGuane rarely comments on his characters' actions; bizarre behavior is simply presented as it happens. Vernor Stanton in *The Sporting Club* foments discord wherever he is; he is also, to a degree, self-destructive. Stealing a dignitaries' bus from a bridge-opening ceremony may seem to be no more than a juvenile prank, but it is also a comment on the pomposity of appointed officials and the ceremonies that surround them. When Thomas Skelton's father (in *Ninety-Two in the Shade*) retreats to his bed for months, he is not a typical hypochondriac; he is actually sick of the world that allows his own father to become successful through political exploitation.

McGuane's humor resembles that of William Faulkner in "Spotted Horses," both in its physical nature and in the fact that it is used to ridicule. In *The Sporting Club*, Earl Olive's dynamiting of the main lodge, the flagpole, and the lifeguard chair sends a group of old men dashing in one direction in pursuit of the perpetrator, only to hear another blast in their rear. Wayne Codd's ineptness in spying on Ann Fitzgerald (*The Bushwhacked Piano*) becomes slapstick when he falls off the roof with his pants down trying to photograph her in bed with Nicholas Payne. In *Something to Be Desired*, Lucien Taylor's efforts to dispose of the body of a customer who dies at his spa are hilarious to everyone but him and his employees, who become frustrated as one glitch after another prevents them from solving the problem.

THE SPORTING CLUB

First published: 1969
Type of work: Novel

Vernor Stanton and James Quinn expose the sordid origins and ancestors of an exclusive hunting and fishing club in northern Michigan.

Thomas McGuane used the woods of northern Michigan as the setting for his first novel, *The Sporting Club*. The Centennial Club, founded by distant relatives of its present members, has been the retreat for highly paid Detroit executives and their families. Hunting and fishing are the accepted manly activities, while the women and children swim and lie in the sun. Into this setting come two characters who eventually destroy the club. James Quinn, who has rescued his father's business from the brink of bankruptcy, appears to be the ideal club member. He longs for the solitude of the woods and the established and honorable rituals of sport. He approaches fishing with care, expertise, and reverence, trying to cleanse himself of the stain of business and the attendant cutthroat competition. Returning to the club after an absence of several years is Vernor Stanton, a friend of Quinn from their adolescent days. Stanton is extremely wealthy and has cast himself apart from those who perform any of the normal tasks of upper-class American life. He wants to "make the world tense" and "foment discord."

Stanton's return is motivated by his desire to destroy the club and to convince the members that they are not the distinguished descendants of grand ancestors who founded the club on lofty ideals. To effect this goal, he must enlist the help of Quinn, who joined him in many a prank in the past. Quinn resists at first, mainly because he sees himself as a responsible businessman—too old, mature, and content to want to disrupt tradition. Stanton's challenges, the force of his personality, and the decadence of the present club members, though, change Quinn from a reluctant spectator into Stanton's accomplice. Stanton can be viewed as a knight in shining armor whose task is to rid the world of evil. Regardless of the reason the Centennial Club was founded, it increased its holdings by driving the surrounding families off their lands, often illegally, through bribes to political figures. Memberships are passed down from father to eldest son in biblical fashion, and most of the present owners act as though they are the rightful heirs of the club's glorious past.

Stanton's plan begins when he gets rid of Jack Olson, the club's manager, who has kept a perfect balance between wildlife, food supply, and hunting and fishing needs within the club's boundaries. When Olson leaves, he hires his replacement, Earl Olive, a man he met in a roadhouse bar. Olive enters with his people—bums, bikers, and floozies—who immediately clash with the club members. In retaliation for getting his nose broken in a duel with Stanton, Olive dynamites the dam, reducing the lake to swamp, and destroys the main building, the lifeguard stand, and the flagpole. Led by the militaristic Fortescu, the prominent club members decide to bring Olive to justice themselves.

A time capsule that is opened in honor of the club's centennial produces a photograph that reveals the decadence of the club's founders, at which point the present members reenact the sexual circus shown in the photograph. When outside authorities finally arrive to restore some semblance of order, Quinn is the only one sane enough to explain what happened. As an acknowledgment of its total destruction, the Centennial Club is put up for sale. Stanton immediately buys it, deeds Quinn's house to him, and uses the club for his own retreat.

In many ways *The Sporting Club* reflects the decadence of society in the same way that William Golding's *Lord of the Flies* (1954) does. Once they decide to solve the Olive problem themselves and shut out any outside help, the club members become irrational, authoritarian, and cruel. By the end, the club members and Earl Olive's people are indistinguishable in their squalor and misuse of authority.

NINETY-TWO IN THE SHADE

First published: 1973
Type of work: Novel

Determined to be a fishing guide, Thomas Skelton pursues his dream in the face of a death threat from a violent, established guide.

Thomas McGuane's third novel, *Ninety-Two in the Shade*, is set in steamy Key West in the world of sport fishing. On the surface, the plot deals with a turf battle between two fishing guides, old-timer Nichol Dance and newcomer Thomas Skelton. The real focus of the novel, though, is a common McGuane theme: the unrest of the protagonist (Skelton) and his search for something that will allow him to remain sane and escape the decadence of American civilization.

Thomas Skelton has quit college as a marine biology major and wants to become a fishing guide at his home of Key West. His despair at what he sees around him, however, has led to drug use, crazy behavior, and the process of discovering a career by elimination. Sport fishing seems to be the only occupation that will keep him sane. The only problem with his decision is that Nichol Dance, one of the guides west of Marathon, feels threatened enough to warn Skelton not to guide in his territory. The conflict revolves around these two men: Dance feels that he must establish "credence"; Skelton feels that his only hope for sanity is to guide.

A series of events leads to a direct confrontation between Dance and Skelton. While in prison for attacking Ray the dockmaster, Dance sends his clients, the Rudleighs from Connecticut, to Skelton. During their excursion, Dance (released from prison because Ray did not die) "kidnaps" the Rudleighs from Skelton's skiff as both a practical joke and a warning. In retaliation, Skelton burns Dance's boat, his only possession of any value; Dance tells Skelton he will kill him if he guides west of Marathon.

Key West and guiding are the ends of the road for both men. Skelton knows that Dance is capable of carrying out his threat, but he orders his boat and continues his plan to guide because there is nothing else for him to do. Dance knows that killing Skelton will, at the least, put him in prison for life, but the alternatives (if Skelton guides) are suicide or loss of credence. Skeltons girlfriend, father, and grandfather all ineffectually try to dissuade him from his plan.

As in all McGuane's novels, there are problems between fathers and sons. In *Ninety-Two in the Shade*, three generations of Skelton males are at odds with one another. Although Goldsboro Skelton finances his grandson's boat, Thomas is disgusted by his grandfather's lust for power and autocratic manner. Skelton's father feels the same way about Goldsboro and the world that Thomas does, and his method of coping is basically the same. He has also looked for a career by the process of elimination, finally withdrawing to a mosquito-net-covered bed where he watches television and plays Jean Sibelius and Hank Williams on his violin.

Skelton's behavior may seem aimless, nonproductive, and even harmful. The method behind his madness, however, is an effort to remain sane by not focusing on the deterioration around him. Skelton has come to Key West to find peace, but he must deal with trendy suburbanites, the Rudleighs, who force the guides to break the rules for sport fishing. He sees a former guide now working as a salad chef at Howard Johnson's because the bank foreclosed on his boat. One of the best fishing lanes is in the flight pattern for a military landing field, and the shattering roar of low-flying aircraft dominates everything at frequent intervals. As part of its efforts to promote tourism, the Chamber of Commerce holds a pie-eating contest in which the contestants gorge themselves to the point of vomiting, the winner to receive a day's guiding from Dance. Skelton can handle these intrusions into his world only by becoming completely involved with guiding.

Other signs of decadence are less obvious but insidious. Skelton's grandfather has become "successful" by exploiting the gaps that exist between deals for power and profit. His father is judged a crackpot and a failure for refusing to compete in a country he believes to be decadent. Within this setting, Skelton and Dance try to stay sane by doing the only thing left for them to do: work as fishing guides and protect their space.

SOMETHING TO BE DESIRED

First published: 1985
Type of work: Novel

Bored with life and lured by the possibility of wild sex and adventure, Lucien Taylor embarks on a voyage of self-discovery.

Something to Be Desired, Thomas McGuane's sixth novel, stands apart from his other novels in that the protagonist, Lucien Taylor, actually reaches a level of contentment and happiness—after abandoning his wife and young son. The "something to be desired," though, turns out to be exactly what he gave up, a life of domestic contentment with his wife, Suzanne, and his young son, James. The discovery process is filled with debauchery and aimless behavior, accompanied by a gradual increase in common sense and maturity and a huge increase in personal wealth.

Lucien's inability to tolerate contentment can be traced to his father, who ran off to Peru with a friend, Art Clancey. A high point in Lucien's life occurred when his father "kidnapped" him from school to camp in the mountains above Deadrock, Montana. Although the trip was a failure in one sense (they spent two days without food or shelter wandering in search of their campsite), Lucien was thrilled to be doing something with his father. When he discovered that his wife had loved Art Clancey (now dead), the elder Taylor had walked out of the house for good, leaving Lucien and his mother dependent on alimony, child support, and handouts from relatives.

During a successful career with the United States Intelligence Agency in Latin America, Lucien returns to Montana without his wife and son to find a more romantic life. He is abandoning what is generally understood as the good life: a beautiful woman who loves him, a son who desperately needs a father, and a good career that gives him the leisure to explore the culture of Latin America. Lucien is drawn to Montana by Emily, the lusty "dark" woman who would not marry him, when he hears that she has murdered her husband. He feels that she can supply his life with the passion, kinky sex, and romance that are missing. After Lucien posts her bail, Emily deeds him the ranch as collateral, which he then owns when she skips the country before her trial. With Emily gone, Lucien engages in aimless behavior and frequent but unsatisfying sex; he becomes the local joke in Deadrock.

The landscape and the physical ranch work keep Lucien from going completely crazy. He seems to recognize the value of the land and his good fortune in living on it. The rituals of mending fences, using horses for work, hunting and fishing begin to provide a small stabilizing force for Lucien.

At his lowest point, physically sick and contemplating suicide, Lucien decides to redeem himself and "set the world on fire." With a huge bank loan, he transforms the natural hot springs on the ranch into a health spa, complete with an airfield and exotic menus. The spa is wildly successful, attracting people whose behavior is as bizarre as Lucien's. Being surrounded by wealthy, dissipated, aimless, and eccentric clients allows him to see his own behavior from an objective perspective and to be more content with his own normality.

Lucien uses his success as a means of convincing Suzanne and James to visit, and it is during this visit that he discovers a fathering instinct, a desire to give James what his own father never gave him. Lucien grows up, casts off his self-destructive behavior, and can even reject Emily when she returns. He does not completely win back Suzanne and James by the novel's end, but the possibility is there for a total reconciliation if they can decide to trust him again.

KEEP THE CHANGE

First published: 1989
Type of work: Novel

Joe Starling tries to recover the family ranch in Montana after becoming disgusted with his aimless life in Florida as an illustrator of operation manuals.

Keep the Change is set primarily in Montana after a brief interlude in Key West and a dizzying dash across the country. The plot concerns Joe Starling's attempt to reclaim his family's ranch after being unsuccessful as a painter in Florida. Starling is a typical McGuane protagonist, caught between his past and future, a man whose good intentions are often thwarted by his bad habits.

Losing the inspiration to paint and working as an illustrator of operation manuals causes Joe to feel disgusted with his rather comfortable life in Florida, where he lives with a ravishing Cuban beauty, Astrid. To escape, he borrows Astrid's car, a small pink convertible, for a trip to the grocery store and ends up in Montana. His destination is his family's ranch, left to him by his father and managed by his aunt and uncle (brother and sister), Lureen and Smitty. The ranch has been leased for years to a neighbor who wants to add it to his own spread. The ranch itself is in financial jeopardy, mainly because Smitty has been siphoning off the lease money for his own use and supposedly brokering seafood shipments from Texas. When Joe returns, he rejuvenates the ranch, rebuilding the springs and fence, buying calves, and eventually selling them at a substantial profit. This profit, however, the money necessary to keep the ranch afloat, is absorbed by Smitty's seafood scam and his general ability to run through a lot of money in a hurry.

The father-son conflict in *Keep the Change* is typical of McGuane. Joe loved and admired his father, a distant and ruthless businessman who essentially sold out even though he tried to instill in Joe a love of the land and a desire to keep the ranch in the family. When Joe returns to Montana to reclaim the ranch, he has to face the fact that his father was not liked by those who did business with him, and for those people the sins of the father are passed on to the son. The only real father figure Joe has had is Otis Rosewell, the foreman who supervised Joe when he was working for the neighboring rancher as a boy.

Joe courts his childhood sweetheart, Ellen Overstreet, as another way of trying to recapture the idyllic days of his past. On his return, he finds her married to his formal rival and sworn enemy, Billy Kelton, a hardworking but land-poor man who basically slaves for Ellen's father. Joe's relationship with Ellen is complicated by her present separation from Billy and the announcement that her child's father is really Joe and not Billy. The possibility of renewing an affair with Ellen leads to antic behavior, especially when she and Billy begin solving their marital problems and Joe learns that Billy is actually the father of Clara. Joe's antics are mild and shortlived for a McGuane protagonist, reflecting his ability to come to grips with his life.

In spite of the loss of the ranch, Joe seems to have wrested some meaning from his spiritual malaise. The novel ends, as does *Something to Be Desired*, on an unresolved but slightly upbeat note. This more mellow conclusion is a reflection of McGuane's changing style; it is less flashy and exudes a degree of warmth that is lacking in his earlier novels. He has not abandoned the dry wit, terse dialogue, and powerful descriptions of nature, but in *Keep the Change* they are integrated into the story and do not stand out as displays of verbal virtuosity.

Summary

Thomas McGuane is a spokesman for what he sees as the decadence of the late twentieth century. His characters experience the confusion that results from the loss of strong masculine values in a world that supports and rewards cleverness and political power. They survive by looking askance at the world and searching for a vocation that will allow them to avoid seeing the deterioration around them. McGuane's humor and bizarre imagination make his novels as entertaining as they are thought provoking and puzzling.

Bibliography

Carter, Allen Howard. "McGuane's First Three Novels: Games, Fun, Nemesis." *Critique* 17, no. 1 (1975): 91-104.

_____. "Speaking Against the Dark: Style as Theme in Thomas McGuane's *Nobody's Angel*." *Modern Fiction Studies* 33, no. 2 (1987): 298.

Gregory, Sinda, and Larry McCaffery. "The Art of Fiction, LXXXIX." *The Paris Review* 97 (Fall, 1988): 34-71.

Harris, Mark. "Tom McGuane: The Former Angry Young Man." *Publishers Weekly* 236 (September 29, 1989): 50-52.

Katz, Donald. "Thomas McGuane: Heroes in 'Hotcakesland.'" *The New Republic* 181 (August 18, 1979): 38-39.

Klinkowitz, Jerome. *The New American Novel of Manners*. Athens: University of Georgia Press, 1986.

Masington, Charles G. "*Nobody's Angel*: Thomas McGuane's Vision of the Contemporary American West." *New Mexico Humanities Review* 6 (Fall, 1983): 49-55.

Wallace, Jon. "The Language Plot in Thomas McGuane's *Ninety-Two in the Shade*." *Critique* 29, no. 2 (1988): 111-120.

David Huntley

LARRY McMURTRY

Born: Wichita Falls, Texas
June 3, 1936

Principal Literary Achievement
McMurtry's novels examine the human consequences when the myth of the Old West, a central component in the American national mythology, loses force and can no longer shape people's lives.

Biography

Larry Jeff McMurtry was born on June 3, 1936, at Wichita Falls, Texas, twenty miles from his parents' home in Archer City, Texas (the Thalia of his books). McMurtry's grandparents had moved into Archer County in the 1880's and established their ranch along a cattle trail in north central Texas. The nine McMurtry boys (Larry's uncles and father, William Jefferson McMurtry) moved westward to work on the huge ranches in the Texas panhandle.

At family reunions, McMurtry heard his elders talk about the golden age of their youth and about such great ranchers and cowboys as Charles Goodnight, Teddy Blue, and Larry's own Uncle Johnny. His hard old uncles, withered and crippled by their long years of cowboying, had been present at the birth of the Western myth, and they lived long enough to see it die. The elder McMurtrys knew, as did Larry, that the new generation could not replace the old. He wrote:

> All of them lived to see the ideals of the faith degenerate, the rituals fall from use; the principal myth become corrupt. In my youth, when they were old men, I often heard them yearn aloud for the days when the rituals had all their power, when they themselves had enacted the pure, the original myth, and I know that they found it bitter to leave the land to which they were always faithful to the strange and godless heirs that they had bred.

McMurtry's books can be read as a parting wave to Old Man Goodnight, Teddy Blue, and Uncle Johnny.

Larry McMurtry and his family moved from the home ranch into the small town of Archer City. He was an honors student in high school and was active in many school activities, but the bitter love affair with the ranching country of his uncles found its companion in his own disillusionment with the small town. Small Texas towns, too, were dying, he later wrote, losing their bold and energetic people to the

cities. McMurtry soon joined the migration to urban America. He was graduated from North Texas State University in 1958 and received a master's degree from Rice University in Houston in 1960. Houston, San Francisco, and Washington, D.C., would be his principal places of residence in the future.

While he was at North Texas State, McMurtry began to write, finishing the first draft of *Horseman, Pass By* in 1958. He taught at various colleges for brief periods and worked as a "scout," locating rare books. In 1964, he moved to the Washington, D.C., area where he opened a bookstore and continued scouting, traveling an average of about a hundred days a year.

Readers can see a pattern to McMurtry's books that matches the flow of his life. His first three books dealt with the small town of Thalia and the surrounding ranch country: *Horseman, Pass By* (1961), *Leaving Cheyenne* (1963), and *The Last Picture Show* (1966). His next three novels make up the urban or Houston trilogy: *Moving On* (1970), *All My Friends Are Going to Be Strangers* (1972), and *Terms of Endearment* (1975). His next few books dealt with displaced people who lived in a variety of settings: *Somebody's Darling* (1978), *Cadillac Jack* (1982), and *The Desert Rose* (1983). In later years, McMurtry returned to the ranch country or to Thalia in *Lonesome Dove* (1985), *Texasville* (1987), *Anything for Billy* (1988), and *Some Can Whistle* (1989). Two books of essays explain the themes of his fiction: *In a Narrow Grave: Essays on Texas* (1968), and *Film Flam: Essays on Hollywood* (1987). The novel *Buffalo Girls* was published in 1990.

McMurtry did not struggle in obscurity. Several of his books were made into Academy Award-winning films: *Horseman, Pass By* (made into the 1963 film *Hud*), *The Last Picture Show* (1971), and *Terms of Endearment* (1983). *Lonesome Dove* brought McMurtry a Pulitzer Prize and was made into an outstanding television miniseries. His books have routinely become best-sellers.

Analysis

As a Texan who writes about Texas, McMurtry focuses on the Western myth of the cowboy and rancher, the cattle drives and the open plains. This myth shapes the self-conception of Texans and other Westerners, and through films, books, and television it has also helped form the national self-image. When Larry's Uncle Johnny was five years old, he sat atop the McMurtry barn and watched cattle drives pass below. During his lifetime, the railroad made drives obsolete, as other machinery would largely replace the cowboy. Years later, his young nephew Larry would explore in his fiction the meaning of the ending of the Old West, which continued to produce such powerful images in American culture. Larry McMurtry quickly found a national audience for his work, because all regions of the United States had at some time undergone a similar passage from frontier to town to city.

McMurtry closely analyzes the Western myth and its human products. The virtues of his rancher-uncles were great. They were independent men who had a deep sense of honor, justice, and respect for the land. Yet they were also intolerant, inflexible, and deeply contemptuous of anyone who did not conform to their values. They disdained such institutions of civilization as churches, schools, farms, and towns. Schools were jails, Larry's Uncle Jeff told him, and life was too short and sweet to lock oneself in jail. These men ridiculed any way of life or values but their own. Yet their way of life was dying, and their values were irrelevant to the more complex urban environment; the Old West did not give its people a usable past when they were forced into a new way of life. McMurtry, both victim and interpreter of this void, writes neither simple nostalgic elegies nor debunking exposés of his homeland; he writes instead of his bittersweet love affair with a homeland in which he cannot live and from which he cannot easily depart.

Recurrent themes mark McMurtry's diverse body of work. Most of his characters have capacities that do not fit their circumstances. The mean-spirited and violent Hud in *Horseman, Pass By* lived in an age (the 1950's) that could not make use of his capacities; in an earlier age, his abilities might have made him a Charles Goodnight. In McMurtry's books, old ranch-country patriarchs struggle to maintain their dignity after their day has passed; strong women cope with weak, purposeless men who cannot find a meaningful role in modern society; young boys, growing up with tales of the old days, see no clear path to the future.

In McMurtry books, one often finds a theme of initiation, as young people pass from childhood into maturity, often introduced into adulthood through sex and death. Loneliness also is central to the life of McMurtry characters, whether they live on a ranch, go with their comrades on cattle drives, or live in towns or cities or on campuses. Marriage does not help end loneliness; failing or empty marriages litter McMurtry's books.

Women especially find themselves in situations that do not fit their capacities. The frontier or the small town offers them few opportunities outside their home, and their homes are filled with insensitive males living without purpose. When the patriarchy of the frontier collapsed, it was not replaced by a new social order based on healthy gender relations. McMurtry's strong women have more patience, wisdom, and optimism than men, but they are not socially oriented or educated enough to become feminists; they are earth-mother types.

HORSEMAN, PASS BY

First published: 1961
Type of work: Novel

Old rancher Homer Bannon and his stepson, Hud, are locked in conflict between frontier-ranching values and Hud's materialistic values of oil-rich Texas.

Homer Bannon, the old cattleman in *Horseman, Pass By*, owns a ranch a few miles south of Thalia, Texas. In his eighties, he has spent his life building a cattle herd of exceptional quality. He is a prosperous rancher, whose joy comes in riding over his land among his cattle. Most of his affection goes to his land, not to his nagging second wife, Jewel, or to her son, Scott "Hud" Bannon. He loves his seventeen-year-old grandson, Lonnie, and tries to pass on to him his feeling for the land and for the traditions of the cowboy past.

Hud Bannon is the best and most reckless cowboy in Texas when he wants to be, Lonnie says, but the thirty-five-year-old Hud spends more time boozing and chasing wild women than working cattle. Hud values the land only for the money it can produce: He wants oil wells on the land, not cattle. Homer's resistance to having holes punched in the land by oil rigs seems to Hud to be mere senility.

Seventeen-year-old Lonnie is narrator of the story. He loves and respects his grandfather, but Homer's stories of the old ranching days can no longer satisfy the lonely and restless boy. At night, after everyone has gone to bed, Lonnie often climbs to the top of the windmill and sits, looking off at the lights of Thalia and Wichita Falls. The future confuses Lonnie. Neither Homer's traditional values nor Hud's materialism seems adequate. Even in love there is confusion. Halmea, the black cook, a strong, wise woman, understands Lonnie's loneliness and his sexual needs, but there is very little that an older, black woman, half sexual object and half mother-surrogate, can do for a young white boy living in Texas in 1954.

The action of the novel starts when one of Homer's cows dies. The state veterinarian tests the herd and finds it infected with the dreaded hoof-and-mouth disease. Homer's entire prize herd will have to be quarantined, then killed and buried. Before the results of the tests come back, a key conflict occurs. Hud wants to sell the herd before it is quarantined. Homer refuses to pass his problem along to some unsuspecting rancher. To Hud, Homer's moral uprightness is a sign of senility. Another defining conflict comes when the state veterinarian gives Homer the bad news and tries to ease the blow by telling him that he can sell some oil leases while he is waiting to rebuild his herd. Homer says:

> If there's oil down there these boys can get it sucked up after I'm under there with it. . . . I don't like it an' I don't aim to have it. I guess I'm a queer, contrary old bastard, but there'll be no holes punched in this land while I'm here. . . . What good's oil to me. . . . What can I do with . . . [oil wells]? I can't ride out ever day an' prowl amongst 'em, like I can my cattle. . . . I can't feel a smidgen a pride in 'em, cause they ain't none a my doin'.

Homer's attitude toward oil confirms Hud's view that the old man is disintegrating, and Hud plots to take the ranch away.

With the herd slaughtered and buried in huge pits, Homer is physically and mentally exhausted. Hud explodes in frustration, raping Halmea, while Lonnie, beaten, watches. The climax comes when Homer falls and hurts himself. Hud and Lonnie find him writhing in pain. Lonnie goes for help. When he returns, he finds that Hud has shot and killed Homer. Did he shoot Homer to take the ranch or did he, in a flicker of love that he had once felt for the old man, kill him to stop his suffering? Lonnie does not know.

At the funeral, Lonnie feels reconciled to Homer's death, knowing that his grandfather is going back into the land he loved. He leaves the ranch, knowing that neither Homer nor Hud has left him a usable past. Perhaps he will become a wanderer, like so many of McMurtry's displaced characters.

THE LAST PICTURE SHOW

First published: 1966
Type of work: Novel

Young people confront conformity and purposeless life in a small Texas town.

Late at night, Lonnie Bannon of *Horseman, Pass By* would sit on top of his windmill and gaze off at the lights of Thalia, the small town that McMurtry describes in his second book, *The Last Picture Show*. There are more people in Thalia than on Lonnie's ranch, but they are equally lonely. People in Thalia in the early 1950's are caught between the dying countryside and the frightening pull of such booming cities as Dallas and Houston. Many people in Thalia had moved in from surrounding ranches (as the McMurtry's had moved to Archer City). Feeling under siege by the strange ways of the steadily encroaching urban United States, they impose their old ways on the town and try to crush any signs of nonconformity.

The story focuses on Sonny Crawford and his friend Duane Moore. It opens as the boys finish their last high school football game and continues over the next year as they search for a new path for themselves. Sam the Lion, once a rancher, now owns the town's movie theater, pool hall, and café. He acts as a father-surrogate for Sonny and Duane, and for other boys in need, including Billy, the mentally retarded boy that Sam took in and reared. Billy sweeps out Sam's businesses. If someone does not stop him, he sweeps to the edge of town and on into the empty countryside, as mindlessly occupied as the rest of the townspeople are as they go about their lives.

Duane dates the town beauty, Jacy Farrow, the daughter of oil-rich Lois and Gene Farrow. Jacy is a narcissistic, selfish young woman whose sense of self depends on the admiration and envy of others. She dates Duane only because he is a handsome high school athlete.

The story focuses mainly on Sonny, an innocent young man much like Lonnie Bannon. During this year, Sonny is initiated into manhood through a sexual relationship with Ruth Popper and through the death of Sam the Lion. Ruth Popper is an attractive woman who has had nearly all the life drained from her when she and Sonny begin an affair. She is the wife of football coach Herman Popper. Herman values a good shotgun more than he does a woman; Ruth tells Sonny, "The reason I'm so crazy is because nobody cares anything about me." Her affair with Sonny makes her see that she is not crazy and that she is an attractive woman with sexual rights.

Lois Farrow, Jacy's mother, is another strong woman who defies the mores of Thalia. The beautiful and rich woman realizes a hard truth that many oil-rich Texans

confront: Having money does not fill their emptiness. She fights off crushing boredom with drink, sex, and spending money; she also enjoys frightening men who cannot cope with assertive women. Both Ruth and Lois are examples of McMurtry
characters whose capacities do not fit their situations.

Sonny matures enough to refuse to join the boys in their sexual escapades with
heifer cows but not so much that the future becomes clearer to him. Nor does he
mature enough to resist Jacy when she seduces him away from Ruth Popper. Duane,
who had been away working in the oil fields, returns, fights with Sonny, and blinds
him in one eye. Duane leaves for the Army. Jacy elopes with Sonny in order to be
the center of attention. She knows that the Farrows will annul the marriage, which
they do, and send her off to college before she wrecks the town.

The outside world intrudes into Thalia in various ways. It pulls Duane and Jacy
away. Television provides too much competition for the picture show, and it closes.
The closing of the movie theater is yet another disappointment for Sonny, following
his loss of Sam the Lion, Jacy, Duane, and Ruth Popper. His final loss comes when
Billy, blindly sweeping the street, is hit by a truck and killed. Later that day, Sonny
tries to leave Thalia. He goes to the city limits and looks at the empty countryside:
"He himself felt too empty. As empty as he felt and as empty as the country looked
it was too risky going out into it." He looks back at Thalia: "From the road the town
looked raw, scraped by the wind, as empty as the country. It didn't look like the town
it had been when he was in high school, in the days of Sam the Lion." Sonny has
matured, but not enough either to leave Thalia or to make a new, viable life in it. He
returns to Ruth Popper; she takes him back, knowing he won't stay.

ALL MY FRIENDS ARE GOING TO BE STRANGERS

First published: 1972
Type of work: Novel

Young author Danny Deck comes to understand that he must choose between
writing about life and living life as a good person and friend.

Larry McMurtry has said that Danny Deck, his protagonist in his fourth novel, *All
My Friends Are Going to Be Strangers*, is close to him in his sensibilities. McMurtry
says: "It is true that the better you write the worse you live. The more of yourself
you take out of real relationships and project into fantasy relationship the more the
real relationships suffer."

In his fourth novel, McMurtry turns from the ranch country around Thalia and
begins what has been called the Houston or urban trilogy. Danny Deck, a young
student at Rice University, is from the ranching country around Archer City, Texas,
but he has cast his lot with an urban way of life beyond the imagination of Homer

Bannon or Sonny Crawford. As the novel opens, Danny meets tall, beautiful, remote Sally Bynum at a party in Austin and, immediately smitten, talks her into going back to Houston with him, where they marry. Sally, like Jacy Farrow in *The Last Picture Show*, is self-centered; she is immune to either Danny's love or his anger. Within a month, Sally has walked out on him several times. In the midst of his perplexity, he receives a telegram from Random House telling him that it will publish his first novel, *The Restless Grass* (which in plot sounds a lot like *Horseman, Pass By*). One dream is coming true even as another may be taken away.

His life is disjointed, both by his sudden marriage and by his publishing success. He turns to his best friends, Flap and Emma Horton. Emma's warm, bright kitchen provides Danny with a sense of order and normalcy, but she cannot keep Danny from feeling that he has been dislodged from his life in Houston and from his friends. Danny and Sally go to San Francisco, where his feelings of displacement grow. Sally, now pregnant, cuts him out of her life. He leaves, moving to a sleazy hotel, where he works on his second book.

Here his crisis deepens. More authors fill San Francisco than Danny knew existed. He realizes that they cannot all be great and wonders whether he can be. If so, he wonders, at what cost? He meets Jill Peel, an intelligent and honest twenty-four-year-old artist who had won an Academy Award for her animated cartoons. She seems to love him but is sexually unresponsive, for reasons she will not explain. She is, she tells him, no longer a woman, only an artist. She has made for herself the decision that Danny is avoiding: to live for one's art rather than for friends or lovers.

Danny returns to Texas, where Sally has gone to have their baby. The trip begins a long, exhausting period of sleeplessness, drink, and drugs. Danny's life is out of control: "My life was no life. It was sort of a long confused drive."

If new ways of life in California had nothing for him, can he return to the ranch country of his ancestors? He visits his ninety-two-year-old uncle Laredo, who, with his cook, Lorenzo, lives forty-seven miles off the paved road, deep in the harshest and most desolate country that Texas offers. Laredo owns a four-story, twenty-eight room Victorian mansion, but he camps behind it and cooks out over an open fire. A hundred years earlier, Laredo would have been a legendary rancher; now he is a bitter parody of those men. He hates cattle and will not let them on his place; he raises goats, camels, and antelope. The half-crazed old man forces his ranch hands to occupy themselves by digging holes in the earth. In a parody of Homer Bannon and his love of the earth, Danny says about his uncle: "My own theory was that he dug the holes because he hated the earth and wanted to get in as many licks at it as he could, before he died."

Danny leaves, not sure that he can get his life under control but convinced that Uncle Laredo's ranch "wasn't the Old West I liked to believe in—it was the bitter end of something. I knew I would never want to visit it again."

Increasingly out of control, Danny goes on to Austin and then to Houston, cutting ties with friends and acquaintances. He fights with Sally Bynum's family, ending any chance of a relationship with his baby daughter. He makes love to Emma, betraying his friendship with Flap and undermining his friendship with her. "Emma and I couldn't talk. My life had gotten that awry. . . . A lot of hope had drained away."

He moves on, toward the Rio Grande Valley. He realizes that he is out of phase with his friends and that they all are going to be strangers. In return for that loss, he is an author—though probably not a great one. As the book ends, Danny, exhausted and distraught, is in the Rio Grande River, drowning the manuscript of his new novel.

TERMS OF ENDEARMENT

First published: 1975
Type of work: Novel

Aurora Greenway and Emma Horton, mother and daughter, buoyantly deal with the details of family life that make up the fabric of human existence.

Terms of Endearment finished the Houston trilogy on which Larry McMurtry had been working for a decade. McMurtry had intended *Terms of Endearment* to be Emma Horton's book, but her mother, Aurora Greenway, took over. Once she was invented as a character, it would have been difficult to keep Aurora under wraps. She is forty-nine years old and three years widowed; she is good-looking, plump, and self-centered. As the story opens in Houston in 1967, Aurora is ticking off her standard list of complaints about her daughter; Emma is overweight (Aurora overlooks her own dietary sins), dresses poorly, and is married to a "drip." Aurora is not really angry, Emma says: "Her mother hadn't really been on the attack; she had just been exercising her peculiar subtle genius for making everyone but herself seem vaguely in the wrong." Aurora goes to pieces—screaming and flailing the air with her hands and finally collapsing—when Emma tells her mother that she is pregnant with her first child. Aurora's blow-up is not a result of concern for her daughter, it is a result of the fact that she is going to be a grandmother and is afraid that her suitors will drop her.

Aurora would have been an easy woman for readers to hate, but she turns into an attractive character as her irresistible, bubbling, and intelligent personality emerges. She is an "emphatic" woman—the kind that McMurtry's male characters are often drawn to and with whom they cannot cope. Her romantic life is confusing. She has various suitors begging her to marry them: a bank vice-president, a retired general, a former opera star, and a wealthy playboy from Philadelphia. None can cope with her: "Only a saint could live with me," Aurora says, "and I can't live with a saint. Older men aren't up to me and younger men aren't interested." She cannot stand men who are frightened of her, and she cannot help frightening them. She wants domineering men, but cannot stand to be dominated.

The only two people who can easily absorb Aurora's criticism are Emma and Rosie Dunlup. Emma sees life clearly. She understands and accepts her limitations and those of the people around her. Rosie has been Aurora's housekeeper for more than twenty years, every one marked by battle. The undaunted Rosie is the only one who can stand up to Aurora and return blow for verbal blow.

Aurora, Emma, and Rosie are tangled with men lesser than themselves; their capacities do not fit their situations. This is also true of the men—a general without any troops, an opera star with an injured throat, and a fiftyish, virginal oil millionaire, Vernon Dalhart—whom Aurora adds to her stable of suitors.

Plot is not very important. Emma has her baby, Rosie copes with a disintegrating marriage, and Aurora has to choose among her suitors. Aurora solves her problem by not choosing. She allows the general to move in with her, but she forces him to allow her to retain her other admirers and pull them into a tight, continuing relationship with one another and with her (her sexual arrangement with the others is not clear). No one man is her equal, but the team together almost copes with her needs.

Part 2, only forty-seven pages long, jumps to the period from 1971 through 1976 and focuses on Emma's life in Des Moines, Iowa, and Kearney, Nebraska. Emma has three children, but her marriage with Flap has disintegrated. Flap is a failure in the academic world (he blames Emma for not nagging him to success) and has affairs with numerous coeds. Emma herself has the strength and stability to have a couple of affairs, bringing some sexual fulfillment and emotional joy into her life.

Then Emma discovers that she has terminal cancer. Rosie, Aurora, and her suitors come to Emma to help her deal with dying. Emma dies with the dignity that she had always had; she does not cling tightly to life. Only Vernon Dalhart understands her needs fully: "He didn't demand that she live." She tries to help Flap cope with her approaching death, but she can not even remember what the terms of endearment between them had been. Ten years later, Flap thinks of her one afternoon and thinks that "he had done something wrong, wrong, wrong, long ago." As she slips toward death, she has them bring Danny Deck's book to her; as the rest of the world fades, Danny returns to her memory.

Emma is buried in Houston. Rosie and Aurora leave the cemetery together to take care of the three children, whom they are going to rear.

CADILLAC JACK

First published: 1982
Type of work: Novel

Antique scout Cadillac Jack McGriff balances his love for beautiful objects with his love of beautiful women.

In *Cadillac Jack*, McMurtry, drawing on his background as a scout locating rare editions of books, takes readers into the world of antique dealers and scouts, flea markets, auctions, and garage sales, a subculture that provides meaning to the lives of thousands of Americans. Like McMurtry, Cadillac Jack is a displaced Texan living in the Washington, D.C., area.

Jack McGriff—called Cadillac Jack because of his pearl-colored Cadillac—is an antique scout. He combs the country locating special items for dealers and collectors. As he gets older he gets pickier, only wanting exceptional items; he is no longer satisfied with the merely first-rate. Exceptional objects can be rare items, such as Billy the Kid's boots or Rudolph Valentino's silver cobra hubcaps, or they can be beautiful items such as the Sung vase he found in a junk barn in De Queen, Arkansas. Cadillac Jack is a legend in his subculture—doing what every flea-market and garage-sale addict dreams of doing: He finds treasure among junk. Jack paid $20 for the Sung vase and sold it for more than $100,000. He buys the objects that he falls in love with, but he keeps them only a short time. If he loses his discipline and cannot bring himself to sell what he buys, then he will become a collector or an antique dealer. He will have lost the calling that gives his life purpose.

Cadillac Jack is not strong on plot. Jack does have a problem with women, however, he falls in love with nearly any (beautiful) woman who is in trouble. As the story opens, Jack has just met the beautiful social climber Cindy Sanders, who owns three fashionable shops, including an antique store. Cindy is a self-centered beauty, with little awareness of anyone or anything outside herself. Her beauty attracts Jack, and her antique shop seems to promise some common interest. Jack finds that she really has no knowledge or appreciation of antiques, but he thinks that if he can get her on his turf he can divert her from her fixation on dominating the Washington social scene. He proposes that she hold a boot show and exhibit an exotic collection that he can find for her, topped by Billy the Kid's boots. Meanwhile, Jack meets Jean Arber and her two charming daughters. Jean owns a little antique shop and knows her business. She is lovely and is a quiet, family-oriented woman. Jack also falls in love with her. This complicates matters, since Jack had not fallen out of love with Cindy—or his two former wives or various other girlfriends.

Jack and his loves provide a slim plot on which McMurtry can hang his satire of Washington. Jack attends parties with the nation's governmental and journalistic elite and finds most of them so bored and boring that it is often difficult to tell whether they are living or dead. Not many congressmen appear, evidently because they spend considerable time cavorting with the prostitutes at places such as Little Bomber's Lounge. In the background are the gray little bureaucrats inhabiting gray little cells in gray office buildings and apartments.

Some of McMurtry's characters are unforgettable. Boog Miller, a fat Texan with slicked-down hair, is a wheeler-dealer on the scale of Lyndon Johnson. He owns Winkler County, Texas, and all the oil underneath it. When he is not manipulating the politicians on Capitol Hill, he is enjoying the beauties at Little Bomber's or reading the works of historians and philosophers. Jack visits legendary collectors, among them Benny the Ghost, who materializes at auctions to buy the one good piece and then dematerializes. Jack is the only one who has visited Benny's five-story home jammed with twenty- to thirty-thousand exceptional antiques. Jack buys boots from the oil-rich, drug-crazed Little Joe Twine, who lives near Archer City,

Texas. Little Joe is the most bizarre of the debris left in the wake of the collapse of the Old West, an extreme symbol of the empty lives of oil-rich, uneducated, former ranchers who have no purpose. He and his cowboys spend their days taking drugs and watching pornographic movies on Joe's wall-size television.

Jack's dream of a life with Cindy falls through when she marries a rich and powerful member of the Washington elite. His relationship with Jean falters when he destroys her trust by lying to her. Jack explains that he only lies to try to reach a higher and "happier truth," but Jean does not understand his ethical concept.

Jack finds peace and sanity by motion, by moving over the open road. The open range is no longer there, but thousands of miles of highway lie under the American sky. Jack leaves Washington for points west. As he drives, he almost comes to an understanding of his relationship with beautiful women and with beautiful objects, he says, but then he starts thinking about the approaching city of St. Louis and loses interest in the question.

LONESOME DOVE

First published: 1985
Type of work: Novel

Augustus McCrae and Woodrow F. Call drive a herd of cattle from south Texas to Montana and establish the first ranch in that territory.

McMurtry dedicates *Lonesome Dove* to the nine McMurtry boys (his uncles and father) and makes perhaps his last farewell wave to Charles Goodnight, Teddy Blue, and the other cowboys of the Old West. The cattlemen helped civilize the West and, in the process, created a mythology that continues to shape the United States. That powerful American myth grew from a very brief era in United States history immediately after the Civil War, a twenty-year period of open range and cattle drives. That period and way of life gave birth to all the dominant images of the Old West. McMurtry has his cowboys take their cattle right through the heartland of America, from Texas to Montana, along the frontier fault line between savagery and civilization. McMurtry quotes T. K. Whipple to define his theme: "Our forefathers had civilization inside themselves, the wild outside. We live in the civilization they created, but within us the wilderness still lingers. What they dreamed, we live, and what they lived, we dream."

This Pulitzer Prize-winning novel is a Western yarn in the old tradition, with cattle stampedes, Indian attacks, and the rescue of a beautiful woman by a heroic cowboy. It is exciting and funny and melancholy; the major criticism of the 850-page novel by many readers was that it was too short.

In the late 1870's, Augustus (Gus) McCrae and Woodrow F. Call, former officers in the Texas Rangers and friends for thirty years, are running the Hat Creek Cattle Company, located near the dilapidated little town of Lonesome Dove, hidden amid the mesquite thickets of south Texas on the Rio Grande River. Life drifts there, in the harsh terrain beneath the burning sun. Call, a man obsessed with duty, has no big tasks left. Gus, who can be gallant and heroic when the occasion demands, now is content to set on his front porch, sip whiskey, and watch his two blue pigs eat rattlesnakes. Perhaps Gus and Call would have turned into Danny Deck's crazed Uncle Laredo if nothing had changed; however, Jake Spoon, an old friend from rangering days, arrives and tells Gus and Call that fortunes are going to be made in Montana, where the grass is deep, the water is bountiful, and the army is about to tame the Indians.

Call decides that they should go north: There is no fun in south Texas anymore, and besides, there is a fortune to be made. Gus points out that Call never had any fun in his entire life and that he does not value money. Gus hopes the drive will be hard enough for Call: "You should have died in the line of duty, Woodrow. You'd know how to do that fine. The problem is you don't know how to live." Yet Gus agrees to go to Montana. There is nothing finer, he says, than riding a good horse into new country; besides, he realizes that he will get to see Clara Allen, the great love of his life, who had left sixteen years before and lives on the Platte River in Nebraska.

They gather cowboys for the drive. These include two former rangers, slow-thinking and steady Pea Eye Parker and the extraordinarily competent black man, Joshua Deets. Young Newt Dobbs, Call's unacknowledged son, goes; he will be initiated into manhood on the journey. Other young cowboys join the drive, many of whom die along the trail. Jake Spoon refuses to punch cattle, but he trails along with the herd for protection and brings with him Lonesome Dove's only prostitute, Lorena Wood, who believes Jake's promise that he will take her to San Francisco.

If *Lonesome Dove* falls within the long tradition of celebration of the myth of the Old West, some literary critics see that McMurtry, while working from that mythology, also reconstructs it by building a firmer and more realistic foundation for it. The reality of the trail drive is almost unceasing discomfort from heat, dust, rain, and injuries, with bad food and hard ground to look forward to at the end of a long day. Death is seldom glorious. It might come quickly, with a bolt of lightning, or horribly, being washed into a tangle of water moccasins, or absurdly, as when the kindly Deets is killed by a starving, frightened young brave who thinks that the cowboy intends to steal an Indian baby. Some Western men idealize women, as the myth says, but hardship ages women, and lack of intellectual life starves their minds. Western chivalry does not prevent women from having to choose between starvation and prostitution. Some are traded for skunk skins, some are brutally raped.

As the herd moves northward, it crosses the Platte River, and Gus calls on Clara Allen, mother of two girls and wife of a man dying of a head injury. Gus is tempted to stay on the Platte, but his destiny is to ride on with his friend Call into the new land.

Together Gus and Call embody all the attributes of the mythological heroes pursuing a quest. Call displays courage and devotion to duty; he is a natural leader. Gus, gallant, courageous, and compassionate, is also a wise man who understands life and death. The land they are riding over is only a boneyard, he says, "but pretty in the sunlight." He tells Call that in wiping out the Indians in Texas, they had been on the wrong side. The Indians had been the interesting people, and Gus and Call had eliminated them to clear the way for bankers and lawyers. First as Rangers and then as ranchers opening Montana, Gus and Call help civilize the West, but that civilization has no place for them.

Gus reaches the beautiful open range of Montana. It is fitting that when he comes across one of the last herds of buffalo, he chases after it as a salute to a passing age and blunders into one of the few remaining bands of wild Indians. In the melee, an arrow lodges in his leg, and gangrene sets in. He gets to Miles City, where, while he is in a coma, a doctor amputates one leg. His other leg should also be removed, but Gus refuses to have it amputated, knowing that his refusal means his death.

Gus also understands that his friend is going to face the most dangerous crisis of his life. What does a hero do once he fulfills his quest? Gus will die a hero's death, but Call is condemned to live. As he lies dying, Gus does his friend a favor by asking that Call return his body three thousand miles to a picnic ground that he and Clara loved near Lonesome Dove: "It's the kind of job you was made for, that nobody else could do or even try. Now that the country is about settled, I don't know how you'll keep busy, Woodrow. But if you'll do this for me you'll be all right for another year, I guess." It was quite a party, he tells Call as he dies.

Call leaves Gus's body in Miles City until spring. He takes the herd on north, to Milk River, and finds the promised land in a beautiful valley with good grass and water. The men build a ranch as winter comes and continue to look to Call for leadership. Call goes through the motions of building a ranch, but his life now is without purpose. He is one of many McMurtry characters who have to pay the consequences of having lived past his day. In the spring, he turns the ranch over to Newt and makes the long trek back to Texas. He completes the task imposed by Gus, and when the book ends, Call is back in the near-empty Lonesome Dove, old and tired, without purpose or challenge.

Summary

Larry McMurtry examines a central myth shaping American consciousness, that of the Old West, of the cowboys and ranchers, the cattle drives and open range. The myth took form from values that Americans brought with them to the West and then took on its own potent life to shape values in new ways. McMurtry also describes what happens to people who live on beyond the age and the social order that spawned the myth.

Ultimately, McMurtry is probing the American Dream. As one looks over his roster of purposeless lives and wrecked marriages, one might ask why American culture and society is not rich enough to provide the ingredients for meaningful lives when the heroic days pass.

Bibliography

Bennett, Patrick. *Talking with Texas Writers: Twelve Interviews.* College Station: Texas A&M Press, 1980.

Lich, Lera Patrick Tyler. *Larry McMurtry's Texas: Evolution of the Myth.* Austin, Tex.: Eakin Press, 1987.

Neinstein, Raymond L. *The Ghost Country: A Study of the Novels of Larry McMurtry.* Berkeley, Calif.: Creative Arts, 1976.

Peavy, Charles D. *Larry McMurtry.* Boston: Twayne, 1977.

Schmidt, Dorey, ed. *Larry McMurtry: Unredeemed Dreams.* Edinburg, Tex.: Pan American University Press, 1978.

William E. Pemberton

NORMAN MAILER

Born: Long Branch, New Jersey
January 31, 1923

Principal Literary Achievement
While there is no critical consensus on the stature of Mailer's novels, he is regarded as one of the most important fiction and nonfiction writers who have appeared since the end of World War II.

Biography

Norman Mailer was born in Long Branch, New Jersey, on January 31, 1923, the son of Isaac ("Barney") and Fanny Mailer. Mailer's mother had family in business in Long Branch, but she and her husband soon moved to Brooklyn, where their son Norman and his younger sister Barbara attended public schools. Mailer has described his home life as deeply nurturing, with his mother taking the lead not only in caring for the children, but also in earning the income (through an oil delivery business) that supported the family during the Depression when his father (an accountant) was sometimes out of work.

Mailer was a precocious child who did extremely well in school. Assembling an impressive model airplane collection and excelling in his mathematics and sciences courses, his early dream was to become an aeronautical engineer. Accepted at Harvard University in 1939 as an engineering student, Mailer was soon captivated by his writing courses, and by the end of his freshman year, he had determined to become a writer. He was graduated in 1943 with an engineering major in deference to his parents' wish for him to have a degree that would qualify him for employment in a profession. He had already written several dozen stories and one unpublished novel. Waiting to be drafted for service in World War II, he wrote in eight months another novel, *A Transit to Narcissus* (published in facsimile in 1978).

Drafted in 1944, Mailer was assigned a number of desk jobs before volunteering as a rifleman so that he could get some experience in combat for the novel about the war that he wanted to write. Originally intended as a short account of a combat patrol, *The Naked and the Dead* (1948), Mailer's first published novel, developed into a long, complex study of the war, the military, and an impressive cross section of soldiers from all regions of the country. It was hailed as the greatest fictional work to have come out of the war, and Mailer found himself at twenty-five on the best-seller lists and launched as one of the most promising writers of his generation.

Mailer enjoyed his sudden celebrity, but it also frightened him, for he had not had time to develop his talent. Success had come with a rush. He floundered in the next few years to find a subject as large as World War II, not wanting to repeat himself by writing a second war novel but afraid that he did not have the experience yet for another major work. He traveled to Europe, visited Hollywood, and dabbled in radical politics. All these experiences found their place in his second novel, *Barbary Shore* (1951), which was heavily criticized as incoherent and excessively didactic. Searching for a new style that was less naturalistic than his first novel, Mailer had tried to write a political allegory that would reveal the fantastic, phantasmagoric, paranoid atmosphere of the Cold War years, when (as Mailer saw it) the United States and the Soviet Union tried to divide the world between them and regarded each other's actions with suspicion.

Demoralized and angered by the negative reviews of *Barbary Shore*, Mailer gradually cultivated a much more aggressive tone, taking on both political and literary establishments, identifying with rebels and hipsters, and defining a new style for himself—that of the engaged, controversial writer who in his own person embodied the conflicting temper of the times. His third novel, *The Deer Park* (1955), a study of Hollywood and the political atmosphere of the 1950's, had a difficult time with publishers, who shied away from its sexual explicitness, and Mailer turned increasingly to the essay form to express his opinions and his imaginative exploration of the American psyche in books such as *The Presidential Papers* (1963) and *Cannibals and Christians* (1966).

Mailer did not return to the novel until 1965, with the publication of *An American Dream*, a disturbing first-person narrative about a hipster hero, Stephen Rojack, whose murder of his wife in the first chapter sets him off on a journey of self-testing and renewal. Several reviewers were outraged that Rojack not only was not caught or punished for his crime but also that the murder of a woman should become the foundation of a life-renewing quest—especially since only a few years earlier Mailer himself had been incarcerated in Bellevue Hospital in New York City after stabbing his second wife, Adele Morales.

From this point, it became difficult for critics to separate Mailer's public and private life, especially since Mailer—after the indifferent reception of his next novel, *Why Are We in Vietnam?* (1967)—turned to nonfiction in which his life and personal voice came to the fore. In *The Armies of the Night: History as a Novel, the Novel as History* (1968), *Miami and the Siege of Chicago: An Informal History of the Republican and Democratic Conventions of 1968* (1969), *Of A Fire on the Moon* (1970), *St. George and the Godfather* (1972), *Marilyn* (1973), and *The Fight* (1975), Mailer covered a protest march on the Pentagon, political conventions, the moon shot, the life of a famous actress, and the Muhammad Ali-George Frazier world championship bout in an inimitable voice and sense of participation that made him and his subjects all of a piece, as though they were part of one continuous nonfiction novel about contemporary life. The trouble was that certain subjects were well within his imaginative grasp—such as the march on the Pentagon, which could be described as though it were a war filled with moments of intense action and exquisite character revelation—and others eluded him—such as the highly technological, impersonal, and even bureaucratic way the astronauts prepared for their trip into space. As comprehensive and subtle as Mailer's own voice had become, he was unable to treat every subject with equal skill, and he (as well as the critics) eventually tired of the way the Mailer ego impressed itself upon everything.

In response to this long period of autobiographical work, Mailer decided to treat the story of Gary Gilmore, a convicted killer who gripped the nation's imagination by refusing to appeal his death sentence and by demanding that the state of Utah execute him, in a scrupulously objective narrative devoid of his usual baroque, metaphorical style. As a result, *The Executioner's Song* (1979) was hailed as a triumph, a return to the panoramic social novel that first earned Mailer his high reputation.

Ancient Evenings (1983), a tour de force history of ancient Egypt, *Tough Guys Don't Dance* (1984), a murder mystery, and the forthcoming *Harlot's Ghost* (1991), a CIA/spy mystery, are all novels that draw upon the fund of ideas Mailer has developed in more than forty years of exploring the meaning of human identity—the individual's relationship not only to society but also to the universe—for Mailer believes it is possible for the novelist to express both the consciousness of his time and an awareness of the eternity of which his time and place are only a part.

Analysis

Mailer has often said that it was his reading of James T. Farrell, especially of Farrell's Studs Lonigan novels (1932-1935), that made him want to become a writer. Farrell wrote in a naturalistic style, vividly describing the society in which a young Irish boy grows up, matures, and dies. An urban novelist, concerned with how institutions press upon individuals, Farrell traced the story of an individual, Studs Lonigan, who dreamed of distinction but died in misery. What gripped Mailer was the idea that literature could be made from a young man's quest for an identity while at the same time exploring the societal forces that conspire against individuality.

Mailer's early short fiction before *The Naked and the Dead* featured young men caught in extremity—in war, in poverty, or in their travels when they threw in with rugged types and tested their mettle. The ethnicity and social backgrounds of his characters were important in defining their sense of the world and in determining their behavior. This is most clearly the case in "A Calculus at Heaven" (1942), set in the Pacific war theater, in which each character stands for a social type and class: Bowen Hilliard, the captain, Ivy-Leaguer and frustrated artist, who looks to war for some kind of resolution of his unfulfilled life; Dalucci, an Italian working-class Midwesterner, puzzled by his ineffectual life and wondering what it is all about; Wexler, a Jewish boy from New Jersey, proud of his football career and spoiling to show his army buddies how tough a soldier he can be. These types and others foreshadow the panoramic method of *The Naked and the Dead*, in which Mailer presents a range of characters meant to represent the country's diversity and to describe the conditions of society.

Mailer's style in this early fiction and in *The Naked and the Dead* was derivative of American writers Farrell, Ernest Hemingway, and John Dos Passos. Indeed, one of the appealing elements of *The Naked and the Dead* is Mailer's deft blending of styles and points of view. Like Hemingway, he is concerned with the fate of individuals, but he links the fate of isolated characters to the destiny of society, showing (as Dos Passos would) how individual character and social class are connected together. Like Farrell, who made the Irish neighborhoods of Chicago a graphic part of his fiction so that Studs was brought into high relief by his surroundings, Mailer made the story of men in war gripping by describing in riveting detail what it was like to slog through the terrain of the Philippines.

Ultimately, it was the influence of Hemingway that prevailed when Mailer decided, after the great success of his first published novel, that it was not enough to know his characters and their environment and to describe them faithfully. He had to have a great theme and significant events by which to measure himself as a writer. *Barbary Shore* and *The Deer Park* thus take on Cold War politics and the motion-picture industry as counters against which his characters must seek their true identi-ties and philosophies. Neither Mailer's second nor third novel is entirely satisfying, because of his difficulty in creating a credible first-person voice. He was drawn to this mode of narration after deciding he no longer had the confidence of the third-person narrator he had used to sum up society in *The Naked and the Dead*. The flaw he had trouble rectifying in *Barbary Shore* and *The Deer Park* was precisely that Mikey Lovett and Sergius O'Shaugnessy, his first-person narrators, were so tentative about themselves. Self-doubt increased the drama of their own quests for identity, but it also lent a certain vagueness and lack of color to the narratives, so that neither Lovett nor O'Shaugnessy was quite believable. They lacked the complex, idiosyncratic style Mailer was to develop in *Advertisements for Myself* (1959).

When Mailer decided to use himself—his troubles, his doubts, his conceits—his style developed and prospered. His theme was still the same, the trials of the individual in his confrontation with society, but now that confrontation was much more convincingly portrayed in light of complicated and often comic personality willing to delve very deeply into his own faults and follies. The impact of Mailer's fiction is palpable in *An American Dream*, in which the first-person narrator, Stephen Rojack, has a mind that is as agile as Mailer's own.

In *The Armies of the Night*, Mailer's discovery of himself as a character capable of representing the conflicting forces of the country receives its most effective treatment. The style is successful because it is Mailer's third-person commentary on himself as he takes up the protest against the Vietnam War by joining a march on the Pentagon. Referring to himself as a "left Conservative" is a canny way of expressing the contradictions in himself, of the middle-aged writer who is reluctant to give up his privileges to play the part of dissenter and yet who realizes that his creative power and insight often come when he finds himself in opposition to the status quo.

None of Mailer's subsequent nonfiction equals the complexity of *The Armies of the Night*, although *Miami and the Siege of Chicago*, *Of a Fire on the Moon*, *Mar-*

ilyn, and *The Fight* all contain extended passages that rival his best autobiographical work. *The Executioner's Song*, however, marks a return to the naturalistic method of *The Naked and the Dead*, and its cast of characters, depiction of the Western landscape, and evocation of the Eastern interests that turn Gary Gilmore's story into a media event far outclass his first novel's understanding of society and politics.

Embedded in *The Executioner's Song* is a quest to understand the very underpinnings of human identity, of the way the American character is related to human nature, and of the way life in the twentieth century United States is but an extension of the eternity of which Gilmore, for example, is sure he partakes. Notions of reincarnation and of karma inform much of Mailer's fiction and nonfiction since the early 1960's; they culminate in *Ancient Evenings*, in which he creates a time and a land (ancient Egypt) that function on magic, telepathy, and reincarnation.

THE NAKED AND THE DEAD

First published: 1948
Type of work: Novel

General Cummings sends a patrol to scale Mount Anaka as part of a strategy to destroy Japanese resistance on the island of Anopopei.

The Naked and the Dead, Mailer's first published novel, was hailed for its riveting depiction of men in war, beset not only by the vicissitudes of battle but also by their social backgrounds and personal problems. Mailer put his brief combat experience to good use, beginning his novel by describing what it feels like to travel on a troop ship, cooped up with men from every part of the country, anticipating combat but not knowing what it would really be like, and reflecting on life back home—traumatic childhood incidents, plans that were never accomplished, and dreams that remain unfulfilled.

Nearly half of the novel is used to build up the complex social context of the soldiers who will be picked for the dangerous mission to scale Mount Anaka behind enemy lines. In characters such as Roth and Goldstein, Mailer reveals the anti-Semitism rampant in the Army and the efforts of Jews either to ignore the prejudice or to prove their courage and loyalty. Slowly the soldiers on patrol learn to work together as a unit even as Mailer interrupts the narrative of their approach to the mountain with flashbacks to their civilian lives. Detailed accounts of the irascible Gallagher's life in Boston, easy-going Wilson's love life in the South, and Croft's rather sadistic life in Texas punctuate the conflict and the cooperation of the men on patrol.

Juxtaposed with the lives of common soldiers is the story of the officers, the higher-ups who give the orders and plot the strategy of the war. General Cummings, a deeply conservative and aloof man, the product of a troubled childhood and of a first-class education, seeks to mold his army into an instrument of his own will. He is opposed in this by Harvard-educated Lieutenant Hearn, who rejects Cummings' incipient Fascism and disputes his authority. Attracted by Hearn's intelligence, Cummings does not believe that Hearn really takes his liberal scruples seriously. Cummings is lonely and would like to groom a protégé, but when Hearn proves resistant and goes so far as mashing his cigarette into the immaculate floor of the fastidious General's tent, Cummings decides to teach Hearn a lesson by dispatching him as leader of the patrol that is charged with climbing Mount Anaka as part of the plan to surprise the Japanese and to take the island of Anopopei away from them.

On patrol, Hearn learns what it means to lead men. He would rather not be a dictator, but Croft—used to having his own way with the men—becomes an adversary. Just when Hearn believes he may have established his dominance, Croft leads him into a Japanese ambush, and Hearn is quickly hit by a bullet that kills him. Cruelly driving the men up the mountain, the maniacal Croft is clearly the counterpart of Cummings, certain that he can impose a pattern on history and make it subordinate to his will. The whole mission finally collapses when the exhausted men accidentally stumble into a beehive and are stung into a terrified run down the mountain.

Eventually Japanese resistance crumbles—not because of Cummings' strategy, but merely because of exhaustion. Cummings is not even present when his second in charge, Major Dalleson, a competent but unimaginative officer, has to take responsibility for handling the rout of the Japanese. Both Cummings and Croft are thwarted, but neither the disaffected men on patrol nor the liberalism represented by Hearn suggest an effective counter to the reactionary forces that appear to be still in control at the end of the novel.

AN AMERICAN DREAM

First published: 1965
Type of work: Novel

Stephen Rojack, a psychology professor and television personality, murders his wife Deborah and sets off on a heroic quest of rebirth.

Several reviewers of *An American Dream* were outraged at the premise of the novel: A man murders his wife and not only gets away with the crime but also actually becomes a better man, finding a new inner strength and appetite for life. Feminist critics attacked Mailer for his misogyny, professing to see a pattern in much of his work that demeaned women while elevating the heroic nature of men. Other critics simply found the novel itself unpersuasive and Rojack a rather ridiculous specimen—like Mailer himself, out to establish some concept of heroism that said more about the deficiencies of the author than about the society or the characters Mailer was ostensibly treating.

Later critics of the novel were much more sympathetic, praising the novel for its stylistic virtuosity and courage in probing the tensions and violence of contemporary life. They were willing to grant Mailer his subject matter and believed that it was beside the point to fret about the morality of Rojack's murder. Mailer had not presented it as simply good or evil, but as an act that reflects Rojack's desperation and extreme desire. He both loves and hates Deborah, and their physical struggle that results in his strangling her is caused by his sudden urge to relieve himself of the grip she has held on his life.

Deborah is vicious. She reminds her husband of everything he has not accomplished, and her words wound a man who came out of the war a hero and with the same kind of promise that put him into politics with John F. Kennedy in Congress. Rojack's career, however, does not prosper. While he gains some stature as an eccentric professor of psychology and television personality, these accomplishments are scorned by his wealthy wife, who turns to more prominent men—perhaps even to Kennedy himself, she seems to imply in referring to her lovers.

The point about Rojack's murder is that it forces him to act on his own, to become his own man, and to jettison all supports—such as his reliance on Deborah and on her father to help him return to politics. In order to justify himself, Rojack engages in the most extravagant actions—toughing out a confrontation with gangsters when he becomes interested in Cherry, one of their women, stomping and throwing Shago Martin (Cherry's black former lover) down the stairs, confronting his father-in-law Barney Oswald Kelly, who would just as soon have Rojack killed for what he suspects Rojack has done to Deborah, and walking the parapet outside Kelly's apartment in an almost mystical effort to prove his courage. Much of this seems foolhardy, even ridiculous, by the very naturalistic standards of character development that Mailer had adopted in *The Naked and the Dead*. Yet Mailer stubbornly sticks by his character's excessive actions, implying that the only way Rojack can remake himself is to seek the death of his former self. The result is a character that transcends the boundaries of social background and individual pathology. Rojack comes to believe that he can indeed become another man, can invent a new style for himself.

The extent to which Rojack will ultimately succeed in sustaining a new identity is not clear. The novel leaves him on the road, traveling to Yucatán, mourning the death of Cherry, who has gotten caught in the revenge of her former lover's friends seeking to murder Rojack for his roughing up of Shago Martin. Rojack has attained his new life at enormous cost to himself and has done nothing to ameliorate the evil of society's powerful figures like Kelly.

THE ARMIES OF THE NIGHT
First published: 1968
Type of work: Novel

A reluctant Norman Mailer joins the march on the Pentagon to protest the Vietnam War and to show solidarity with a younger generation of dissenters.

With *The Armies of the Night*, Mailer received the best reviews since the publication of *The Naked and the Dead*. Reviewers found his third-person treatment of himself as a character utterly convincing. Mailer's narration seemed so credible because he dealt with all the important aspects of his character in conjunction with the complexity of events surrounding the march on the Pentagon. In other words, his original aim in *The Naked and the Dead* of showing the convergence of character and society was amply demonstrated in a mature, comic, and subtle work.

Mailer begins *The Armies of the Night* with his own reluctant agreement to participate in the march. He is at home trying to write when he gets a call from Mitchell Goodman, a friend urging him to come to Washington. At first, Mailer is petulant, advising Goodman that it behooves writers to write, not to engage in events that only take them away from their work. Mailer has to admit to himself, however, that he is not writing anything important at the moment and that he is really looking for excuses to duck a commitment.

Mailer's ambivalence and early efforts to dominate events result in his drunken antics as master of ceremonies at the Ambassador Theater, where Robert Lowell, Dwight Macdonald, Paul Goodman, and other literary luminaries have gathered to read their work and to express their support for the march on the Pentagon. Mailer makes a spectacle of himself by trying to act the role of a literary Lyndon Johnson, trying to bully the crowd and mold it—like General Cummings—into an instrument of his will. This is a new generation, however, impressed with Mailer but hardly willing to have him dominate events. He is booed as much as he is cheered.

Sobering up and realizing that his attitudes toward draft resisters are ambivalent, Mailer joins the marchers with a newfound sense of modesty, hoping only to be arrested and quickly released to make a symbolic point. Instead, he is detained for many hours and is forced to probe his feelings about himself and about his middle-class life. *The Armies of the Night* becomes, in part, a coming to terms with his middle-aged self and his left conservatism, which is sympathetic to the young protestors but is not willing to take revolutionary action to change the fundamental bases of society. Instead, Mailer is comfortable moving within the power structure, trying to bore from within and examine its complacent beliefs and his own sometimes fatuous convictions.

The first half of *The Armies of the Night*, then, is what Mailer calls "the novel as history." Through his personal lens, events unfold and are interpreted in the novelist's quest for meaning. The second and shorter half of *The Armies of the Night*, "history as a novel," is a more objective study of accounts of the march on the Pentagon, which shows how the march was planned and reported; it dwells on the discrepancies of press reports and demonstrates that those who purport to write "history," no less than those who write novels, make constructs of events—imaginative projections of what they think happened, of what they saw from different points of view. The armies in Mailer's title refer, therefore, not only to the clash between the protestors and the guardsmen at the Pentagon but also to different modes of perception. History and the novel are distinct genres, but they also have more in common than their practitioners are usually willing to admit. In writing both history and a novel, Mailer combines fiction's immediacy and drama with history's documentary quest for verification.

THE EXECUTIONER'S SONG

First published: 1979
Type of work: Novel

A vivid third-person account of the life and execution of murderer Gary Gilmore and of the societal forces that inform and are attracted to his singular story.

The Executioner's Song appeared at a time when critics (and Mailer himself) had become tired of the way his personality tended to dominate everything he wrote. He wanted to find a subject and a style that would be bigger than his ego and that would force him to write in a different style. Presented with a massive amount of material by Larry Schiller, who had bought the rights to Gary Gilmore's story, Mailer found that he had hundreds of characters to work with, speaking on tape and in documents that amounted to a massive social novel that would ultimately cover virtually every region in the country through the voices of people describing their involvement in Gilmore's life. Conducting several new interviews and immersing himself in the thousands of pages of court record and press coverage, Mailer developed an objective, precise, spare voice that had the ring of authenticity, for it was a voice that did not seem to make any more of the experience than what a reader could observe in the accounts on the page.

The Executioner's Song is divided into two parts, "Western Voices" and "Eastern Voices." The first part begins with the release of Gary Gilmore from prison and the efforts of his relatives to find him a decent job and place to live. Gilmore has trouble adjusting, coping with the everyday necessities of working, shopping, eating, and so on. He falls in love with Nicole Baker, a young woman he is sure he has met in another life, and whom he binds to himself with an intensity that drives him to despair when she leaves him. Committing two murders for no apparent reason—except for the implication that he shoots two clean-cut Mormon men rather than turn the gun on himself and Nicole—Gilmore decides in prison that he should be executed.

The second part of *The Executioner's Song* details the media attention that Gilmore's resolution to die inspires. Gilmore is articulate, determined, and contemptuous of the state. His defiance and his willingness to accept punishment fires the public imagination and provokes the interest of Larry Schiller, who sees both book and film possibilities in Gilmore's saga. In many ways, Schiller becomes Mailer's surrogate, for in his previous books Mailer has put himself forward as the sensibility reporting on and shaping events. Now it is Schiller who assembles every piece of the story, getting exclusive rights and dealing directly with Gilmore. As in Mailer's use of the third person to describe himself in *The Armies of the Night*, his third-person depiction of Schiller is a brilliant way of showing how the reporter both reflects and shapes the events he covers.

A huge critical and popular success, *The Executioner's Song* was praised as a great social novel giving a panoramic view of the whole country. Mailer himself confessed that he could not have invented better characters. They were presented with a density and wealth of social detail that surpassed *The Naked and the Dead*, thus making *The Executioner's Song* Mailer's most comprehensive and convincing work.

Summary

Many critics have suggested that Mailer's greatest achievement has been in nonfiction, where he has had a plot ready made and a cast of characters about which he can report with uncanny accuracy and insight. At the same time, in turning to nonfiction he has adapted the techniques of fiction to show how much of history—once it is reported—can be seen as a novel. To dismiss his novels, however, would be a mistake, since *The Naked and the Dead* and *An American Dream*, for example, express and often superbly realize the way he has tried to shift between and balance the countervailing forces of the individual and society.

Bibliography

Adams, Laura, ed. *Will the Real Norman Mailer Please Stand Up?* Port Washington, N.Y.: Kennikat Press, 1974.

Braudy, Leo, ed. *Norman Mailer: A Collection of Critical Essays.* Englewood Cliffs, N.J.: Prentice-Hall, 1972.

Gordon, Andrew. *An American Dreamer: A Psychoanalytic Study of the Fiction of Norman Mailer.* London: Associated University Presses, 1980.

Lennon, J. Michael, ed. *Conversations with Norman Mailer.* Jackson: University Press of Mississippi, 1988.

_____, ed. *Critical Essays on Norman Mailer.* Boston: G. K. Hall, 1986.

Lucid, Robert F., ed. *Norman Mailer: The Man and His Work.* Boston: Little, Brown, 1971.

Manso, Peter. *Mailer: His Life and Times.* New York: Simon & Schuster, 1985.

Mills, Hilary. *Norman Mailer: A Biography.* New York: Empire Books, 1982.

Poirier, Richard. *Norman Mailer.* New York: Viking Press, 1972.

Solotaroff, Robert. *Down Mailer's Way.* Urbana: University of Illinois Press, 1974.

Wenke, Joseph. *Mailer's America.* Hanover, N.H.: University Press of New England, 1987.

Carl Rollyson

BERNARD MALAMUD

Born: Brooklyn, New York
April 26, 1914
Died: New York, New York
March 18, 1986

Principal Literary Achievement
Universally recognized as one of America's greatest writers, Malamud transcends the Jewish experience to champion the triumph of the human spirit and the brotherhood of man.

Biography

Bernard Malamud was born on April 26, 1914, in Brooklyn, New York. The older of two sons of Max and Bertha (Fidelman) Malamud, who had emigrated from Russia early in the century and ran a grocery store, he enjoyed a relatively happy childhood. Both Yiddish and English were spoken in the Malamud household, and a great emphasis was placed on the cultural aspects of Judaism. His early years were spent going to the Yiddish theater on Manhattan's Second Avenue and reading novels by such favorites as Horatio Alger. Doubtless his later writings were influenced also by his father's stories of life in czarist Russia.

Indeed, his father, along with his teachers, encouraged the young Malamud to develop his obvious talent for storytelling. One of his most cherished gifts was the multivolume *Book of Knowledge* encyclopedia that his father gave him after the boy's recovery from pneumonia when he was nine. Many of his boyhood nights were spent in the back room of the family store putting on paper the stories he made up to amuse his friends. He would later confess a lifelong love for short fiction even over the novel, since "if one begins early in life to make up and tell stories, he has a better chance to be heard out if he keeps them short." His interest in literature continued through high school at Erasmus Hall in Brooklyn, where he was an editor of the literary magazine and involved in dramatic productions.

In 1936 Malamud was graduated with a B.A. from City College of New York. He had written a few stories while in college, and after graduation he continued to write in what little spare time he had from jobs in a factory, a variety of stores, and as a clerk with the Census Bureau in Washington, D.C. While working on an M.A. at Columbia University, he taught English at Erasmus Hall Evening High School, devoting his days to studying and writing. He continued his teaching at Erasmus for

several years after receiving his graduate degree in 1942.

In 1945, Malamud married Ann de Chiara. His father was quite upset by his marrying a gentile but was later reconciled—on the birth of the couple's son, Paul. During the 1940's, Malamud's stories appeared in several noncommercial magazines, a fact that made him happy even though he received no payment. In 1949, he sold "The Cost of Living" to Pearl Kazin at *Harper's Bazaar.* In that same year, he and his family left New York for Corvallis, Oregon, where he had accepted a position at Oregon State University.

A lifelong city dweller, Malamud was overwhelmed by the vastness of the Pacific Northwest. Although it took him a while to get his bearings, the change of scenery and lifestyle permitted him a new perspective on his life and his writing. In those early years at Oregon State he developed a weekly routine that allowed much time for writing: He taught three days a week and wrote four. This disciplined approach helped him zero in on those things about which he really yearned to write. His teaching was not as satisfying, since, without a Ph.D., he was allowed to teach composition but not literature. His most gratifying teaching came during a night workshop in the short story, which he offered for townspeople who wanted to take a writing course. Malamud later admitted that he did not care what he taught as long as he had time to write. Some of his fondest memories of those early days at Oregon State were of his wife pushing a stroller as she handed him lunchtime sandwiches through the window of the Quonset hut where he wrote and taught. During those years, his work appeared in such noted magazines as *Partisan Review* and *Commentary* in addition to *Harper's Bazaar.*

In 1952 his first novel, *The Natural,* appeared to mixed reviews. Some critics were put off by what they saw as an obscure use of symbolism, while others applauded its masterful use of fable and its art of ancient storytelling in a modern voice. In 1956, the *Partisan Review* made him a fellow in fiction and recommended him for a Rockefeller Grant, which allowed him to take a leave of absence from Oregon State to spend a year in Europe. In 1957, his next novel, *The Assistant,* was published. More Jewish in its characters and theme than *The Natural,* this work firmly established him as a major American Jewish writer. Malamud was presented with the Daroff Memorial Award and the Rosenthal Award of the National Institute of Arts and Letters for his second novel.

In 1958, thirteen of Malamud's previously published short stories appeared in his first collection, *The Magic Barrel.* Including such notable short stories as "The Magic Barrel," "Angel Levine," and "The Last Mohican," the collection strengthened Malamud's position as a major Jewish voice in American letters. *The Magic Barrel* won a National Book Award in 1959. A fellow in the Ford Foundation's humanities and arts program from 1959 to 1961, Malamud wrote his third novel, *A New Life* (1961). Also in 1961 he left Oregon State to take a position in language and literature at Bennington College in Vermont, where he taught for more than twenty years, with the exception of a two-year visiting lectureship at Harvard University from 1966 to 1968.

In 1963, he published another collection of short stories, *Idiots First*, followed by his fourth novel, *The Fixer*, in 1966. *The Fixer*, which won him a second National Book Award and a Pulitzer Prize in 1967, was researched by a trip to Russia and six months of uninterrupted study.

From 1969 until his death in 1986, Malamud continued to publish both novels and short stories. His works include *Pictures of Fidelman: An Exhibition* (1969), a collection of stories about one character; *The Tenants* (1971), a novel about the conflicts between an old Jewish writer and a young black one; *Rembrandt's Hat* (1973), another collection of stories; *Dubin's Lives* (1979), a novel about a writer at midlife; *God's Grace* (1982), a novel; *The Stories of Bernard Malamud* (1983), another collection; and a host of stories published separately in prestigious magazines.

Additional awards and honors included Vermont's 1979 Governor's Award for Excellence in the Arts, the Brandeis Creative Arts Award (1981), and the American Academy and Institute of Arts and Letters' Gold Medal in Fiction (1983). From 1979 to 1981 he was president of the PEN (International Association of Poets, Playwrights, Editors, Essayists, and Novelists) American Center. Bernard Malamud died in Manhattan on March 18, 1986.

Analysis

Malamud first came to prominence during the late 1950's and early 1960's, a period when fiction was preoccupied with the "new novel." In part, his writings can be seen as a reaction to this school, which devalued form, presented weak, atypical characters, offered a negative view about the future of humankind, and often provided an amoral view of the world. Taking an opposite stance, Malamud was absolutely adamant about the role of fiction: "The purpose of the writer is to keep civilization from destroying itself. But without preachment. Artists cannot be ministers. As soon as they attempt it, they destroy their artistry."

Indeed, Malamud's literary roots extend deeply into the nineteenth century narrative method. He is foremost a storyteller. "I feel that story is the basic element of fiction," he claims, "though that idea is not popular with disciples of the 'new novel.'" He admits to being influenced by the great European realists such as Gustave Flaubert, Thomas Hardy, Anton Chekhov, Leo Tolstoy, and Stendhal as well as modern Americans such as Ernest Hemingway and William Faulkner. Malamud tells a story in the traditional manner. He is a great believer in form, which he calls an "absolute necessity . . . the basis of literature." At the heart of every story stands character. In fact, Malamud is devoted to the development of the individual:

> The sell-out of personality is just tremendous. Our most important natural resource is Man. The times cry out for men of imagination and hope. Instead, our fiction is loaded with sickness, homosexuality, fragmented man, "other-directed" man. It should be filled with love and beauty and hope. We are underselling Man.

Like his literary forebears, especially the American writers, Malamud favors the initiation story. A typical Malamud story follows the maturation pattern: A young man who has led an unfulfilled life fraught with failed relationships, undeveloped emotions, and questionable morality undertakes a journey. Most often this odyssey involves physical movement—from a rural setting to the city, or the reverse. There, the young man encounters a series of father figures—some false and some true— and by asking questions, suffering for past inadequacies, facing new experiences, and accepting responsibility for himself, he grows.

The quintessential Malamud format, then, is mythic. Joseph Campbell, the eminent scholar and myth critic, reduced the basic structure of myth to "separation-initiation-return." Certainly Malamud's most familiar protagonists follow this pattern. Roy Hobbs and Yakov Bok separate from their bucolic innocence for the urban experience, S. Levin departs New York City for a small town in rural Oregon, and Frank Alpine journeys from the West to New York City. All four protagonists are male, young, and without parents; furthermore, all four search for father surrogates to guide them through the difficult passage to adulthood. In their new world they are initiated through a series of trials; encountering deception, often in the form of a female temptress, they make mistake after mistake and are forced to suffer. Iris Lemon, the heroine of *The Natural*, teaches the essential Malamud lesson when she says, "We have two lives, Roy, the life we learn with and the life we live with after that. Suffering is what brings us toward happiness." The returns are varied. Each novel ends after a decisive moment in which the youthful protagonist is at the threshold of maturity. Roy Hobbs cuts off his involvement with gamblers by returning the bribery money and stalking off. Frank Alpine replaces Morris Bober in his tomb of a grocery store. S. Levin loads up the car with his new family to return to the East. Yakov Bok leaves the prison cell of his self for a trial, now willing to shoulder the load of communal suffering. While these novels are open-ended (the reader has no idea of any protagonist's ultimate fate), the important thing is that these characters have come to a sense of who they are, have clarified their relationship to the world, and have willingly accepted their responsibility.

Ultimately, in the battle between humanism and nihilism, Malamud's novels are an affirmation of life. As Malamud himself has said, "Literature, since it values man by describing him, tends toward morality. . . . Art celebrates life and gives us our measure." Though starting in the gloom, all of his lead characters search for "possibilities," "a better life," "a new life," "opportunities," and to some degree they find them. They may live in a modern wasteland—a world of suffering, toil, and degradation—but they persist. They learn to turn suffering into a positive value rather than letting it crush them. His *schlemiels* prosper.

While Malamud's heritage is undeniably Jewish (his father was a Jewish immigrant, and, like Sholom Aleichem and I. L. Peretz, he is part of the tradition of Yiddish storytelling), to see him as wholly a fixture in the so-called contemporary Jewish Literary Renaissance is to limit him. "I write about Jews because I know them," he says. "But more important, I write about them because Jews are absolutely the very stuff of drama." Malamud does not envision the Jew as unique, as primarily a product of the Judaistic culture and consciousness in the manner of Saul Bellow and Philip Roth. The Jew is a metaphor for all men, a modern-day Everyman—as Malamud's oft-quoted remark "All men are Jews" suggests. As a humanist, Malamud seeks through his synecdochic method to examine the whole human race.

Malamud's works are essentially an affirmation of the community of man. Despite his protagonists' varying ethnic, geographic, educational, and national backgrounds, Malamud emphasizes not their differences, but their similarities. His plots, themes, characters, and mythic underpinnings all combine to stress the essential community of man. Moreover, Malamud is full of hope: "My premise is that we will not destroy each other. My premise is that we will live on. We will seek a better life. We may not become better, but at least we will seek betterment."

THE NATURAL

First published: 1952
Type of work: Novel

In the contemporary world, heroism is a difficult struggle for a young man.

The Natural, Malamud's first novel, initially received mixed reviews but is now generally regarded as a superb piece of literature. The novel is both an anomaly for and an introduction to the author. The book differs from the typical Malamud novel: Its style is not as realistic; its central protagonist, Roy Hobbs, is not Jewish; it closes on a note of defeat; and it centers on a sport, professional baseball. As such, *The Natural* is generally viewed in the top echelon of sports novels, such as Robert Coover's *The Universal Baseball Association, Inc., J. Henry Waugh, Prop.* (1968) and Mark Harris' *Bang the Drum Slowly* (1956). *The Natural* is also one of the two Malamud books to have been made into a film (though in this case, to ensure the film's popularity, the ending is more optimistic, with Hobbs' hit winning the play-off game). The book follows the traditional Malamud initiation story pattern, has a mythic structure, uses an Everyman figure as protagonist, and utilizes a mixed tone of comedy and tragedy.

The Natural has many levels. On the surface, it is a sports book about the rise and fall of Roy Hobbs, a young man with the potential to be a baseball superstar and hero. Malamud knows the diamond sport, and he has infused his tale with actual events from baseball lore. With his being an orphan, his tendency to overeat, and his hitting a homerun for a dying boy, Hobbs is obviously based on Babe Ruth. Hobbs' being shot in a hotel room by a deranged woman echoes the fate of Eddie Waitkus, and his ultimate succumbing to the gamblers' desire to throw a game is highly reminiscent of Shoeless Joe Jackson. Thus, Hobbs symbolizes the best and the worst baseball has to offer.

On another level *The Natural* is an initiation story. Roy Hobbs, whose name means "bumpkin king," is a white-faced pitcher one year out of the Northwest High School League. After striking out the American League batting champion, he hubristically announces that he wishes to be "the best there ever was in the game." His pride and immaturity bring him a silver bullet in a Chicago hotel room. Fifteen years later he tries the major leagues again, but his carnal lust, materialism, and immaturity lead him to throw a game. At the novel's conclusion, Hobbs, feeling old and grimy and filled with overwhelming self-hatred, realizes that "I never did learn anything out of my past life, now I have to suffer again."

On perhaps the deepest level, Roy Hobbs is the archetypal protagonist on a heroic quest. Malamud borrows from many legends, but mostly from the Grail myth. Like Sir Perceval, the youthful Hobbs sets out alone for the Grail (baseball champion- ship) armed with a marvelous weapon—his bat, Wonderboy (seemingly magical and carved from a lightning-blasted tree). Along the way, he tries to aid a dying Fisher King figure, Pop Fisher (manager of the New York Knights). Unable to dis- cern the temptresses (Memo Paris and Harriet Bird) from the Lady-in-the-Lake (Iris Lemon)—that is, to see the distinction between carnal lust and true love—Hobbs succumbs to the evil figure (Judge Goodwill Banner) in the Chapel Perilous (here the Judge's dark tower). Hence, Hobbs is not granted a vision of the Grail (the right to play in the World Series), and neither the urban wasteland nor the dying Fisher King is saved or replaced.

On a psychological level, Hobbs never matures. Narcissistically fixated on his athletic career, he mistakenly pursues the sterile and feeble-breasted (Memo Paris and Harriet Bird) instead of the fertile Iris Lemon, who is pregnant with his child, and who appropriately breaks his phallic symbol, Wonderboy. Hobbs, though in his thirties, is likewise a broken child. Though aided by various father figures (scout Sam Simpson and Pop Fisher), he is unable to become a real father himself. On a moral level, Malamud stresses Hobbs's failure to develop a suitable moral code. The protagonist is preoccupied with himself. Unable to recognize the need to live for other people (Iris Lemon, Pop Fisher, or his public) as well as the value of love, self-sacrifice, and suffering, Hobbs ends up alone, defeated.

The Natural is a book of blends. The reality of American baseball is mixed with heroic myth. Moments of sheer terror are rendered in a very poetic style. When Harriet Bird shoots Roy Hobbs, the narrator's description is vivid, almost lyrical: "The bullet cut a silver line across the water. He sought with his bare hands to catch it, but it eluded him and, to his horror, bounced into his gut." At the same time, however, the narrator seems detached and ironic: "She pulled the trigger (thrum of bull fiddle)." *The Natural*, then, is much more highly symbolic and lyrical than Malamud's later novels, closer to the traditions of the romance than the realistic novel. Rather than being viewed as flawed, even inconsistent, the novel is probably best read as an experiment, a harbinger of forms and themes that in later works will be better rendered.

THE ASSISTANT

First published: 1957
Type of work: Novel

After a series of mistakes, a man matures through suffering and the acceptance of responsibility.

The Assistant, Malamud's critically acclaimed second novel, is a realistic look at the Jewish community. Malamud, however, transcends the Jewish experience by revealing on a universal moral level what it means to be a man. His protagonist learns about the regeneration of the self and the process of individual redemption.

The focal point of this initiation novel is Frank Alpine, a twenty-five-year-old orphan who has recently come from the West to New York City. Typical of his always making the wrong decision, Frank falls in with a thug and helps him rob and beat a poor Jewish grocery store owner, Morris Bober. Later, after falling in love with the grocer's daughter, Helen, Frank rescues her from a would-be rapist (the same thug), but then completes the act of rape himself. Clearly at the nadir of his existence and unacknowledgable about himself, Frank finally begins to learn.

Deciding that he is, after all, "a man of stern morality," Frank takes the place of the grocer he injured. He works sixteen hours a day in the grocery, supplements this with a night job, and secretly gives the Bober family money from his savings account. He also cuts his ties to Ward Minogue, the thug, and stops his voyeuristic behavior toward the woman he loves, Helen Bober. Through discipline, love, and suffering, Frank becomes a responsible adult such that even Helen realizes that "he had changed into somebody else, no longer what he had been." Appropriately, at the end of the novel, Frank has himself circumcised and, after Passover, becomes a Jew.

On the surface, Malamud seems to be suggesting the moral supremacy of the Jewish belief; however, the writer does several things to suggest that he is really interested in establishing a general humanistic code of ethics. First, Frank's role model, Morris Bober, is not an orthodox Jew (he never goes to synagogue and fails to follow the dietary code). Second, Frank actually traces the Catholic pattern of sainthood; Malamud takes care to indicate that Frank parallels his namesake, Saint Francis of Assisi. Early in the novel, Frank describes Saint Francis as a man of poverty feeding birds in a natural setting. By the middle of the novel, Helen notices Frank in the park feeding peanuts to pigeons. On the last page, Frank has a vision of himself as Saint Francis working in poverty in the grocery store. Thirdly, Malamud also has Frank follow the mythic pattern of the questing knight. As he journeys through the blighted land, Frank asks the traditional questions, faces the various temptations, and ultimately replaces the dead king. As a result, Frank embodies the basic patterns of moral growth in Western culture, not only Jewish law.

Another pattern used by Malamud is that of the father replacing the son. Morris' grocery is repeatedly described in negative images—a prison, a cave, a tomb, and a coffin. Later, when Frank takes over the store, he uses the same imagery, even going so far as to say that, like Morris, he has a perpetual stink (failure) in his nose. At Morris' funeral, Frank falls into the grocer's grave and must climb out. Like Morris, Frank uses the grocery to help Ida, Morris' widow, survive and help Helen attain her desire—going to college.

The Assistant is also a muted criticism of the American Dream. Morris, a Russian immigrant who has come to America to seek his fortune, is instead buried (first in his grocery store, and then in the ground) a poor man. Morris' problem is that he is an honest man who, despite Frank's prodding, refuses to cheat his customers. Morris is foiled against Charlie, his former partner who cheated him, and Julius Karp, who trades on people's miseries with a liquor store and lies to Morris about to whom he will rent his property. Because they lack scruples, Charlie and Julius have become rich.

Frank Alpine is not the novel's only "child" of a family. One reason Malamud uses the omniscient method of narration is to explore other characters. In fact, the novel employs several other father-child relationships. Much of the novel focuses on Helen Bober, who has had to relinquish her dream of college and work as a menial secretary at Levenspiel's Louisville Panties and Bras to support her father. Unable to develop her possibilities, she has become very unhappy. Similarly, Louis Karp is unable to take over his father's liquor store, Nat Pearl seems to be a perpetual law student, and Ward Minogue, in reaction to his father, a police detective, has turned to a life of crime. Ironically, the only successful transmission of knowledge from father to son is through Morris to his surrogate son, Frank, the orphan.

Perhaps the real strength of this novel lies in Malamud's ability to make his fictional universe so real. One way he accomplishes this is his steady flow of minor characters: Breitbart, the light-bulb peddler; Al Marcus, the paper-bag salesman stricken with cancer; Nick Fuso, the upstairs tenant. Malamud carefully describes the gray-haired Polish woman who appears every morning at 6:00 A.M. to buy her three-cent roll. The Yiddish speech patterns ring true: when Leo the cakeman says, "Bad all over," Morris replies, "Here is the worst." The language is replete with words such as *schmerz* and *landsleit*.

A NEW LIFE

First published: 1961
Type of work: Novel

After a painful struggle toward self-definition, a man ironically gains freedom and triumph by choosing responsibility and defeat.

A New Life continues Malamud's treatment, begun in *The Natural* and refined in *The Assistant*, of the search for self-definition. This most picaresque of his works follows the struggles of S. Levin, a young professor from New York who hopes to redeem what he perceives as a failed life through relocation to a technical college in the Northwest. Set in the 1950's, the novel substitutes the mythic placelessness of Malamud's earlier novels with a Stendhalian realism replete with topical allusions to the Cold War, McCarthyism, and liberalism versus loyalty oaths.

The novel is actually two books in one. On one level, *A New Life* functions as a satire on academic life. Amid a world of drab parties, hateful faculty meetings, and dull classes, Malamud introduces a cast of mentally crippled faculty members whose only goal seems to be to hang onto their jobs no matter what sacrifices of intellectual or moral principle must be made. The students are no better; they find little interest in things intellectual and see no ethical problem with cheating to pass their classes. On the second, and more important, level, Malamud deals with his ever-present theme of the quest. The characters and incidents that Levin encounters at Cascadia College are the obstacles in his mythic journey to self-discovery. As in all Malamud's novels, the hero must ultimately make a choice that will determine his destiny. In *A New Life* this choice involves, as always, a definition of freedom. To complete his quest, Levin must come to terms with the suffering involved in gaining true freedom.

Malamud's satirical pen is sharp, with barbs directed both at the academic establishment and at his hero's excessive idealism. From Levin's arrival in Eastchester, the home of Cascadia College, it is apparent that this former drunkard and professed liberal is out of his element in the stifling atmosphere of this land-grant institution devoted to giving its students a practical education. He is told flatly that the liberal arts (which he believes "feed our hearts") have no place in the school's conservative English department, devoted to drilling students with the anachronistic chairman's text, *The Elements of Grammar*.

Against this backdrop Levin encounters a series of disillusionments as he attempts to shape a new life filled with success in his academic career and a oneness with the beauties of the natural world. Be it teaching, departmental relationships, or encounters with nature, Levin's lofty expectations arising from his overblown, often comic romanticism doom him to comic failure. A modern-day Don Quixote, he sees his efforts to impose his ideals on an insensitive world end in bumbling disaster: Attempting to inspire his students with his own enthusiasm for learning, he lectures with his fly unzipped; thinking he has found a role model in a "liberal" colleague, he discovers only an arch anti-feminist reduced to trivial causes such as opposing "indiscriminate garbage dumping and dogs that run loose and murder his chickens." Filled with an intoxicating joy in the beauties of a pastoral scene, he steps in cow dung.

Indeed, Malamud fashions Levin as a more intense version of Roy Hobbs or Frank Alpine—the hero who is his own worst enemy. Levin's attempts to escape the ghosts of a failed love affair, the suicide of his mother, and a two-year lapse into drunkenness have proved futile. Relocation to another part of the country and a beard grown over the face he cannot stand to look at fail to exorcise the old self that haunts his every action. Levin is given to fitful dreams and long bouts of melancholy in his room. So intense are these battles between what he desires and what he realizes he must accept instead that Levin at times seems at the point of insanity.

Levin's disillusionment with the academic life leads to loneliness and a need for female companionship. Even in the arena of love, however, Levin's romanticism dooms him to an almost clownlike failure. Counselled during his first meeting with the departmental chairman against sexual escapades with women from town, colleagues, students, or faculty wives, Levin launches into a series of affairs with exactly these types—with predictable results. His conquest of a waitress in a barn is interrupted by her boyfriend, who steals their clothes. His liaison with Avis Fliss, a single member of the department, ends abruptly in his office one night when, during frantic foreplay, he discovers her damaged breast and becomes impotent. Even his consummated affair with Nadalee Hammerstand, a student, ultimately ends in disappointment, when, after a madcap journey involving comic confrontations straight from a picaresque adventure, he arrives at their rendezvous by the ocean only to encounter a series of slapstick events that ruin any chance of sexual fulfillment.

The novel's turning point comes when Levin, a failure both academically and with women, falls in love with the wife of Gerald Gilley, the director of composition and the antithesis of everything for which Levin stands. It is through his relationship with Pauline that Levin discovers who he is and gains the courage to break free from the bonds of his false idealism. After months of struggle during which Levin (torn between his romantic ideas and practical reality) rejects Pauline and then takes her back, the affair culminates when Levin agrees to tell Gilley about the relationship. His admission, during the heat of his campaign against Gilley for department chairman, leads to his dismissal from Cascadia.

His future uncertain, Levin must confront Gilley to ask for custody of the Gilleys' adopted children. After failing to dissuade the aspiring husband and father by detailing all the problems Levin is bringing upon himself with such a neurotic woman and endlessly sick children, Gilley places a final stipulation on his willingness to let them go: Levin must renounce the teaching profession. When Levin agrees, Gilley asks him why he is willing to shoulder such a burden. Levin's answer, "Because I can, you son of a bitch," marks him as the Malamudian hero who finds freedom in the acceptance of responsibility, inner triumph in outward defeat.

THE FIXER

First published: 1966
Type of work: Novel

Against a backdrop of early twentieth century Russia, a man gains self-definition by accepting suffering as a means to freedom.

The Fixer is perhaps Malamud's finest novel. A best-seller and Literary Guild Selection, it won for him both the Pulitzer Prize and the National Book Award for

Fiction. In addition, it was cited for excellence by the American Library Association and was adapted into a film.

Malamud continues his theme of the quest for self-definition. *The Fixer*, however, replaces the more contemporary settings of his earlier novels with the historical backdrop of early twentieth century Russia. In fact, the novel's plot is based on an incident that occurred in 1911 in Kiev, the setting for most of the book. The work is by no means a slavish reportage of actual events; rather, Malamud uses the situation of Mendel Beiliss, a Kiev worker who was imprisoned for the ritual murder of a Christian boy, as the basis for his fictional account of the struggles of his hero, Yakov Bok.

Underlying the plot of *The Fixer* is Malamud's familiar attempt to define true freedom in an insensitive, seemingly irrational world. Yakov Bok, a poor fixer (or handyman), grows disenchanted with his humble life in a run-down village. An orphan who was taught his trade in an orphanage and apprenticed at age ten, Bok has served in the Russian Army and taught himself some history, geography, science, and arithmetic in addition to learning the Russian language on his own. Considering himself a freethinker, he feels trapped in his situation (even his childless wife has deserted him) and longs for the new opportunities that life in the city might afford. He sells all that he owns except his tools and a few books and journeys to what he believes will be freedom in Kiev.

Malamud uses Bok's journey to reveal the character's basic humanity. For all his shortcomings, Bok is a good man, and it is his spirit of giving that constantly embroils him in trouble. Like Roy Hobbs, Frank Alpine, and S. Levin before him, Bok is his own worst enemy. At times his troubles are comical; feeling sorry for an old woman walking on the road to Kiev, he offers her a ride in his run-down cart only to have the cart break down under their weight. At other times, however, his humanity leads him into more devastating circumstances. His false imprisonment for the ritual murder of a Christian boy is a direct result of his rescuing the anti-Semite Nikolai Maximovitch from smothering in the snow after passing out in a drunken stupor and his sheltering an old Jew suffering from the cold. Maximovitch, at first thankful for the rescue and not knowing Bok is a Jew (a fact Bok conceals), gives his savior a room in his house and a job managing his brickworks. Later, however, after discovering Bok's Jewishness and hearing the false accusations of assault by his daughter, who has tried unsuccessfully to seduce Bok, Maximovitch acts as a central witness against Bok in the death of the boy. Bok's sheltering of the old Jew also provides evidence against him when the situation is misinterpreted by the authorities.

The majority of the novel treats Bok's imprisonment. For more than three years he endures almost unbearable physical and mental suffering. Paramount to his anguish, of course, is the injustice of his fate; an innocent man, he has been cast into the prison's hellish confines with little chance to defend himself and with little real hope of being cleared of the charges. Bok's isolation becomes a time for reading and reflection, as he attempts to understand his role in such an irrational situation.

Malamud uses a well-drawn cast of characters to aid Bok in his movement toward self-definition. During his confinement Bok comes in contact with people from the outside, as well as those of the prison community, who offer either torment or support. Each of these minor characters contributes to Bok's understanding of himself and his relationship to the world in which he must live. Perhaps Bok's most important visitors are the two members of his family. Shmuel, the skinny old peddler with the talent for selling the seemingly worthless, attempts to get his son-in-law to open his heart to God and accept some responsibility for all his troubles. Tugging at the Jewishness which Bok has earlier tried so hard to deny, Shmuel claims that even in the face of great trouble God will always provide if only a person will let him. For all his efforts, however, a disappointed Shmuel finally leaves his son-in-law. It is left to Raisl, Bok's unfaithful wife, to help him open the door to understanding the nature of suffering and responsibility. At the novel's beginning, she has deserted Bok for a stranger she met at the village inn, leaving her husband with feelings of anger and guilt, since she failed to bear him a child. Ironically, she visits Bok in prison with the sole purpose of getting him to sign a paper acknowledging his paternity of a child she has conceived by another man. Raisl's comment, "Whoever acts the father is the father," helps bring about Bok's epiphany on the relationship between responsibility and freedom.

He comes to a realization that only through accepting the sometimes irrational suffering that responsibility to others brings can one find true freedom. No longer fearful of his prison cell, he concludes that the freedom he has so long sought is in reality a state of mind that must be actively pursued. At the novel's conclusion he drinks in the crowd's cheers as he heads to trial a hero of the downtrodden. With a newly discovered spirit he shouts, "Where there's no fight for it there's no freedom."

THE MAGIC BARREL

First published: 1954
Type of work: Short story

Love is a redemptive force earned through suffering and self-knowledge.

"The Magic Barrel" is another fantasy, this time mixing elements of the traditional fairy tale with Jewish folklore. Like most fairy tales, the story begins with "Not long ago there lived. . . . " Leo Finkle, the rabbinical student searching for a wife, is the prince; Salzman, the marriage broker with the magic barrel and sudden appearances, is the supernatural agent; and Stella, his prostitute daughter, is the princess. As in a typical fairy tale, the prince finally meets the princess and through the intervention of the supernatural agent has a chance at a happy ending.

The fairy tale combines with elements from Jewish folklore. The characters are stereotypic: the marriage broker, the *schlemiel*, and the poor daughter. The setting is the usual lower-class milieu. With Leo helping Salzman at the end, the plot has the familiar reversal. Even the theme is the easily recognizable one of redemptive rebirth through love. Malamud also infuses the story with humor. Aside from the stock characters and stock situations, he utilizes puns, hyperbole, and juxtaposition (women are described in the jargon of a used-car salesman).

The story is also social criticism directed at the Jews. Leo Finkle has learned the Jewish law, but not his own feelings. He takes refuge in his self-pity, he wants a wife not for love but social prestige, and he uses his religion to hide from life.

ANGEL LEVINE

First published: 1955
Type of work: Short story

In recognizing another's divine essence as well as the bond of brotherhood between himself and the person, a man is redeemed.

"Angel Levine," part fable and part fantasy, is yet another example of Malamud's brotherhood theme. Manischevitz, a typical Malamudian Job-like victim, seeks relief from his suffering and aid for his sick wife, Fanny. In the Malamudian world, help comes from a human rather than divine source, which here is a Jewish black man/angel, Angel Levine. Manischevitz can only wonder why God has failed to send him help in the form of a white person. The tailor's subsequent refusal of aid, which is saturated with egotistical pride, fails to lead to relief.

Eventually, Manischevitz, in pursuit of aid, roams into Harlem, where, finding Angel Levine in Bella's bar, he overhears the essential Malamudian lesson about the divine spark in all men: "It de speerit," said the old man. . . . From de speerit arize de man." . . . "God put the spirit in all things."

Colorblind at last, Manischevitz can now believe that the same spirit dwells within every human, uniting all. Manischevitz is rewarded by the sight of a dark figure flying with dark wings. The final meaning of his experience he conveys to Fanny when he admits, "Believe me, there are Jews everywhere." Here he is Malamud's *raisonneur* mouthing the familiar theme of brotherhood.

THE GERMAN REFUGEE

First published: 1963
Type of work: Short story

A teacher of communication ironically fails to communicate with his language student.

"The German Refugee," one of the few first-person stories in the Malamud canon, illustrates the familiar theme of brotherhood. The narrator, Martin Goldberg, relates his attempts to teach English to a German refugee, Oskar Gassner, who is to give a lecture in English about American poet Walt Whitman's relationship to certain German poets.

Two distinct stories emerge: Oskar's anguish and his failure to learn English, as well as the irony of the narrator's failure to understand why. While Martin teaches Oskar English, the German Army begins its summer push of 1939. What the narrator fails to realize is his pupil's deep involvement with his former country's fate and that of his non-Jewish wife, whom he left there.

Malamud emphasizes the irony through the references to Whitman. Oskar ends up teaching the important lesson when he declares about the poet that "it wasn't the love of death they [German poets] had got from Whitman . . . but it was most of all his feeling for *Brudermensch*, his humanity." When Oskar successfully delivers his speech, the narrator feels only a sense of pride at what he taught the refugee, not the bonds of *Brudermensch* that have developed between them. When Oskar commits suicide, the narrator never sees that he is partially responsible.

Summary

Although undeniably part of the Jewish Literary Renaissance, Malamud is quintessentially a humanist. His novels and short stories, quite possibly some of the finest literary achievements of the latter half of the twentieth century, argue for the dignity and brotherhood of man. Occasionally experimental, Malamud basically utilizes traditional forms to stress traditional values. "My work, all of it," he claims, "is an idea of dedication to the human. If you don't respect man, you cannot respect my work."

Bibliography

Astro, Richard, and J. Benson, eds. *The Fiction of Bernard Malamud*. Corvallis: Oregon State University Press, 1977.

Bloom, Harold, ed. *Bernard Malamud*. New York: Chelsea House, 1986.

Field, Leslie, and Joyce Field, eds. *Bernard Malamud and the Critics*. New York: New York University Press, 1970.

Hershinow, Sheldon. *Bernard Malamud*. New York: Frederick Ungar, 1980.

Richman, Sidney. *Bernard Malamud*. New York: Twayne, 1966.

Hal Charles

DAVID MAMET

Born: Chicago, Illinois
November 30, 1947

Principal Literary Achievement

Capturing the rhythms and idioms of working-class American speech and dramatizing the business world in conflict with personal values, Mamet has enriched the stage with penetrating character studies of postmodern life.

Biography

To call David Mamet a "Chicago boy, bred and born" would not be entirely accurate, but he did live the formative years of his childhood and youth in the embrace of that giant Midwestern hub of the free enterprise system—the "hog butcher of America." Mamet was reared in a Jewish neighborhood on the South Side of Chicago, and he attended grade school and high school in the city. Following his parents' divorce, his high school education was split between a suburban high school and Francis W. Parker School in Chicago. His father, Bernard, a Chicago lawyer, was an early influence in Mamet's sensitivity to the musical rhythms of natural language. Various odd jobs taught Mamet how the working world operated and exposed him to the rough and colorful language of the streets. Much has been made of his early experience at Second City (an improvisational comedy group) as a busboy, where he saw the improvisational artists and, more important, learned the language of the stage. As a backstage volunteer in neighborhood playhouses, he furthered his interest in the theatrical world.

Although his father had a law degree in mind for Mamet, the young high school graduate preferred the broadening education of Goddard College in Vermont (where he received a B.A. in English in 1969), where the liberal arts were taught in an experimental atmosphere. He intentionally interrupted his graduate education to spend more than a year in New York City, taking acting classes at the Neighborhood Playhouse by day and working at night as house manager for an Off-Broadway musical, the long-running success *The Fantasticks* (1960). This coincidence, together with his earlier accidental discovery of Second City in Chicago, convinced him that the theater world had something to offer him, and although he was never successful as an actor, he continued in the theater from that time on.

His stage writing had begun in college with a musical revue called *Camel*, but his first serious stage effort was *Lakeboat* (1970), written on demand for an acting class

he was teaching at Marlboro College. When that teaching job was over, Mamet returned to Chicago for a series of non-theater jobs; once again, his sensitivity to the rhythms of business were to stay with him during his playwriting hours. Especially notable was his stint with a real estate development company selling Florida lots from Chicago, an experience that was to be dramatized in Mamet's Pulitzer Prize-winning play, *Glengarry Glen Ross* (1983). College teaching still appealed to him, however, and he returned to Vermont, this time to his alma mater, Goddard College; for three years he taught theater and served as artist-in-residence. During these years his writing became more clearly articulated, and he began to write scenes for his students to work with in acting classes.

As an offshoot of his combining actor training with playwriting, he formed the St. Nicholas Company, but he moved to Chicago in 1972 (this company, under the name St. Nicholas Players, was re-formed in Chicago in 1974). Mamet began in earnest his grassroots research into the nature of human discourse, wandering the streets of the city, visiting his father's law offices, trying out on paper the dialogues and ideas that flooded into his head. From that period came *Duck Variations* (1972), actually produced in Vermont in 1972, a nondramatic dialogue between two elderly gentlemen on a park bench, watching and feeding ducks. Its form helped Mamet find a writing style that freed him from elaborate stage directions and the other paraphernalia of stage scripting, allowing him to concentrate on the spoken (and unspoken) rhythms of speech and pause, and at the same time giving actors the respect they deserved for finding the sense of the line without parenthetical assistance. Similar in style is *Sexual Perversity in Chicago* (1974), again essentially a series of simple dialogues, in bars and on the beach, in which the two main characters reveal the complexity of their relationships without directly addressing them. In this play, more elaborate than *Duck Variations*, three of the four characters share the dialogue series from time to time. There is also a love relationship in this play, a theme Mamet would not examine again until *The Woods* (1977).

Mamet combined these two plays as his first attempt at a New York success, at the Off-Off-Broadway showcase house St. Clements Theatre, in 1975. It moved to the Off-Broadway Cherry Lane Theatre in 1976, opening June 16, and Mamet enjoyed his first recognition from the difficult New York theater community.

Back in Chicago, Mamet's play *American Buffalo* had been staged with great success in 1975 at Stage 2, an adjunct to the Goodman Theater, a prestigious not-for-profit theater. The three-character play moved to Broadway in early 1977; in that same year Mamet married actress Lindsay Crouse. The play marks the beginning of an important new theme for Mamet (although *Sexual Perversity in Chicago* hinted at the possibilities): the examination of the world of business and enterprise. Here, three crooks plan a burglary, but the setting and plot are larger metaphors for the absence of moral principle in business. Far from a symbolic play, it is an ultra-realistic look at the life-styles of its three colorful if self-destructive characters.

A period of intense playwriting and production activity followed. Of the plays of these few years, which included *Dark Pony* (1977), *The Water Engine* (1977), and

Mr. Happiness (1978), perhaps the most completely realized was *A Life in the The-ater* (1977), a two-character drama about the waxing and waning of two theater actors' careers; this story, too, is told in the short-scene, blackout style that had already worked so well for Mamet. The mise-en-scène of backstage theater life, with its combination of art and commodity, continued his study of the conflict of business and friendship (or, as some critics view the play, love).

A steady stream of strong plays began to emerge from Mamet's imagination. Occasionally suffering from adverse critical opinion, they nevertheless contain pow-erful characterizations and stunningly convincing dialogue. *Lone Canoe* (1979), a musical/historical study of Indian life versus advancing civilization, was not suc-cessful but continued the daring verbal experimentation that has come to be asso-ciated with Mamet's work. *Edmond* (1980) is a dark look at the descent of an average man, from his tame married life to a new if subterranean view of love in a prison.

In 1984, after a run in London, *Glengarry Glen Ross* came to Broadway, an event that announced the maturing of Mamet's work. Here, he had found his voice and his subject and joined them in a powerful, unforgettable theater experience. That year it won for him the Pulitzer Prize, as well as the virtually unanimous praise of the New York critics. *Speed-the-Plow* (1988) examines the world of Hollywood film "prod-uct" development (a world to which Mamet had been introduced through his screen-play for the 1981 remake of *The Postman Always Rings Twice*). The cast of *Speed-the-Plow*, another three-character play, dominated the press because of the presence of rock star Madonna, and much of the criticism and publicity centered on her rare stage appearance. Whether the play itself carries the full weight of Mamet's talent is a matter of critical debate, but some of the dialogue illustrates Mamet at his best.

Mamet's screenplays have been successful as well. Often working on rewriting classic films, such as *We're No Angels* (1989) and *The Postman Always Rings Twice*, Mamet has also written original screenplays, such as *The Verdict* (1982) and *House of Games* (1987), in which his wife Lindsay Crouse starred. An informal book of essays on theater and other subjects, *Writing in Restaurants*, was published in 1986.

Analysis

In David Mamet's dialogue, the American language of informal discourse be-comes a tool for combat and defense, a song of near meanings, and a sanctuary in slang for the dangerous exposure to true feeling. He has perhaps caught the rhythms of the spoken language as no one has since William Shakespeare, and his characters are true to their speech. He is often compared to Eugene O'Neill, and some critics believe that he surpasses that great American playwright in his ability to make be-lievable the speech patterns of common street life. Several observers of Mamet's canon have used a musical analogy, calling his dialogue "Chicago jazz" or "a fugue" or otherwise underlining the sense of rhythm that his speeches seem to evoke.

Some critics, while noting the strength of the dialogue, interpret the talking scenes as static or undramatic. While it is true that "action" in its basic sense is often missing or concentrated at the end of the plays, the "action" inside the dialogue is complex and multilayered. All speech is in fact "speech-act," the establishing of relational strategies by means of speech. The dialogue in a Mamet play, then, is a series of defenses, justifications, explanations, probing into opinions, and establishing common ground, and underneath all the talk is an action as dramatic as any more obvious or physical action. Mamet's characters admit, deny, offer, accept, deceive, sell, plead, reveal, and conceal in their language. Many times, as critics have noted, the dialogue conceals the emotional content of the scene, as though (in Voltaire's words) "words conceal meaning." In this respect, Mamet, more than any other contemporary playwright, finds his true genre in stage writing in which the action is carried almost exclusively in the character dialogue.

Mamet's views of personal relationships, a theme important to his work, are easily revealed in the content and the mise-en-scène of his plays: Love is treated not as a gentle or honest relationship but as a hard-fought conclusion. Usually love is seen as it collapses, as a relationship breaks apart. In *Sexual Perversity in Chicago*, for example, the getting together of Dan and Deborah takes place briefly and almost offstage; their break-up, however, is open and on the stage. Even the scene in which Deborah moves in with Dan is not placed in a neutral or happy setting, but in her former apartment, with her former roommate Joan angrily concealing her own bitterness and unhappiness with a series of smart-aleck rejoinders. In every play, love is shown in off-handed, negatively connoted scenes.

Where Mamet stands in terms of business and enterprise is not so easily revealed in a single examination of one play or scene. While it is certainly true that the shoddy, "grifter" side of business takes center stage, the question remains whether Mamet applauds that attitude or finds fault with it. In one sense, the dynamics of a business transaction are like drama, but in another sense, the phoniness and false intentions of business dealings are antithetical to true communication. Mamet has chosen to dramatize the inability or reluctance of the characters to enter into an honest negotiation but at the same time their willingness to join in friendships and bonds that transcend simple business dealings. In the play *Glengarry Glen Ross*, Roma's best scene is a brutally honest rephrasing of the principles of existentialism, and for a moment the audience thinks that this is Mamet himself speaking. When Roma turns salesman, however, the audience realizes that his apparent frankness was only the warm-up to the duplicitous business of selling Florida property to an unwilling restaurant owner. *The Water Engine* dramatizes the inventor's dilemma of finding financial security without selling out to the free enterprise system; both this idea and the theme of *Speed-the-Plow* are reminiscent of some themes of playwright Sam Shepard in this respect, showing the artist at odds with the world of enterprise.

More viscerally important than either love or business is Mamet's prevailing theme of language as defense, as shield against encroachment by honest emotion. In *American Buffalo*, the affection between Donny and Bobby is never spoken of outright, but it is there in Donny's long-suffering patience, in his attempt to include Bobby in the scheme (against Teach's wishes), and his defense of Bobby when Teach hurts him in the final scene. Teach is all alone in the world, with no friends; even Ruthie, an offstage presence, hurts his feelings when he asks for a piece of her toast. Bobby and Donny, however, have developed an awkward, unspoken father/son relationship in the dingy setting of the junk store. Bobby's devotion to Donny (as witnessed by his attempts to buy the coin) is an example of how simple, less articulate persons show their affection. Donny, on the other hand, a bridge between the world of business and deceit and the world of human interaction, has none of the verbal brittleness of Teach. Teach is all words; he is adept at using talking as a shield, a defense, and an aggressive agent.

If the harsh language of virtually all the characters suggests that Mamet is always coarse in his treatment of relationships, it is a mistake to see Mamet's plays as devoid of warmth. The play *A Life in the Theater* is touching in many instances, and at base is a pas-de-deux of two like souls. Told poignantly and sensitively, it is a graceful work. While not entirely devoid of the rough language of Mamet's other plays, the dialogue moves through a more sophisticated vocabulary, because the characters are educated actors in the midst of the world of theater rather than people in a working-class environment.

The Woods is a love story as well, despite the harshness of its conclusion. *Sexual Perversity in Chicago*, on the surface about the coming together and breaking apart of the couples, is also a story of male bonding, however crude and insensitive Bernie is to Dan's problems. It is a play about the inability to love, and as such shows the influence of Samuel Beckett, Harold Pinter, and other absurdists, showing characters caught in the dilemma of a need for love and a world that sees love as a weakness. In the big city life that pervades Mamet's work, love has no permanent place. In fact, business is not so much a subject as a metaphor for all human relationships: intimate contact for personal gain, duplicity and deceit for protection. The love stories are always concerned with implied and stated contracts, with the unspoken rules, with an ineffable morality that transcends the gutter talk of the dialogue itself.

Storytelling is an art both for Mamet's characters and for Mamet himself. In every play, at least one long monologue is devoted to telling a story of the past, both as a protective device and as a form of bravado on the part of the speaker, to hide or to reveal his inner self. It is as though the speaker tells his story to avoid revealing himself, yet reveals himself at the same time accidentally. Whether that can be said of Mamet himself is open to question. An open, talkative, witty, and accessible personality, Mamet often appears with a large cigar, a "prop" behind which he successfully hides his personal life.

AMERICAN BUFFALO

First produced: 1975 (first published, 1977)
Type of work: Play

Three petty thieves try to steal back a possibly valuable buffalo nickel from the man who purchased it.

The scene is a sleazy junk store, run by Donny, in a run-down urban setting. Donny runs the shop in a low key, using Bobby to run errands for him. The world of the shop is cluttered and arbitrary, an organic construction rather than a carefully designed one. The financial stakes are low here; an occasional sale to a passerby is enough to sustain the two men in their unambitious lives.

Into this mix comes Teach—angry, "wired," full of venomous energy—with a plan, a scheme, a project of the will (to use Henrik Ibsen's term). It is not enough for Teach to plan and carry out the crime; his innate secretiveness, paranoia, and distrust must extend to his partners, Donny and an offstage figure (Fletch) who eventually deserts the project. Teach brings an anger with him that has become emblematic of the kind of vicious energy that drives Mamet's plays forward. One sees the same kind of energy in Bernie (*Sexual Perversity in Chicago*) and in Roma (*Glengarry Glen Ross*), although Roma is closer to a hero than other destructive Mamet characters.

Driving the minor-key greed of the two more passive characters (Bobby is slightly simple, helpful, and, in a scheme of his own, determined to please Donny) is the possibility of stealing back a coin Donny sold to a customer some time previously. Apparently the coin, a buffalo-head nickel, has some value, because the customer paid fifty dollars for it. Rather than taking delight in Donny's windfall, Teach sees the customer as a cheat who probably knows the coin was worth even more. Thus, as a kind of angry revenge, they can steal the coin back with a clear conscience—the customer has somehow turned into the villain and the trio become, in their own minds, the Robin Hood-like righters of wrongs.

What goes wrong with the burglary is distrust and lack of sophistication. First, the victim is not away from the house; the thieves have been misinformed by Bobby, because he left his observation post. Also, their silent partner has not shown up, and they suspect that he has preceded them in the theft and betrayed them. In fact, he is in the hospital, but they do not believe the story. At the end of the play, Donny shows that he is not another Teach but a friend of a more compassionate order.

The play is not exactly an indictment of all business. The question of trust, of partnership, is examined, and the conclusion is double-sided. The agreements between Donny and Teach are suspect because they are based on distrust; however, the relationship between Donny and Bobby is more genuine. In the opening scene, when Bobby is sent to get food for Donny, there is a sense that the way business works best is by trust—Donny tells Bobby to buy some food for himself as well and does not quibble about the money. When Teach enters, his first lament is about an incident that occurred in the same restaurant—an argument over half a piece of toast. While the scenes are immediate and dynamic, on reflection they represent two ways of "doing business" (which for Mamet means joining in any relationship). Either the business arrangement is the only connection between partners, in which case duplicity and trickery are parts of the agreement, or else the business arrangement is part of a larger relationship, one of affection and mutual trust, in which case the automatic self-serving attitudes of the business person have no place.

Now widely done on the regional stage, this play is often the center of controversy regarding appropriate stage language for more conservative audiences. Its success as drama has invariably won the argument in favor of language verisimilitude, and the rest of Mamet's works have subsequently been widely accepted.

GLENGARRY GLEN ROSS

First produced: 1983 (first published, 1984)
Type of work: Play

High-pressure Florida real estate salesmen fight for leads to promising clients, losing their own principles and values in the process.

In this play, Mamet has found his strongest metaphor for the complexity of human relationships. A group of salesmen, vying for "leads" to hot prospects for a Florida land scheme, make use of language not only to "close" their prospects but also to obfuscate their actual intentions, which include robbing the "leads" from the real estate office. On the surface, every salesman is a man for himself, and the last emotion one would expect is friendship and loyalty among them. They can only judge their success by the sales they make, and the "board" of the contest is the measurement of that success. The best leads get the best closes, and if a man is too far down on the list of persons getting leads, he never has a chance to catch up. In this respect, the play is reminiscent of Arthur Miller's *Death of a Salesman* (1949), because the American Dream of success is separated from the method, from the moral premise behind success.

The first-act scenes in the restaurant are hard-edged dialogues, almost monologues with a responding listener. Moss and Aaronow, whom the audience originally suspects for the office break-ins, are an example of the intimidation relationship in which Mamet excels. Aaronow is drawn into the robbery by dint of Moss's ability to "sell" his guilt to him. As in *American Buffalo*, the criminal turns his crime around into a sort of revenge against someone who did not play by the rules—here it is Moss, showing Aaranow that to steal the leads is a just punishment for Williamson, whose job is to give the leads out. Williamson, it is noted, has never closed a sale, has never been out there in the field, but is a pawn of the offstage owners, Mitch and Murray. In a sense, there is something besides Florida real estate being sold: reputation, one's place on the sales board, even one's loyalty to the police, are all for sale.

At the center of the play is Roma's and Levene's friendship, despite their competition for the Cadillac. When they are both winners, when the sales are closing, they share a frenetic energy and understanding of the almost sexual exaltation of success. When Levene defends Roma to Williamson, the audience sees a side of him that is soft and more likeable; however, the revealing of that very softness is the undoing of Levene, when he accidentally lets Williamson know that he was the actual burglar in the previous night's incident. Williamson immediately pounces on the flaw, and Levene is discovered as the crook. In the meantime, Roma does not even realize what his friend has done for him, as he pursues a lost sale.

The fast-talking world of Florida (and Arizona) real estate sales is a world where the men function only in direct proportion to their ability to hide themselves, to seek the fast buck. It is a hollow relationship, but one with certain unspoken rules. The three-day rule, in which a customer has three days to cancel his deal, is a rule imposed from outside. The customers who are never serious, such as the Indians and the Nyborg family (famous for writing bad checks), are looked down on by the salesmen as unfair players, as wastes of time. Stealing the leads and selling them to a competitor is a way of breaking the rules of the business they are in, but more importantly, it confuses the order of success among the men.

Mamet found inspiration from his own brief work in such a sales office and from "those guys you see on planes" who are the businessmen at work, artificial in their own relationships, competing daily either directly or indirectly for the same dollar. Very little daydreaming is actually done about spending the money, about eventually relaxing and enjoying the fruits of their labors. At the moment, like racehorses, they are in the race and every bit of energy must go into winning it.

Events such as Levene's triumphant entrance and depiction of his grand sale to Bruce and Harriet Nyborg (underscored by Aaranow's disgruntled "I had them on River Glen") are the highlights of these men's lives—the moments when they can announce their successes to one another. The fact that the Nyborg deal will fall through when the check is shown to be fraudulent caps the deadly day of deceit and hopelessness in the ruined office. The other deal gone sour, the sale to Lingk, occurs at the office itself, when Lingk, prompted by his less gullible wife, demands a retraction of the deal. The support character of the detective, Baylen, the only one not involved in the real estate scheme as seller or buyer, is not fully developed—he represents a "finding out," a revealing not of who broke the law but who broke the unwritten code by which these men work.

The storytelling abilities of Mamet's characters, especially the salesmen, are a reflection of Mamet's own ability to tell a good story. The quick-talking defense mechanism of the salesman prevents real contact. As in *American Buffalo*, where the physical object of the buffalo nickel is a carefully chosen symbol (of the lost American West, perhaps, as one critic notes), so the valueless Florida real estate the men are hawking is a symbol of the uselessness at base of the efforts of the men and their world. What they have to sell is worthless; their lives are made worthless as a result.

SPEED-THE-PLOW

First produced: 1988 (first published, 1988)
Type of work: Play

A pair of motion picture producers decide whether to make a sure-fire hit or a high-risk but thematically valuable script recommended by their temporary secretary.

In this play, the question of the worth of a commodity is made the center of the conflict. Far from being useless, worthless property, as in *Glengarry Glen Ross*, here the "product" is a film script more or less guaranteed to make money versus a very questionable project that has no real value but is valuable to the spirit of the men involved.

Bobby Gould, a newly promoted production executive, is visited by an old "friend and associate," Charlie Fox. Gould has "a new deal" with the money man, Ross (offstage). In a power position, Gould is constantly "promoted" by other producers who want him to approve their film deals. He is wary of being "promoted," but Fox, an old friend and business associate, brings him a perfect project—a name actor has agreed to "cross the street." Fox does not "go through channels"—a metaphor for the disguises, the safeguards between people and their emotions—not because he trusts his friendship with Gould, but because he is sure that his film opportunity will appeal to Gould on a business level.

Money versus people is the theme, as Gould and Fox themselves agree: When the "deal" starts to slip away, what are the real values? The question of loyalty and friendship versus the world of business, as in *Glengarry Glen Ross* and *American Buffalo*, comes up again. "It's only words unless they're true," says Fox. Another property, by an Eastern philosopher, has taken the fancy of Karen, a temporary secretary, who visits Gould and sleeps with him in exchange for consideration of the new project.

The audience must consider whether Gould was truly converted to the new book or was tricked into believing in the ideas of the book. The theme that concerns Mamet once again is the interface of business (by which he means cold, distrustful relationships with unwritten rules) and friendship (by which he means trust without boundaries). Two scripts compete for one "green light" from the head of the studio. One script, clearly a moneymaker, is trite and exploitive and imitative. The other script is a large idea from an Eastern author, purveying a notion that radiation was sent by God to change the world. Its value as box-office revenue is very questionable, but Karen's explanation of it, coupled with her offer of sexual gratification, is too much for Gould, and he changes his mind in favor of the radiation book. When his friendship with Fox, a friendship bordering on "old boy" camaraderie, is threatened, Fox shows Gould that Karen was simply using him for her own ambitions.

When Gould sends Karen away and goes to the meeting with Fox, the audience realizes that Gould has abandoned his soul and his only chance for true greatness. On the other hand, the duplicity and confused nature of love is also in question: If Karen had been clearly the good influence, the play would have been melodramatic, but with Karen's motives under question, the play becomes much more insightful and complex. This sense of possible betrayal, coupled with a swing in power from one person to another, is at the base of the play's drama.

Karen is an unusual character for Mamet—an attractive woman who presents the idea of noble principles to an otherwise superficially insensitive businessman. Usually the women in Mamet's plays are impediments to a man's business, asking for personal commitment (as in *The Woods*) in place of the retreat of the emotions that Mamet sees as a masculine trait. Here, again, the woman is asking the man to be himself, to go against the rules of business (including the first rule of guarding himself from damage in friendship), to project himself outside the safe business deal into a film based on belief. Where Mamet stands on the question of real value is not immediately clear, since the radiation text in question is at once profound and nonsensical. As in all of his plays to date, Mamet stays neutral regarding the nature of truly principled action.

Summary

If Mamet's plays appear on the surface to be all rough language, superficial relationships, static plots, and unpleasant characters, they deserve a closer look. The language is often quite beautiful when heard with a sensitivity to the rhythms of ordinary speech. Relationships that appear to be superficial are in fact deep and complex. Actions of a very subtle kind drive the plays forward, embedded in speech and in unspoken bonding. Often the violent climax of the play comes as an inevitable release of tensions built up through the whole play's structure. Mamet can never be said to be loveable, but behind his façades and protections, he is an astute observer of the human parade and, ultimately, a believer in life.

Bibliography

Bigsby, C. W. E. *Beyond Broadway.* Vol. 3 in *A Critical Introduction to Twentieth Century American Drama*. Cambridge, England: Cambridge University Press, 1985.

_____. *David Mamet*. London: Methuen, 1985.

Cohn, Ruby. *New American Dramatists: 1960-1980*. New York: Grove Press, 1982.

Dean, Anne. *David Mamet: Language as Dramatic Action*. Rutherford, N.J.: Fairleigh Dickenson University Press, 1990.

Mamet, David. *Writing in Restaurants*. New York: Penguin Books, 1986.

Ruas, Charles. *Conversations with American Writers*. London: Quartet Books, 1986.

Thomas J. Taylor

EDGAR LEE MASTERS

Born: Garnett, Kansas
August 23, 1869
Died: Melrose Park, Pennsylvania
March 5, 1950

Principal Literary Achievement
Masters owes his literary fame almost exclusively to the finely crafted epitaphs in his 1915 book of poems entitled *Spoon River Anthology*.

Biography
Edgar Lee Masters was born on August 23, 1869, in Garnett, Kansas. He was the son of Emma and Hardin Masters. When Masters was still an infant, his parents returned to Illinois. He spent his childhood and adolescence in the Sangamon Valley of central Illinois, largely in the towns of Petersburg and Lewiston.

In Petersburg, Hardin Masters developed a successful law practice and was elected several times to local political offices. In his 1936 autobiography, *Across Spoon River*, Edgar Lee Masters recalled that his parents had argued very frequently. He felt more loved by his grandmother than by either of his parents. Although Masters admired his mother's refinement and interest in literature, he resented her harsh criticism. His relationship with his father was strained. He appreciated his father's intelligence but thought that Hardin Masters was excessively concerned with law and politics and remained emotionally distant from his wife and children. The most painful event of his childhood was, however, the death in 1878 of his five-year-old brother Alex from diphtheria. When he wrote his autobiography almost six decades after Alex's death, Edgar Lee Masters still felt intense grief.

After his undergraduate studies at Knox College in Illinois, he moved to Chicago and studied law. He was admitted to the bar in 1891, and he practiced law for four decades in Chicago. In 1898, he married Helen Jenkins. She divorced him in 1923, presumably because of his numerous adulterous affairs. From his first marriage, he had two daughters, Marcia and Madeline, and one son, Hardin, who published in 1978 a very personal series of reflections on the family life and career of his father. After his divorce, Masters almost never wrote of his first wife. In his 1936 autobiography, he referred by their first names to sixteen of his mistresses, but the index to *Across Spoon River* contains no reference to Helen Masters. In his 1978 book, Hardin Masters wrote of his deep love and admiration for his mother, whom Mas-

ters had left. In 1926, Masters married Ellen Coyne; they had one son, Hilary. They moved to New York in 1931, where they lived for most of the last two decades of his life. During the 1930's and 1940's, Masters became an important figure in New York literary circles. He became ill in the late 1940's, and he died on March 5, 1950, in a convalescent home near Philadelphia.

Edgar Lee Masters was a prolific writer. Between 1898 and 1942, he published more than fifty books in such diverse genres as poetry, autobiography, theater, biography, and short fiction, but he has remained famous solely for his *Spoon River Anthology* (1915). His autobiography, *Across Spoon River*, shows him to be a rather vain, libidinous, and unsympathetic person. Hardin Masters assured his readers that his two sisters, Marcia and Madeline, felt very alienated from their father for decades after the 1923 divorce.

When he wrote in his own literary voice, Masters was a terribly repetitious writer. In *Spoon River Anthology*, however, he composed 246 epitaphs, which revealed the extraordinarily diverse ways in which the dead inhabitants perceived the reality of life in the mythical village of Spoon River. Although this very moving and well-structured book of poems clearly owes much to Masters' own experiences in the Sangamon Valley of central Illinois, the feelings of joy, frustration, anger, grief, and love that it expresses have moved readers not only in the United States but in many other countries as well. Hardin Masters wrote with evident pride in 1978 that his father's masterpiece had been reprinted more than a hundred times and had been translated into numerous foreign languages.

Analysis

After the publication of *Spoon River Anthology* in 1915, several critics believed that Edgar Lee Masters would develop into a major visionary poet. His later books of poetry, including his 1920 *Domesday Book* and its 1929 sequel, *The Fate of the Jury: An Epilogue to Domesday Book*, reminded numerous readers, however, of narrative techniques and stylistic devices that he had utilized with greater diversity and effectiveness in *Spoon River Anthology*. Although less original than *Spoon River Anthology*, his other works in such diverse genres as poetry, biography, autobiography, fiction, and drama are certainly not negligible.

Although he did publish more than fifty books, his major works written after 1915 were his long narrative poems, *Domesday Book* and *The Fate of the Jury*, his autobiography, *Across Spoon River*, and his biographies of Abraham Lincoln (1931) and Walt Whitman (1937). In his autobiography, he referred to himself as "an omnivorous reader" who admired not only American literature but also the Greek classics and modern writers of his own literary sensitivities. He identified closely with.German poet Johann Wolfgang von Goethe and frequently praised Goethe's ability to see through appearances and grasp the very essence of reality. In his biography of Walt Whitman, he affirmed that Whitman had been the American Goethe. Masters argued that Whitman had expressed with unsurpassed clarity profound aspects of the American experience just as Goethe had explored the true nature of the German spirit.

Masters may well have exaggerated similarities between Goethe and Whitman, but he did help readers to understand why Whitman was the preeminent American visionary poet. Although Masters also wrote books on such important Americans as Abraham Lincoln, Vachel Lindsay, and Mark Twain, these are highly impressionistic works that tell a reader more about Masters' own views on American culture than they do about their subjects.

After his *Spoon River Anthology*, Masters wrote two major poetic works: *Domesday Book* and *The Fate of the Jury*. Critics have frequently compared the *Domesday Book* to Robert Browning's *The Ring and the Book* (1868-1869). Both narrative poems describe legal proceedings undertaken to determine the cause of a woman's death and relevant details about her life. Masters denied even having read *The Ring and the Book* before 1920, but the critic John Flanagan has argued persuasively that "the denial seems a bit disengenuous."

In his *Domesday Book*, Masters used his extensive experience as a lawyer in order to show how a county coroner named Merival and the members of his coroner's jury obtained testimony from diverse witnesses before concluding that Elenor Murray, whose body had been found in a wooded area, had died from natural causes. *The Fate of the Jury* describes the emotional suffering endured by Merival and the members of the jury in the years that followed their deliberations concerning the death of Elenor Murray. In one sense *Domesday Book* reveals very effective uses of deductive reasoning in order to show that a crime had not been committed. As a detective story, the *Domesday Book* is very successful, but Masters also believed that this book about the hopes, loves, and suffering of Elenor Murray and those who knew her somehow constituted "a census spiritual" of American society. Masters was clearly sincere, but he never shows convincingly that his remarks on Elenor Murray represent profound insights into the nature of American culture. A reader is left with the definite impression that Masters made excessive claims for the significance of the book.

Although the characters in *Domesday Book* and *The Fate of the Jury* come from diverse social classes and have very different personalities, these books are very repetitious and do not always retain the reader's interest. Masters presents a consistently pessimistic view of life, society, politics, and the law. Once readers realize that Masters did not believe in the existence of true love, honest businessmen, or upright lawyers, readers are not surprised that his characters behave in a terribly predictable manner. Despite initial positive reactions to the *Domesday Book* and *The Fate of the Jury*, these books have not aged well. They merely serve to remind readers that the *Spoon River Anthology* was his only aesthetically successful work.

SPOON RIVER ANTHOLOGY

First published: 1915
Type of work: Poetry

Interconnected epitaphs spoken by people buried in the local cemetery tell of life in the fictional town of Spoon River, Illinois.

The *Spoon River Anthology* encourages and almost demands the rereadings of epitaphs, because almost all these poems make references to characters and events mentioned in other poems. The reader soon comes to appreciate that each inhabitant of Spoon River expresses a partial and very personal perception of reality. The speakers, who are all now dead, will never understand that their views of themselves differ greatly from the opinions held by their fellow villagers. Each rereading of epitaphs helps one to see beyond appearances in order to discover the hidden and complex emotional and social realities in this village.

His *Spoon River Anthology* is certainly not merely a work of historical interest about life in small American towns in the late nineteenth and early twentieth centuries. These 246 epitaphs express a microcosm of almost any town—be it in America or elsewhere—from any century. Successive generations of readers have discovered many different levels of meaning in these poems. Masters began this book with a powerful poem entitled, "The Hill." As its title suggests, this poem is spoken by the cemetery itself, which is located on a hill overlooking the town. The cemetery asks repeatedly "where" certain villagers now are; the answer is not that they are in heaven. The cemetery repeatedly answers its own question by responding: "All, all are sleeping on the hill." This eternal "sleep" has brought little consolation to those whose lives were filled with unhappiness. The solitude and loneliness of those "whom life had crushed" have become permanent.

Although the dead speakers in the *Spoon River Anthology* are extremely diverse in their social backgrounds and personalities, Masters included several similar sets of poems that are spoken by spouses and by other members of the same family. These series of poems show clearly that personality conflicts or an unwillingness to communicate can doom a marriage to failure. Some critics have suggested that Masters was thinking about his own unhappy first marriage or of the profound incompatibility of his parents.

Among the most effective epitaphs spoken by spouses are those by Mr. and Mrs. Benjamin Painter. He was a successful but vain lawyer who would have the reader believe that he was the innocent victim of an insensitive wife who forced him to leave their house and to live "in a room back of a dingy office." Such an explanation, however, is not plausible. Despite divorce or separation a wealthy lawyer would never have to live in such unbecoming quarters. Readers sense that Benjamin Painter is concealing an important fact. The townspeople felt pity for him. Masters de-

scribes Mrs. Painter as a lady "with delicate tastes" who could not stand his alco-
holism or crude behavior. Separation was essential for her emotional well-being.
Despite their wealth, the Painters were bitterly unhappy and lonely people. Benjamin felt so alienated that he asked to be buried not near other family members, but
with his dog, Nig, whom he describes as his "constant companion, bed-fellow, com-
rade in drink." This lawyer whom most people in Spoon River admired so highly
was, in fact, a psychologically unstable man with a serious drinking problem. Readers come to empathize with his wife, whom the townspeople considered to be a
snob. The druggist Trainor expresses a curious assessment of the Painters. He affirms
that they were "Good in themselves, but evil toward each other: He oxygen, she hy-
drogen." This chemical comparison suggests that the Painters might well have attained happiness and inner peace if they had never married each other.

Although the Painters clearly had a disastrous marriage, it would be wrong to
conclude that Masters presented a consistently negative view of love and marriage.
A very moving epitaph is spoken by a couple named simply "William and Emily."
Their surnames, social class, and professions are irrelevant; they represent any couple whose mutual love matured over the years. Emily and William speak with one
voice. Their love for each other began with "passion" and "the glow of youthful
passion" and grew until they both started "to fade away together." They feel, however, no anger at death. They aged together in mutual love, and it seemed only
natural to them that the "fire" of passion and life be extinguished "gradually, faintly,
delicately." Emily and William felt inner peace when it was their turn to leave "the
familiar room" of their earthly abode in order to live together for eternity.

The love of which Emily and William speak refers not only to one's family but
also to society as a whole. Love of country is a theme frequently treated in the *Spoon
River Anthology*. Masters never confused love of country with admiration for politicians. He was a Populist and consistently questioned the motives of politicians and
members of the ruling class. He portrayed the leading figures in Spoon River, such
as Mayor Blood, the circuit judge, Judge Somers, and state legislator Adam Wein-
rauch, as amoral individuals who abused their authority for personal gain by selling
their votes or judicial decisions to the highest bidders. These vain men still do not
understand why the townspeople held them in such low esteem. While they possessed power they were feared; in death, however, these members of the ruling class
have received poetic justice.

The self-righteous Judge Somers is angry because he was buried in an unmarked
grave, whereas an impressive marble tombstone was erected over the grave of the
town drunkard, Chase Henry, who is amused by this unexpected and undeserved
honor. He was a Catholic, and the local Catholic priest would not permit the burial
of Henry in consecrated ground. For reasons that Henry has never understood, certain Protestants took umbrage at this reasonable decision and decided to honor him
with an expensive tombstone. Chase Henry appreciated the irony of this situation.
He tells his listeners:

> Take note, ye prudent and pious souls,
> Of the cross-currents in life
> Which bring honor to the dead, who lived in shame.

Henry knows that his tombstone topped with a large urn means nothing. It was erected by irrational people angered by the Catholic priest's refusal to permit the burial of Chase Henry in a Catholic cemetery.

Another speaker also knows all too well that one should not mistake appearance for reality. Barney Hainsfeather was a Jewish businessman whom the Christians in Spoon River never really accepted as their equal. Because of an absurd but understandable error, Barney Hainsfeather is now buried in the Protestant cemetery of Spoon River, whereas the body of John Allen was sent to the Hebrew Cemetery in Chicago. Barney and John both died when the train to Peoria crashed and burned; their bodies were burnt beyond recognition. Barney now finds himself under a tombstone with Christian prayers carved in the marble. He concludes his epitaph with this lament:

> It was bad enough to run a clothing store in this town,
> But to be buried here—*ach*!

Although Edgar Lee Masters had a healthy distrust of those who possessed political power, he did remain an extraordinary idealist. Masters felt that people would become and remain morally upright if they avoided the destructive temptations of power and wealth. He firmly believed that wealth and power would corrupt almost everyone. One could object that Abraham Lincoln governed wisely without compromising his moral principles. Masters would argue that Lincoln was the exception and not the rule among politicians.

Perhaps the most famous epitaph in the *Spoon River Anthology* is the one spoken by Anne Rutledge, whom Lincoln had loved before his marriage to Mary Todd. In her simplicity and honesty, Anne Rutledge imagines that her altruistic love for Lincoln inspired in him a desire to uphold the ideals of "justice and truth" on which American society is based. In a mysterious but real way her love for Lincoln and his love for humanity made possible "the forgiveness of millions towards millions." Love alone put an end to the hatred provoked by the American Civil War. Without love, a republic "shining with justice and truth" would have ceased to be meaningful to many citizens. Anne Rutledge ends her epitaph with these eloquent lines:

> I am Anne Rutledge who sleep beneath these weeds,
> Beloved in life of Abraham Lincoln,
> Wedded to him, not through union,
> But through separation.
> Bloom forever, O Republic,
> From the dust of my bosom!

A mystical and almost religious union connects all those, both great and small, who live their lives so that the republic may flourish for the good of all of its citizens.

Summary

Edgar Lee Masters' literary reputation rests solely on his 1915 masterpiece, *Spoon River Anthology.* Its 246 epitaphs constitute a unique contribution to American literature. The fictional speakers present very personal perceptions of what life in Spoon River meant to them. Readers come to the realization that Spoon River represents any small town in America or elsewhere. For generations, readers have appreciated the refined artistry by which Masters gave each speaker a unique poetic voice.

Bibliography

Flanagan, John T. *Edgar Lee Masters: The Spoon River Poet and His Critics.* Metuchen, N.J.: Scarecrow Press, 1974.

Hallwas, John E., and Dennis J. Reader, eds. *The Vision of the Land: Studies of Vachel Lindsay, Edgar Lee Masters, and Carl Sandburg.* Macomb: Western Illinois University Press, 1976.

Masters, Edgar Lee. *Across Spoon River.* New York: Farrar and Rinehart, 1936.

Masters, Hardin W. *Edgar Lee Masters: A Biographical Sketchbook about a Famous American Author.* Rutherford, N.J.: Fairleigh Dickinson University Press, 1978.

Primeau, Ronald. *Beyond Spoon River: The Legacy of Edgar Lee Masters.* Austin: University of Texas Press, 1981.

Yatron, Michael. *America's Literary Revolt.* Freeport, N.Y.: Books for Libraries Press, 1969.

Edmund J. Campion

PETER MATTHIESSEN

Born: New York, New York
May 22, 1927

Principal Literary Achievement

Naturalist Matthiessen's principal concern is with the human species' place in and impact on the natural world—in particular with its negative impact on the balance of life on earth.

Biography

Peter Matthiessen was born in New York City to Erard A. and Elizabeth C. Matthiessen on May 22, 1927. He developed his lifelong interest in nature and the environment early in life. His father, an architect, was a trustee of the National Audubon Society, and his son soon developed a passion for the natural world, spending much of his youth in the Connecticut and New York countryside.

After serving in the United States Navy, Matthiessen attended the Sorbonne, University of Paris, from 1948 to 1949 and received a bachelor of arts degree from Yale University in 1950. After teaching creative writing at Yale in 1950, he returned to Paris and developed friendships with a variety of American expatriate writers, including James Baldwin, Richard Wright, William Styron, Terry Southern, and Irwin Shaw. With Harold L. Humes, Matthiessen founded the *Paris Review* in 1951. He married Patricia Southgate in 1951; they divorced in 1958. In 1963 he married Deborah Love, who died in 1972. In 1980 he married Patricia Eckhart; they live on Long Island, New York.

While in Paris, he wrote his first novel, *Race Rock* (1954). His other novels include *Partisans* (1955), *Raditzer* (1961), *At Play in the Fields of the Lord* (1965), *Far Tortuga* (1975), and *Killing Mister Watson* (1990). In 1989, Matthiessen published *On the River Styx and Other Stories*, a collection of short stories. He published a second collection of stories, *Midnight Turning Gray*, in 1984.

Matthiessen worked as a commercial fisherman and a captain of a deep-sea charter fishing boat between 1954 and 1956. He has traveled widely, and these experiences—as well as his lifelong commitment to sharing his concern for the preservation of the wild—inform all of his writings. In 1956, Matthiessen took off on his first lengthy trip with the intention of visiting every wildlife refuge in the United States, because he wanted to see this country's untamed places before they all disappeared. This journey resulted in *Wildlife in America* (1959). Since then, he has

1310

made anthropological and natural history expeditions to Alaska, the Canadian Northwest Territories, Peru, New Guinea, Africa, Nicaragua, and Nepal. Since the 1961
publication of *The Cloud Forest: A Chronicle of the South American Wilderness*,
Matthiessen has produced many books that reflect his interests in human and natural
history, including *The Shorebirds of North America* (1967), *Oomingmak: The Expedition to the Musk Ox Island in the Bering Sea* (1967), and *Blue Meridian: The
Search for the Great White Shark* (1971). *The Tree Where Man Was Born: The
African Experience* (1972) examines the people and animals of East Africa; *Sand
Rivers* (1981) focuses on a trek he made in one of Africa's largest remaining game
preserves, the Selous Game Reserve. *The Snow Leopard* (1978) describes his Nepal
trek; this book won both the National Book Award for contemporary thought (1979)
and the American Book Award for its paperback edition (1980).

   Matthiessen also writes about human history, particularly about current events
that reflect issues which he sees as being central to the environmental and political
problems that humankind now faces. *Sal Si Puedes: Cesar Chavez and the New
American Revolution* (1970) examines the farm labor organizer's efforts to gain equality for American migrant workers. *In the Spirit of Crazy Horse* (1983) looks at the
issue of racism as it has affected Native Americans; *Indian Country* (1984) further
explores this same topic.

   Matthiessen won recognition for *Sand Rivers*, which received both the John Bur-
roughs Medal and the African Wildlife Leadership Foundation Award in 1982 and
the gold medal for distinction in natural history from the Academy of Natural Sciences in 1985. In addition, Matthiessen received the American Academy Award
(1963), a National Institute/American Academy of Arts and Letters grant for *The
Cloud Forest* and *Under the Mountain Wall: A Chronicle of Two Seasons in the Stone
Age* (1962), and National Book Award nominations for *At Play in the Fields of the
Lord* and *The Tree Where Man Was Born*. His book *Wildlife in America* is in the
permanent collection of the White House library. Matthiessen has also contributed
many articles, essays, and short stories to such publications as *The New Yorker, The
New York Review of Books, The Atlantic, Esquire, Audubon, Newsweek*, and *The
Saturday Evening Post*.

Analysis

   Peter Matthiessen is considered one of America's foremost environmental writers.
Both his fiction and nonfiction devote themselves to considerations of the fragile
planet humans share with other life forms. Matthiessen's subject is life on earth; he
takes his materials wherever he finds them, no matter how remote the locale. His
writing reflects his passion for travel, his interest in human nature—both innocent
and destructive—and his commitment to calling others' attention to the pressing
problems associated with the environment. Yet, although Matthiessen characterizes
himself as a romantic, he does not give into what could be a temptation to romanticize nature: He describes both the beauty and the brutality of the natural world.

   Matthiessen is especially noted for his unflinching consideration of the damage that industrial imperialism is causing or is about to cause the world's fragile eco-system, in particular, damage to those underdeveloped or undeveloped portions of the globe most vulnerable to the devastating effects of such things as clearcutting, pollution, and overpopulation. Thus, the journeys that Matthiessen shares with his readers are not simply travelogues for armchair tourists wishing to see exotic places; rather, his books first challenge his reader to think about what they see and, second, ask them to develop a shared concern for the continued well-being of a threatened environment, ecosystem, or ancient culture that he describes. His books again and again reflect his fear that industrial greed threatens to wipe out cultures, creatures, and whole geographical areas. Such fiction as *At Play in the Fields of the Lord* and *Far Tortuga* and most of his nonfiction, such as *Indian Country, Sand Rivers,* and *Men's Lives: The Surfmen and Baymen of the South Fork* (1986) all take this per-spective as their controlling focus.

Wildlife in America launched Matthiessen's career as a traveler to far places, an activity that was to be the main thrust of his life for the next twenty years. His travels inform all of his work, fiction and nonfiction alike. For example, *Far Tortuga* chroni-cles the voyage of a Caribbean turtling schooner. Yet Matthiessen does not always write of faraway places; he also addresses the problems faced by the vanishing or victimized cultures of North America with the same intensity that he brings to his exploration of the more remote corners of the world. While such a book as *Under the Mountain Wall: A Chronicle of Two Seasons in the Stone Age* looks at the culture of the New Guinea Kurelu tribe; *Sal Si Puedes: Cesar Chavez and the New American Revolution* focuses on Chavez' work to organize migrant workers in California. Books such as *The Cloud Forest: A Chronicle of the South American Wilderness* and *Oom-ingmak: The Expedition to the Musk Ox Island in the Bering Sea* examine cultures far from the immediate influence of the United States, but in his books *In the Spirit of Crazy Horse* and *Indian Country,* Matthiessen examines the effects of the modern age on Native American cultures and peoples.

Always present in Matthiessen's nonfiction is a strong sense of the writer's per-sonality. Matthiessen is not an invisible observer clinically reporting what he sees; his personal voice and the strength of his commitment can be heard very clearly in all that he writes. His farflung travels not only afford him the opportunity to show his readers other cultures and locales but they also allow him to reveal his own personality, his emotions, and the interior journeying for which the external expedi-tion is an emblem. *The Snow Leopard* is perhaps the best example of this aspect of Matthiessen's writing; in it he journeys through Nepal with George Schaller, a wild-life biologist on the trail of the endangered snow leopard. Yet the book is as much— if not more—about Matthiessen's need to find internal answers and silence as it is about the two men's pursuit of the leopard. The book details Matthiessen's struggle to achieve an interior peace and acceptance; the leopard eventually becomes an ex-ternalized version of that elusive Zen silence.

Besides *The Snow Leopard,* Matthiessen has written another autobiographical work, *Nine-Headed Dragon River: Zen Journals 1969-1982* (1985) which discusses his journey toward and practice of the Zen philosophy and way of life.

Matthiessen's fiction explores the moral landscape in much the same way that his nonfiction examines the human species' lack of moral commitment to the planet on which it lives. For example, his second novel, *Partisans*, reflects the liberal Left's disillusionment with Communism. Set in Paris, it concerns American newsman Barney Sand's search for Jacobi, a Communist who has been rejected by his own people. *Raditzer* examines the ambiguities associated with the friendship of two Navy men during World War II: the narrator, Charles Stark, and the morally corrupt Raditzer. Matthiessen confesses that Joseph Conrad and Fyodor Dostoevski have been major influences on his writing; *Raditzer* reflects the same moral focus and bleak interior landscapes so often the focus of both these writers. Critics see his subsequent novel, *At Play in the Fields of the Lord*, as expressing these same interests.

AT PLAY IN THE FIELDS OF THE LORD

First published: 1965
Type of work: Novel

Contact with a modern civilization can only bring about the destruction of primitive cultures.

At Play in the Fields of the Lord, set in the jungles of South America, has received much critical recognition. An aboriginal tribe of Amazonian Indians—the Niaruna— lives so far up the headwaters of the Amazon that they have never seen "modern" men, except the anthropologist who has been there to observe them. Once discovered, however, they become the focus of a number of groups' attempts to bring civilization to them. The Niaruna will never be the same after modern man comes on the scene, but neither will the Americans who go there. This novel expresses Matthiessen's central concern with the negative impact that modern technology has, not only on the less "advanced" cultures on which it encroaches, but also on the people who take their own advantages for granted. It also describes the tension that arises when the innocent "savages" are confronted by an essentially corrupt civiliza- tion—in this case, Catholic and Baptist missionaries and two American mercen- aries.

The Niaruna are causing problems for the governor of their state; although they usually live peacefully in their remote villages, they occasionally cause trouble for the civilized South American Indians who are their neighbors. The prefect of Ori- ente State wants them "pacified" by whatever means is effective. Although he per- sonally favors bombing the Niaruna and driving them across his country's borders, he cannot afford a scandal. Since he holds two American soldiers of fortune as detainees (Wolfie and Moon), he coerces them into taking the job.

Not only does *At Play in the Fields of the Lord* show readers what can happen to the Indians once they are introduced to the twentieth century, it also examines the effect that going into the jungle has on people for whom a life of modern convenience has been one that they have always taken for granted. In the jungle, many pretensions are stripped away, and people such as the (perhaps well-intentioned) missionaries cannot handle the result. Being face-to-face with nature and primitive tribes can terrify, as it does Hazel Quarrier, wife of Martin, one of the Baptist missionaries. While most of the characters are far from mad, they do show the effects of their removal from the protective shelter of the modern world. The piranhas, the filth and disease, the local infighting, the brutality of the Niaruna, and their own innate brutality all conspire to test these characters in ways they have never imagined possible in their "safe" modern world. The portrait Matthiessen offers is hardly flattering, for, although the Niaruna are predictably changed from their encounters with modern people, the people who come to civilize them—mercenaries and missionaries alike—are affected in more savage ways.

It is not the missionaries who offer the most complicated response to the Niaruna; Lewis Meriwether Moon, a Cheyenne Indian who grew up on an American reservation and who has since become a soldier of fortune, displays the most complicated response to these people. At first he looks on fulfilling the prefect's demands to subdue the Niaruna as merely another job. Yet, once he becomes involved with these other Indians, he begins to see himself as their savior. In them he sees his own people; under the influence of a hallucinogenic drug, Moon hijacks a plane originally intended for bombing the tribe and parachutes into the Niaruna's forest. They look upon him as a sort of god; he struggles to live like a native, but has trouble walking barefoot. Completely alienated by his experiences at home, he dreams of successfully leading the Niaruna in their battle to defend their territory. Given Matthiessen's pessimistic outlook, it comes as no surprise that Moon fails in his efforts to organize the Niaruna's resistance to the missionaries and the prefect.

Matthiessen clearly believes that the downfall of these remote cultures will only be a matter of time and that, no matter how well-intentioned the people who go to them are, contact with the outside modern world will destroy them. Even in the modern desire to "do good" lies the destruction of the world's remaining innocence and the debasement of the very people who thought that their work would help.

FAR TORTUGA

First published: 1975
Type of work: Novel

A crew of Caribbean fishermen battle against nature in their hunt for turtles.

In *Far Tortuga*, Peter Matthiessen blends poetic form with the novel to create a hybrid whose form helps to tell the story of the crew of the schooner *Lillias Eden* and their search for the elusive green turtles. The story is one familiar to readers of tales of the sea: man against the elements. Raib Avers, the captain of the decrepit turtle-fishing boat, is determined to prove that he is the best captain alive in the Caribbean; his driving will endangers the lives of his entire crew and is strongly reminiscent of perhaps the most famous sailor, Herman Melville's Captain Ahab of *Moby-Dick* (1851). Like Ahab, Captain Avers is angry, compelled, and reckless with the lives of those who work alongside him. His desire to find the turtles is responsible not only for his own death but also for those of all but one of his crew. Hoping to use the money earned from a good haul to refit his boat, Avers sets out without a chronometer, life jackets, fire extinguishers, or a radio capable of calling for help. The boat and crew are doomed from the start. The crew itself seems typical of such a story: a drunk, a stowaway, a stranger, a malcontent, and so on. Captain Avers is determined that his plans will succeed despite the fears of his crew. In the end, piracy, shipwreck, and the death of all but one person are what actually occur. Critics liken Matthiessen not only to Herman Melville but also to Joseph Conrad, who is famous for his brutally pessimistic stories of men who go to sea.

Far Tortuga resembles Matthiessen's other work in that it, too, is about the people of a dying culture. The book also demonstrates Matthiessen's careful observations and understanding of the area about which he writes: In 1967, he spent an extensive period of time sailing with the turtle fishermen of the Grand Caymans. *Far Tortuga* describes these people's way of life and examines a livelihood that is rapidly vanishing and a locale that has now been exploited and irreversibly altered by the tourist industry, at the expense of the indigenous culture. The novel provides stunning descriptions of the native wildlife, sea, and weather, all related in Caribbean dialect. Matthiessen follows the crew of the *Lillias Eden* as they leave Grand Cayman Island to go after turtles in the southwest Caribbean off the coast of Nicaragua. Because it is the end of the turtle season, Avers and his crew are unable to locate many of the creatures; frustrated, he heads for Far Tortuga, the name given by West Indian turtle-fishing men to an island supposedly located south of Cuba that is reputed to be the last sanctuary for green turtles; it is also a place that may or may not exist, one that is not even recorded on modern charts. Whether or not the *Lillias Eden* actually ever arrives there is not clear.

As a novel, *Far Tortuga* is experimental; Matthiessen forgoes many of the conventional strategies of fiction. The book is organized as a series of conversations in which the speakers are never identified by name; a reader must learn to recognize the different dialects and speech mannerisms in order to know who is talking. Matthiessen also does not allow himself the luxury of describing the characters' physical or emotional states; all the reader has to go on is the conversations that are reported. In addition to this spare form of reporting, Matthiessen experiments with the physical form of the book. In the early pages of the novel, Matthiessen includes a ship's manifest and a diagram of the *Lillias Eden*'s layout. This provides the only real description of the boat, and it is up to the reader to interpret the information that has been given. The book's endpapers offer charts for the area where the *Lillias Eden* sails; the reader must use them to follow the course of the boat as Captain Avers searches farther and farther afield for the turtles. Elsewhere, Matthiessen draws a straight line to indicate the horizon; he surrounds words with a page of white space; he indicates the death of a shipwrecked crew member with a black blot with the character's name under it on an otherwise blank page. These tactics serve to eliminate the author almost completely from the book. For some readers such strategies will be troublesome, yet these techniques capture the feel of the journey, the isolation, and the futility. They also make *Far Tortuga* a very contemporary novel, one that some critics have called a cross between poetry and novel.

THE SNOW LEOPARD

First published: 1978
Type of work: Nonfiction

The external search for the elusive snow leopard mirrors a spiritual quest for inner peace.

Unlike his earlier books, Peter Matthiessen's *The Snow Leopard* is intensely personal, revealing the man himself—the individual who is so passionately interested in understanding the world around him, who is committed to imparting the knowledge that he does gain to interested readers. In his earlier work, Matthiessen the person was always remote—an observer who let his descriptions speak for themselves. In *The Snow Leopard*, however, what he describes is both his journey through Nepal and his quest to find inner peace.

In 1973, he accompanied wildlife biologist George Schaller on a trek to the Crystal Mountain in northern Nepal near its border with Tibet. Schaller, a dry, stoic man, is intent on locating a herd of bharal—blue sheep, a rare animal that could be a close ancestor of both sheep and goats that had lived twenty million years ago. The trek covered over 250 miles and took Matthiessen, Schaller, and their sherpa guides over snow- and ice-covered mountain passes, through breathlessly high elevations to the Land of Dolpo. Not only did they intend to find the blue sheep, they also had hopes of sighting the rare snow leopard, a creature that is seldom seen and about which little was known. Much of *The Snow Leopard* is Matthiessen's recounting of this trek, based on the extensive journal he kept while in Nepal. As such, his travel narrative is in the tradition of such explorers as Sir Richard Burton, Sir Henry Morton Stanley and Sir Ernest Henry Shackleton. Matthiessen brings the reader face-to-face with the land and the people of Nepal. One learns precisely what it was like trekking in harsh weather, living in a small tent, dealing with the native population, and existing in an environment whose enormity dwarfs its human inhabitants.

Although Matthiessen makes use of his trained observer's eye to create a detailed picture of the Himalayas' natural history, *The Snow Leopard* is much more than a travelogue. Matthiessen is as interested in chronicling his interior spiritual quest as he is in describing his and Schaller's search for the snow leopard. A year prior to his departure on this trip, Matthiessen's second wife, Deborah Love, had died a brutal death from cancer. His trek through Nepal becomes a means by which he searches for peace and healing. A student of Zen Buddhism, Matthiessen looked upon his turmoil as a Zen problem in achieving inner quiet. He sought to capture a sense of unity with the natural world around him, a world that included the death of the woman he had loved. *The Snow Leopard* attempts to explain the manner in which such inner Zen harmony is achieved. If one goes looking for a preconceived answer, one will be disappointed; it is necessary to become almost passive and allow whatever the answer is to emerge of its own accord, prompted by one's experiences on the journey. That is what Matthiessen attempted to do in Nepal. The snow leopard itself becomes the emblem for that quest: It is a creature that both Matthiessen and Schaller very much wish to see. Yet it remains hidden, almost refusing to show itself precisely because they are looking for it. Similarly, as long as Matthiessen struggled against and with the fact of his wife's death, he could not attain inner harmony. At the book's conclusion, the snow leopard has never been seen: There is some indication that it may have fleetingly appeared, but Matthiessen can never be sure. In fact, it is no longer important that the leopard was not sighted, for the journey's real purpose had not been to find it. In looking for one thing—the snow leopard—Matthiessen found something he had despaired of ever attaining: acceptance of Deborah's death, the Zen perspective that the world was as it should be.

As in his other books, Matthiessen takes the opportunity to examine the Western attitude toward the world and toward nature. He reflects on his countrymen's desire both to love nature and to subdue it for the sake of "progress" and monetary gain. This type of progress is one Matthiessen always questions vigorously and one he ends up rejecting as wrongheaded. While some critics find *The Snow Leopard* to be less satisfying than Matthiessen's earlier books, they confess that what causes them the most trouble is the mystical vision quest that is a key aspect of the book, the sections that may make the book difficult to understand but, at the same time, are what lend it such an intensely personal tone.

INDIAN COUNTRY

First published: 1984
Type of work: Nonfiction

In fragmenting Native American cultures, Americans have destroyed their last contact with primal nature.

The themes of vanishing wilderness, of a world in which humans are only an insignificant part, and of the rape of the land are all a part of Peter Matthiessen's *Indian Country.* In that sense, the book reflects concerns he has expressed throughout his writing career. This time, Matthiessen tackles a subject closer to home: the loss of Native American lands and traditions. Matthiessen sees the Native Americans as the last representatives of a life tied to the land and in harmony with nature.

Juxtaposed with that is American capitalism: big business taking over more and more of the land and destroying more and more of the environment in its greed for materials and profit. Most victimized by this voracious appetite, Matthiessen feels, are the Native American tribes, whose best interests have not been represented by the Bureau of Indian Affairs (BIA).

Indian Country begins in inland Florida, with Native Americans in conflict with the American energy industry. Matthiessen then visits reservations in Florida, Tennessee, New York, California, North and South Dakota, and the Southwest. Included among the tribes that he visits are the Hopi, Navajo, Cherokee, Mohawk, Muskeegee, Sioux, Apache, and Comanche. With the help of a Native American "guide," Craig Carpenter, who describes himself as a detribalized Mohawk in search of genuine Native American culture, Matthiessen finds people whose culture is dying, whose young people are leaving, and whose land is desolate and difficult. The people seem to be split into two groups: the traditionals, who want to preserve the old ways, and the tribals, who wish to achieve some blending with the white culture. Not only do the Native Americans appear to be at odds with the whites, whom Matthiessen portrays as selfish opportunists, they also seem to be divided among themselves. For Matthiessen, the BIA, which should work to protect Native American interests, is only another means by which these indigenous cultures and their lands are rapidly being destroyed.

Once again, Matthiessen is a moralist, whose main objective is to alert readers to the damage done to the environment at the hands of greedy capitalist technocrats. Wherever he looks on Native American land, Matthiessen sees evidence of the encroachment of destructive technologies: Energy conglomerates steal or buy oil and mineral rights and leave behind a landscape littered with strip-mine debris, poisonous uranium tailings, and oil rigs. Matthiessen views the Native Americans as the representatives of the way in which life should be lived: in harmony with nature.

Some critics observe that, unlike his earlier books, in *Indian Country* Matthiessen shows a tendency to idealize his subject, presenting the Native Americans as the symbol for all that is noble and pure, ignoring the fact that these peoples are not simple savages but are members of a variety of complex and confusing cultures in which the environment as much as the people themselves seem to be threatened. He does not make an attempt to draw distinctions between the more than three hundred separate tribes, ignoring the very different social, religious, economic, political, and environmental circumstances that differentiate these peoples. The book has also been criticized both because he has chosen to exclude anthropological and historical sources from his work and because he does not discuss key internal issues that Native American tribes now face, such as the role of tribal members living off the reservation or the concerns of tribal members of mixed race.

Summary

One of the most respected twentieth century American writers expressing natural history and environmental concerns, Peter Matthiessen focuses on threatened and vanishing environments and on human cultures. He sees modern technology as the chief threat and cause of destruction. He has traveled widely and brings his careful attention to everything that he observes and records. His writing is powerful and evocative and does not shy away from unpleasantness. Matthiessen can hardly be called simply a writer of travelogues or "nature books," for his work also records his pursuit of moral vision, reflecting his own deep journeyings—interior explorations that take place while he contemplates and reports.

Bibliography

Harrison, Jim. *The New York Times Book Review*, May 17, 1981, pp. 1, 26.

Hughes, Robert. *The New York Review of Books*, October 23, 1986, pp. 21-23.

Nabakov, Peter. "Return to the Native." *The New Republic* 31 (September 27, 1984): 44-45.

Nichols, D. *Peter Matthiessen: A Bibliography, 1951-1979.* Canoga Park, Calif.: Orirana Press, 1980.

Parker, William, ed. *Men of Courage: Stories of Present-Day Adventures in Danger and Death*. New York: Playboy Press, 1972.

Smith, Wendy. "Peter Matthiessen." *Publishers Weekly* 229 (May 9, 1986): 240-241.

Styron, William. "Portraits and Farewells: Peter Matthiessen." In *This Quiet Dust and Other Writings*. New York: Random House, 1982.

Zweig, Paul. "Eastern Mountain Time." *Saturday Review* 5 (August, 1978): 44-45.

_____. "Vanishing Tribes." *The New Republic* 190 (June 4, 1984): 36-38.

Melissa E. Barth

HERMAN MELVILLE

Born: New York, New York
August 1, 1819
Died: New York, New York
September 28, 1891

Principal Literary Achievement

Although the full value of Melville's literary achievement was unrecognized until a half century after his death, he has become known as one of the greatest American novelists of the nineteenth century.

Biography

Herman Melvill, who did not add the final *e* to his name until after his father's death, was born in New York City, New York, on August 1, 1819, to Allan and Maria Melvill. His father, a relatively prosperous merchant and importer, was an open-minded, optimistic man whose Unitarian beliefs contrasted with his wife's sterner Calvinism. His grandfathers were both Revolutionary War heroes: Thomas Melvill had participated in the Boston Tea Party and Peter Gansevoort had led the forces that defended Fort Stanwix.

In 1830, Allan Melvill went bankrupt and was forced to move his family up the Hudson river to Albany, New York. Two years later he died, leaving his eldest son Gansevoort to support Maria and the seven younger children. When Gansevoort's fur business failed during the Panic of 1837, Herman Melville abandoned any hope for further formal education and began a frustrating search for steady employment. He worked as a bank clerk, a farm laborer, and a schoolteacher. He briefly studied surveying in the hope of being employed on the Erie Canal. When this prospect failed, Melville signed on as "boy" aboard the merchant ship *St. Lawrence* for a voyage to Liverpool.

After returning from Liverpool, Melville traveled to Illinois in another unsuccessful effort to find employment and once again tried teaching. On the last day of 1840, unable to find another opportunity, he signed on as a common sailor aboard the whaling ship *Acushnet*, bound for the South Seas. After eighteen months of hard labor, short rations, and harsh treatment at sea, Melville and a companion jumped ship at Nuku Hiva in the Marquesas Islands. For about three weeks Melville lived with the reputedly cannibalistic Typee tribe before being picked up by the Australian whaler *Lucy Ann*. Conditions aboard the *Lucy Ann* were even worse than they had

been aboard the *Acushnet*, and Melville became involved in a mutinous work stoppage that landed him in a Tahitian jail. He and a companion escaped and, after traveling about the nearby islands, he shipped out on the whaler *Charles and Henry*, from which he was discharged in Hawaii in 1843. Concerned that he would once again be arrested, Melville signed on to the warship *United States* and was released from service when the ship docked in Boston in October of 1844.

Almost immediately, Melville began to write of his adventures in the South Seas. *Typee: A Peep at Polynesian Life* (1846) was a great critical success, although Melville's American publishers pressured him to remove several passages in which he had condemned the behavior of missionaries. His second book *Omoo: A Narrative of Adventures in the South Seas* (1847), was completed after his marriage to Elizabeth Shaw, daughter of Lemuel Shaw, Chief Justice of the Massachusetts Supreme Court. Like its predecessor, *Omoo* was well received, and although Melville did not make much money from either of his first two books, he was understandably confident about his literary future.

After publishing *Mardi and a Voyage Thither* (1849), an allegory of political satire that was rejected by the reading public because of its experimental approach, Melville quickly wrote two realistic narratives based on his sea experiences, *Redburn: His First Voyage* (1849) and *White-Jacket: Or, The World in a Man-of-War* (1850). In 1850 Melville purchased a home, called Arrowhead, near Pittsfield, Massachusetts. There he became friends with Nathaniel Hawthorne.

During his first year at Arrowhead, Melville completed his masterpiece *Moby-Dick: Or, The Whale* (1851); however, the work did not win recognition nor earn for him the money he needed to support his growing family. Desperately, Melville tried to imitate the successful romances of the era by publishing *Pierre: Or, The Ambiguities* (1852), but the work, which hinted at incest and attacked the hypocrisy of Christian moralists, brought Melville scathing reviews that generally concluded that the author had gone mad.

With the serial publication of *Israel Potter: His Fifty Years of Exile* (1854-1855), Melville entered a brief period in which he contributed fiction to the leading monthly magazines of his day. Stories such as "Bartleby the Scrivener" (1853) and "Benito Cereno" (1855) appeared in *Putnam's* and *Harper's* before being published in a collection, *The Piazza Tales* (1856). *The Confidence Man: His Masquerade* (1857), Melville's dark picture of the United States on the brink of civil war, was the last of Melville's prose fiction to be published during his lifetime.

Concerned for his son-in-law's health and sanity, Judge Shaw financed a trip to Europe and the Middle East for Melville. When he returned, Melville unsuccessfully tried for three years to support his family on the lecture circuit, finally selling Arrowhead in 1863 and moving to New York City. There his frustrating search for employment ended when he accepted a position as a customs inspector in 1866, but the difficult years had taken a toll. In 1867, believing that Melville had gone mad, Elizabeth threatened to leave him. In that same year, their son Malcolm killed himself at the age of eighteen.

Melville kept his position as a customs inspector for nineteen years until a small legacy allowed him to retire in 1886. During his time at the custom house, Melville abandoned fiction and turned instead to poetry. He published *Battle-Pieces and Aspects of the War* (1866), *Clarel: A Poem and Pilgrimage in the Holy Land* (1876), *John Marr and Other Sailors* (1888), and *Timoleon* (1891) in small private editions. The manuscript of *Billy Budd, Foretopman* (1924), which Melville evidently wrote during the last five years of his life, was discovered after his death of a heart attack on September 28, 1891. The work was not published until Melville was "rediscovered" in the 1920's.

Analysis

Herman Melville died in 1891 as a forgotten author. His death came almost forty years after he had stopped publishing fiction and more than thirty years before the discovery of the manuscript of *Billy Budd* and its posthumous publication began the revival of Melville's literary reputation. By the middle of the twentieth century, the significance of his work was recognized, and his novel *Moby-Dick* was viewed as one of America's literary masterpieces. Although Melville's poetry has received increasingly favorable attention, his literary reputation is firmly based on the remarkable series of novels and stories that he created during eleven years in the 1840's and 1850's. Melville's fiction is varied, written in different genres, for different purposes, and with differing degrees of success, but his work is unified by themes and techniques that allow readers to trace the remarkable development of his literary skills during this brief period.

If the term is used in its broadest sense, all Melville's major themes spring from his lifelong concern with the question of authority. His treatment of this subject would be less interesting if he had been a polemicist arguing from a set viewpoint. Instead, Melville explored ideas and was often driven between opposing viewpoints. One of his favorite transitional words was "nevertheless," an indication of the contrariness of his thinking. Because Melville was open and sympathetic to sometimes contradictory ideas, the themes that derive from his interest in the limits and applicability of authority are far-ranging, touching on questions of self-awareness, civil obedience, and moral verities.

Individual liberty is one recurrent theme that derives from Melville's interest in authority. Writing at a time when slavery was the most discussed political issue in the United States, Melville examined the struggle for personal liberty from a variety of viewpoints, acknowledging the necessity of liberty to human development while warning against its abuse. Melville's young protagonists strain against the limitations imposed by authoritarian rule, usually represented by tyrannical ship captains. They also dream of escaping the moralistic restrictions of societal codes. Ironically, their positions as common seamen make Melville's protagonists both rootless wanderers of the open seas and victims of the most repressive working conditions in nineteenth century America. The books also demonstrate that individual liberty depends upon freedom from want. *Redburn*'s portrayal of a mother and child starving in the streets of Liverpool, and *Typee*'s exposition on the benefits of a moneyless society exemplify Melville's indictment of capitalism's inequality. Yet Melville also showed the dangers of individual liberty. For characters such as Captain Ahab in *Moby-Dick*, Taji in *Mardi*, or Pierre in *Pierre*, the pursuit of personal desire becomes a monomania that cuts off the possibility of happiness. Bartleby's preference not to work is a sign of despair. For Melville, the idea of individual liberty implied the dark possibility of misanthropy, madness, and alienation. Worst of all, it could mean becoming a renegade, a person who cuts himself off from his societal and familial connections.

The extent to which an individual should subordinate personal desires in order to be civilly obedient is another theme that evolves from Melville's consideration of authority. Melville's novels demonstrate his sensitivity to the social ills of his time and his commitment to protesting injustice. He chastised Christians for supporting the imperialistic and racist actions of missionaries in *Omoo*, satirized the inefficiency of bureaucrats in *Mardi*, deplored governments' failure to meliorate urban poverty in *Redburn*, argued against the naval policy of flogging in *White-Jacket*, criticized the United States' failure to support its veterans adequately in *Israel Potter*, questioned the conditions of women factory workers in "The Tartarus of Maids," and exposed the exploitative working conditions of seamen in several books. Melville's anger was, however, tempered by the terrible threat of civil war and the violent rebellions that were changing European governments. Although sympathetic to rebels and dissenters, Melville feared rebellion that could become anarchy. Thus, in *Typee* and *Omoo*, his protagonists elect to return to the oppressive seafaring exploitation from which they have escaped. In the epilogue to *White-Jacket*, Melville urged his reader to reject mutiny even if the ship of state seemed mishandled. In "Benito Cereno" he contrasted the evil of slavery with the darker evil of anarchy. In *Billy Budd* he sympathized with Captain Vere's terrible decision to hang Billy Budd for the accidental murder of Claggart because the larger issue of order in society took precedent.

Divine authority was another important theme for Melville. After being visited by Melville in Liverpool in 1856, Nathaniel Hawthorne wrote that Melville "can neither believe, nor be comfortable in his unbelief; and is too honest and courageous not to try to do one or the other." Melville could not ignore the reality of evil in the world nor could he easily accept the authority of a paternalistic God; thus, he imagined a character such as Ahab, who tries to strike at the mystery of omniscience in the form of the white whale, but showed how such unbending pride leads to destruction. Like his weary pilgrim in *Clarel*, Melville unsuccessfully pursued a divine authority that he could accept wholeheartedly.

Melville's prose is enriched and complicated by his use of symbolism and allusion. His best books provide readers with symbols of provocative resonance: the tattooed bars on the faces of the Typees, the delicate glass ship in *Redburn*, the protagonist's odd jacket in *White-Jacket*, the mysterious and ominous white whale in *Moby-Dick*, and the blank walls outside the lawyer's windows in "Bartleby the

Scrivener." In his early work, Melville freely used informative passages taken from other sea narratives or scientific works, exposition that he interjected to increase his narratives' credibility and to respond to his readers' desire for information about the exotic lands and people he was describing. In later works, Melville's writing is more allusive, reflecting his voracious reading in theology, history, philosophy, and literature.

Most of Melville's novels can be read as initiation tales in which young, innocent and idealistic men, who are orphaned by circumstances or conscious choice, brave the tempests of the world's open seas. Yet Melville wrote with incredible range, and his novels utilize the themes and techniques of many genres: the Gothic romance of *Typee*, the picaresque satire of *Omoo*, the fantasy and allegory of *Mardi*, the social commentary of *Redburn* and *White-Jacket*, the patriotic tale of *Israel Potter*, the sentimental romance of *Pierre*, and the absurdist drama of *The Confidence Man*. In some cases Melville was desperately trying to find an audience, for he was always short of money and his writing never paid his expenses. In a letter to his friend Nathaniel Hawthorne, Melville complained that "dollars damn me. . . . What I feel most moved to write, that is banned,—it will not pay. Yet, altogether, write the *other* way I cannot. So the product is a final hash, and all my books are botches." Perhaps the diversity of Melville's work is best explained by his consuming desire to go beyond what he had previously written. Soon after completing *Moby-Dick*, he wrote to Hawthorne, "Lord, when shall we be done with growing? As long as we have anything more to do, we have done nothing. So, now, let us add Moby Dick to our blessing, and step from that. Leviathan is not the biggest fish;—I have heard of Krakens."

TYPEE

First published: 1846
Type of work: Novel

After living among savages, a young deserter from a whaling ship returns to the civilization he has initially spurned.

Typee: A Peep at Polynesian Life is based on Melville's experiences in the South Seas, specifically his desertion of the whaling ship *Acushnet* in the Marquesas Islands and his subsequent stay with a tribe of reputedly cannibalistic islanders. He wrote the novel when he was twenty-five, soon after returning from his sea journeys, and he later told his friend Nathaniel Hawthorne that "from my twenty-fifth year I date my life." The reviews of this first novel were almost unanimously favorable, convincing Melville that he was going to be a literary success.

Typee is narrated by a dreamy young sailor who is weary of the conditions aboard the whaling ship *Dolly*. He combats the tedium of the voyage by constructing fantasies of tropical adventures. When the *Dolly* anchors in Nuku Hiva harbor in the

Marquesas Islands, he convinces himself and a companion named Toby to ignore the fearful tales of murderous cannibals and jump ship. Their escape from the ship to the island's interior is a harrowing and symbolic initiation rite, forcing the young deserters to survive chills, fever, hunger, and perilous heights in order to earn their entry into the enigmatic paradise of Typee Valley. Their trial ends when they exhibit their determination by leaping from a cliff into the top of a tree in the valley below.

In Typee valley they discover a society free from the necessity of work and the restrictions of civilized moral codes. They are taken in by the tribe, and the protagonist, who names himself Tommo, is adopted by a family that provides for all of his needs. Tommo and Toby spend their time learning about the valley and bathing with the young girls of the tribe. Tommo develops a special relationship with a beautiful girl named Fayaway, and the young couple share blissful canoe trips on the valley's lagoon.

Yet Tommo cannot trust this tropical paradise. A mysterious leg injury, suffered during his escape, plagues him throughout his stay with the Typee, functioning as a measure of his psychological state, particularly his continuing suspicions of the natives' cannibalistic intentions. Tommo's fears are heightened by the linguistic barriers that make full communications impossible and by a series of ambiguous events that fuel his Gothic imagination.

After Toby is allowed to leave the valley, Tommo's anxiety increases, and when the Typees begin to pressure him to be tattooed, Tommo panics. The tattooed facial bands seem like racial prison bars to Tommo. Although he repeatedly argues the superiority of Typeean culture and praises the beauty and gentleness of the Typees themselves, the thought of becoming one of them and cutting himself off from his own cultural heritage drives him to escape.

Because of his leg, Tommo must be assisted in his escape. Fayaway, his adopted father Marheyo, and his Typeean friend and guide Kory-Kory take him to the beach, where a ship has been sighted. Their reluctant assistance and their obvious sadness at his departure exemplify the selfless innocence of the Typee, but the cannibalistic side of the tribe is represented by Mow-Mow, a fierce chief who has opposed letting Tommo leave. Mow-Mow tries to prevent Tommo's escape by swimming after the longboat that has picked him up. When Mow-Mow reaches the longboat, Tommo slashes the savage's throat with a boat hook, baptizing himself in blood in order to return to civilization. *Typee* is Melville's first effort at portraying the enigmatic character of moral truth. Despite the melodrama of its conclusion, which might lead some readers to assume that Mow-Mow's desperate pursuit discloses the true barbarism of the Typee, *Typee* does not solve the basic enigma of good and evil; instead, it suggests that any moral judgment is relative and open to question.

The novel's romantic narrative is interrupted by informative chapters that explain native customs and argue the merits of Typeean culture. Although these expository interruptions offer an alternate way of viewing Typee Valley, their connection to the narrative is sometimes artificial. Indeed, many of these chapters were added after the completion of the manuscript in response to the publisher's concern for authenticity.

MOBY-DICK

First published: 1851
Type of work: Novel

A young seaman survives a disastrous whaling journey led by a megalomaniacal captain who is pursuing a powerful white whale.

Moby-Dick: Or, The Whale is Melville's masterpiece, the book in which he most thoroughly used his experiences in the South Seas to examine the human condition and the metaphysical questions that were at the center of the author's troubled worldview. From the novel's famous opening line, "Call me Ishmael," the reader is addressed directly by the book's youthful but embittered narrator. Unlike many of Melville's youthful narrators, Ishmael is not presented as a young innocent, although he does face an initiation into the ways of the world. Instead, he is depicted as a young man with a past, who takes to the sea to avoid taking some more drastic action in response to the difficulties he has faced.

Ishmael comes to New Bedford, Massachusetts, to sign on to a whaling ship, but before sailing he is confronted with comic and foreboding events that suggest the broad range of the novel. First, Ishmael shares a bed with a tattooed South Seas islander named Queequeg. Despite his initial comic horror, Ishmael demonstrates his open-mindedness by overcoming his fears and becoming friends with the cannibal. Ishmael also attends the famous whaleman's chapel, where he hears Father Mapple deliver a sermon based on the story of Jonah and the whale, a sermon that emphasizes the dangers of human pride. After selecting the *Pequod*, a ship named after the Indian tribe that was massacred by the Puritans, the narrator and his new pagan companion are confronted by a strange old man who warns them of dangers to come.

The *Pequod* sails on Christmas, but Captain Ahab remains in his cabin for many days. Meanwhile, the ship is managed by the three mates, Starbuck, Stubb, and Flask. Ishmael describes the careful hierarchy of the ship, whose ethnically diverse crew composes a microcosmic vision of the world. When Ahab does reveal himself to the crew, his scarred face and whalebone peg leg present a sobering image of a physically and mentally damaged man.

Ishmael, who is a reflective young man, open to all ideas, provides the reader with a wealth of information regarding whales, whaling, and whaling ships. His approach to the gathering of knowledge is eclectic, ranging from scientific classification to imaginative association. As the *Pequod*'s crew hunts for whales and Ahab hunts for Moby-Dick, Ishmael hunts for meaning.

In the pivotal chapter entitled "The Quarter-Deck," Ahab reveals his purpose to the men. In a masterful display of persuasive oratory, he stirs the crew to dedicate themselves to assist him in his vengeful pursuit of the white whale and nails a gold doubloon to the mast as the prize to the man who sights Moby-Dick. When Starbuck, whose name suggests his struggle against fate, questions Ahab's personal pursuit of vengeance against a dumb animal, Ahab reveals his belief that the world is operated by a malicious force that works through visible objects. Thus, Ahab's quest is not only a matter of individual vengeance but an effort to strike at the controlling force of nature.

During the journey around the Cape of Good Hope and across the Indian Ocean, the Pequod's crew lowers boats to pursue whales. Ahab then reveals the special boat crew, led by the demonic Fedallah, that he has kept hidden. The *Pequod* also meets other vessels. Before the novel is over, the *Pequod* has met nine other ships (*Goney, Town-Ho, Jereboam, Jungfrau, Bouton-de-rose, Samuel Enderby, Bachelor, Rachel,* and *Delight*), and each meeting adds perspective to Ahab's mad quest. As he begins to hear direct testimony about the white whale from sailors on other ships, Ahab's obsession intensifies. He orders his men to ignore opportunities to capture other whales and frantically studies his charts.

Before the final tragic confrontation, the African-American cabin boy, Pip, is lost overboard and goes insane before he is finally rescued by the *Pequod*. Touched by the lad's condition, Ahab takes Pip under his personal care, and Pip returns Ahab's kindness with an innocent devotion that almost distracts Ahab from his vengeful course. It is clear that in order to persevere in his quest, Ahab must sever all ties of human affection. In the end, the crew of the *Pequod* wages a three-day battle against Moby-Dick, a struggle that concludes with the whale's destruction of the ship and all the crew except Ishmael. The narrator ironically escapes aboard Queequeg's coffin and survives to tell the tale.

Moby-Dick is an expansive book in which Melville utilizes diverse styles. The book incorporates a wide range of dialects and rhetorical models as different as the sermon and the tall tale. As in *Typee* and other earlier novels, Melville inserts autonomous chapters, such as the chapter on cetology, that interrupt the narrative; in *Moby-Dick*, however, the interrelation of these chapters to the themes of the book is closer. Moreover, most of the autonomous chapters that interrupt the narrative in *Moby-Dick* use a particular subject, object, or event to present Ishmael's musings on the meaning of experience.

THE CONFIDENCE MAN

First published: 1857
Type of work: Novel

A masterful confidence man toys with a ship full of passengers on a journey down the Mississippi River.

The action of Melville's *The Confidence Man: His Masquerade* takes place on April Fool's Day aboard the *Fidéle*, a steamship heading down the Mississippi River.

The novel introduces the reader to a bewildering array of characters, one of whom is a skilled confidence man who appears throughout the book in a variety of disguises.

The theme of *The Confidence Man* is trust—the limits of belief in modern society. Melville examines the heart of man and finds it as corrupt as Mark Twain did in his later works. Aboard the *Fidéle,* which is presented as a microcosm of human society, with an incredible diversity of human types, self-interest is the only human motivation. Perhaps more disconcerting is the near impossibility of ascertaining the true character of anyone on board. The protean confidence man is only the prime example of the rule of pretense. The world of *The Confidence Man* is a world of deception and deceit; each of the confidence man's swindles demands that the dupe display confidence, and each parallels the Fall of Man. The confidence man toys with his victims until he discovers the weakness that he can use against them.

The confidence man appears in a bewildering series of disguises: a mute wearing cream colors, a crippled African-American beggar named Black Guinea, a Man with a Weed, an agent from the Seminole Widow and Orphan Asylum, the President of the Black Rapids Coal Company, an herb doctor who sells Omni-Balsamic Reinvigorator and Samaritan Pain Dissuader, the Happy Bone Setter, an agent for the Philosophical Intelligence Office, the Cosmopolitan (who wears a strange outfit pieced together from the national costumes of several nations), and Frank Goodman. The novel presents a number of recognizable regional types, particularly the rough-and-ready Westerner and the sly Yankee peddler, and frequently sets one region's representative against another. Melville provides scant clues for the reader to determine the identity of these characters, thus placing the reader in a position similar to that of the confidence man's victims, who are sometimes accosted by more than one of his manifestations.

There is very little action in the novel, which consists almost entirely of the confidence man's discussions with his victims. Thus, the narrative consists of the dialectical working of ideas. The passengers with whom he interacts are themselves shown to be engaged in a variety of confidence games; at least, they are frequently shown to be self-interested people who rarely reveal their true thoughts or intentions. As in any confidence game, the novel's protagonist is able to play on the selfish motives or inflated egos of his victims.

For the most part, the confidence man is successful, but his monetary gain is generally slight. The fact that he works so hard for little gain emphasizes the book's contention that evil has its own purposes. His toughest opponents are Westerners such as Pitch and Charles Arnold Noble who are hardened against the human geniality on which the confidence man feeds, or soulless intellectuals such as Mark Winsome, Melville's scathing caricature of Ralph Waldo Emerson. Thus, the novel seems to maintain that the only defenses against deception are misanthropy or vacuousness.

As the novel nears its conclusion, the confidence man goes below decks, where he discovers an old man reading the Bible by the dim light of a single lamp. Around the cabin in the darkness are other men in berths, whose comments interrupt the confidence man's conversation with the old man. After buying a counterfeit detector and a money belt from an innocent-looking boy and subsequently realizing that he has been sold inferior merchandise, the old man is led away by the confidence man, who extinguishes the lone remaining light in the cabin, ending the book in smoky darkness.

Critics have struggled with *The Confidence Man*, and perhaps no other book of Melville's has been judged as variously. Some view it as Melville's greatest achievement next to *Moby-Dick*; others maintain that it is a brilliant failure, a "non-novel" lacking plot or character development. It has been read as social criticism, religious allegory, and a commentary on the history of optimistic philosophy.

BILLY BUDD

First published: 1924
Type of work: Novella

A ship's captain sentences a young seaman to hang for accidentally killing an officer.

Billy Budd, Foretopman was written during Melville's final years. He may have begun it after reading "The Mutiny on the *Somers*" in *The American Magazine* in June, 1888. Melville's cousin Guert Gansevoort had been a lieutenant on the U.S. brig-of-war *Somers* in 1842 and had been a member of the military court that condemned a young seaman accused of mutiny. Melville may have wanted an opportunity to reinterpret the situation. The manuscript was discovered after his death and it was not published until 1924. Many critics have suggested that *Billy Budd* represents Melville's most mature vision of the metaphysical questions that troubled him throughout his life. They suggest that in this novella Melville came as close as he could to reconciling the confrontation between free will and authority.

William Budd is a young handsome sailor aboard the *Rights-of-Man* who is impressed into service aboard H.M.S. *Indomitable* in 1797. Although the ironically named ships comment on the tyranny of such an act, Budd accepts his enforced change of ships with good spirits. Indeed, Budd is a character of remarkable innocence. Neither stupid nor weak, he nevertheless is untouched by the knowledge of evil. He is an image of man before the Fall, marred only by his tragic flaw, a tendency to lose the capacity to speak during times of emotional stress.

The captain of Budd's new ship, Captain Vere, is a thoughtful, well-read man who takes an immediate liking to his new recruit, but the *Indomitable's* master-at-arms, Claggart, is a different case. From the start, Claggart, an embodiment of satanic malice toward virtue, shows an unreasoning dislike for the new recruit, whom he mockingly calls Baby Budd. Unable to conceive of innocence such as Budd's, Claggart assumes that Budd returns his hatred and plots the young sailor's downfall. Unable to taunt or tempt Budd into actual crime, Claggart baldly accuses him of mutinous activities. Budd, who is unable to speak in response to the accusation, strikes Claggart in the temple and kills him.

Captain Vere is left with a terrible decision. It is a time of war, and Vere accepts the importance of maintaining authority. Recent mutinies aboard other British warships make his decision more critical. Vere can see no way to avoid hanging Budd, and he makes it clear to the officers who convene to decide Budd's fate that they cannot respond to human sympathies but that they must perform their duty to preserve order and the rule of law. If Budd can be seen as an image of Adam before the Fall, and Claggart can be seen as an image of Satan, Vere can be seen as a model of God, a stern but righteous father. He orders the execution, but the story portrays Vere as a sensitive man who sentences Budd to die despite his deep sympathy for the boy. Before being executed, Billy cries out "God bless Captain Vere!" and his final act of forgiveness is echoed by the crew assembled to witness the execution.

Soon after Budd's execution, the *Indomitable* engages another ship in battle, and Vere receives a fatal wound. As he dies, he murmurs the name Billy Budd, but his final words are affectionate and sad rather than remorseful, for he knows that he has played his tragic part faithfully. *Billy Budd* is Melville's final examination of authority, and in the story he resigns himself to the tragic necessity for authority to preserve the greater good even at the expense of individual rights.

BARTLEBY THE SCRIVENER

First published: 1853
Type of work: Short story

A confident and self-satisfied lawyer discovers the limits of his melioristic impulses.

"Bartleby the Scrivener: A Story of Wall Street" was one of the first stories that Melville published during the brief period when his work was accepted by the major monthlies. It has become his most widely known story, praised for being ahead of its time. The story focuses on a prosperous lawyer, who prides himself on being a "safe man." Ensconced in his Wall Street law offices, the lawyer manages an office of complementary contrasting scriveners (law copyists) who represent opposing types. The lawyer works around the limitations of his employees in the optimistic belief that this is the enlightened and most effective way to lead life. In effect, he attempts to avoid conflict and promotes compromise. He stands as a representative of nineteenth century American optimism, an outlook that Melville questioned in much of his writing.

When a cadaverous man named Bartleby approaches him for employment, the lawyer, pressed for extra help at the time, gladly puts the new employee to work. Bartleby is clearly capable of doing acceptable work, but before long he exhibits an annoying refusal to engage in certain tedious activities such as proofreading documents. Pressed for time, the lawyer works around this unusual refusal, but before long he discovers that Bartleby is living in the offices at night, subsisting on ginger nuts that he stores in his desk. The lawyer's uneasiness is compounded when Bartleby begins to refuse all work, refuses to leave the premises, and spends much of his time staring out a window at the brick wall only inches away from him.

The lawyer's melioristic optimism is pushed to the limit. He tries to discuss the situation with Bartleby, attempts reasoning with him, even attempts bribing him. He invites him to stay at his home. Bartleby's maddening response is always the same: "I would prefer not to." The lawyer eventually surrenders, trying to escape his responsibility for this strange, broken human being by moving his offices and leaving Bartleby behind, but before long the new residents of the building are complaining about the strange character who lives in the hallways. The lawyer renounces any responsibility and Bartleby is hauled off to the Tombs, the city prison, where he is surrounded by walls such as those he stared at from the lawyer's window.

The lawyer tries to bribe a jailer to assure that Bartleby is treated well, but upon his return weeks later, he discovers that Bartleby has been refusing to eat and has died of malnutrition. At the story's end, when the lawyer sighs "Ah Bartleby! Ah humanity!" the reader recognizes the universal implications of the story and knows that the lawyer will be unable to approach life with the same simplistic optimism he had before.

As an epilogue of sorts, the narrator adds a bit of information about Bartleby's past, explaining that he had been previously employed in the dead letter office of the post office. In this position he was repeatedly faced with the tragedies of miscommunication. This revelation should not serve as an easy explanation for Bartleby's condition, however, for Melville's story depicts the mystery of despair and argues that some suffering is beyond melioration. Melville's "story of Wall Street" has been praised for its modernity. Certainly, "Bartleby" foreshadows the twentieth century theme of urban alienation and describes a dehumanized environment of brick and mortar that is shut off from the consolations of the natural world.

BENITO CERENO

First published: 1855
Type of work: Short story

An optimistic sea captain is deceived by a cunning and diabolical slave.

Melville's story "Benito Cereno" was originally published serially in three parts. There is some indication that he considered making it into a novel but was discouraged by his potential publisher. Melville drew much of his material from Amaso Delano's *A Narrative of Voyages and Travels in the Northern and Southern Hemispheres* (1817); in fact, much of the court deposition material is transcribed exactly from the original.

The story is set in August of 1799 off the coast of Chile, where the "singularly undistrustful" captain of an American sealer, *Bachelor's Delight*, Amaso Delano, comes upon an erratically sailing ship that is flying no colors. Against the advice of his mate, Delano approaches the mysterious vessel in a longboat and discovers that she is the *San Dominick*, a Spanish merchant ship carrying slaves from Buenos Aires to Lima. Upon boarding her, Delano meets the captain, Benito Cereno, a sickly invalid who tells Delano a tale of disease and bad sailing weather that has killed much of his crew.

Delano is puzzled by the lack of discipline on the ship, the mysterious actions of the crew and slaves, the over-solicitousness of the servant Babo, and the mercurial behavior of Don Benito, who switches from gentleness to harshness without warning. He studies the unusual mix of sailors and slaves on deck, sensing that all is not as it seems; however, he is unable to reach any reasonable conclusion as to the actuality of the situation. Although he takes pride in his enlightened attitude toward the Africans on board, Delano's racist assumptions regarding the limited capabilities of Africans lead him to suspect that the Spaniard is plotting some evil. In general, Delano has no capacity to discern evil, and his ethical blindness, which parallels the pragmatic optimism of nineteenth century America, prevents Delano from perceiving the situation until the truth is thrust upon him. Like the lawyer in "Bartleby the Scrivener," Delano is an optimist who is indisposed to countenance evil; therefore, he repeatedly assures himself that his suspicions are illusory.

After resupplying the *San Dominick*, Delano prepares to depart and promises to tow the disabled ship to safe anchor next to the *Bachelor's Delight*. As Delano casts off, Don Benito leaps into the longboat, pursued by the knife-wielding Babo. For a moment, Delano believes that he is being attacked by Don Benito, but a "flash of revelation" makes the situation clear. He realizes that the slaves have rebelled, killed most of the Spaniards, and are plotting to capture Delano's ship in order to continue their journey to freedom. Their leader, Babo, is revealed to be a cunning and violent deceiver rather than the loyal servant that Delano had imagined him to be.

Delano overcomes Babo, rallies his crew, and manages to overwhelm the slaves who hold the *San Dominick*. The rebellious slaves are brought to trial, and the last portion of the story is a reconstruction of the court proceedings, retelling the narrative in cold, legalistic terms. Cereno is ruined by the experience. Delano's efforts to console the Spaniard are futile, and Don Benito retires to a monastery, where he soon dies. Babo is executed, but his head, which is placed on a pole, still smiles in warning after death. The story shows that evil—dark metaphysical evil, an evil that cannot be repaired, meliorated, or ignored—is real in the world. Don Benito recognizes this, and the realization crushes him. Delano's optimism is tempered but not conquered by the experience.

The story uses color imagery to emphasize the idea that truth is difficult to interpret. White represents good, although, as in the case of the skeleton that the murderous slaves place on the *San Dominick*'s figurehead, good is sometimes in decay. Black represents evil, although the story also recognizes the correctness of the slave's impulse toward freedom and disputes the stereotype of blacks as incompetent and happy-go-lucky. Gray is the other frequently used color in the story, and it represents the ambiguous mix of good and evil that faces man in the world.

CLAREL

First published: 1876
Type of work: Poem

A young intellectual fails to find spiritual regeneration during a tour of the Holy Land.

Melville wrote *Clarel: A Poem and a Pilgrimage in the Holy Land* during the twenty years following his journey to Europe and the Middle East in 1856-1857. Just as Elizabeth Melville hoped that her husband's extended tour would ease his debilitating depression, Clarel, the protagonist of the narrative poem, searches for spiritual renewal, attempting to regain the faith that he has lost during his years of study.

The poem is divided into four parts, and each part culminates in death. In part 1, Clarel is repulsed by the barrenness of Jerusalem and overwhelmed by feelings of loneliness. His need for a companion is answered when he meets Ruth, falls in love with her, and impulsively asks for her hand in marriage. Their courtship is interrupted by the death of Ruth's father, and Clarel decides to pass the time of mourning by joining an odd assortment of pilgrims who are traveling toward the Dead Sea.

In part 2, Clarel and the other pilgrims journey through the wilderness. His companions represent a range of opinions, and much of the poem recounts their discussion of theological matters. Set amid the formidable and barren landscape of the Siddom Gorge, part 2 builds toward the group's encampment on the shores of the Dead Sea. There the aged mystic Nehemiah, who has been traveling with them, dies after having a visionary dream and walking into the water.

In part 3, the pilgrims travel to Mar Saba, the ancient monastery and oasis. In Mar Saba, the starkness of their journey is relieved by the conviviality of the monks, the comfortable quarters, and the plentiful food and drink. The humanism of this center of Christian belief stands in contrast to the closed doors and dust-covered shrines of Jerusalem that Clarel had first encountered; however, this part of the poem also ends in death, as the pilgrims discover the corpse of Montmain, one of their companions, with its eyes open, staring at the sacred palm.

In part 4, the pilgrims return to Jerusalem, completing their symbolic circular path. Clarel, who has had second thoughts regarding his betrothal to Ruth while on his journey and has even exhibited some homosexual interest in Vine, one of his companions, discovers that Ruth has died while he has been traveling. Confused and alone, Clarel is last seen joining another band of pilgrims. Critics have argued over the implications of the poem's epilogue. Some see in it a Melville who, near the end of his life, had made peace with the conflict between disbelief and belief. Others, however, see in it a reaffirmation of Melville's lifelong inability to resolve the conflict and a conviction that it could not be resolved.

Summary

As perfumes were made from the ambergris formed in the intestines of whales, so Herman Melville transformed his gritty experience as a sailor into a body of fiction that addresses the most difficult questions of human existence. Thus, *Moby-Dick*, a lengthy and often obscure story about the anachronistic business of hunting whales, transcends its limitations to stand as one of America's proudest contributions to world literature.

Melville's determination to explore the meaning of existence through his fiction, his ability to transform the objects and events he describes into resonant symbols of profound metaphysical significance, and his unbiased examination of the social questions of his time compose his greatness.

Bibliography

Brodhead, Richard, ed. *New Essays on Moby-Dick*. Cambridge, England: Cambridge University Press, 1986.

Bryant, John, ed. *A Companion to Melville Studies*. New York: Greenwood Press, 1986.

Dillingham, William B. *An Artist in the Rigging: The Early Work of Herman Melville*. Athens: University of Georgia Press, 1972.

_____. *Melville's Later Novels*. Athens: University of Georgia Press, 1986.

_____. *Melville's Short Fiction 1853-56*. Athens: University of Georgia Press, 1977.

Duban, James. *Melville's Major Fiction: Politics, Theology, and Imagination*. Dekalb: Northern Illinois University Press, 1983.

Karcher, Carolyn L. *Shadow over the Promised Land: Slavery, Race, and Violence in Melville's America*. Baton Rouge: Louisiana State University Press, 1980.

Seelye, John. *Melville: The Ironic Diagram*. Evanston, Ill.: Northwestern University Press, 1970.

Shurr, William H. *The Mystery of Iniquity: Melville as Poet, 1857-1891*. Lexington: University Press of Kentucky, 1972.

Stern, Milton. *The Fine Hammered Steel of Herman Melville*. Urbana: University of Illinois Press, 1957.

Carl Brucker

JAMES MERRILL

Born: New York, New York
March 3, 1926

Principal Literary Achievement
Merrill was recognized in his twenties as a skilled young poet; he continued to publish poetry of more and more significance. His career reached a high point with his epic trilogy, *The Changing Light at Sandover*, published in 1982.

Biography
James Merrill was born in New York City, the son of Helen (Ingram) Merrill and Charles E. Merrill, one of the founders of the brokerage firm Merrill, Lynch, Pierce, Fenner, and (at one time) Beane. His parents divorced before his eleventh birthday, at which time he discovered a love for opera and music.

Merrill attended Lawrenceville School in New Jersey, where he began to write, privately printing *Jim's Book: A Collection of Poems and Short Stories*. After graduation, he entered Amherst College, but after a year there, he entered the U.S. Army, where he spent another year (1944-1945). He then returned to Amherst, where he was elected to Phi Beta Kappa, had various poems published, and starred in a school production of Jean Cocteau's *Orphee*. He wrote a senior thesis on Marcel Proust, the famous modernist French novelist, a writer who was always to have much influence on him. He received his B.A. summa cum laude in 1948 and stayed on to teach a year at Amherst, but then left to become a writer. He decided that Manhattan was not the proper atmosphere in which to write, so he first traveled throughout Europe, finally settling down in a house he purchased in Stonington, Connecticut, in 1954. In the mid-1960's, however, he bought another house in Athens, Greece. Throughout these years he shared both houses with his companion, David Jackson.

He published his first book of poems, *First Poems*, in 1951. The book was well-received and launched Merrill on a lifelong career of writing. Before publishing another book of poems, however, he wrote two plays, *The Immortal Husband* (1956) and *The Bait* (1960), and a novel, *The Seraglio* (1957). *The Bait* was acted off-Broadway in 1953. *The Immortal Husband* was presented at the Theatre de Lys in Greenwich Village in February, 1955; reviewers found it well-written but confusing.

His novel, *The Seraglio*, received mixed reviews: It was considered to have style, humor, and shape but to be shallow in character and insubstantial in story. Although these attempts in forms other than poetry led to comparative failure, these works do

1337

illustrate Merrill's skill in narrative and dramatic writing which will later inform some of his most ambitious attempts and better achievements; after these partial failures he temporarily swore off prose.

Very soon after, he published his next book of verse, which was enthusiastically received; it was entitled *The Country of a Thousand Years of Peace and Other Poems* (1959). The country is Switzerland. Earlier Merrill had met a young Dutch writer, Hans Lodeizen, and had become close friends with him. Lodeizen soon afterward became ill with leukemia, and Merrill visited him in the hospital in Switzerland. Lodeizen was very ill and soon died; the title poem of the volume is an elegy written for him.

During the 1960's and 1970's, Merrill, living both in Connecticut and Athens, published five more books of poetry and was often lauded as one of the top poets of the time. He published *Water Street* in 1962, *Nights and Days* in 1966, *The Fire Screen* in 1969, *Braving the Elements* in 1972, and *The Yellow Pages: 59 Poems*, made up of previously uncollected poems, in 1974. *Nights and Days* won the National Book Award for poetry in 1967. Although reviewers of his earlier poems praised his verbal and formal skills, they often criticized him for lacking serious subject matter. These were the days of the Vietnam War protests, it should be noted, and many a poet was criticized for lacking "relevance" to the events of the day and the troubles of the times. Later in the 1970's, the critics found that his poems took on more substance and that his "relevance" quotient was rising.

His next book was quite a departure. Called *Divine Comedies* (1976), it contained six somewhat long poems and three short ones, followed by the "Book of Ephraim." The latter purported to be an account of a conversation, through a Ouija board (and with the help of David Jackson), with a first century Greek slave named Ephraim, who worked on the staff of the emperor Tiberius and was later strangled to death while still young for attempting to make love to the young Caligula. The poem is an amazing tour de force, primarily because it immediately engages the reader's interest and curiosity and because the poetic writing (both of "Ephraim" and Merrill) is so good. The book won the Pulitzer Prize for Poetry.

Two sequels immediately followed "The Book of Ephraim": *Mirabell: Books of Number* (1978), which won the National Book Award for Poetry, and *Scripts for the Pageant* (1980), which won the Bollingen Prize. The three poems were later combined with a "coda" and published in 1982 as *The Changing Light at Sandover* (1982), a trilogy of poems based on Merrill's and Jackson's encounters with a Ouija board. Since then Merrill has published more volumes of poetry: *From the First Nine: Poems 1946-1976* (1982); *Santorini: Stopping the Leak* (1982); *Souvenirs* (1984); *Bronze* (1984); *Late Settings* (1985); and *The Inner Room* (1988). He won the National Book Critics Circle Award in 1984.

Analysis

James Merrill is a difficult poet, but he does not write difficult poetry to forbid the reader access to his work; he is a poet with W. H. Auden's sense: one who simply likes to have fun with words and is deeply sensitive to the multiple valences, the mercurial surfaces, that words present. His early poetry was often accused of being merely clever. Indeed, the early poems are among the small number of true modernist poems written in the United States besides those of Wallace Stevens, the great American poet of the 1920's and 1930's. These poems are congeries of imagery surrounding a central intuition, often not clearly stated, creating a feeling where none existed before.

Unfortunately for Merrill, the age of the modernist poets was passing, and the critics harped on the lack of substance in his poetry. Indeed, many of his early poems (such as "The Mirror") are symbols of the relationship between poetry and its subject. The reigning poetic fashion of the 1970's, however, was confessional poetry: trying to make some personal experience relevant for society. Perhaps this fashion inspired Merrill. He began writing longer poems, more influenced by the narrative technique he had shown in his early novel, *The Seraglio*, and they began to be about (rather than chance meetings and symbolist confrontations) James Merrill's deeper life. "Broken Home," for example, is a reminiscence of his parents' divorce and of his own frightening Oedipal encounter with his mother. In this period, certain images dominate. Fire imagery increases in importance; the house itself becomes a synecdoche for the identity of its occupants. Most of all, the mirror comes to the fore as an image of poetry, that reflection of reality that is supposed to tell readers something about themselves. The image appears everywhere in Merrill's poetry—subtly, as a pond, a lake, skies, or even broken glass, or directly, as in the earlier poem, "The Mirror."

After Merrill set up his winter home in Athens, the landscapes of his poetry became more and more Greek and more mythological. The Greek house gets its own treatment, especially after a fire forced its thorough reconditioning. Merrill begins to combine his mythic sense with a perhaps even stronger animism, and one hears a black mesa and a stream bank speak in soliloquy. Intimations of immortality appear here and there in his poems as long poems appear more frequently.

All of this seems like a preparation for *The Changing Light at Sandover*, certainly the most individual book of poetry published in the United States since Walt Whitman's *Leaves of Grass* (1855). The technique of this book, of transcribing (actually, more or less editing) the messages of the Ouija board into poetry, allows Merrill the freedom to create a dramatic epic. The voices of the Ouija board bear witness to a world of the spirit to which Merrill the witness can act as either a skeptic or a believer, and a true dialogue can be set up between the voices of the board and the reflections and responses of the poet.

Dotted throughout *The Changing Light at Sandover* are set pieces showing some remarkable prosodic advances over his earlier poetry. He had always shown a skill at creating unique verse forms, often some combination of quatrains in tetrameter or pentameter, especially with his favorite rhyme scheme (*abba*), but with the long poem came some even more memorable set pieces. For example, there is the W section of "The Book of Ephraim," written in a masterful terza rima, reinforcing its allusions to Dante, the medieval Italian epic poet. These allusions begin with the title of the book, *Divine Comedies*, in which "The Book of Ephraim" first appeared. There is a section of pentameters with random rhymes reminiscent of the meditative poems of W. H. Auden, the brilliant modern British-American writer. *Scripts for the Pageant* contains a modernist set piece called "House in Athens," written in six-line stanzas of trochaic trimeter broken by a fourth line in pentameter, rhymed haphazardly, sometimes with consonance. The same book also includes a poem, "Samos," written in the form of a medieval canzone or sestina, with five twelve-line stanzas repeating the sounds of "sense," "light," "water," "fire," and "land," arranged abaacaaddaee. The sounds change in each stanza so that a different sound ends the first line of each one.

On the surface, Merrill's poetry is difficult, exploiting the modernist device of not specifying his nouns—his characters and places. His goal is to render, as exactly as possible, the movements of the human spirit in its encounter with reality, the world, or other people. In doing so, he acts as if the word as medium contains the realities it names. His work, as a result, has a profound civilizing function. Merrill also wants to know how he feels toward (and among) his own poetry, that wisdom of the imagination which gives value to life. He stands in a line of great writers including Auden and Proust, who taught him how each sensation is a seed which, if properly nurtured, can turn into a work of art.

THE BROKEN HOME

First published: 1966
Type of work: Poem

Merrill reminisces about his old house and his parents' divorce.

"The Broken Home" uses a unique form, a combination of seven different types of sonnet, to explore the meaning of family in the life of a child. The first sonnet is unrhymed; it begins with the apparent genesis of the poem: He is going home one night and sees a family through the windows of the apartment above his. He goes to his own room and, trying to read a book of maxims, asks if his lonely life has any value.

The second sonnet, written in pentameters and rhyming abba cddc effe gg, talks about his father's world. His father had two goals—sex and business—and a desire to "win." "Time was money." He married "every thirteen years," but when he was seventy, he died: "Money was not time."

The third sonnet is in a sort of free verse, rhymed abba cddc efg efg. It comments on what Merrill says was a popular "act" when he was a boy. A woman would accost a famous man and, after calling him names, would demand that he give women the vote; he would, in return, implicitly tell her to go back to homemaking. The last three lines of the sonnet turn it into an allegory of what Merrill feels is the eternal battle of the sexes between "Father Time and Mother Earth." He begins to see his own parents' divorce as part of a larger rift in the world between the male and female principles, a theme he will further develop in his famous trilogy.

The fourth sonnet is written in a sort of tetrameter, rhyming abba bccb dee bdb, and is the celebrated center of the poem. The young boy, led by his dog, enters the bedroom of his distraught mother; she is in bed, sleeping, "clad in taboos." He wonders if she is dead; she jumps and reaches for him, and he runs from the room in terror. This Oedipal incident seems to color the whole poem. The fifth sonnet is again in free verse, rhyming abc db cdc eee fef; the rhyme scheme includes many slant rhymes. The poem centers on the conceit of a lead toy soldier. The parents decide to separate; he feels that they were full of passions but that everything is now cold and heavy.

The sixth sonnet, rhyming (or slant rhyming) abba cddc eff ghh, tells what he believes is the result of his parents' divorce: He refuses to be like his father, active and competitive, or like his mother, nurturing, a gardener.

The last sonnet is the closest to the Petrarchan model, rhyming abab cdcd efg efg. The octave celebrates the whole event, telling of the little boy and his dog frozen back in time. The sestet points out that the house is now a boarding school; perhaps its inhabitants will learn more there than he did. The poem is not didactic or condemnatory; it merely delineates a history and relates it to today and to the world.

18 WEST 11TH STREET

First published: 1972
Type of work: Poem

The poet treats an accidental bomb explosion by antiwar protesters as symbolic of mankind's troubles.

"18 West 11th Street" seems to have been inspired by a newspaper report: Certain anti-Vietnam War protesters had a house blow up around them while they were trying to make bombs. The only survivor was a girl named Cathy Wilkerson, seen running from the building naked and covered with blood.

The poem is one of Merrill's most difficult—at least partially because it tries to tell three stories at once. The first is the story of the bombing: The five revolutionaries are fed up with society and its warmongering leaders. They have given up trying to use words to get their message across and are now resorting to bombs, a means of "incommunication." Instead of bombing "The Establishment," however, they end up bombing themselves, leaving only the unfortunate girl, fleeing naked and wounded into the night.

The second story turns on a marvelous coincidence: 18 West 11th Street was Merrill's childhood home. The story is of little Jimmy coming down with a cold on his birthday. The story is not clear, but the mood is one of disappointment: No one seems to care except the maid. The Merrills had three children, making the total official population of the house five. The story also makes much use of fires, mirrors, furniture, a "parterre" or garden, and a clock on the mantel. There are references to a mysterious woman who seems to be a double object of affection, and the story hangs heavy with the lack of communication.

The third story is the myth of the garden of Eden. The house's garden with its one tree made leafless by the explosion becomes the primal garden. The girl escaping was heard to exclaim the name "Adam" as she was running away, so the poem suggests that lack of communication, leading to an explosion, is the proper mythical explanation for all humankind's ills. When one can no longer communicate with others, one resorts to violence of some kind, whether civil, domestic, or religious. Further, the poem suggests that the division is incurable and that therefore these explosions are inevitable.

The poem seems to be grow from the two lines at the exact center of the poem printed in caps:

NIX ON PEACE BID PROPHET STONED
FIVE FEARED DEAD IN BOMBED DWELLING.

The opening line points out that there is no peace, blaming it on then President Richard Nixon. The prophet seems to be the revolutionaries, who listed smoking marijuana as part of their sins against society. The five dead in the dwelling are also Merrill's family. The boy on his birthday apparently rattled off some poems to his family which were "duds"—they were ignored by his family members.

The poem is written in a series of tercets emphasizing the triple nature of the theme, and the style is gnomic; it takes the concept of functional ambiguity to its extremes, all the while resembling the notes of a mad newspaper reporter on a fast-breaking story. Each word seems to try, by the use of pun and multiple meaning, to apply to all three stories, making the puzzling out of the poem difficult in the extreme.

THE CHANGING LIGHT AT SANDOVER

First published: 1982
Type of work: Long poem

An encounter with a spirit on a Ouija board leads to a 560-page poem consisting of conversation with spirits and commentary by the poet.

The Changing Light at Sandover is one of the more remarkable poetic works to have been published in the West since T. S. Eliot's *The Waste Land* (1922). Its genesis is interesting enough: James Merrill and his lover, David Jackson, had been experimenting with a Ouija board with little results when, one day in 1955, a spirit named Ephraim answered the ritual question: "Who's there?" After a long time conversing with Ephraim, Merrill decided to take the notes he took from their "conversations" and turn them into a poem. The resulting work, "The Book of Ephraim," contains a series of twenty-six poems, each beginning with a separate letter of the alphabet, one for each of the twenty-six capital letters on the board.

Merrill solves the difficult problem of separating the words of the "spirits" from his own by putting the former in capital letters; words of people other than himself are in italics. Each of the poems uses a slightly different poetic form, so the longer poem can be viewed as a book of forms. Narrative sections fall into blank verse, and didactic commentary tends to slip into heroic couplets. There are meditative sections that use stanza forms reminiscent of Percy Bysshe Shelley or William Wordsworth, the great British romantic poets of the nineteenth century, and there is a section of 127 lines in terza rima, the length of a typical Dantean Canto, that narrates a long discussion on life and art with his nephew.

The primary problem of the poem is that of what credence one should be expected to give to the garbled transmissions of a Ouija board. Merrill tackles the problem in various ways: He sees his psychiatrist, who calls the exercise a *folie a deux*, an attempt by him and his lover to communicate on some higher plane; he also expresses his own skepticism, pointing out that Ephraim knows no more about what he says than Merrill or Jackson does. Yet the tone of the poem in some way demands belief if it is not to break down into an elaborate folly.

"The Book of Ephraim" also contains large sections of a very murky novel concerning characters in the southwestern United States who are trying to settle on a remote piece of land. Ephraim at one time tells Merrill to forget it, but Ephraim is somehow in the novel himself, for the heroine of the book carries around a Ouija board. There are many other things in *The Changing Light of Sandover*, such as tributes to Merrill's friends Auden, Maya Deren, and Maria Mitsotáki and to Merrill's mother. There is a beautiful elegy for Venice, the dying city, and the discussion with his nephew on art. Ephraim himself is a springboard to many other things.

With book 2, *Mirabell: Books of Number*, all is quite different. The spirits "write" most of this book; moreover, they seem to demand belief much more that they did in "The Book of Ephraim." One meets new spirits here—fourteen black batlike creatures who claim to be creatures of a past world; they also claim to be speaking "science" rather than merely reporting otherworldly gossip, as Ephraim did. Their "science," however, turns out to be as metaphorical as the account of creation in the Bible, despite an elaborate numbering scheme which owes more to Pythagoras, the ancient Greek numerological philosopher, than it does to Einstein. In fact, their chief spokesman is first called 741. Later, he changes his bat form and becomes a peacock; Merrill then names him Mirabell, after the hero in *The Way of the World* (1700) by William Congreve, the witty seventeenth century British playwright. Mirabell elaborates a system of creation and salvation through what he calls "labwork" and "V" work, and describes the creation of soul substance out of materials from former humans, animals, and trees. He posits five super-souls who guide the world, being reincarnated in each generation, and hints at higher beings, including those in charge—called 00, god B (for biology), and in the end, a guardian of the sun, Michael.

The poem is divided into ten sections headed by the ten numerals on the Ouija board, 0 through 9. Sprinkled throughout are more delightful lyrics, odes, elegies, and didactic couplets. The book ends with a glorious and peremptory speech by the white angel of the sun, Michael, who apparently announces that Jackson and Merrill must stay even longer, for there is more work to be done.

The third section is called "Scripts for the Pageant"; it is the longest and most complex of the three sections, taking up exactly half of *The Changing Light at Sandover*. It is here that one learns, for the first time, what "Sandover" means: Merrill's childhood home, after he moved out of it, was turned into a boarding school called Sandover, and the central dining room became a ballroom. While Jackson and Merrill operate the Ouija board at Stonington, the spirits gather, by means of an antique mirror, in the ballroom at Sandover, a "place of learning." The result is the "pageant" that is part of the trilogy.

If this form of the first book was conversational and the second, catechetical, the third book is epic-dramatic. The speakers' names are often lined up at the left margin as one would expect in a playbook, and the style has been raised. The book is organized, again according to the Ouija board, into ten "YES" sections, five "&" sections, and ten "NO" sections. The book, like the two others, is dotted here and there with set pieces, stanzaic blank verse, and terza rima—the latter, like the two sections in terza rima before it, ending with the word "stars," a quiet but effective tribute to Dante. Then comes a piece called "Samos," opening the "&" section, a beautiful double canzone in the medieval manner, celebrating the desire of poets everywhere to make the best of the material they are given.

In content, there is immense variety: The reader meets the four archangels who rule the four elements of Earth, from whose struggles comes the drama of human history. The reader then learns the names of the five super-souls: Akhnaton, Nefertiti, Homer, Montezuma, and Plato; then one discovers that Maria Mitsotáki was Plato reincarnate and that she will be reborn in India soon as a Hindu sage. One learns that god B has a twin sister, whom humans call Nature and whom readers meet at Sandover dressed like a Victorian belle. God B himself speaks, saying that his children (Michael and Gabriel) have shown the light and dark: Make a V work out of it, he says to Merrill.

The entire book ends with a coda: Auden and Maria will be released from their waiting room when Jackson and Merrill break the mirror; they do so and the correspondents say good-bye to one another. There is one more scene, however; Merrill gathers at the ballroom at Sandover with all those who took part in the pageant. They await his reading of the book the reader has just finished.

LOSING THE MARBLES

First published: 1988
Type of work: Poem

This poem is a meditation on old age, concentrating on the aspects of decaying mental and physical abilities.

"Losing the Marbles" is a seven-part poem meditating on the various aspects of old age, especially as they relate to poetry. Section 1 is written in the manner of a romantic meditation, indicating the impetus for the poem. The poet has lost his date-calendar and cannot remember what he is supposed to do that day—nor can he remember what he and his friends discussed at lunch. He comments: "another marble gone." Then he remembers; they were describing what each one's "Heaven" would be. His was to be an acrobat in old Greece when the Parthenon was a living building. The coming of dusk brings to mind a line of the famous twentieth century Welsh poet, Dylan Thomas: "Rage, rage against the dying of the light." He puns, saying that evenings were graces allowing a man to tumble gracefully "into thyme,/ *Out* of time."

Section 2 is in the style of a metaphysical ode. Complicated metaphors fill it—a storm like a silver car, a rivulet of ink in which the poet must dip, mouth to mouth resuscitation by means of the *Golden Treasury*. It is an ironic comment on the inability of poetry to stem the storm of old age. Section 3 at first is a puzzle: It is a series of disconnected phrases arranged helter-skelter on the page. It seems to be describing a passionate sexual encounter at first, then it modulates into a lament not only for the body's ineptitude but also for the good memories that present failures obscure.

Section 4 is in rhymed couplets. It begins by insisting that old age should not blot out the artistic achievements of the past. "My text is Mind," he says. He first points out the monetary value of even an inch of a Cézanne canvas, and then creates what appears to be the central aphorism of the poem: "Art furnishes a counterfeit/ Heaven" where ideas are immortalized, even if those who hold them cannot be. The section concludes with puns on marble ("All stone once dressed asks to be worn"; "topless women" choose worn stones at the beach "To use as men upon their checkerboards.")

Section 5 solves the puzzle of section 3: It is written in modified sapphics and contains, in the exact same spot on the page, all the words of section 3. It turns out to be a rational comment on the passion and lament of section 3. It begins by pointing out that the human body is the preferred symbol of young poets and that a majority of them scorn "decrepitude/ in any form." In old age, the body "plunders what we cannot," and the poem presents images of death. Merrill concludes that old poets learn how to make poems of homecomings, even though the "marble" for such works comes from "no further off/ than infancy."

Section 6 begins with three stanzas in ballad form, pointing out that "pattern and intent" make up for aphasia. The second half is in free verse and chronicles the return from a voyage on an ocean liner. The passengers are full of gossip, especially about friends who have "flipped" or who have died; but, they say, do not mention death.

Section 7 is in blank verse and relates that the poet's lover gave him a pack of marbles for his birthday, and he in response embedded them in the slats about the pool. The pool then is described as a "compact, blue, dancing,/ Lit-from-beneath oubliette." Both the marbles and the pool reflect the stars, and the poet sits near them talking about the heavens (as in section 1). The pool and the marbles become an image for art of all kinds which, by reflecting the heavens above, provides spiritual knowledge nowhere else available.

Summary

James Merrill seems to have ensured himself a place in the line of great American poets. He began as a disciple of the Symbolist poets and, after publishing a series of books of very good small poems, launched into deep waters with a major work, *The Changing Light at Sandover*. Although the content of the book irritates many, the deeper subject matter and the poetic skills with which it treated make most who read it respect it as a grand attempt. Merrill is a successful postmodernist poet in that he pushes poetry past its Symbolist stage to a place where it can deal with the questions of his time.

Bibliography

Berger, Charles, ed. *James Merrill: Essays in Criticism*. Ithaca, N.Y.: Cornell University Press, 1983.

Bloom, Harold, ed. *James Merrill*. New York: Chelsea House, 1985.

McClatchy, J. D. "DJ: A Conversation with David Jackson." *Shenandoah* 30 (1979): 23-24.

Moffett, Judith. *James Merrill: An Introduction to the Poetry*. Rev. ed. New York: Columbia University Press, 1984.

Yenser, Stephen. *The Consuming Myth: The Work of James Merrill*. Cambridge, Mass.: Harvard University Press, 1987.

Robert W. Peckham

JAMES A. MICHENER

Born: New York, New York
February 3, 1907?

Principal Literary Achievement

Known as one of the most popular writers of the twentieth century, Michener is generally considered to be the best writer of historical fiction today.

Biography

James Albert Michener claims to have been born in New York City on February 3, 1907, although the actual history of his birth is obscure. Abandoned as an infant in Doylestown, Pennsylvania, Michener was adopted by a Quaker woman, Mabel Michener, who boarded children. She supported the children in her care by taking in laundry and by sewing buttonholes; James helped make ends meet as a child by working as a soda boy, paperboy, and hotel watchman. Nevertheless, the Michener family was evicted frequently, and James spent four months in the poorhouse. Mabel made these bad times bearable for James by instilling in her adopted son a love for books and music. He also acquired a sympathy for poor people and an admiration for hard work that resurfaced years later in his novels.

Michener was enrolled in Doylestown Grammar School but was overcome with wanderlust at the age of fourteen, an impulse that is still with him. After bumming his way across forty-five states and staying with more than fifty families, Michener returned to high school and became a sports columnist and an amusement-park spotter at fifteen. Even though he was very active in basketball, baseball, tennis, and acting, Michener was graduated first in his class and was awarded a scholarship to Swarthmore College; he was graduated summa cum laude and Phi Beta Kappa in 1929.

Michener continued to pursue his intellectual goals after college. A traveling scholarship, the Lippincott Award, sent him to St. Andrew's University in Scotland. While in Europe, he also found time to collect rare songs in the Hebrides, study painting in Siena, Italy, tour Spain, and ship out as a seaman in the British merchant marine. Returning to the United States in 1933, Michener taught English for three years at a Quaker institution called George School near Philadelphia. After marrying Patti Koon in 1935, Michener became a professor at the state teachers college at Greeley, Colorado. In 1936, he began his six-year tenure with the educational press, which marked the beginning of his writing career. In 1940, he became a visiting history

professor at Harvard University and then a textbook editor at Macmillan in New York.

Michener's promising career at Macmillan was interrupted by the bombing of Pearl Harbor. After he enlisted in the Navy, Michener's ability as a writer came to the attention of his superiors, and he was sent to officers' school, where he was trained for service in the Mediterranean theater. Ironically, though, when Michener requested active duty, he was sent to the Pacific. He visited forty-nine Pacific islands, collecting material for a novel about the South Pacific. Eventually, he became senior historical officer for the area from New Guinea to Tahiti. At the end of the war, Michener was discharged with the rank of lieutenant commander, and he returned to his position at Macmillan.

Michener's career as a novelist began in 1946 with the publication of two chapters of his South Pacific novel in *The Saturday Evening Post*. Michener was still working in Macmillan's educational department when *Tales of the South Pacific* was published in 1947 and won the Pulitzer Prize. That same year, he divorced his first wife and married Vange A. Nord, a *Time* magazine writer and interior decorator. Financial liberation for Michener came both from the sale of the musical and film rights to *South Pacific* and from his appointment as roving reporter for *Reader's Digest*. Nevertheless, he continued to work at Macmillan while working on his second novel, *The Fires of Spring* (1949), until a literary agent, Helen Straus, persuaded him to quit his job and become a full-time writer.

The knowledge of Asia that Michener had displayed in his first two novels led to other responsibilities. In 1953, he was named president of the Asia Institute, the only graduate school in the United States devoted exclusively to training in Asian affairs. In 1954, he also helped to found the Fund for Asia, a non-profit organization that he disbanded two years later. After Vange sued for divorce, Michener married a Japanese American woman named Mari Sabusawa in 1955.

A series of global reporting assignments soon followed. The National Broadcasting Company sent him to Java, Bali, Malay, Cambodia, Vietnam, Thailand, and Burma in 1956 to film a documentary. That same year, *Reader's Digest* sent him to Hungary to cover the Hungarian Revolution, an experience that he recorded in *The Bridge at Andau* in 1957.

Between writing novels, Michener also found time for politics. He had supported Adlai Stevenson's bid for the presidency in 1956 and pleaded for the election of John A. Burns for governor of Hawaii in 1959. Michener's own political career began in 1962, when he ran unsuccessfully for congress from the Eighth Congressional District in Pennsylvania. Between 1967 and 1968, he served as secretary of the Pennsylvania Constitutional Convention and head of the Pennsylvania electors.

Two books were the direct product of his involvement in politics during the 1960's: *Report of the County Chairman* (1961) and *The Drifters* (1971). Michener's political activity continued in the 1970's, with his appointment to the United States Advisory Commission on Information (1970-1974) and his trip to China with Richard Nixon in 1972. On February 1, 1979, he testified before the U.S. Senate on the topic of space exploration.

Michener contributed millions of dollars to universities and institutes in the 1980's to give back a little of what he believes he has received from education. He also reached out to universities in an entirely different way during that decade. To assist with the writing of *Texas* (1985) and *Alaska* (1988), he asked university students from those states to help him with the mammoth task of conducting the necessary research. He also continued to travel; in 1989, for example, he went to Havana, Cuba, to collect facts for *Caribbean* (1989). As a testament to his continuing popularity, *Caribbean* received a 35,000-copy first printing, the largest in the history of Random House.

Analysis

James Michener is certainly one of the most successful and unique writers of fiction in the twentieth century. Unlike many best-selling authors, Michener has amassed a huge following, not by filling his novels with gratuitous sex and violence, but by writing huge, carefully researched books that create their own universes. Each of his epic novels gives the reader a *Weltanschauung*, or a view of life, through the myriad details he presents pertaining to the history, archaeology, religion, language, geology, wildlife, agriculture, and social and economic lore of a region. Michener's background as an educator is reflected in this factual quality of his books, which has made each one a "history course" for the average American, many of whom have little time or interest to delve into history books. With Michener's novels, one can learn a great deal without much effort.

It is the epic quality of Michener's fiction, however, that has brought him under fire from the critics. His desire to involve his characters in as many historical events as possible results in what many perceive to be contrived situations. In addition, the vast time frames that his novels span give Michener little room for character development. Thus, his characters are often stereotypes or one-dimensional beings who converse in somewhat stilted dialogue. Even though Michener has never claimed to be a stylist such as John Updike or Saul Bellow, critics have lambasted his workmanlike prose, which is devoid of paradox, irony, or ambiguity. Moreover, since Michener interprets facts as he gives them, he has been accused of preaching to his readers, telling them how to think about historical events.

Michener's mass appeal, however, indicates that the general public has overlooked these shortcomings. Not only do many people feel enlightened by his facts, but they are also enthralled by his themes. The fact that Michener possesses a blend of liberal and conservative tendencies has helped him reach out to a broad audience.

Racial discrimination is a moral issue in all of Michener's novels except for *The Bridges at Toko-Ri* (1953) and *The Drifters*. In *Hawaii* (1959), Michener attributes the zeal of the missionaries and their descendants in Hawaii to an implicit belief in the superiority of white Christianity and the ways of the Western world. This ideological conflict intensifies with the arrival of Chinese, Japanese, and Polynesian immigrants to Japan. In *The Source* (1965), Michener points out that the Hebrews' faith in their status as God's Chosen People bolstered their spirits and prevented them from capitulating in the face of overwhelming opposition; however, in the modern world, Michener argues, this archaic (even egotistical) way of thinking is still nurturing ancient antagonism between the Jews and the Arabs. *Centennial* (1974) dramatizes the decimation of the Indians in nineteenth century America and the exploitation of the Japanese and Mexican field laborers in the twentieth century to demonstrate the bigotry that accompanied the winning of the West. In these novels and others, Michener demonstrates that because discrimination diminishes the potential of a large segment of a society, the society as a whole suffers for it.

The environmental issue is another major target of Michener. In many of his novels, Michener discusses the fragile bond that exists between the land and the people who live on it. *Hawaii* dramatizes the drastic changes that take place in the lives of the inhabitants through the depletion of the islands' only natural commodity, sandalwood. Arrogance, Michener says, is primarily responsible for the failed promise of paradise in *The Source*, *The Covenant* (1980), and *Texas*. Although the environmental crisis is only one of several issues in these novels, it is at the core of *Centennial*. Throughout that novel, Michener demonstrates that respect for the land is essential if humans expect it to support them in the twenty-first century.

Michener's conservative leanings manifest themselves in his solid belief in the Puritan work ethic. The slothful natives in *Hawaii* lose control of their islands to the more industrious Chinese and Japanese. In *Centennial*, Michener applauds the resourcefulness and ingenuity of immigrants such as Potato Brumbaugh and his Japanese and Mexican workers who are able to coax productivity out of a barren land. In fact, Michener is so convinced of the enabling power of hard work that even some of his villains, such as the soldier Skimmerhorn in *Centennial* and the pirate Bonfleur in *Chesapeake* (1978), command respect because they are men who are able to achieve their goals through the sheer force of their own will. If a society such as those which existed in Virginia (*Chesapeake*) and Hawaii (*Hawaii*) begins using slaves to do all the work, moral and economic bankruptcy soon follow. Michener clearly admires the self-made millionaires in *Hawaii* and *Centennial* who, he argues, are entitled to their vast riches because they, like Michener himself, pulled themselves up from humble beginnings.

Finally, Michener's emphasis on the wisdom and courage of the young reflects his acceptance of change as a fact of life. Adherence to tradition is commendable, Michener says, but such behavior also impedes progress, causing rigid societies to stagnate and die. It is the freethinkers, such as the children of the Japanese immigrants in *Hawaii*, who revitalize the culture by changing with the times. Such changes, Michener warns, must not be made impulsively; many of his heroes and heroines reach a point where they have to decide which values are worthy of preservation.

TALES OF THE SOUTH PACIFIC

First published: 1947
Type of work: Novel

In the face of overwhelming odds, American military personnel display amazing courage before and during combat.

Michener's first novel, *Tales of the South Pacific*, appears at first to be a collection of nineteen casually related episodes. Upon closer inspection, however, a coherence becomes apparent, produced by a chorus of common themes and characters that resonate throughout the work. In this way, Michener's novel is reminiscent of William Faulkner's *Go Down, Moses* (1942), which achieves unity through the same devices. The classification of the book, though, is still so nebulous that the Pulitzer Prize authorities felt compelled to change the category of "novel" to "fiction in book form" before awarding it the Pulitzer Prize in 1948.

Michener is more successful at attaining narrative unity in this book than he is in most of the others, largely because *Tales of the South Pacific* is so much shorter. The unidentified first-person narrator describes himself as a "paper-work sailor." The observations that he makes in the first two tales, "The South Pacific" and "Coral Sea," reveal Michener's primary goal, which is to discuss the human side of the war.

Although several stories, such as the first two, are no more than journalistic sketches, "Mutiny" has true literary merit. The narrator has been sent to Norfolk Island to oversee the cutting down of a strip of pine trees so that an airstrip can be built. The title refers both to *Mutiny on the Bounty* (1932) and to the resistance of an old lady named Teta Christian and a retarded fifteen-year-old girl; both of their ancestors migrated to Norfolk Island from Pitcairn Island in 1856 and planted most of the pines. The organic symbol of the trees, a "cathedral of pines," is contrasted with the cold, heartless, mechanistic symbol, the bulldozers, one of which is blown up by the two women. Through Tony Fry, a sympathetic Navy lieutenant, Michener is saying that victory is hollow if the spirit of free individuals is trampled.

"Our Heroine" is one of two stories on which the musical *South Pacific* (1949) was based. Nellie Forbush is attracted to a wealthy French planter named Emile DeBecque. Although she is enchanted by the bright hues of the foliage on the island, however, she has trouble accepting the same variations in DeBecque's eight illegitimate children. This is the first appearance of what was to become a major theme in Michener's later novels: the need for racial tolerance.

The effects of long periods of inaction on virile young men are demonstrated in the next three stories. In "Dry Rot," eight hundred men who are afflicted with a fungus growth also "itch" for action with the enemy and, in a different sense, with women. "Fo' Dollar" is the second story that inspired *South Pacific*. After the girl he had been writing to in "Dry Rot" dies, the frustrated Joe Cable falls in love with a beautiful Tonkinese girl named Liat; however, he cannot marry her because he is to be part of the invasion of Kuralei. The theme of racial intolerance resurfaces in Cable's reluctance to bring Liat back to the United States and in the way Liat is ridiculed by the French girls at the convent.

Bus Adams is the narrator of "A Boar's Tooth" and "Those Who Fraternize" and is the main character in "Wine for the Mess at Segi." In "A Boar's Tooth," a gruesome native ritual reminds Dr. Benoway of the revolting emphasis that all religions place on appurtenances, such as the importance some American churches place on the height of a church steeple. In "Wine for the Mess at Segi," the dangers that the men encounter in their search for whiskey provide as much relief from boredom as does the whiskey itself. "Those Who Fraternize," which is narrated by Bus Adams, focuses on the desperate attempts of four of the half-caste DeBecque sisters to attain security by marrying sailors. The futility of trying to establish a permanent, meaningful relationship during wartime is underscored by the fact that all the girls' lovers are killed in battle.

The stir-crazy sailors finally encounter the enemy in the last four stories—"The Strike," "Frisco," "The Landing on Kuralei," and "The Cemetery at Hoga Point." Even though the narrator is personally involved, his commentary is oddly restrained. The commander of the Navy Supply Depot in "The Strike" is Captain Kelley, a no-nonsense officer who likes to imitate Captain Bligh in the film *Mutiny on the Bounty* (1935). Unlike the descendants of the mutineers in "The Mutiny," sailors such as Polikopf rebel against authority by burlesquing naval life. In "Frisco," the crew of a landing craft headed for Kuralei form a loose bond through their shared memories of the last American city in which they spent time. "The Landing on Kuralei" is a minute-by-minute account of the American assault, during which more than nine hundred Japanese and more than two hundred American soldiers are killed. The narrator fully comprehends the senselessness of war when he discovers that the courageous Tony Fry is killed during the landing and that the cowardly Bill Harbison has avoided the conflict altogether. The elegiac tone of "A Cemetery at Hoga Point" is tempered by the assertions of the narrator and the two black gravediggers that there will never be a shortage of good men when duty calls.

Even though *Tales of the South Pacific* was considered by many critics to be a poor choice for the Pulitzer Prize in 1947, the novel is noteworthy for its small-scale approach to an epic conflict. The Pacific theater of war as recorded in this book is a learning experience for both the readers and the military personnel. Michener implies that people such as Nellie Forbush and Joe Cable survive by questioning the values that they brought with them and adapting to their new circumstances.

HAWAII

First published: 1959
Type of work: Novel

The history of Hawaii illustrates Michener's belief that all civilizations advance at racial crossroads.

Hawaii, the first of Michener's "blockbuster" novels, was also the first of a new type of historical novel. Although Honoré de Balzac, Émile Zola, and John Dos Passos had all written novels that span several decades, none of their works had the epic scope of *Hawaii*, which covered several hundred years of human history. Another innovation was the attention that Michener paid to historical accuracy, which makes the novel as instructional as it is entertaining.

The novel begins with the birth of the Hawaiian islands in a section entitled "From the Boundless Deep." These "new" lands, totally devoid of life, can only be tamed by the arrival of what the narrator terms a "new breed" of men. This first-person narrator, whose identity is unknown until the end of the novel, is Hoxworth Hale, a direct descendant of several of the families depicted in the novel.

The second section, "From the Sun-Swept Lagoon," deals with the first human inhabitants. In the ninth century, King Tamatoa and his younger brother flee Bora Bora in the middle of the night for fear that they will be sacrificed to a new god, Oro. Blown off course by a terrible storm, they land on a mountainous island that appears to be habitable. Many of the rituals that the missionaries will confront hundreds of years later are introduced in this section.

The narrator then jumps forward one thousand years to document the arrival of the first Caucasians—missionaries from Yale University. The title of this section, "From the Farms of Bitterness," refers to the "fire and brimstone" that Abner Hale, the stereotyped embodiment of Calvinistic Congregationalism, preaches as he converts the natives. Hale's preaching also makes subtle references to the inherent superiority of the white race and Western culture. By contrast, Hale's wife, Jerusha, preaches a message of love in the school that she sets up to bring literacy to the islands. In a few short years, Jerusha dies from overwork, a fitting death for the woman from whose body would spring a line of men and woman who would devote their lives to bringing civilization to the islands.

To introduce the arrival of the Chinese immigrants in "From the Starving Village," Michener begins with the birth in 1847 of one of the most fascinating characters in the novel, Nyuk Tsin. In 1865, her parents are killed by the invading Tartars; soon thereafter, Nyuk is abducted. A Punti cook named Mun Ki, who works at the brothel where Nyuk has been sold into prostitution, decides to take her with him to Hawaii, where he intends to sell her. During the ocean voyage that Mun Ki and Nyuk share with three hundred other conscripted Chinese, Mun Ki appreciates her potential as a good wife, even though she is a Haaku. Both people, Michener says, are victims of tradition.

Once in Hawaii, Mun Ki and Nyuk Tsin are not in John Whipple's employ for very long before they absorb the old Yankee virtues of thrift, family solidarity, scholarliness, and common sense. Nyuk's willingness to spend her off hours earning money to buy land convinces Whipple that the Chinese will revitalize the indolent Hawaiians. Yet Nyuk's most sterling qualities become apparent only after her husband contracts leprosy and is sent to a leper colony; Nyuk goes there with him. Like Jerusha Hale, Nyuk Tsin and the other "kokuas" who accompany their diseased relatives to the leper colony demonstrate that the word "love" has what Michener calls a "tangible reality." Just before he dies, Mun Ki, in one of the only sentimental scenes in the novel, calls Nyuk his real wife, a belated acknowledgment of her worthiness.

When Nyuk returns to Honolulu, the first thing she does is to reunite herself with her sons, who have been cared for by a charitable Hawaiian woman named Apikela. In time, all of Nyuk's sons, including the one who was adopted by the governor while she was at the leper colony, become community leaders.

Despite the increasing fortunes of the Chinese, the haoles, or whites, control Hawaii during the remainder of the nineteenth century. Rafer Hoxworth's grandson, "Wild" Whipple, stands for all the ruthless American entrepreneurs of the nineteenth century. Michener's re-creation of the deposing of Queen Liiuokalani and the admission of Hawaii as a territory by U.S. President William McKinley takes liberties with the facts.

Michener's love of the Japanese is evident throughout the entirety of "From the Inland Sea." His account of the beauties of the Inland Sea and the island of Kauai has a lyrical quality that is quite striking. One of the workmen imported from Hiroshima, Kamejiro Sakagawa, exhibits persistence, obedience, endurance, and industriousness in all the menial jobs that he is given. Of all the Japanese characters in this section, he is the best developed. Another quality that Michener admires in the Japanese, their patriotism, drives four of Sakagawa's sons to enlist in the 222nd Combat Team (the fictional equivalent of the 442nd). Racial discrimination is a major theme in this section. World War II marks the decline of the whites and the emergence of the orientals as the ruling class in Hawaii.

The final section of the book, "The Golden Men," is generally considered to be the weakest. Instead of developing each scene, Michener provides brief synopses of a staggering number of postwar conditions in Hawaii. Many readers were offended by his portrayal of a descendant of generations of Hawaii as a surfer who preys on wealthy women. The title of this section refers to Hawaii's population. The narrator recapitulates the ancestor worship and the insistence on racial purity by all the races in Hawaii and then, on the last page, observes that all Hawaiians are "products of the mind," the beneficiaries of the cross-fertilization of ideas from different cultures.

Hawaii is the novel on which Michener's reputation most firmly rests. Although critics still complained about his "cardboard characters," they were impressed by the scope and narrative power of his novel. Charles Sutton dubbed him the "Pepys of the Pacific," after the seventeenth century English diarist, Samuel Pepys. In addition, the ending of *Hawaii* is much more satisfying than the endings of his other novels. Whereas the evidence of disorder and unreason contradicts the narrator's optimistic affirmation about the future in books such as *Centennial*, Hoxworth Hale's prediction regarding the ultimate brotherhood in which all men will live seems to be warranted by the novel it concludes.

THE SOURCE

First published: 1965
Type of work: Novel

Suffering and obedience to the law characterize the development of the Jewish culture.

Of all Michener's novels, *The Source* is certainly the most ambitious and complex. Conceived while Michener was on a visit to Israel, the novel traces the history of the Jews from their primitive origins thousands of years ago to the establishment of Israel in 1948. The chapters in which each stage of the history is illustrated are, for the most part, independent narratives; however, like *Hawaii*, partial continuity is achieved through the repetition of familiar family names.

In *The Source*, Michener employs a variation on the narrative technique that he had used in *Hawaii*. The historical events in *The Source* are put into contemporary perspective by a frame story that is set in 1964. In the frame story, a team of three archaeologists is excavating a Tell, or mound, at the site of the fictional crossroads of the ancient world called Makor, or the Source, because of its spring. The narratives correspond with the unearthing of each successive level of human habitation, beginning with the earliest level—Level XV. At the end of each chapter, the archaeologists evaluate the finds that correspond to the events that have previously been related. The chapter entitled "The Bee Eater" begins in 9831 B.C. and introduces Ur, the progenitor of the Family of Ur that appears in the next four chapters. Ur is primarily a hunter, but his son's experiments with planting presage a new way of life for Ur's descendants. When his son-in-law is killed by a wild boar, Ur begins probing the mysteries of life and death by asking himself questions such as "Why do I live?" By the year 2202 B.C., the people of Makor have attempted to answer those questions by creating gods, in "Of Death and Life." When the time comes for Urbaal to sacrifice his first-born son to the Canaanite god of Death, he does so willingly in spite of the protests of his wife.

"An Old Man and His God" introduces the Haibiru, who are the forerunners of the Hebrews. After arriving in Makor, the Haibiru diplomatically respect the local gods but cling to the belief that El Shaddai is the most powerful god. This theological conflict is dramatized in the dilemma faced by the leader of the Haibiru, Zadok, whose granddaughter is impregnated by Zibeon, the son of the Canaanite leader.

The third historical chapter, "Psalm of the Hoopoe Bird," takes place during the reign of David. By this time, El Shaddai has been replaced by Yaweh, who controls the heavens and the hearts of man. A descendant of Zibeon named Jabaal is an engineer who builds a massive tunnel that King David places below the more abstract accomplishment of a psalmist named Gershon. In 1964, though, the rediscovered tunnel is itself hailed as a psalm of those who do God's work.

In "The Voice of Gomer," a theme that had been an undercurrent in the previous chapters—suffering for one's religious beliefs—receives its first major exposition. Gomer, a poor widow, becomes a heroine because she does as Yahweh commands, regardless of the hardships she must endure. When Yahweh tells her to defy the governor and drive out the priestess-prostitutes of Baal, she does so. Imprisoned in a well shaft, Gomer predicts that Yahweh will use the Babylonians to punish the Hebrews for their pagan ways. The Jews' passive acceptance of God's punishment becomes an integral part of their character.

"King of the Jews" is the only chapter of the novel that is told in the first person. The narrator is a Roman soldier named Myrmex who admires his superior, Herod, because Herod kills his beloved Jewish wife when ordered to; however, obedience, Michener implies, is admirable only when the command is from God. Although Myrmex does not construe Herod's disfigurement by a horrible disease to be a sort of divine punishment, the evidence provided by the author forces the reader to draw this conclusion. Five hundred years later, the Jews continue to resist any attempt to change their beliefs. In "Yigal and the Three Generals," the Jews organize a successful protest against the bringing of a statue of the god Caligula to Makor. For their defiance of Nero, many are crucified.

The harshness of Jewish law is exposed in "The Law," which is set in the Byzantine period. Rabbi Asher declares Menahem a bastard because his widowed mother remarries before the fifteen-year waiting period has elapsed. Barred from participating in Jewish rituals, Menahem converts to Christianity. While the arrival of the Muslims in A.D. 635 does not disperse the Jews, it does add to their suffering in "A Day in the Life of a Desert Rider." After eight hundred Jews of Medina are beheaded for refusing to convert, military units are dispatched all over the Middle East to do the same everywhere, if need be, to spread Islam. The next two chapters recount the invasion of the Holy Land by the Crusaders. In "Volkmar," Michener draws a clear parallel between the slaughter of Jews in Europe and in the Middle East in the eleventh century and the systematic extermination of European Jews by Adolf Hitler in the twentieth century. Two hundred years later, in "The Fires of Ma Coeur," the Crusaders are on the decline.

The first example of "modern" persecution occurs in the chapter entitled "The Saintly Men of Safed." The three men who take center stage in this episode are saintly because each suffers mightily for his belief. Michener's description of the tortures endured by Jews in the Spanish Inquisition is just as horrifying as his explanation of the shocking plight of the lepers in Hawaii. The chapter ends with

Michener's observation that Judaism has had a tendency to be protected from common understanding when too much emphasis is placed on mysticism and legalism.

The need for religious tolerance is the central theme of "Twilight of an Empire." In 1880, a Russian Jew named Schumuel Hacohen attempts to escape the anti-Semitic atmosphere of his homeland by establishing a colony of transplanted Russian and Polish Jews along the Jordan river. The once-dispersed Jews return to their homeland in larger numbers than ever before. "Rebbe Itzik and the Sabra," the last of the historical narratives, is an account of the evacuation of the British from Palestine. The chapter ends with the Jews' assertion that they will never again submit to oppression or dispersion, thereby adding a new dimension to the Jewish character.

The novel comes full circle in the last chapter with the discovery of the well and prehistoric flints by the archaeologists in the frame story. The Jews' strict adherence to tradition, Michener says, has been a heavy burden, but it has preserved and defined the Jewish character down through the centuries. The novel ends with the optimistic pronouncement that the Arabs and Jews are closer than they realize because they share land and the same partnership with God.

CENTENNIAL

First published: 1974
Type of work: Novel

Violent conflict, heroic struggles, and cruel injustice characterize the lives of the people and the animals that inhabit Colorado throughout its turbulent history.

Published two years after his nonfiction examination of the Kent State shootings—*Kent State: What Happened and Why* (1971)—*Centennial* returns to the genre upon which his reputation rests. Like *Hawaii* and *The Source*, *Centennial* is a fascinating blend of historical fact and fiction. Unlike his previous novels, though, which are set in exotic lands, *Centennial* takes place in the continental United States.

In *Centennial*, Michener employs the same type of narrative artifice that he had used in *The Source*, but which he believed was unnecessary in *Chesapeake*, *The Covenant*, and *Space* (1982). The contemporary presenter of the historical episodes in this novel is the fictional Professor Lewis Vernor, who is commissioned by *US* magazine to validate a series of articles on a town in Colorado called Centennial.

As in *Hawaii*, Michener provides a dramatic and historically verifiable explanation of how the land was created and populated. It is in his exposition of the prehistory of Colorado that Michener introduces two themes that run through the entire novel: the survival of the fittest and the persistence of the past into the present. The first human inhabitants of Colorado followed the woolly mammoths across a land bridge from Asia to Alaska thirteen thousand years ago. Michener then moves to the second half of the eighteenth century to introduce the progenitor of many of the characters in the novel, Lame Beaver, who inadvertently makes the area attractive to white men when his golden bullet falls into their hands.

Despite the plethora of Indian lore that Michener provides, Lame Beaver's story is strangely uninteresting. The thrilling exploits of the first two white men who come on the scene, however—Jacques Pasquinel, a trapper, and Alexander McKeag, a fugitive from Scotland—help to bring the novel alive in chapter 5. McKeag, Pasquinel's fellow trapper, is a much more complex character; he breaks with Pasquinel after a knife fight with Pasquinel's half-breed son, Jake. This dispute foreshadows the racial tensions that permeate the remainder of the novel.

The next two chapters document the two forces that contributed to the vanquishing of the culture of the American Indian: the settlers and the United States Government. The central character of chapter 7 is Levi Zendt, a former member of a Pennsylvania Dutch community who is ostracized for flirting with his brother's girlfriend. In his flight from injustice, Levi bears an ironic resemblance to the Indians in chapter 8 who are forced to leave their homeland after their treaties are broken. The courage of Levi and his sixteen-year-old bride, Elly, is underscored by their naïveté, which is revealed early by Levi's insistence that horses be used instead of oxen to pull his huge Conestoga wagon. Thus, his journey is also a rite of passage, and his tutors are the people who join with them. After Elly dies, he starts a store that becomes the focal point of the town of Zendt's Farm, later renamed Centennial.

In chapter 7, the whites are firmly established as the dominant race in Colorado by the machinations of the U.S. Government and the instrument of its will, the U.S. Cavalry. The domination of the whites is ratified in a treaty during the Civil War that reduces the Indians' lands to forty-acre allotments on reservations. The degradation of the Indians culminates in a massacre of the Arapaho that is instigated by the fanatical Frank Skimmerhorn.

The novel then moves to its third phase, the civilizing of the West. Chapter 8 is probably the most successful because of its unity and because of the verisimilitude that is achieved by its detailed and authentic portrayal of life on the range. In order to stock the 670,000 acres of range, a transplanted Englishman, Oliver Seccombe, hires a Confederate general and the son of the infamous Frank Skimmerhorn to drive longhorn cattle from Texas to Colorado. The story focuses on a fourteen-year-old boy named Jim Lloyd. Because of Jim's inexperience as a cowboy and his overall naïveté, it is appropriate that the reader view the trip through his eyes. Throughout the drive, Jim exhibits those qualities that Michener contends were essential in the winning of the West: responsibility, courage, and skill.

Chapter 9 dramatizes the struggles among the various forces of civilization to control the prairie. An immigrant from the Ukraine named Hans Brumbaugh finds farming to be more profitable after he begins irrigating the land to produce potatoes first, then beets. Although Oliver Seccombe maintains an uneasy truce with Brumbaugh, he declares war against the sheepherders and their leader, Messmore Garrett. The tragedy of this conflict is pointed out by Paul Garrett years later, as he observes Herefords and sheep grazing together with no apparent harm to the grass.

Michener's epic narrative culminates in chapter 11, which illustrates what Michener calls the "dark side of western history." To make ends meet, a destitute actress named Maude Wendell lures a Swede to her bedroom in hopes of blackmailing him. When he protests, she kills him, and she and her son conceal the corpse in an ancient beaver cave. Ironically, the Wendells prosper: Maude becomes a socialite, and her husband and son become unscrupulous real estate agents.

Chapter 12 and 13, which bring the novel into the twentieth century, add a whole new set of characters. Chapter 13 concerns the efforts of Mervin Wendel, the railroad, and an agronomist named Dr. Thomas Dole Creevey to attract farmers to Colorado in 1911. Despite the warnings of Lloyd and Brumbaugh, the immigrants implement Dr. Creevey's system of dry farming, only to find the promise of the first few years shattered by crop failure in the 1920's and by the dust storms of the 1930's.

Like chapter 1, chapter 14 is composed entirely of the frame narrative. In Paul Garrett, Professor Vernor finds a man who epitomizes the history of the West. In Garrett, the genetic strains of many of the main characters converge (although a bit too conveniently to be believable). Yet Paul is also a product of the West in his love and respect for the land. Another frontier quality, courage, surfaces in Paul's decision to marry a Mexican girl despite the social constraints prohibiting such a union. Paul acts as Professor Vernor's guide and introduces him to changing aspects of the West. Looking to the future, Paul tells Professor Vernor that Colorado will be in trouble if it does not acknowledge the fact that mankind and nature have always existed in precarious balance and begin protecting all of its components.

Despite its shortcomings, *Centennial* is an impressive work. The novel clearly benefits from the years that Michener spent in Colorado. The desert scenes, for example, are much more vividly described than the desert scenes in his earlier *The Covenant*. Michener must also be praised for avoiding the big, easy subjects such as gold mining and railroad building and choosing, instead, the more challenging subjects such as irrigation and farming.

Summary

In terms of book sales, James A. Michener can be said to be one of the most successful American writers of the twentieth century. The immense popularity of his novels is made all the more amazing by the fact that the subjects of his novels are not in tune with what the public generally seems to want. People read Michener's novels not only to escape but also to learn. Each of his massive, epic novels reflects his obsession with geographic and historical detail.

Although his characters are, for the most part, stereotyped representatives of certain types of people, his most heroic characters embody those virtues that Michener has tried to cultivate in himself: hard work, courage, resourcefulness, and independence.

Bibliography

Becker, George. *James A. Michener.* New York: Frederick Ungar, 1983.

Bell, Pearl K. "James Michener's Docudramas." *Commentary* 71 (April, 1981): 71-73.

Bruccoli, Matthew J., ed. *Conversations with Writers.* Vol. 2. Detroit: Gale Research, 1978.

Day, A. Grove. *James A. Michener.* New York: Twayne, 1964.

James, Caryn. "The Michener Phenomenon." *The New York Times Book Review,* September 8, 1985, pp. 44-46.

Kakutani, Michiko. "Michener: The Novelist as Teacher." *The New York Times Book Review,* November 23, 1980, p. 3.

Michener, James. "Historical Fiction." *American Heritage* 33 (April/May, 1982): 44-48.

Mitgang, Herbert. "Why Michener Never Misses." *Saturday Review* 7 (November, 1980): 20-24.

Poulton, Terry. "A Miner in the Bedrock of History." *Macleans* 93 (December 15, 1980): 8-9.

Shahin, Jim. "The Continuing Sagas of James A. Michener." *The Saturday Evening Post* 262 (March, 1990): 66-71.

Alan Brown

ARTHUR MILLER

Born: New York, New York
October 17, 1915

Principal Literary Achievement
Considered one of America's foremost dramatists, Miller has penetrated the American consciousness and gained worldwide recognition for his probing dramas of social awareness.

Biography

On October 17, 1915, Arthur Miller, son of Jewish immigrants, was born in Manhattan. His father Isadore ran a prosperous garment business, and his mother, Augusta Barnett Miller, was at one time a schoolteacher. When his father's firm began to fail in 1928, the Millers moved to the suburban area of Brooklyn, an area that would be the model for the settings of *All My Sons* (1947) and *Death of a Salesman* (1949). From his mother, he inherited a strong sense of mysticism that would inform his later work. As a young boy, Miller came to resent his father's withdrawal, caused by failure. The figure of the failed father would play a significant role in Miller's plays.

The young Miller came of age during the Great Depression. Seeing once-prosperous people on the streets begging for work deeply affected Miller. To him, the Depression signified the failure of a system and the tragedy of a generation of men who would blame this failure on themselves. The events of the Depression and their impact on personal success and failure would lead Miller to probe the individual's relation to his work and the price that must be paid for success or the lack of it.

Like Biff Loman in *Death of a Salesman*, Miller was more of an athlete than a scholar. He read mostly adventure novels and some Charles Dickens. Unable to get into college, he worked for his father, where he first became moved by the sad plight of salesmen. After a series of odd jobs, Miller worked in an automobile parts warehouse, where he was able to save five hundred dollars for college on a fifteen-dollar-a-week job. He re-created this experience in *A Memory of Two Mondays* (1955). While working, Miller became an avid reader and was especially impressed with Fyodor Dostoevski's *Bratya Karamazovy* (1879-1880; *The Brothers Karamazov*, 1912), a novel which focuses on a failed father, fraternal rivalry, and a trial motif, themes that would repeatedly occur in Miller's works.

After much convincing, Miller finally got the University of Michigan to accept

him. At the university, Miller became interested in social causes and began to form his liberal philosophy. He studied playwriting under Kenneth Rowe and won two Avery Hopgood Awards, in 1936 for *No Villain* and in 1937 for *Honor at Dawn*. In 1938, he won the Theater Guild National Award for *They Too Arise*. Following the style of the 1930's, Miller's early plays focus on young idealists fighting to eliminate social injustice. After college, he worked for the Federal Theater Project and wrote radio scripts. In 1944, he tried to re-create the feelings of the ordinary soldier in his screenplay "The Story of GI Joe" but was thwarted by motion-picture executives who wanted him to romanticize his work. That same year, he had his first Broadway production, *The Man Who Had All the Luck* (1944), but his drama of a man dismayed by his incredible success was a flop.

In 1947, Miller finally achieved success with *All My Sons*, a much tighter and more topical work. In 1949, *Death of a Salesman* achieved unprecedented critical acclaim and established Miller as a significant American playwright. Disturbed by the repressive climate of the 1950's Cold War, the scare tactics of Senator Joseph McCarthy, and the betrayal by his one-time liberal friends who cited names before the House Committee on Un-American Activities, Miller wrote *The Crucible* (1953), which connected the witch hunts of seventeenth century Salem with the Red hunts of the 1950's. *The Crucible*, however, did not achieve immediate success. His next works were two one-acts, *A Memory of Two Mondays* and *A View From the Bridge* (both 1955). An expanded version of *A View From the Bridge* (1956) told the story of Eddie Carbone, a longshoreman who is driven by incestuous desires for his niece to inform on his niece's boyfriend and other illegal immigrants living with him.

During the mid-1950's , Miller entered a troubled period of his life. After divorcing his first wife, Mary Grace Slattery, Miller married film star Marilyn Monroe and became involved in her turbulent career. He was also cited for contempt of Congress for refusing to name names before the House Committee on Un-American Activities. Although acquitted on appeal, this ordeal took a financial and emotional toll on him. In 1961, his marriage to Marilyn ended in divorce, and in 1962, he married *Magnum* photographer Ingeborg Morath.

After a nine-year hiatus from the American stage, Miller wrote *After the Fall* (1964) and *Incident at Vichy* (1964); both plays dealt with the universal guilt associated with the genocide of the Jews. Miller returned to the form of family drama with *The Price* (1968), a drama depicting the rivalry of two brothers.

Continuing to experiment, Miller wrote *The Creation of the World and Other Business* (1972), a comedy based on Genesis; *The Archbishop's Ceiling* (1977), a play about power and oppression in a European Communist country; *The American Clock* (1980), a montage view of the Depression focusing on the trials of one family; and *Danger Memory* (1986), two short symbolic dramas exploring the mysteries hidden in past actions. Despite the fact that these dramas have not received the critical acclaim of his earlier works, the continual revivals of his dramas both on stage and on television and his burgeoning international reputation have kept Miller in the forefront of American theater.

Analysis

A serious dramatist who believes in drama's ability to effect change, Arthur Miller explores the social as well as the psychological aspects of his characters. For him, individual dilemmas cannot be removed from their social contexts. His dramas attempt to go beyond simple protest pieces or self-absorbed psychological studies to deal with moral and ethical issues. He is interested in how an ordinary individual can live in unity and harmony with his fellow humans without sacrificing his individual dignity.

Most of Miller's dramas locate the family as the central unit for exploring social and ethical issues, and central to Miller's family drama is the image of the failed father. In selling out his fellow men to protect his family business, Joe Keller in *All My Sons* indirectly causes his own son Larry's death. In *Death of a Salesman*, Willy Loman forces his false dream on his son, with disastrous consequences. Both fathers commit suicide. Quentin's father in *After the Fall*, like Victor Franz's father in *The Price* and Moe Baum in *The American Clock*, loses money in the Depression and goes into decline.

Miller's sons are striving to break the bonds of the father. Chris Keller, like Biff Loman, becomes disillusioned with the false values of his father. Quentin can see through his father's phoniness, and Victor realizes his father's betrayal. The father often represents the misguided and self-centered dream of material success that must be attained at any cost. The son must break away from the father and his world in order to realize his own identity and to lead a more authentic life.

In the family dramas, the mother has two sides. Kate Keller, like Linda Loman, both supports and defends her husband at all costs. In Miller's later plays, the mothers refuse to accept the failure of the father. Quentin's mother treats the father with contempt, and Victor's mother vomits on his bankrupt father. Although the mother is a source of stability that props up the father, she can also be a source of disillusionment.

Although some critics disagree, Miller sees his common heroes as tragic figures willing to sacrifice everything for their convictions even though those convictions may be based on false ideals or private delusions. Willy Loman is a washed-up salesman; Eddie Carbone, a troubled longshoreman; and John Proctor, a simple farmer. Yet each is willing to die for his beliefs. Miller's heroes proudly confirm their individual identity. Willy screams, "I am Willy Loman." Eddie must defend his name, and John Proctor in *The Crucible* would rather die than lend his name to an evil cause. Naming names and accusing others is a serious offense; to die anonymously in death camps is an abomination.

Miller's heroes are not victims of inexorable social forces. Ultimately, they bear the responsibility for their own actions. Embedded in them is a sense of guilt, usually for sexual infidelity. Willy's affair in a Boston hotel room haunts him, and Proctor's adultery fills him with shame. Proctor, like Quentin, stands accused before his wife. The Puritan strain of sexual guilt, a recurring theme in American literature, is an undercurrent in Miller's work.

Guilt for Miller, however, goes beyond sexual transgressions. It is centered in a more serious crime: betrayal, either of oneself or of others. Miller's characters often live in a world of illusion and denial, and those who escape from tragedy must undergo a process of self discovery. In Miller's cosmos, the individual must act upon his own conscience without betraying his fellow men for private gain. His plays, which often involve litigation, put society itself on trial. In a post-Holocaust world, no one is innocent. After the Depression, a shadow has been cast on capitalism and its promise of salvation through material prosperity. Socialism, which once held out the dream of a universal brotherhood, has given way to totalitarianism. In this fallen world, the individual must learn how to live with dignity and honesty in an age of disillusionment.

Although labeled a realist, Miller has experimented with a number of innovative dramatic techniques. In *Death of a Salesman*, he intersperses time sequences from the past and present without using flashbacks. In *After the Fall*, he employs expressionistic stage techniques in a stream-of-consciousness narrative. The device of a narrator in *After the Fall* and *A View From the Bridge* and the authorial comments in *The Crucible* add a distancing effect to his dramas. The montage effect in *The American Clock* and the Pinteresque absurdist style employed in *Danger Memory* demonstrate his ability to handle a variety of dramatic styles. Also, Miller's poetic use of idiomatic speech and his subtle deployment of dramatic symbols show that his drama has moved beyond photographic realism. Using a variety of approaches, Miller most often puts characters in confrontation with their past actions in order that they may define themselves not only in terms of their social situation but also in terms of their moral convictions.

ALL MY SONS

First produced: 1947 (first published, 1947)
Type of work: Play

A man who sacrifices the lives of others for personal wealth becomes responsible for the death of his own son.

All My Sons is a realistic drama with tragic overtones. The play has a tight structure: It takes place in one day and is located in one place. Following the tradition of Henrik Ibsen, Miller slowly unravels past events to reveal a moral wrong or sinister crime. Joe Keller is a prosperous manufacturer enjoying the fruits of his wealth. He is a jovial man with a loyal wife, Kate, and a devoted son, Chris, who will inherit his father's business. Miller said that he started the first scenes slowly, without much action, but hints of menace appear early in the play.

Despite its realistic tone, the play has the air of a fatalistic tragedy. Larry, Joe's son, was missing in action in World War II. After three years, he is presumed dead, yet Kate refuses to accept his death. As son, brother, and lover, Larry's haunting presence is felt throughout the play. The night before the play opens, a storm knocks down Larry's memorial apple tree, a sign of hidden guilt and the fall from innocence. Anne, Larry's old girlfriend, is staying in his room, which still contains Larry's clothes and his freshly polished shoes. Chris wants to marry Anne, but he is not sure that she has accepted Larry's death. Even after Anne has accepted his proposal, Chris still kisses her like Larry's brother. Also, as long as Kate will not accept Larry's death, Chris cannot marry Anne with his mother's blessing.

Larry's death is linked to a hidden crime: Joe Keller knowingly sold defective engines to the Army, causing the deaths of twenty-one pilots. Joe has pushed the blame onto his innocent partner, who is serving a jail sentence. Kate will not accept Larry's death because Larry's death will make Joe the murderer of his own son. Since Larry did not fly any of the defective planes, Joe considers himself innocent in his son's death; however, Anne reveals a letter from Larry in which Larry condemns his father for the deaths of the pilots and declares his intent to fly a suicide mission. Thus, Joe, who bears not only responsibility for his own son's death but also for the deaths of the other pilots, commits suicide.

In *All My Sons*, Miller explores the hidden order of the universe. The crime that Keller tried to avoid comes back to haunt him. From the grave, his son's voice condemns him. Although it is often criticized for its melodramatic effects, *All My Sons* gives a tragic dimension to a realistic drama.

DEATH OF A SALESMAN

First produced: 1949 (first published, 1949)
Type of work: Play

An unsuccessful salesman relives his past, trying to discover the reasons for his failure, then commits suicide in order to leave his son the legacy of his insurance.

More effectively than any other American drama, *Death of a Salesman* probes the nature of the American Dream and its promise of success. America was established as a new Eden, a place where one could transform the wilderness into a paradise of riches. The American myth created the pioneer hero who was always moving to greener pastures. One side of Willy Loman is firmly grounded in this myth. Willy's father was a traveling man who got rich peddling gadgets in South Dakota and then headed for Alaska. Willy's brother Ben is a true adventurer who walks into the jungles of Africa at seventeen and comes out rich. Ben, who is constantly on the move, shunning civilization and its laws, is the self-reliant hero of the American myth who conquers the wilderness and makes his fortune. As a salesman, Willy also sees himself as an adventurer who opens up new territories in New England—once the original frontier.

The play focuses on a longing for the lost Eden. Willy admires the scenery on his trips to New England. He longs to smell the lilacs and wisteria that once grew in his suburban idyll, now overshadowed by dingy apartment buildings. He wants to build a house in the country where he can buy chickens and grow things. In the end, this American Adam is reduced to the tragic figure of a down-and-out salesman planting lettuce in a barren garden in the dead of night as he contemplates suicide.

The theme of the Edenic garden coincides with the theme of the outdoorsman and the Western myth of open spaces. Willy is not only a gardener who wants to remain close to nature like Henry David Thoreau, he is also a man who can chop down branches, build porches, and remodel ceilings. His sons long to leave cramped offices and go swimming. Biff wants to go west to raise horses or be a carpenter.

Willy holds onto two other American myths. The myth of "having it made" is embodied in Dave Singleman, who at eighty-four can sit back and make sales from his hotel room. Dave is the popular hero who has throngs of people come to his funeral. Dave projects the image of the man who has "made it" in the system and who can make money without effort. The second American myth to which Willy subscribes is the "get rich quick" scheme. Like Ben, he hopes to find diamonds. He encourages his sons to open up a million-dollar sporting goods business with no capital and little experience.

Willy has based his notion of success on popularity and appearances, but Willy himself does not make a good appearance. Both he and his sons are out of place in a competitive world. The business world is changing; old promises are worthless. When Willy is no longer productive, he is fired. In the end, he "sells" his life for a twenty-thousand-dollar insurance policy in order to stake his son's fortune. In other words, he tries another "get rich quick" scheme. Charley and Bernard, Willy's neighbors, prove that success can be achieved, but for Willy Loman, who has absorbed too many American Dreams, the system inevitably becomes destructive.

In 1949, *Death of a Salesman* won the New York Drama Critics Circle Award and the Pulitzer Prize. The play ran for 742 performances. In 1966, a television production played to seventeen million people. In 1975, it was successfully produced at the Circle in the Square theater with George C. Scott in the lead, and in 1984, it played Broadway again with Dustin Hoffman in the lead. In 1985, Hoffman was featured in another television production of the play. *Death of a Salesman* has been produced around the world. In his book *Salesman in Beijing* (1984), Miller documents an unprecedented Chinese production. The play still appears in most college anthologies and continues to be taught as an American classic.

THE CRUCIBLE

First produced: 1953 (first published, 1953)
Type of work: Play

In a repressive Puritan society that is killing innocent people as witches, a simple farmer refuses to barter his conscience for his life.

The Crucible is about the right to act upon one's individual conscience. In Puritan New England, Roger Williams, the founder of Rhode Island, claimed his right to act upon his conscience. In the nineteenth century, Henry David Thoreau considered the exercising of this right a moral obligation, even if it meant breaking the law. The individual's right to follow his conscience is part of the American heritage. In *The Crucible*, Miller shows how an ordinary individual living in a repressive community gains tragic stature by sacrificing his life rather than betraying his conscience.

Salem is a divided and disturbed community. Hidden behind its sacred crusade are the petty grievances of the self-interested and the vengeful. The town's minister, Reverend Parris, is desperately trying to stabilize his power and is more interested in maintaining his social position than in ministering to his congregation. When his daughter Betty, with Abigail Williams, Tituba, and other young girls are seen dancing naked in the forest, he fears the scandal will bring down his ministry. Thomas Putnam is disturbed because he wants an excuse to confiscate his neighbor's land. His wife Ann is jealous of Rebecca Nurse, who has more children than she. Abigail Williams consciously seeks to revenge herself on Elizabeth Proctor, who dismissed her from the Proctors' service.

Miller clearly shows that in such a community, which is at odds with itself, all that is needed to set the community into hysteria is the specter of Satan, the epitome of insidious evil behind which small-minded people hide their own hostility and their quest for power. Soon experts such as John Hale are called in from the outside to find evil, even where it does not exist. Next, a high court invested with infallible judgment acts on the testimony of finger-pointing witnesses who indiscriminately accuse innocent people. Miller shows how judges at a purge trial lead witnesses to give the appropriate testimony. Tituba, a Barbados native, confesses to witchcraft because she knows what the authorities want to hear. The young girls accuse innocent people to deflect blame from themselves and to gain power and publicity.

In this climate of hysteria, John Proctor, a simple farmer, is called upon to act. Proctor, an independent man who is not afraid to oppose his minister and to work on the Sabbath, knows that the young girls are lying. At first, Proctor is reluctant to act. He withdraws from the town and tries to prevent his wife from incriminating herself. He not only knows that the young girls are making a sham of human justice, but he also knows that, deep down, he does not believe in witches—yet he will not confess to heresy.

Moreover, Proctor is a guilty man, a sinner, with hidden sin gnawing at his conscience. He has betrayed his wife and has committed adultery with Abigail Williams, so he also faces the judgment of his wife and has shaken her trust in him. Miller follows a theme in American literature, one which is especially pronounced in the works of Nathaniel Hawthorne. This theme examines the way in which private sin and nagging guilt intermingle with public sin. To save his wife and the town, Proctor must discredit Abigail, but to do so, he would have to expose his own guilt.

Proctor's battle with the court is doomed, for the repressive court is implacable. He first tries to present concrete evidence, but in the Puritan court such evidence is suspect. A list of character witnesses becomes a source for suspicion and further interrogation. To question the court is blasphemy. In times of political and religious hysteria, everyone is on trial, even the witnesses. Mary Warren, a young girl who tries to do what is right, breaks down under the pressure of the court and the hysterical antics of Abigail. Proctor tries to expose Abigail as a whore and openly implicates himself as an adulterer, but his wife lies to protect him. Even though Governor Danforth can see that the accusations of witchcraft are questionable, he continues to commit himself to a course of injustice rather than admit a mistake and discredit the court.

Not being a saint like Rebecca Nurse, Proctor is willing to lie and confess to witchcraft so that he can live and rear his family; however, when he is asked to name names and sign a public confession, his conscience will not allow him to ruin the names of others nor to have his name used to justify evil. Only if he can keep his individual dignity can he pass on anything of value to his children. Proctor, an ordinary man, takes extraordinary action and is willing to die for his convictions.

The Crucible opened on Broadway in 1953 to a lukewarm reception, but it was later revived Off-Broadway with more success. Jean-Paul Sartre wrote the screenplay for the French film version of *The Crucible, Les Sorcieres de Salem* (1955). In 1961, *The Crucible* was converted into an opera, and in 1967, it was adapted for television with George C. Scott in the lead role. According to Miller, *The Crucible* is his most frequently produced work both in America and abroad.

AFTER THE FALL

First produced: 1964 (first published, 1964)
Type of work: Play

A lawyer relives scenes from his past that test his ability to relate to the women in his life, and he comes to accept his responsibility for his actions.

After the Fall shows one man's struggle to survive in a fallen world. The fall from Eden is a recurring theme in American literature—America, after all, was established as a kind of New World Garden, a bountiful paradise that would yield endless riches. It would bring forth an ideal community in which all individuals could live together in harmony and prosperity. The Puritan commitment to the individual's natural propensity for evil, however, always left open the possibility of a fallen Eden. Some of the greatest American authors—Nathaniel Hawthorne, Herman Melville, Henry James, and William Faulkner—have treated the theme of the fall. In *After the Fall*, Miller explores this theme in the light of the modern world. Quentin, the main character, is an alienated man on trial who feels that there is no God to judge his actions. He tries to plead his case to a sympathetic Listener who is neither seen nor heard.

Quentin, a once-successful lawyer, examines his own conscience and becomes aware of his own fall from innocence. Through Quentin, Miller explores the historical context which has lead humanity into a state of universal guilt. With his new girlfriend, Holga, Quentin visits a Nazi concentration camp. At the site, he realizes that human beings built such atrocities to slaughter nameless victims. According to Miller's ethics, a hero dies affirming his identity by holding onto the dignity of his name. Anonymous slaughter is anathema. The atrocities of the camps have made everyone, especially the survivors, guilty. Innocence is no longer possible, for the Holocaust of the Jews has violated all the principles of Judeo-Christian morality. The image of the concentration camp, a constant reminder that the world has fallen, haunts Quentin throughout the play.

Quentin also experiences the guilt inherent in being part of a family. His father went bankrupt in the Depression, another symbol of the fall—a fall from economic stability that changed the American system and made once-successful men feel guilty for their own fall from prosperity. Quentin's mother blames his father for the father's failure to avoid economic disaster. Quentin becomes an accomplice as he picks up her contempt for his father, along with the message that he himself must succeed. Dan is the brother who has remained loyal to the family while Quentin, who sees through his father's phoniness, has separated himself from the family. In his quest for self-knowledge, Quentin tries to go beyond blaming his troubles on the actions of his parents. Quentin tries to see family life as part of a fallen world where there is betrayal and loss of faith.

Quentin is also defending his friend Lou, who is caught in the national hysteria promoted by the investigations of the House Committee on Un-American Activities, another sign of the fall. The American system is being distorted by petty publicity seekers who are destroying people's lives. People are breaking faith and naming names in absurd public confessions and selling their consciences for economic security. The guilt, however, lies not only with the Committee. Lou, who once believed in the ideals of a Communist brotherhood, has written a book distorting the facts about Russian life. The great idealistic cause of leftist sympathizers, such as Lou and Mickey, has been a fraud. The utopian vision that has been so much a part of the American consciousness has again failed; everyone is a "separate person." Mickey is willing to betray Lou; Max, Quentin's boss, will not easily tolerate Quentin's support of a Communist. Quentin finds himself stymied by the breach of communal fidelity and is groping for answers in a fallen world.

Another sign of the fall from Eden is seen in the sexual fall and in the presence of Eve as temptress and betrayer. In *After the Fall*, betrayal has its locus in women. Quentin comes to realize that his wife Louise is not his innocent, unfallen Eve. Quentin's mother holds his father in contempt and refuses to share in the responsibility of their failure. Louise tries to separate herself from Quentin and to maintain her innocence. Maggie, the star singer that Quentin subsequently marries, always sees herself as an innocent victim and forces Quentin to realize that he cannot save her from herself. The women in Quentin's life are judgmental and often label men as idiots. Only through Holga, a survivor of the Nazi concentration camps, does the alienated Quentin learn to accept the responsibility for his actions and to persevere.

After the Fall was partially inspired by Albert Camus's *La Chute* (1956; *The Fall*, 1957), which Miller saw as a book about troubles with women and about the impossibility of rescuing a woman who does not want to be rescued. The critics, however, could not divorce Miller's play from its author. Miller was accused of being cheap and sensational in publicly exploiting his relationship with Marilyn Monroe. The play was labeled a self-indulgent confession. Others found it confusing and uneven. Miller, in turn, accused the critics of not seeing beyond certain autobiographical allusions in order to penetrate the deeper meaning of the play. *After the Fall* opened on January 23, 1964, as the first production of the new Lincoln Center Repertory Theater. The play was adapted for television in 1974 and was revived Off-Broadway in 1984, with Frank Langella in the leading role.

Summary

Miller examines both the psychological and sociological make-up of his troubled characters. His heroes are common men who relentlessly pursue either their firm convictions or their misguided illusions. Using family relationships as a starting point, Miller's plays confront moral dilemmas, focusing on the individual's responsibility to be true to himself as well as his responsibility to be a part of the human race. His concern with the ordinary individual's struggle to define himself in a troubled world has not only made him a renowned American playwright but has also gained for him worldwide attention. He is one of the most frequently studied playwrights in the American canon.

Bibliography

Bhatia, S. K. *Arthur Miller: Social Drama as Tragedy.* New Delhi, India: Arnold-Heinemann, 1985.

Carson, Neil. *Arthur Miller.* London: Macmillan, 1982.

Hayman, Ronald. *Arthur Miller.* New York: Frederick Ungar, 1972.

Martin, Robert A., ed. *Arthur Miller: New Perspectives.* Englewood Cliffs, N.J.: Prentice-Hall, 1982.

Miller, Arthur. *Timebends: A Life.* New York: Grove Press, 1987.

Moss, Leonard. *Arthur Miller.* Rev. ed. Boston: Twayne, 1980.

Panikkar, N. Bhaskara. *Individual Morality and Social Happiness in Arthur Miller.* Atlantic Highlands, N.J.: Humanities Press, 1982.

Schlueter, June, and James K. Flanagan. *Arthur Miller.* New York: Frederick Ungar, 1987.

Welland, Dennis. *Arthur Miller: The Playwright.* London: Methuen, 1983.

Paul Rosefeldt

HENRY MILLER

Born: New York, New York
December 26, 1891
Died: Pacific Palisades, California
June 7, 1980

Principal Literary Achievement

Writing with enormous energy and unparalleled frankness in a style derived from extensive self-education and a sharp ear for the American vernacular, Miller extended the boundaries of imaginative prose while bringing psycho-surrealism into American fiction.

Biography

Henry Valentine Miller was born in the Yorkville section of Manhattan's Upper East Side the day after Christmas in 1891. His father, Heinrich Miller, was an affable raconteur who ran a tailor shop, while his mother, Louis Marie Nieting, liked the stability and order of a stolid community of merchants and conventional shops. Before Miller was a year old, his family moved across the East River to the Williamsburg section of Brooklyn, where young Henry spoke German until he entered school. He was a good student, ranking second in his high school class, and upon graduation in 1909, he entered City College of New York but dropped out after only one term. For the next few years, he worked at a variety of jobs, traveled to California (where he met Emma Goldman), read widely, and began to dream of becoming a writer. Financial restrictions kept pulling him back to Brooklyn and his parents' home, and after a number of affairs, he married Beatrie Wickens, a piano teacher, in 1917. Two years later, his daughter Barbara was born, and in that same year, his first written works were published—a few reviews for a small short story magazine called *The Black Cat*, based in Salem, Massachusetts.

Miller succeeded in getting a job as an employment manager for Western Union Telegraph Company in 1920, a position he used as the basis for the first part of *Tropic of Capricorn* (1939), and over a three-week vacation in 1922, he wrote the manuscript for a novel to be called *Clipped Wings* about telegraph messengers. The novel was never published, but he felt that March 22, 1922, was his "first day of being a writer." In 1924, he divorced Wickens when he met June Smith, a dancer in a Brooklyn club; June was the basis for the Mara/Mona figure of his autobiographical romances. Miller and Smith were married as soon as his divorce was granted,

1374

and for the next few years, he tried several methods of earning a living while unsuc-cessfully pursuing a career as a writer. In 1927, while his wife was traveling in Europe with a female friend, Miller wrote a twenty-six-page outline of what would become *The Rosy Crucifixion* epic—including *Tropic of Capricorn*, *Sexus* (1949), *Plexus* (1953), and *Nexus* (1960)—and began a revised version of his Western Union novel, retitled *Moloch*, which was never published.

One of his wife's male friends sent the Millers to Europe in 1928 to find a pub-lisher, but Miller was uncomfortable there, and as his marriage was beginning to de-teriorate, he returned to the United States where he began a third novel in 1929 called *Crazy Cock*, which was also never published. As his marriage drifted toward a complete collapse in 1930, Miller returned to Paris alone to begin a decade of expa-triatism. He subsisted on hand-outs, the generosity of friends, and occasional news-paper work. Although the first wave of expatriates had returned to America, Miller became friends with an interesting group of international avant-garde artists. In 1931, the year he began his intense friendship with Anaïs Nin, he started another novel, which he saw as a "Parisian notebook" and which was to appear eventually as *Tropic of Cancer* (1934).

Miller's wife arrived unexpectedly in Paris in October, 1931, and while she and Miller were unable to rescue their marriage, her involvement with Nin led to the transformation of the Miller/Nin relationship from one of mutual admiration and encouragement to a secret sexual attachment as well. Nin and Miller corresponded steadily throughout the 1930's, and Nin provided the money from a personal loan to assist in the publication of *Tropic of Cancer*. The book was widely admired by some leading literary figures, such as Ezra Pound and T. S. Eliot (who wrote that it was "a rather magnificent piece of work"), but because of its sexual expressiveness, it was banned in every English-speaking country. Miller divorced Smith in 1934 and re-turned briefly to New York in 1935 before spending the remainder of the decade in Europe, where he wrote *Black Spring* (1936), a book of essays called *Max and the White Phagocytes* (1938), a study of D. H. Lawrence which was not published until 1980, and *Tropic of Capricorn*. As World War II threatened to engulf Europe, Miller left Paris (with a ticket purchased by Nin) to visit the British writer Lawrence Dur-rell in Greece, which became the setting for his rhapsodic travel journal, *The Co-lossus of Maroussi: The Spirit of Greece* (1941). Arriving in New York in 1940, broke and unable to find an American publisher for the books he had been writing, Miller toured the United States with the artist Abraham Rattner, a trip which be-came the basis for *The Air-Conditioned Nightmare* (1945). In the early 1940's, Mil-ler began to write the trilogy which formed the body of *The Rosy Crucifixion*, the epic account of his life with June Smith in the 1920's; James Laughlin, the visionary American publisher of New Directions Press, began to send Miller steady advances against royalties for books he could legally publish in the United States.

Miller journeyed to the West Coast in 1944, hoping to find some kind of work in Hollywood, and when this failed, he settled in the rugged California coastal country of Big Sur and married Janina Lepska. Miller's daughter Valentine was born in

1945, and although *Tropic of Cancer* had been selling steadily in Europe, Miller was unable to collect any royalties and continued to struggle financially. When *Sexus* was published in 1949, the year after Miller's son Tony was born, the extreme frankness of its account of sexual behavior upset even some of his longtime supporters such as Durrell, and in 1950, the book was banned worldwide. Miller and Lepska were divorced in 1952, the year he wrote *The Books in My Life*, and in the following year, Miller married Eve McClure. During the 1950's, Miller was gradually being recognized by some conventional critics as an important writer, and the publication of *Big Sur and the Oranges of Hieronymus Bosch* in 1957 enabled readers to see his more genial, less rebellious side. He was elected to the National Institute of Arts and Letters in 1958, and concluded his exploration of his life in the 1920's with *Nexus* in 1960, although he maintained for many years that there would be a sequel.

Barney Rosset of Grove Press challenged the restrictions on the rights of writers and publishers by issuing *Tropic of Cancer* in an American edition in 1961, and the book immediately became a best-seller. Miller and McClure were divorced in 1963, and *Tropic of Cancer* was finally ruled not to be obscene after two years of trials. Miller bought a residence in Pacific Palisades in the mid-1960's and began to publish shorter books of recollections and reflections with Noel Young's Capra Press. In 1967 he married Hoki Tokuda, a marriage that lasted three years and led to Miller's *Insomnia: Or, The Devil at Large* (1971), and he spent the 1970's writing only on occasion but finally being celebrated by friends and admirers who recognized him as an honored sage and important figure in American literary history.

Analysis

Miller's work was misunderstood from the very beginning not only because of its startling candor and sexual explicitness but also because Miller was one of the foremost exponents of many of the modernist techniques which traditional commentators were unprepared to evaluate or understand. For one thing, Miller (like artist Pablo Picasso and the composer Igor Stravinsky) challenged the limits of conventional composition, refusing to be bound by the "rules" of unity or the linear demands of chronology. His books were not exactly "novels" or "autobiographies" or "journals" or "essays," instead blending those forms into a mutant or hybrid amalgam that combined some of the elements of various genres which were generally kept separate. Also, his "voice" ranged from the conversational to the oratorical, with many variants along the scale, and his use of language ranged from his mastery of American colloquial speech to his proficiency with many different modes of rhetorical declaration. At the root of all these elements, Miller drew on—indeed, plunged into—the depths of his subconscious mind in an effort to create as complete and accurate a picture of his sensibility as it evolved across the middle decades of the twentieth century as his means allowed. The narrative consciousness of his "auto-novels" was an archetype of the artist-as-hero, a replacement for the more traditional adventurer, athlete, soldier or industrialist of earlier American fiction, and because this artist/hero grew and changed with the author, he was never completely captured in any single volume Miller wrote.

For this reason, critics have often suggested that Miller's books lack form and structure, but Miller worked throughout his career from a rough outline he developed in the 1920's, a sprawling chart which mapped the direction of two progressive narratives. The first and more specific one would be an epic of artistic and emotional development, in which the extraordinary sexual maelstrom he inhabited with June Smith would be explored in unprecedented depth. This track was called "Capricorn" in his notes, and eventually came to include *Tropic of Capricorn, Sexus, Plexus*, (which was a failure and a distraction) and *Nexus*, and remained incomplete in Miller's mind until his death. The other track, which eventually disclosed its form as it was written, derived from Miller's ideas about how an artist might live in an ideal social community, and it had its origins in the world of childhood which he recalled as a kind of paradise he had lost long ago and hoped to regain in another form through the self's revelation in artistic perceptions.

Miller took as his model Walt Whitman's "Song of Myself" (1855), and the form of the work is determined by the collision of the phenomena of the universe and the evolving artistic consciousness of the author. This track began with *Tropic of Cancer*, a book which declared the fully formed but still developing self of the author in opposition to a landscape of blight and erosion; it then moved both back toward a dreamlike past in *Black Spring* and outward to a more congenial environment in *The Colossus of Maroussi*. Eventually it moved on to a semi-conclusion in *Big Sur and the Oranges of Hieronymus Bosch*; this track actually includes many of Miller's letters to Durrell, Nin, and others.

In the first group (a triad if *Plexus* is discarded), the author is the prime agent of the action, a character in flux whose future is unclear, whose present is in turmoil, and whose life is instinctual, immediate, and often psychologically devastating. In the second group, a quartet, the author is more of an observer than an actor, prepared by the events of the triad to comment on, evoke and describe, and evaluate everything he sees. The crucial link between the two tracks is the fact that the triad should explain the artist who erupts into being and song in *Tropic of Cancer*, but in *Nexus*, the tone and mood of the narration (Miller writing in 1960) is hardly like the defiant snarl that proclaims a unique, dangerous and compelling new creation. This failure of sorts is typical of Miller's inability to realize his aspirations completely, but the mysteries that remain are a part of the appeal of his work, and the struggle toward clarity and self-understanding is as fascinating in its dead ends and tortured turnings as in its occasional moments of satisfaction and fulfillment. Miller's attempts to understand and express the feminine equivalent of his traditionally masculine sensibility is part of a goal he never really reaches, but—as is the case in much modernist art—the journey is as important to the traveler as the destination.

Two additional related factors further complicate Miller's work. One is his use of the "I" narrator, a device which was valuable for the process of self-creation but confusing to critics who tended to assume that there was a fairly specific equivalence between the author and his central character. Miller however maintained, "If I lie a bit now and then it is mainly in the interest of truth," and his essential point is that any technique for establishing "reality" is appropriate and justified. Similarly, many readers have been troubled by his treatment of women. In actuality, the attitudes of various male characters are not representative of the author at all, and in many cases, they are used as indications of the failure of the speaker to find love and his neurotic retreat into physical gratification as a substitute for a more complete relationship. It is necessary to see passages which exhibit anxiety and hatred as reflecting a national psychosis that is part of the society Miller constantly criticizes in his desire to see a utopian America. This does not mean that Miller is entirely free from some of the attitudes he expresses but that, as in most aspects of his work, everything is more complex than any single instance might suggest.

TROPIC OF CANCER

First published: 1934
Type of work: Novel

Fortified with gleeful anger and the energy of creative awareness, an underground artist prowls the streets of Paris recording human erosion and redemptive beauty.

More than half a century after its initial publication, *Tropic of Cancer* still has the power to startle and overwhelm a reader. Its wild, violent language, its immense force, its radiant paeans to the historic beauty of Paris, and its unsettling descriptions of a society in an advanced state of decomposition reflect a bottom dog's sense of the world that is still relevant and disturbing. Even the fairly explicit sexual passages retain the power to shock and disturb, not because of their pornographic content, but because they show the psychotic self-absorption of people ruined by social stratification and personal egocentricity. Miller wrote the book as a declaration of his own survival after a wrenching psychic experience, and his exuberant embrace of nearly every aspect of existence is a reflection of his discovery that he had found a voice and a form appropriate to the ideas and ambitions he had been harboring for his entire adult life. Before the book was published, Nin read the manuscript and accurately described the protagonist as "the mould-breaker . . . the revolutionist," and the revolution Miller was proclaiming was part of the modernist enterprise of challenging conventional but no longer viable authority.

One aspect of this challenge was the form of the book itself. It was begun originally as a kind of journal called "Paris and Me," and Miller eventually divided the book into fifteen sections; however, it has little character development beyond the narrator's personal journey, a discontinuous sense of chronology, no plot in any familiar sense, no real dramatic events, and no conclusion. Instead, the narrative drifts and drives from "the fall of my second year in Paris" (in 1929) and continues in rhythmic lurches to the spring of 1931, but time is elastic, and days and months have no particular meaning, since the narrator has no regular job or any other specific schedule. This enables him to roam freely, at random primarily, so that he is able to avoid all the traps which have led his companions to spiritual destruction.

Certain motifs recur throughout the book. There are many scenes of male bonding, including men eating, drinking, arguing, complaining, and womanizing together. One of the most striking among these is section 8, in which Miller describes Van Norden, a nonspiritual man as mechanical monster who is something of a double for the protagonist. These sections are often bracketed with descriptions of women from the perspective of male lust, and in passages such as the one in section 3, where the protagonist celebrates the qualities of Germaine, a whore he finds admirable, Miller is criticizing the narrowness and self-centered posturing of the men in the book. These passages are often also apostrophes to the mythic beauty and mysterious power of Woman, what Norman Mailer calls Miller's "utter adoration," reflecting "man's sense of awe." A third motif includes an introduction of the comic into almost everything so that mundane difficulties become a source of humor rather than a cause for concern. This capacity for appreciating the comic aspect of a generally frustrating and discouraging pattern of searching for food, love, friendship, and so on is what separates the protagonist from nearly everyone else, and this gives Miller, as his fourth motif, a pure vision of ecstasy generated by the almost delirious contemplation of beauty in many forms, particularly in the city itself.

Section 13 offers Miller's powerful tribute to artist Henri Matisse, constructed in terms of the artist's use of light—a continuing fascination for Miller, who sets it against the darkness and sterility of the cancerous world. The fact that the protagonist can emerge from a realm of human decomposition with his sense of wonder at the phenomena of the universe intact is what makes the book exhilarating in spite of all the failure it examines. As the book moves toward a conclusion, or at least an ending or stopping, Miller becomes more and more rhapsodic, exclaiming "I love everything that flows," in a tribute to James Joyce; on the last pages of the book, after a bizarre interlude spent teaching at a boys' school in Dijon (a job Nin helped Miller obtain), the protagonist steps out of a doomed culture and into a landscape of serenity. For a moment, as he regards the Seine, he is able to imagine himself merging with the great flow of cosmic energy that animates the universe, his own manic energy temporarily spent and his psychic demons relegated to the realm he has left. The culmination of the artist's development at the end of *Tropic of Cancer*, is as Jay Martin says, proof that he is now the man who can write the book.

TROPIC OF CAPRICORN

First published: 1939
Type of work: Novel

A man is rescued from a desolate existence by a woman whose romantic allure is as powerful as it is mysterious.

Henry Miller planned to explore his relationship with June Smith in a multi-volume proto-epic that covered his life in the 1920's in extraordinary detail. While his plans were never completely carried out, *Tropic of Capricorn* is the first book in the series, an introduction to the world in which he was living and a prologue to the later volumes, which concentrated on his life with Smith. It is divided into three parts, beginning with the protagonist employed by the Cosmodemonic Telegraph Company, an apt name for the metaphorical conceit he developed to dramatize the bureaucratic insanity of modern industrial society. As an employment manager, the protagonist is able to meet and describe a staggering variety of people, representative of a full range of strange and fascinating characters in the United States.

After the failure of his marriage, the narrator is thrown into a kind of sexual-psychic hell that almost destroys his mental stability. Then, he is redeemed by a woman he barely knows but who promises to lead him from (as Jay Martin puts it) "the Inferno of civilization and the Purgatorio of sensuality into the Paradiso of the liberated imagination." The book concludes with the protagonist so totally absorbed by his idealized sense of love that it is clear that he is on the verge of further psychic calamity, but the aura of romance is so great that it overwhelms everything else, including judgment and perspective.

BIG SUR AND THE ORANGES OF HIERONYMUS BOSCH

First published: 1957
Type of work: Journal

Toward the end of his career, a writer finds peace and serenity amid personal and public distraction in a landscape of wonder.

In 1944, Henry Miller settled in what he called "my first real home in America," a cabin on Partington Ridge, located in the rugged beauty of the Big Sur region of the California coast. He lived there for the next twelve years, and in *Big Sur and the Oranges of Hieronymus Bosch*, he tried to combine his vision of an ideal community with the somewhat less perfect situation of his life. In a painfully honest and often mundane report of his day-to-day life as a writer, parent, counselor, and local explorer, Miller produced what Norman Mailer calls a "wise record" of psychic survival. Still dedicated to his work (this is the time when Miller wrote *Sexus*, the heart of the triad that covers his life in the 1920's), Miller was not as animated by the fire of wrath that drove his earlier work, and much of what he covers is amusing but not widely significant.

For readers familiar with Miller's life and work, the book is like visiting an old friend, and Miller's sense of style and language is still impressive enough to make his descriptions of the landscape and his observations about the world captivating.

Except for the last hundred pages, though, there is little narrative suspense, and Miller's occasional pronouncements as the Sage of Big Sur, the center of an artistic gathering of serious and talented writers, are dissipated by frequent homilies and banal commentary. Too often, the genial ironist becomes the coy famous writer (as in references to "my quaint biographical romances"), but in the last part of the book, originally published separately as "The Devil in Paradise," Miller provides the only real portrait of evil in his work.

A visit from an old acquaintance from his Paris days, the astrologer Conrad Moricand, brings an infusion of Old-World decadence into this New World of semi-innocence. Moricand is a monster of self-obsession, vain, supercilious, and haughty, and Miller presents him as a parasitical creature controlled totally by an icy egotism. The contrast between the two men is an effective demonstration of how far Miller himself is now from the cancerous world of the 1930's when he began his "song" and how much more he is capable of creating than the erotica which made him notorious.

Summary

Henry Miller became famous for the wrong reasons and stayed famous for the right ones. Although his books have never been studied in American schools, he is one of the United States' most widely read authors. Beyond the shock of his examinations of previously forbidden aspects of human behavior, readers have discovered his erudition, his insight into every aspect of human nature, his mastery of an appealing style of expression (what George Orwell called his "friendly American voice"), and his judicious critique of contemporary society. His work, although uneven, eccentric, sprawling, and not always tasteful, remains compelling in accordance with Ezra Pound's definition of literature— "News that stays news."

Bibliography

Brown, J. D. *Henry Miller.* New York: Frederick Ungar, 1986.
Gordon, William A. *The Mind and Art of Henry Miller.* Baton Rouge: Louisiana State University Press, 1967.
Lewis, L. H. *Henry Miller: The Major Writings.* New York: Schocken Books, 1986.
Mailer, Norman. *Genius and Lust: A Journey Through the Major Writings of Henry Miller.* New York: Grove Press, 1976.
Mathieu, Bertrand. *Orpheus in Brooklyn.* Paris: Mouton, 1976.
Mitchel, Edward, ed. *Henry Miller: Three Decades of Criticism.* New York: New York University Press, 1971.
Wickes, George, ed. *Henry Miller and the Critics.* Carbondale, Ill.: Southern Illinois University Press, 1963.

Leon Lewis

N. SCOTT MOMADAY

Born: Lawton, Oklahoma
February 27, 1934

Principal Literary Achievement
Of Kiowa-Cherokee ancestry, Momaday successfully transmutes the rhythms and the power of the Native American oral (storytelling) tradition into American English poetry, fiction, and autobiography.

Biography
Born in the Kiowa and Comanche Indian Hospital, Momaday was registered as having seven-eighths Indian blood (with the remaining one-eighth attributable to pioneer ancestry); his name was registered as Novarro Scotte Mammedaty, born to Mayme Scott (Natachee) and Alfred Morris (Huan-toa) Mammedaty. It was Momaday's father who simplified the surname to its current spelling.

Native Americans believe that the act of naming has the special significance of bringing the named one into existence and helping to chart his life course. Momaday has been granted the gifts of three separate namings. At six months of age, he was given his first Indian name by Pohd-lohk, stepfather of Mammedaty, Momaday's grandfather, who died of Bright's disease two years before Momaday was born. Devil's Tower (Tsoai), Wyoming, according to Kiowa oral tradition a sacred site of mystical power, was the basis by which he was named Tsoai-talee (Rock Tree Boy) by the old man. Before Momaday was five, a Sioux elder gave him his second Indian name, Wanbli Wanjila (Eagle Alone). Later in his life he received yet a third name, Tso-Toh-Haw (Kiowa for Red Mountain).

Momaday's mother was a teacher and a writer; his father, a teacher and an artist. Throughout his early years, his mother shared her love of English literature with him. Although both parents reared him to view English as his first language, they also encouraged him to immerse himself in the tribal cultures of the reservations on which they lived. Consequently, Momaday sees his childhood as an enriching experience.

He considers his early formal education, however, including attendance at several Catholic schools, as unremarkable and substandard. At twelve, Momaday moved with his parents to Jemez Pueblo, New Mexico, which remained his home until his senior year in high school. For his graduation year, Momaday decided to seek a more rigorous education at Augusta Military School, Virginia, in preparation for college.

In 1958, Momaday was awarded his A.B. in English from the University of New Mexico. Although he thinks of himself primarily as a poet, he has stated that until his graduate studies at Stanford University he knew little about classical poetic perspectives; he received his Ph.D. from Stanford in 1963. There, Momaday credits Yvor Winters, a professor and a friend, with having a profound influence upon his writing. In addition to his 1959 Stanford University creative writing fellowship, in 1962 Momaday won the Academy of American Poets prize for his syllabic poem "The Bear."

Having written his doctoral dissertation on the poet Frederick Goddard Tuckerman, Momaday served as editor for the 1965 Oxford University Press edition of *The Complete Poems of Frederick Goddard Tuckerman*. Since that time, the concentration of Momaday's prose and poetry has reflected both his Native American heritage and the Southwestern landscape.

After assuming an assistant professorship for two years at the Santa Barbara campus of the University of California, Momaday was awarded a 1966-1967 Guggenheim Fellowship. During this time, he wrote and published a limited edition of Kiowa folklore, *The Journey of Tai-Me* (1967). A revised edition, with illustrations by his artist father appeared in 1969 under the title *The Way to Rainy Mountain*. Describing a personal quest inspired by the death of his grandmother, Aho, Momaday's chronologue of Kiowa tribal history from emergence to demise coalesces racial memory, legend, and personal experience into a life-giving renewal of Kiowa spirituality.

Momaday has stated that for those few years he focused on prose writing, setting aside his poetry. One of the results was the 1969 Pulitzer Prize for *House Made of Dawn* (1968), his first published novel, written intermittently over a period of two years. *House Made of Dawn* is a non-chronological presentation of human growth through the main character's isolation and alienation and his ultimate healing restoration.

Momaday regards university/college teaching as an ideal profession for a writer because of its flexible schedule. In fact, he has stated that he prefers to teach afternoon classes so that he can set aside four or five hours in the early morning for his writing. Despite being a self-proclaimed unhurried writer, during his years at Stanford University (from 1973 to 1982) as a full professor, Momaday published three major works as well as articles for periodicals.

The early- to mid-1970's mark his return to poetry and art as forms of expression. His first two publications following *The Way to Rainy Mountain* were collections of his poetry, *Angle of Geese and Other Poems* (1974) and *The Gourd Dancer* (1976), which he illustrated himself. As an artist, Momaday has sketched in both graphite and pen-and-ink. He has also worked in acrylic and in watercolor. For Momaday, the spontaneous process of creating visual pieces is in direct counterpoint to the intense deliberation with which he writes.

In 1976, *The Names: A Memoir* was published. Although labeled an autobiography, this text contains far more than is traditional for that genre. One function of the Native American oral tradition is to perpetuate tribal legend and memory through the telling of its stories. Once the stories have been truly heard, they become part of the listener's experience. Supplementing his text with pictures from his mother's family album, Momaday has transformed the tradition into a recounting by the written word.

Momaday's profound attachment to the Southwest is clear. Since 1982, he has served as a full professor in the University of Arizona's English department, a move he has described as coming home again. In 1989, Momaday published *The Ancient Child*, a novel based upon a Kiowa legend that has long fascinated him, the legend of Devil's Tower and the boy who becomes a bear.

Although he has declined to function in an official capacity as a spokesman on Native American issues, Momaday is an active reviewer of topics related to the American Indian. In his storytelling pieces for periodicals, he has also shared such unique personal experiences as his membership in the Gourd Dance Society, the Taimpe, which performs an annual celebration in Oklahoma.

Analysis

N. Scott Momaday's vital identification with the Southwest and with Native American nations (particularly the Kiowa) is consistently reflected in his choice of locations, subject matter, and protagonists. Unwilling to write about anything that he has not examined and does not know intimately, Momaday's focus is restrained yet powerful.

Momaday has described himself as a "word walker," a storyteller who uses language on his life's journey in a way that transverses dimensions. If language is so powerful that, as Momaday believes, by speaking words one can create their reality, then precision, awareness, and harmony with the rhythms of nature are essential to their appropriate expression.

Consequently, Momaday's distinctive juxtaposition of what may initially appear to be fragmented scenes is actually designed to reveal essences rather than simple chronological sequences. In *House Made of Dawn*, for example, the shattering of Abel's body after his beating by Martinez is dramatically reinforced by the abrupt intrusion of prison memories, childhood experiences, and a peyote ceremony.

Such is the Native American concept of "seeing"—to recognize the facet of creation existing on this plane and beyond to its essence as an integral part of the Great Mystery (God). Momaday's central concern is man's harmonious and awe-filled relationship with all existence. When mankind denies this relationship or his responsibility for it, the inevitable results are isolation, alienation, and disintegration. The blindness motif in *House Made of Dawn* is only one example of the consequences of self- or other-alienation.

To Momaday, any separation from nature causes deterioration of the human spirit. Lack of positive female relationships, disregard for ancestral heritage, and denial of tribal memory are capable of promoting an individual's, or a culture's, extinction. As a result, Momaday moves again and again from crises to vividly detailed descriptions of landscapes, because an intimate connection with "place" is vital to human awareness and understanding. In *The Way to Rainy Mountain*, the historical description of an important ceremonial tipi's destruction by fire is followed by a slow, soothing description of silence and shadow at the end of a day.

Light and shadow, sound and silence, circular imagery, water and animal symbolism, and the four directions of the Medicine Wheel are recurrent stylistic instruments with which the author heightens his reader's awareness. According to Native American philosophy, the Medicine Wheel reflects the process of life from birth to death. Each direction possesses its own integral characteristics. The healing of Abel's dawn run at the conclusion of *House Made of Dawn* is an example of Medicine Wheel symbolism. The color for the East is the red of dawn; its season, spring; its spiritual quality, understanding; its animal totem, the eagle, which represents a direct connection to the Great Mystery achieved as the result of successful passage through major life crises.

Momaday's prose writing style is most often described as "lyrical." This quality is evidenced in his stress upon the rhythm and sound of his word choices designed to reflect both the content and the substance of his subject matter. The following brief passage from *The Way to Rainy Mountain* describes dawn's stillness: "It is cold and clear and deep like water. It takes hold of you and will not let you go." The mystical quality of this language deftly captures the author's sense of wonder and reverence.

Although he has written in traditional iambic form, Momaday's most compelling poetry is either chant or syllabic rather than metered. A chant, such as "Plainview: 2," involves what might appear to the eye as monotonous repetition; however, when read aloud as if to the beat of an Indian ceremonial drum, its impact increases dramatically. Despite its being considered experimental poetry, the chant is firmly rooted in Native American oral tradition. Use of parallelism and repetition increases the power of the words. Furthermore, these techniques serve as memory aids for the listeners so that other levels of awareness may be more easily reached.

Syllabic poetry, of which "The Bear" is an example, depends upon a specific pattern of syllables per line, concrete imagery, and most often the use of rhyme. The advantages of this poetic form are that its rhythms are less artificial than a fully metered poem and that the phraseology is less cluttered and more direct. For Momaday, syllabic poetry appears to reflect more accurately his mystical awareness of, and attunement to, the elements of nature.

Even in the most dire of circumstances, such as the demise of the Kiowa tribal identity, N. Scott Momaday's Native American vision enables him to surge toward the hope of resurrection and rebirth. One foundation upon which he bases his perception of life is the historical failure of externally imposed restrictions to alter internal value systems. Recognizing the exigency of establishing a tribal/family memory, whether experienced or imagined, is another. The final step that he repeatedly presents in his writing is accepting the responsibility to feel wonder and joy in communion with the "giveaway" that is this universe.

HOUSE MADE OF DAWN

First published: 1968
Type of work: Novel

An alienated young Native American undergoes the initiation trials crucial to his reemergence as an actualized human being.

House Made of Dawn, Momaday's first novel, is divided into four major sections with dated chapter subheadings. In keeping with the Native American sense of history, the narrative is episodic rather than chronological. Thus, Momaday evokes both a sense of timelessness and a concentration on the essence of each experiential piece, gradually forming a healing pattern for Abel, the protagonist, as he moves toward an internal congruence with the earth.

Part 1, "The Longhair," opens and closes with Francisco, Abel's grandfather. A drunken Abel arrives by bus and is taken home. The ensuing flashbacks from Abel's childhood are both pleasant and fearful. His lack of attunement with nature is evidenced when, as a young child, he refuses to accept the moaning of the wind and responds instead with fear. The death of his brother Vidal is juxtaposed with Abel's coming-of-age rites.

Memories of The Eagle Watchers Society, survivors whom disaster had molded into medicine men, are next to surface. Abel catches a great eagle during the hunt but cries when he thinks of the implications of its captivity. Recognizing that the bird is no longer able to retain its natural state of grace, he strangles it. Once again, death is paralleled to life.

As the novel continues, Father Olguin, a priest fascinated by the perverted journal of Fray Nicholas, whom he sees as a saint, and Mrs. Martin St. John are introduced. Despite her pregnancy, Angela St. John plots to seduce Abel. Neither of these antagonists has made appropriate life accommodations for his or her role. Abel himself is too spiritually fragmented to meld with the rhythms of his horse in the annual rooster-plucking contest. The evil albino, however, retrieves the rooster and beats Abel with it. Thus, Abel is directly confronted with his alienation from himself and others.

Following a description of the unique gifts of animals on the land, Abel begins to reexperience nature's rhythms but discovers that he is not yet healed enough to have words for a creation song. Nevertheless, he does have the power to bed Angela, who sees in him the bear, thereby starting down her own path of healing, which is reinforced by her craving for the cleansing rain. Abel kills the albino, then kneels beside him to honor the dying process and to soak in the purifying rain.

Part 2, "The Priest of the Sun," is set in Los Angeles. The Right Reverend John Big Bluff Tosamah opens a serious sermon on the power of the word and how modern man has diluted that power, but midstream he begins to interject his own dilutions in the form of colloquialisms, irony, and blatant humor.

Against this is the reader's first indication of Abel's critical physical condition as he lies near the water. He flashes back to his childhood healing by Josie, a medicine woman, and to his trial for the albino's murder. Still, Abel has no words. Instead, he coughs blood as an owl, the sharp-sighted night bird, watches.

Remembrance of the dawn runners against evil and death unblocks Abel's awareness. He recognizes his isolation from self and from creation and, now open for healing, returns to the water. The peyote episode is also curative, as Ben Benally is revealed to be a healer through his vision of the horses and the "house made of dawn."

Abel remembers Josie's nurturance after his mother had died. He realizes that his generalized chronic fear is paralyzing his potential for integration. Flashing back to a time when he had wanted to share the extraordinary sight of twenty-four geese rising in formation from the river, Abel relives Millie's story of abandonment, isolation, and grief. Then he rises to journey home. As Abel travels, Tosamah reveals the story of the Kiowa migration and the steps that led to their demise. Part 2 concludes with Tosamah's tale of the sojourn to Rainy Mountain.

Part 3, in Los Angeles, is narrated by Ben Benally after he has given Abel his own coat for Abel's train ride home. The night before, Ben had created a future in words for the two men so similar in background that they are brothers. He had privately sung the healing "House Made of Dawn" chant. Considering Abel's history in Los Angeles, Ben concludes that Abel did not fit. He interacted little with others and appeared withdrawn, lost. After his failed drunken attack on Tosamah, during which the other poker players laughed, Abel had isolated himself totally.

The tension of the foregoing scenes is alleviated by the comic story of the venerable Indian who fell into the river. Moreover, this story bridges to the "Turquoise Woman's Son" song, a chant to restore wholeness to the incomplete, the means by which Abel prepares for change. Angela's brief street appearance introduces her to Ben, who will call her while Abel is recovering in the hospital. The symbolism of Abel's reappearance after three days lends credibility to the theory that he is progressing toward wholeness. Similarly, Angela's tale of the bear and the maiden represents her healing connection to the Earth Mother.

Part 4, "The Dawn Runner," in Walatowa (which means Village of the Bear), opens as Abel returns to his dying grandfather. After spending two days in a drunken stupor, Abel acknowledges the chronic state of his own illness. Even though he wants to speak to his grandfather, once again he has no words. Francisco, however, does. Transmission of his own honorable experiences on the bear hunt empowers Abel.

After his grandfather dies, Abel prepares him for burial and notifies Father Olquin. Although the priest has almost deluded himself into believing that he has successfully adapted to the Native culture surrounding him, his protestations of understanding ring false. In fact, Father Olquin's capacity for self-deception has increased. Preparing for his own dawn run to wholeness, Abel rubs his upper body with ashes. Then, as dawn strikes the horizon, he runs beyond his own pain, beyond evil, beyond death. By repeating the words of Ben's healing song, Abel indicates his acceptance of integration with nature.

THE WAY TO RAINY MOUNTAIN

First published: 1969
Type of work: History and folklore

Momaday recounts Kiowa legend and history from tribal memory.

The Way to Rainy Mountain, illustrated by Al Momaday, is both a eulogy for the demise of an active tribal identity and a celebration of the potential for its perpetuity in individual tribal consciousness. Divided into three major parts, "The Setting Out," "The Going On," and the "Closing In," the text has twenty-four numbered sections.

Each section is also separated into three passages, clearly delineated by three unique typescripts. Until section 20, the first passage is a translation of Kiowa myth, the second concerns Kiowa history, and the third is from the author's own experience. (Momaday's sources for the first two excerpts originate in both familial and tribal heritage.) A gradual composite begins to form as the author claims the elements for his own mythic heritage.

The book both begins and ends with a poem. The introductory poem, "Headwater," is a lyric description of the Kiowa emergence into the world. The Kiowa became what they dreamed. They were what they saw. Coming down from the mountains, never an agrarian people, the tribe adapted to its new environment as nomadic warriors and horsemen. Although they learned quickly from the Crow and were befriended by Tai-me, who became the focal point of their Sun Dance culture, the Kiowa did not long flourish. Tribal division and a series of disasters in the 1800's decimated the tribe. A meteor shower was taken to symbolize the destruction of the old ways. Epidemics raged. The buffalo and the Kiowa horses were massacred. Their slow surrender to the soldiers at Fort Sill was spiritually devastating to tribal consciousness.

The myth of the arrowmaker in section 13 is a recurrent theme in Momaday's writing. Artistry and precision are aesthetically essential to an appropriate balance with nature. They are also essential to survival. Because the arrowmaker is a craftsman, he knows that his arrow will fly true. His stalking awareness (as much a part of the Native American tradition as is dreaming) alerts him to an alien presence. Taking "right action" and moving cautiously, the arrowmaker allows the stranger the opportunity to declare his intentions. When the stranger does not, he becomes the enemy. Momaday uses ambiguity to heighten curiosity, and the anonymity of this fallen presence is intriguing.

The warrior society of section 3 illustrates Momaday's emphasis upon mastery and right action. If an individual is attuned to himself and his surroundings, self-aware but not self-preoccupied, then his behaviors will be effortless and true. The dog who leads the warriors is not as attuned to his own nature as is the dreamer who counsels him simply to be a dog.

The concluding poem, "Rainy Mountain Cemetery," eulogizes the ancient ones who have traveled to dimensions beyond this earthly existence. That they had survived is not the issue; those left behind blend the ancestral memories with their personal identities in order to preserve the collective tribal consciousness.

THE NAMES

First published: 1976
Type of work: Autobiography

A narrated account of the writer's experiences, both actual and metaphysical.

The Names: A Memoir differs from the traditional autobiographical account in both its approach and its subject matter. Again, Momaday has structured his writing to reflect the essence rather than the chronology. Across a cultural continuum of his own and his ancestors' experiences, Momaday weaves imaginative re-creations.

Naming is a process by which one identifies and reinforces predominant characteristics of a situation or an individual. In this memoir, Momaday sustains a mythic familial and tribal consciousness by naming the significant events that shape their distinctive spirit. For Momaday, active participation in a life experience does not necessarily imply that he is the protagonist in that event. He adheres to the Native American beliefs in the timelessness of the universe and the vital union of the physical and the spiritual worlds.

Therefore, his memoir serves two purposes. First, his assimilation of the collective memory through his contribution as a listener in the oral tradition perpetuates the heritage of his people. Second, his sharing of this heritage by creating an avenue to express oral traditions through the written word increases the tribe. His memories become the reader's memories.

As Momaday studies a picture of Mammedaty, the grandfather who died two years before the author was born, Momaday experiences with full sensory impact the great Sun Dance giveaway in which a young boy joyfully led his black horse into the circle for Mammedaty. The author describes the feel of his own hands upon the horse. In the time-ridden physical universe, this event is an impossibility; in dimensions of the metaphysical universe, it is a reality.

Employing visual symbolism as a catalyst to shifting levels of awareness is a technique crucial to Momaday's potency. Minute detail of landscapes, animal behaviors, characteristics of the aged in a synesthetic presentation of his emotional response evoke like awarenesses in his readers. The genealogy of his family encourages a nurturance in others of their histories.

Directly and succinctly, Momaday reaffirms the timelessness of his universe with the statement, "Notions of the past and future are essentially notions of the present." Similarly, family trees are mirrors rather than extensions of an individual. Momaday then names the idea that he is defining himself, thereby giving physical existence to the process. The subsequent flow of his stream-of-consciousness musings is uninterrupted by punctuation. His paragraphing reflects that the only boundaries he places upon his creation of self are those of ideas.

In the epilogue, Momaday closes the metaphysical circle of his Kiowa identity with his return to the hollow log from which the Kiowa entered this world.

THE BEAR

First published: 1961
Type of work: Poem

Unrecognized by humans out of harmony with nature, the bear is a moral animal in balance with the physical and spiritual world.

"The Bear," winner of the 1962 Academy of American Poets prize, is a five-stanza syllabic poem. Momaday devotes the first two stanzas to the question of the processes employed by humans to distort their visions of the natural world. The remaining three stanzas depict the bear without distortion, as an integral element in the cycle of life.

Humans consciously pervert their perception of the bear because of their unwillingness to face the potential of what they might have been had they opted for nature rather than civilization. One of the defenses humans favor is the misuse of their imagination to create artificial barriers rather than accepting what already exists. A second technique is the fragmentation of their capacity to penetrate directly to the essence so that they can deny it.

In stanza 2, Momaday expresses his incredulity regarding human insensitivity. That anyone could so delude himself as to misperceive the grandeur of the bear, one of nature's most graced, appears to be beyond the parameters of Momaday's belief system. To the author, the aged bear is a warrior, a moral animal with courage and dignity.

The absolute stillness of stanza 3 is a striking poetic device to reinforce the bear's immense power. He dominates without action. Thoughtful and discerning, he does not react. He waits. Mythic healer and destroyer, he simultaneously exists in all times, all dimensions.

The bear's power in the physical world is now limited by age and injury. The consequent imbalance of his spiritual and his bodily potency is symbolic of his imminent return to the Earth Mother. In the final stanza, the bear has magically disappeared, without apparent sound or movement. Nature, in the form of buzzards, shows her respect.

Summary

An award-winning poet, novelist, autobiographer, and scriptwriter, N. Scott Momaday has concentrated his literary attention on that which he holds closest to his heart: the Southwestern landscape and his Native American heritage. The minute detail within his passages on human and nonhuman facets of nature is masterful. His reverence for nature and his insistence that all mankind must recognize its responsibility to heal the physical and spiritual earth is unmistakable. Equally clear is that humans must first balance themselves in relation to their universe. The pioneer in creating a means to share Native American oral tradition accurately through the written word, Momaday is an intermediary whose giveaway is his writing.

Bibliography

Berner, Robert L. "Trying to Be Round: Three American Novels." *World Literature Today* 58 (Summer, 1984): 341-344.

Lincoln, Kenneth. "Tai-me to Rainy Mountain: The Makings of an American Indian Literature." *American Indian Quarterly* 12 (Spring, 1986): 101-117.

Momaday, N. Scott. "A MELUS Interview: N. Scott Momaday—Literature and the Native Writer." Interview by Tom King. *MELUS: The Multi-Ethnic Literature of the United States* 10 (Winter, 1983): 66-72.

_____. "N. Scott Momaday: An Interview." Interview by Joseph Bruchac. *The American Poetry Review* 13 (July/August, 1984): 13-18.

Scarberry-Garcia, Susan. *Landmarks of Healing: A Study of "House Made of Dawn."* Albuquerque: University of New Mexico Press, 1990.

Woodard, Charles L. *Ancestral Voice: Conversations with N. Scott Momaday.* Lincoln: University of Nebraska Press, 1989.

Kathleen Mills

MARIANNE MOORE

Born: Kirkwood, Missouri
November 15, 1887
Died: New York, New York
February 5, 1972

Principal Literary Achievement

Acclaimed as one of the major American poets of the twentieth century, Moore is recognized for her innovations in poetic technique, use of detail, and exploration of paradox.

Biography

Marianne Craig Moore was born in her maternal grandfather's home in Kirkwood, near St. Louis, Missouri, on November 15, 1887. She never knew her father, an engineer and inventor, because earlier that same year he suffered a nervous breakdown and was committed to an institution. Her mother, Mary Warner Moore, and brother John then moved to Kirkwood to live with Marianne's grandfather, the Reverend John Riddle Warner, a Presbyterian minister.

Moore spent her first seven years in an affectionate, close-knit environment. Her grandfather and her mother encouraged serious reading and a tolerant attitude toward diverse religious beliefs. They both believed in the education of women. From her mother, she learned a verbal decorum and precision, but her mother's influence extended much further. Moore never married, and with the exception of her four years in college, she lived with her until her mother's death in 1947.

When her grandfather died in 1894, Mary Moore took the children to Carlisle, Pennsylvania, to live. Her small inheritance was insufficient to support the family, so she took a job as an English teacher at Metzger Institute for Girls, where her daughter began school in 1896. Moore especially remembered an art teacher who encouraged her to draw natural objects. She retained this interest throughout her life, and techniques of the visual arts influenced her poetic style.

Upon graduation in 1905, Moore entered Bryn Mawr College. Her first two years were difficult academically. During this time, she began to write poetry, and in 1907, the Bryn Mawr literary magazine published two poems, "To Come After a Sonnet" and "Under a Patched Sail." They published five more in her last two years of college. In those early poems she used run-on lines and a natural colloquial style, techniques that later became characteristic of her poetry. She said that she felt too

immature to study English, but courses in comparative literature and art history opened her eyes to new developments in Europe in the early 1900's. She majored in biology and histology. Later she commented that the precision, the disinterested logic, and the economy of statement in those laboratory studies enhanced her imagination. When she was graduated in 1909 with an A.B. degree, she was uncertain as to her direction in life and said she would perhaps continue with her early interest in art and become a painter.

After graduation, Moore returned home and, during the next year, took a secretarial course. From 1911 to 1915 she taught business subjects at the United States Industrial Indian School in Carlisle. During these years, she continued to write, contributing ten poems to the Bryn Mawr alumnae magazine.

In 1915, two of her poems, "To the Soul of Military Progress" and "To a Man Working His Way Through a Crowd," appeared in the April issue of the *Egoist*, a London literary magazine that was publishing the Irish writer James Joyce. With that, Moore burst upon the literary scene. During that same year, the *Egoist* published five more poems. Her work also appeared in the New York publication *Others* and in *Poetry*, a Chicago magazine.

The appearance of her work in these magazines coincided with other important events in her life. In 1916, she moved to New Jersey with her mother to keep house for her brother. During their stay in New Jersey, Moore made frequent trips to New York; in 1918, she and her mother moved to an apartment in Greenwich Village, where they lived until 1929. Moore worked briefly as a secretary and as a private teacher, while continuing to write. She also met artists and other writers such as William Carlos Williams and Wallace Stevens, who gathered at parties and frequented museums and galleries. During those years Moore published fewer poems. One, "The Fish" (1918), signaled a turning point in her development. She used the syllabic verse, stanzaic arrangement, and artist-like description that were later known as her unique style. She also wrote her well-known poem, "Poetry," with its opening line, "I, too, dislike it."

At this time in her career her work began to be collected. Her first book, *Poems* (1921), containing twenty-four early pieces, was published without her knowledge by friends in England. In 1924, Moore assembled fifty-three of her own poems in *Observations*. This book received *The Dial* Award, which included $2,000 in prize money. Included were the long poem, "Marriage," "The Octopus," and "Sea Unicorns and Land Unicorns." With this publication, she became an established poet, noted for range and versatility.

From 1921 to 1925, Moore worked as an assistant at a branch of the New York Public Library. In July, 1925, following publication of *Observations*, she became acting editor of *The Dial*. In 1926, she assumed full editorship, a job which she continued until *The Dial* ceased publication in July, 1929. In this capacity, Moore not only edited but also wrote editorials and more than a hundred reviews.

Editing helped her to win recognition, so after the demise of *The Dial*, Moore was able to support herself and her mother by writing poetry, reviews, and essays.

They moved to a larger apartment in Brooklyn. In 1935, friends urged her to bring out *Selected Poems*, which included forty-two poems from *Observations* and nine others. It sold only 864 copies by 1942, but it contained some of her best verse: "The Steeple-Jack," "The Buffalo," and "The Jerboa." It also won the Ernest Hemingway Memorial Prize. In 1936, she published *The Pangolin and Other Verse*. In 1940, she received the Shelley Memorial Award.

Other books followed, many of which included poems published in earlier books. *What Are Years* came out in 1941; *Nevertheless*, which won two prizes, appeared in 1944. In 1945, Moore received a Guggenheim Fellowship and in 1946, a joint grant from the American Academy of Arts and Letters and the National Institute of Arts and Letters. She then began translating seventeenth century French poet Jean de La Fontaine's *Fables*, a project which took eight years to complete.

The final illness and death of her mother in 1947 caused a significant change in Moore's poetry. Her grief for her lifelong companion was intense. *Collected Poems* (1951) was dedicated to her and among the nine new poems was a brief elegy, "By Disposition of Angels." During the following seven years, she spent much of her time working on the fables and writing essays. In 1952, when modern poetry had begun to gain acceptance, she won the prestigious National Book Award, the Pulitzer Prize for Poetry, and the Bollingen Prize. Her translation of La Fontaine's *Fables* came out in 1955. Also in 1955, she published *Predilections*, a group of twenty-two essays and reviews selected from pieces written beginning in 1916.

During the 1950's and 1960's, Moore's zest for learning and her lively responses on a wide range of subjects attracted a certain amount of public interest. Ford Motor Company asked her to suggest names for a new car. She continued to learn dances like the tango, and, famous for loving baseball, she threw out the first ball for opening day at Yankee Stadium in 1968. In 1966, she moved back to Greenwich Village.

In 1967, *Complete Poems of Marianne Moore* appeared. This volume solidified her status as one of America's greatest poets, and in 1968 she received the National Medal for Literature. On February 5, 1972, she died in her sleep in her Greenwich Village apartment at the age of eighty-four.

Analysis

Randall Jarrell, the modern American poet and critic, said that Marianne Moore discovered a new subject and a new structure for poetry. T. S. Eliot, the twentieth century British writer, felt that Moore was one of the few poets who have used the English language inventively. These sentiments are not unusual. Moore is a poet other writers admire. She had her early detractors because of her innovative rhythms and stark imagery. By the 1950's, however, when modernism became more widely accepted, Moore emerged as a major poet alongside William Carlos Williams and Wallace Stevens.

Moore's work has several distinct stylistic qualities and themes. Her main contribution is precise imagery created by a disciplined use of language. Throughout her career, she also dealt with discipline as a theme, advocating a set of values that included courage, independence, responsibility, and simplicity. Moore believed that mankind is besieged by threats to these principles, so must be constantly on guard. In many poems, particularly her later ones, she advocates creating emotional barriers to repel these threats. Throughout her career, Moore explored paradoxical situations, and seeming contradictions underlie many of her poems.

Tracing Moore's poetic career presents difficulties, for, as critic Bonnie Costello notes, her work does not conform to chronological development. Throughout her life, Moore continually revised. Each book she published contained reworked material, so each book includes different styles and themes. For example, her frequently anthologized work "Poetry" (1919), a statement of her belief in the honest and genuine in art, underwent three reworkings. The same holds true for many others. The verse that she wished to preserve appears in *Complete Poems of Marianne Moore*, which conforms as closely as possible to her stylistic and thematic intentions.

Moore's precise style is one of controlled excitement. Her work affects the reader visually as well as emotionally and intellectually. She achieves this by presenting concrete images of ordinary objects. For example, in *The Pangolin and Other Verse*, "The Pangolin" describes a scene near a willow tree where three hungry wide-eyed mockingbirds as big as their mother wait for food. Whatever her subject—fish, jerboa, octopus, nectarine, baseball, art—she gives clusters of precise colorful images, always grounded in particulars. In "The Wood Weasel," the animal is an "inky thing/ adaptively whited with glistening/ goat fur." All Moore's images are visual, because she was interested in design and pattern as well as meaning.

Moore's prosody is also unique. Rather than the regular rhyme and rhythm of a form such as the sonnet, Moore uses syllabic verse. She counts the total syllables in a line and then arranges lines in balanced patterns. For example, in "The Frigate Pelican," the opening line of each stanza has fifteen syllables. This allows her to do a number of things. She is free to use normal prose syntax, and she frequently has the title as the first word in a poem. She can also use the run-on line. She is not under pressure to use masculine rhyme, because the stress can be on syllables other than the rhyming ones. She does rhyme words, but she works with internal correspondences more than end-rhymes.

Moore's basic unit, then, is the stanza rather than the line. She frequently parallels line length stanza by stanza. In "The Jerboa," for example, the third line of the first stanza has the same number of syllables as the third line of the second, third, and following stanzas. She indents to put together lines with end rhymes. This technique results in the stanzas themselves having a regularly controlled visual pattern on the page, one that is usually consistent within each poem. The pattern enhances the visual effect already created by her images. Even though the poems sometimes read like prose, they nevertheless require a dexterous reader. Because she valued restraint and precision, Moore sometimes omitted connections. She used ellipses and juxtapositions, and incorporated allusions, quotes, and other notes into the poetry.

Because Moore's style and subject matter is so precise, some critics classify her with the Imagists of the early twentieth century, who held precision as their watchword and believed that suitable poetic subject matter was whatever the senses experienced. Moore's poetry, however, differs from that of the Imagists. She not only describes things and what surrounds them literally but also merges that detail with what surrounds them imaginatively. Imagination was fundamental to Moore, and the reality she creates by fusing the two is where she finds her ethical principles. In "Apparition of Splendor" the porcupine is partially literal and partially imaginative. Combining these into one animal enables Moore to comment on her theme, order within chaos. Moore therefore takes the Imagists one step further by adding moral and intellectual convictions.

Moore developed certain themes early in her poetic career and continued working with them throughout her life. Mankind, she believed, lives in danger. People's ignorance of the significance of things and events makes them vulnerable. Nature is indifferent to man, so people must be hard and, like the cliff in "The Fish," must be on guard. One must armor oneself like the porcupine in "Apparition of Splendor," must be an "intruder," "insister," and "resister."

One protection is decorum and restraint, disciplines that avoid excesses in all areas of life. "Poetry" makes a strong case for stripping away all extraneous things and getting to what is honest; "The Octopus" reiterates this theme. Delight will arise from espousing values such as honesty, simplicity, and courage. Striving for them requires restraint, but the result, harmony with nature, will be protection in a harsh world.

As her career proceeded, Moore added poems that dealt with other themes, including the belief in a supreme being and the love and spiritual grace that results. "The Pangolin" details qualities of animals, architecture, and man, interrelating the power of grace in all their features. "What Are Years" is perhaps her most direct statement, and it shows that man can maintain the spiritual strength to keep going by being aware of something beyond the mortal. Later in her career, she also wrote poetry for particular occasions. "A Piece for Messr. Alston and Reese" (1956) was dedicated to the Brooklyn Dodgers baseball team; "To a Giraffe" she wrote for a book published in 1963 by the Steuben Glass Company. In this sort of poetry, she continued both her restrained experimental style and her thematic interests.

To speak of Moore's style and themes without mentioning her preoccupation with paradox would omit one of her major concerns. Even "Poetry" seems contradictory, as do such poems as "The Mind Is an Enchanting Thing." The paradoxes inherent in life are not problems to be solved, however: They present situations to be explored for whatever significance they present. Moore's whole career was an exploration of these situations, whether literally or imaginatively experienced. The result is genuine poetry that renews the spirit, making her one of the greatest of the modernists.

THE FISH

First published: 1918
Type of work: Poem

Sources of life contain forces of treachery and death that one must guard against even though one cannot completely understand them.

"The Fish" marked a turning point in Marianne Moore's development. Even though she would later write poems that were as good, critics note that she never excelled in achieving a more perfect integration of images and ideas. She creates precise images of natural things in terms that also denote human characteristics. These build upon one another to express an eternal truth—that all life forces contain death.

Moore always observed natural phenomena, both at first hand and in pictures and photographs. Her early education in art and the natural sciences provided her with a trained eye for details. In "The Fish," this observation results in images—colors, shapes, and textures—so precise that critic William Pratt included the poem in his book, *The Imagist Poems* (1963), the definitive text on the Imagist movement. Like the Imagists, Moore bases the poem on common objects of nature. One fish "wades through black jade" as it moves near the treacherous cliff. The "sun,/ split like spun/ glass," invades every crevice, leaving nothing hidden. It reveals colors—the "turquoise sea/ of bodies" of fish, the "rice-grains" of jellyfish, and crabs like green lilies. Moore also introduces alien images such as "ash-heaps." These, like the verbs "wade" and "split," describe the surroundings, yet they also suggest natural and human forces of destruction.

She organizes these details so that they build to an ending that comments on the ethical significance of her images. In the first section, she describes the aquatic world surrounding the cliff: fish, shells, barnacles, starfish, jellyfish, crabs, and toadstools. Following these images, she moves to a general statement about the nature of this world. "All/ external/ marks of abuse" show on the defiant cliff, all the physical signs of nature trying to destroy it; they show the foreboding presence of death within life. The sea itself, a source of life, also contains powers which threaten. Its creatures exist within it, unconscious of the magnitude of these forces; the cliff remains, a fortress against them. In the last stanza, Moore states the ethical significance of this scene. The cliff, a symbol of defiance and strength, can live on, existing and recording the history of abuses, even feeding upon this harshness.

This paradox, that life and death grow stronger at the same time, is one of Moore's favorite themes; "The Fish" contains some of her most important ideas. The cliff represents an ideal, the capacity of the courageous spirit not only to survive but also to prevail. The ocean, as it batters the cliff, represents the peril of existence that any life form battles, but it also represents the source of all life. The fish and other creatures precariously balance between the two. All these images of life in the sea contain some hint of peril, suggesting nature's impersonal harshness and mysterious purpose. The verbs used in the images suggest man's unwelcome intrusions—also forces of death. Like the cliff, human beings caught in this predicament should not hide, but should face these forces defiantly. In the poem, Moore explores the human predicament, using the scene as a theater to expose ideas that are harder to clarify in a human context.

Her poetic techniques complement her ideas. The line breaks and stanzaic arrangements combine to keep the reader from scanning through too fast. It is a laborious, not an easy, movement, as is the interaction of the water and the cliff. Each stanza follows the same pattern. Each parallel line has the same syllabic count. The rhyme scheme is elaborate, but because of the run-on lines, it does not intrude. Moore also relies on the sounds to carry the meaning, quick consonants such as "crow-blue mussel-shells," rather than alliteration. She liked strict proportion and symmetry, so in each line and each stanza, she balances the key words.

This emphasis on pattern and stability in style further shows the precise integration of image and idea. The cliff is stable against constantly threatening forces; the poem itself has a strong formal arrangement. In "The Fish," Moore attempts to make sense out of the eternal problem of maintaining a resilient spirit in a world that nourishes, yet also threatens at every turn. It is a theme with which she grappled her whole life, sometimes retreating to a position of hiding. Here, the ethical situation is clearly laid out imagistically. Like the cliff, man has no place to hide.

POETRY

First published: 1919
Type of work: Poem

A poet must present an object for itself but must also enhance it by imagination so that the poem illuminates a universal truth.

"Poetry," a poem Marianne Moore reworked several times, states her aesthetic beliefs. She published the first version in 1919, but in 1925 she stripped it from thirty lines to thirteen to comply with her principles of clarity and precision. In the *Selected Poems* of 1935, she returned it to the original. Then, in 1967, after she repudiated the syllabic verse she used in much of her poetry, she reduced it to the three lines that appear in the *Complete Poems of Marianne Moore* published that same year. (The original version appears in the "Notes" of that book.)

The poem is best known for the shocking first line in which Moore states that she dislikes poetry. The remaining two lines of the 1967 version present some problems because she does not exemplify the word "genuine" after stating that there is "a place for the genuine" in poetry. In the original version, however, Moore illustrates precisely what poetry she repudiates and what poetry she admires.

Moore dislikes poetry that she calls "fiddle"—poetry written about stereotypical poetic subjects such as nature in high-sounding tones. These become so abstract that they cannot be understood. Poets who write this way, the "half-poets," take standard opinions as truth, then embroider them with pretty or overly intellectual language. The result is that truth, the "genuine," if it is there at all, becomes obscure.

What she admires and what she attempts in her own poems is, first, the presentation of objects for themselves. Things, such as hands, eyes, and hair are honest subjects because they are useful things. She also develops images of things such as elephants pushing, horses rolling, and baseball fans cheering. Readers understand these subjects because they have experienced them. She renders her subjects accurately and precisely, and then enhances them with the poetic imagination. The imagination rearranges the details, giving an aesthetic order so that the universal truths can emerge. Where the imaginative concept and the object rendered coincide lies pure realism of ideas.

If the rendering is precise and the imagination alive, readers will comprehend the truths and admire the poem because they understand it. A poet who writes this way is a "literalist of the imagination," a phrase Moore borrowed from the Irish poet William Butler Yeats. This poet will rise above trivial things to present true poetry, "imaginary gardens with real toads in them." Only those demanding raw material such as toads will even aspire to real poetry; only those with imagination will transform this raw material into truth.

This longer version follows Moore's common pattern. After the blunt opening, "I, too, dislike it," the beginning is casual in pace. To illustrate the abstract topic, she details specific images of people and nature. The poem reaches a climax in the next-to-last sentence. She ends off-handedly with a direct comment to summarize: If readers will not settle for less than the process she describes, then they are interested in real poetry.

Moore sets high standards, ones that she herself constantly sought through the revision process. Considering her emphasis on precise rendering of raw material before the poet synthesizes it by imagination, it is perhaps surprising that she so trimmed "Poetry" for the 1967 collection.

THE JERBOA

First published: 1932
Type of work: Poem

In art as in life, the simple and natural things are virtuous; the extravagant and artificial are dangerous.

"The Jerboa" is a poem in two sections. In the first, Moore weaves together references to Egyptian art and the animals kept by Egypt's royal courts. In the second, she juxtaposes those articles of opulent living with the jerboa, a tiny desert rat who uses natural powers of survival. These contrasting images illustrate one of her favorite themes: the value of the natural unity of form and function over the tendency of human cultures to perfect, transform, or possess nature, both in art and in life.

The opening stanza of the first section, "Too Much," contains the word "contrive," indicating that what follows will be unfavorable. Moore's images describe a picture of wasteful and artificial luxury. An ancient Roman fashions an indeterminate shape, a "pine cone/ or fir-cone," to serve as a fountain. Since Moore values precision, this indicates the first serious fault. This piece "passed for art" since it looked like something the ancient Egyptians would have liked for their courts.

The remaining fifteen stanzas describe the excesses of wealth, waste, and artificiality of the Egyptian pharaohs. They exploited animals by making them into possessions. They kept crocodiles and put baboons on the necks of giraffes to pick fruit. They bred "dog-cats," unnatural creatures to chase other small animals. They viewed all nature as theirs: impalas, ostriches, cranes, and geese. They liked "small things" and made playthings of nests of eggs and carved bone. These people destroyed the grace and form of nature by parodying it, by elevating some animals to the status of gods and degrading others.

Meanwhile, they were insensitive to human life. Slaves built colossi, dying in the process. Drought plagued the poor. Amid famine and death, the court kept dwarfs to make life a "fantasy." The whole environment, in fact, perverted what life should be. In games, they continued this masquerade by having men and women dress as each other. The pharaoh himself was the height of this fakeness, for he "gave his name" to images of serpents and beetles and was also named for them. He was no different than the other lifeless parodies.

The last three stanzas in "Too Much" are transitional. They introduce the pharaoh's mongoose, kept to kill snakes used in court rituals and games. This mongoose is restless under the restraint of its artificial existence. Unlike this animal, the jerboa has rest and joy in its desert home, "a shining silver house/ of sand" that lacks the artificial comforts of the court. Moore's meaning is clear: The life of the jerboa is preferable.

The second section, "Abundance," begins with a reference to Africanus, the native blacks who live like the jerboa when they are untouched by men motivated by greed and pride. Nine stanzas detailing the life of the jerboa follow. Moore does not moralize, but presents exhilarating images of an animal living harmoniously with its surroundings. Its color blends perfectly with the desert surroundings; it runs in a fashion that is musical. The jerboa approaches true artistry of simplicity and harmony.

Moore's poetic style enhances this theme. In the first section, the pace is slower, as though she wanted to make sure that the scorn in her lines is clear. The metrics of the second section are the same as the first—the same number of syllables in parallel lines, the same number of lines in stanzas, the same rhyme scheme. It moves faster, however; the imagery drawn from music and nature creates a lighter, more flowing effect. This contributes to the celebratory tone praising the animal that lives best because it lives in true harmony and true abundance rather than in artificial plenty.

In this poem as in many others, Moore puts forth her value system by celebrating this uncomplicated life of an animal. Survival in the world depends on honesty in function and behavior, simplicity, modesty, and courage. Threats are ever-present, but the jerboa survives because it is fast, resourceful, and self-reliant; it is an ideal creature.

Human culture cannot realize this perfect condition, and Moore is aware of the paradoxical situation of the poet. In writing the poem, she, too, has transformed the world to suit her purposes. What saves the poet from the same fate as the Egyptians is that she acknowledges that her comparisons are purely imaginary, having no power or authority. Instead, they allow the mind to imagine and pursue its own needs.

THE MIND IS AN ENCHANTING THING

First published: 1944
Type of work: Poem

The mind, a miracle of complexity and inconsistency, possesses the power to enchant and be enchanted at the same time.

"The Mind Is an Enchanting Thing" appeared in the 1944 publication of *Nevertheless*. Both technically and thematically it is a central poem in Marianne Moore's work. In it, she uses intricate syllabic verse and stanzaic arrangements. Through a series of similes and metaphors, she alternates between details and generalities, integrating the two in the last line. The poems deals with a complex paradox: The mind is both subject and object, both enchanter and enchanted. It has the power to dissolve unities into multiplicities and also to synthesize those different facets into new unities. It has the power to transform dejection into joy, death into life. Moore is celebrating the miracle of the poetic process.

She introduces the paradox at the beginning by changing a single syllable; the "enchanting" of the title becomes "enchanted" in the first line. A series of similes follows, each focusing on the contradiction inherent in being both subject and object. Having established the paradox, Moore uses an animal, the kiwi, to lead to the central part of the poem, the concept of the mind that "walks along with its eyes on the ground." Kiwi is the name New Zealand natives give to the apteryx, a flightless bird with a long beak that walks looking downward. It, too, is a paradox. It is a bird but does not fly. The mind is like the kiwi—it focuses intently, but it also "has memory's ear." It is in touch with the history it has stored, and in that sense, it can fly anywhere.

The sequence of similes that follows describes strange phenomena that bring this contradiction to life: "Like the gyroscope's fall," and "like the dove-/ neck animated by/ sun." Forces of the universe move the gyroscope. Like the mind, it possesses those memories. The last line of the fourth stanza sums up these images: "It's conscientious inconsistency." Things are fixed and not fixed at the same time, just like the mind.

The concluding lines deal with the outcome of being a "conscientious inconsistency." The mind "tears off the veil" that the heart wears. Like the veil that separated the holy from the truly elect in the temple at Jerusalem, the veil the heart wears gets in the way of understanding. The veil represents certainty and, for Moore, the opposite of insight, so this process of liberating the heart to pursue truth is as important as the truth itself. The mind is also flexible. It resembles "unconfusion [that] submits/ its confusion to proof." Unlike King Herod, who refused to change his oath, the mind has nothing to do with death. Instead, the mind sustains life by its power to change sensation into understanding, to abstract from multiple detail by listening to inward as well as outward surroundings. The mind possesses all these powers and can delight itself even in a dull world; it perceives the unusual amidst the ordinary. As long as it has these qualities, poetry is possible.

Moore enhances this theme by giving the poem a songlike quality. Changing "enchanting" to "enchanted" sets a rhythm. Throughout the poem, the hard consonants and rhyme scheme suggest a musical composition. Her reference to composer Domenico Scarlatti in the opening stanza reinforces this. Music liberates the spirit, but it is a controlled technical medium. Her prose technique, regular syllables per line and a precise stanzaic pattern, is also tightly controlled, yet Moore employs it to express a liberating idea.

Moore valued simplicity, but she attacked complex issues. The mind is worthy of celebration if it has faculties beyond simply perceiving stored memories. It can perceive hidden truths; it is not a weak, unchanging faculty, but grows as life unfolds. It accepts the inevitable confusion of experience. Its connection with the spirit enables it to create poetry.

IN THE PUBLIC GARDEN

First published: 1958
Type of work: Poem

Art has a public function, but the artist needs to retain a freedom of expression that exists in an absence of public demands.

Marianne Moore wrote "In the Public Garden" for the 1958 Boston Arts Festival, where she read the poem to an audience of five thousand people. In it, she considers art both in its public function and as an expression of individuality. To emphasize the importance of artistic freedom, she arranges her ideas in a series of paradoxes.

The first stanza introduces the duality. The festival "for all" takes place near Harvard University, which has made "education individual." Moore considers one individual, an "almost scriptural" taxicab driver who drove her to Cambridge. He wisely remarks: "They/ make some fine young men at Harvard." This comment suggests the beauties of the landscape, but Moore disrupts the reader's expectation by going backward from summer to spring to winter. She notes the weathervane with gold ball glittering atop Boston's Faneuil Hall in summer. Spring brings pear blossoms, pin-oak leaves, and iris. Winter, instead of death or hibernation, exhibits snowdrops "that smell like/ violets."

Moore next moves inside King's Chapel to contemplate gratitude. She quotes a traditional Southern hymn about work as praise of God. A chapel and a festival are alike; they both involve an exchange. The festival-goer expects to get art or inspiration in exchange for pay or attention. Instead, Moore cites some unexpected givings: black sturgeon eggs, a camel, and, even more unusual, silence. Silence is as precious as freedom. This comment leads to another unexpected statement, that freedom is for "self-discipline." In the next lines, Moore explores this paradox. She cites a quote from President Dwight Eisenhower, who remarked that schools are for the "freedom to toil." She mentions the determination of inmates to gain their freedom by selling medicinal herbs, a strategy that would backfire if they themselves became ill.

At this point, Moore interrupts to return to the occasion at which she is speaking. She is grateful because the audience is there "to wish poetry well" by the fact of their attendance. She is grateful for religious, intellectual, and artistic freedom. She ends with that sentiment, now capitalizing "Art." Even though it is "admired in general," Art is "always actually personal." This is the exchange mentioned earlier. The artist, in exchange for the self-discipline that comprises freedom, gets in return silence, the absence of restraints. The public enjoys the freedom to hear the highly personal voice of the artist.

This poem typifies some of Moore's later works. She addresses the occasion, but she also continues to explore personal themes. The paradox of freedom as discipline is a central concern. She also refines stylistic devices. The syllabic verse is less exacting in the number of syllables per line than in her earlier poetry. She uses run-on lines but varies the regular five-line stanza by interjecting a three-line stanza at the point she addresses the occasion directly. Moore also employs an interesting rhyming device. She uses forty variations on a single rhyme, the "-al" found in "personal" and "festival." Perhaps she meant to suggest a pealing of bells appropriate to a celebration of artistic freedom. In varying her expected style to explore the truth of the paradox, she illustrates concretely what she came to Boston to say.

Summary

In keeping with the principle of restraint that she espoused throughout her career, Marianne Moore did not presume to have any extraordinary vision; critics and fellow poets have disagreed. James Dickey, the American poet and Moore's contemporary, believes that her poetry reached new conclusions. She accomplished this by weaving together particulars that people see but do not understand. To Dickey, her poetry presented moments of perception to renew the spirit.

Moore explored the nature of paradox. She insisted on strong values; determination and independence permeate all of her poems. She practiced the restraint that enables strong values to develop, devising new forms of poetic technique and constantly reworking to pare down to the simple yet elegant image and line.

Bibliography

Costello, Bonnie. *Marianne Moore: Imaginary Possessions.* Cambridge, Mass.: Harvard University Press, 1981.

Engel, Bernard F. *Marianne Moore.* New Haven, Conn.: Twayne, 1964.

Garrigue, Jean. *Marianne Moore.* Minneapolis: University of Minnesota Press, 1965.

Hadas, Pamela. *Marianne Moore: Poet of Affection.* Syracuse, N.Y.: Syracuse University Press, 1977.

Stapleton, Laurence. *Marianne Moore: The Poet's Advance.* Princeton, N.J.: Princeton University Press, 1978.

Tomlinson, Charles, ed. *Marianne Moore: A Collection of Critical Essays.* Englewood Cliffs, N.J.: Prentice-Hall, 1969.

Willis, Patricia. *Marianne Moore: Vision into Verse.* Philadelphia: Rosenbach Museum and Library, 1987.

Louise Stone

WRIGHT MORRIS

Born: Central City, Nebraska
January 6, 1910

Principal Literary Achievement
Morris' fiction, essays, and photographs convey his ideas about the human
imagination as they depict the inhabitants of the Midwest.

Biography

Wright Morris was born in Central City, Nebraska, on January 6, 1910, the son of
William Henry and Grace Osborn Morris. Morris' mother, the daughter of a Seventh-
Day Adventist preacher, was born on a farm near the south shore of the Platte River.
Six days after Wright's birth, she died, leaving an emotional scar that would in one
way or another shape the direction of all of his fiction. Since Morris never knew his
mother, she becomes a nebulous figure in his writings, often made conspicuous by
her absence and frequently suggested by way of contrast with the many shallow, distant, and largely dysfunctional motherly types who people his novels.

William Morris had come to Nebraska from Ohio, lured west to work as a station
agent for the Union Pacific railroad. The "jovial good-natured" man to whom Morris refers in his memoirs was also something of a speculator, never sticking with one
job for long. Shortly after Grace's death, Will was remarried, to a young woman
named Gertrude, left his position with the railroad, and took up chicken farming in
an attempt to make a fortune supplying the railroad with day-old eggs. The enterprise failed when Morris' father lost his entire stock of pullets to a fatal disease.
This episode appears, thinly disguised as fiction, in *The Works of Love* (1952).

In 1919, Morris moved with his father to Omaha. William's fortunes continued
to be bad, eventually leading Gertrude to abandon him and nine-year-old Wright,
who by now was spending most of his time with the Mulligans, a foster family. In
1924, Morris and his father moved on to Chicago. Forced to live without much help
from his father, who was struggling to find steady work, Morris learned rugged self-
reliance the hard way, by supporting himself doing odd jobs and working at the local
YMCA.

In 1926, in response to his father's need for a "new start," Morris made the first
of several unsuccessful trips to and from California in search of better prospects.
After returning to Chicago, Morris, though faced with virtually no home life, somehow managed to graduate from high school. In 1930, he enrolled in Pomona College

in Claremont, California. In 1933, however, he left Pomona after deciding to spend some time traveling in Europe. After a soul-searching, adventurous year spent wandering in France, Italy, and Austria, Morris returned to the United States in 1934, convinced of his calling to become a writer.

By 1934, Morris had also married his first wife, Mary Ellen Finfrock, a teacher and native of Cleveland. As early as 1936, Morris had begun to take photographs, which would later be published in his "photo-text" volumes, *The Inhabitants* (1946), *The Home Place* (1948), and *God's Country and My People* (1968). During the winter of 1941, while living in Los Angeles, Morris wrote his first novel, *My Uncle Dudley* (1942), a picaresque tale giving fictive form to Morris' many travels in the United States. During the 1940's, Morris received the first two of his three Guggenheim Fellowships, allowing him to complete *The Inhabitants* and *The Home Place*. In addition to the two photo-texts and *My Uncle Dudley*, Morris found time to publish two other novels, *The Man Who Was There* (1945) and *The World in the Attic* (1949).

From 1944 to 1958, Morris lived in suburban Philadelphia, experiencing his most productive period and publishing some of his best work. The urban experience provided the impetus for *Man and Boy* (1951) and *The Deep Sleep* (1953). While in Philadelphia, Morris also became a neighbor and close friend to another Nebraskan, Loren Eiseley, the distinguished anthropologist, naturalist, and author of such books as *The Immense Journey* (1957), *The Firmament of Time* (1960), and *The Innocent Assassins* (1973). Eiseley's influence proved to be profound, and he helped Morris formulate aesthetic notions about man and nature—how human consciousness and intellectual growth depend on the ability to come to grips with one's past and the inevitable passage of time, a ubiquitous theme in much of Morris' fiction.

During the 1950's, Morris published *The Works of Love* (1952), a book that contains his quintessential statement not only about his father but also of the playing out of the American Dream of success on the Great Plains; *The Huge Season* (1954), a fictional account of his days at Pomona College; *The Field of Vision* (1956), a book that won the National Book Award; *Love Among the Cannibals* (1957), his most complete confrontation with the quotidian present; and *The Territory Ahead* (1958), an ambitious collection of essays on the major figures in American literature.

Morris ushered in the 1960's with the publication of what many feel to be his most sophisticated novel, *Ceremony in Lone Tree* (1960), a multivoiced narrative about how time, place, and perspective shape the American experience. In 1961, he divorced Mary Ellen and married Josephine Kantor, a Los Angeles art collector and dealer. In 1962, he published *What a Way to Go*, his first major novel about Europe, and began teaching creative writing at San Francisco State University, where he remained until he retired in 1975. In 1963, Morris released *Cause for Wonder*, another novel set in Europe; in 1965, *One Day*, a book about the effects of the Kennedy assassination on a small California town; in 1967, *In Orbit*, a book about violence and crime in America's heartland; and in 1968, *A Bill of Rites, A Bill of Wrongs, A Bill of Goods*, a collection of social criticism and witty commentary about the contemporary scene.

During the 1970's and 1980's, Morris continued his impressive production of fine fiction and critical essays by publishing *Fire Sermon* (1971), *War Games* (1972), *A Life* (1973), and *About Fiction: Reverent Reflections on the Nature of Fiction with Irreverent Observations on Writers, Readers, and Other Abuses* (1975). After a brief stint in 1976 as novelist-in-residence at the University of Nebraska, Morris completed *The Fork River Space Project* in 1977 and went on to write *Plains Song: For Female Voices* (1980), a novel that earned for Morris the American Book Award for Fiction in 1981.

Since 1981, Morris has been intent on publishing his memoirs. Starting with *Will's Boy*, a story of Morris' childhood, he has progressively traced his maturation as a writer through successive autobiographical writings such as *Solo* (1983), a recapturing of his 1933-1934 *wanderjahre* in Europe, and *A Cloak of Light* (1985), a memoir that covers the writer's middle years and ends with his second marriage (to Josephine).

Analysis

In his long and productive literary career, Wright Morris' fictional practice has remained consistent with the theoretical concerns he expresses in his essays and interviews. Morris is one of the few contemporary writers to combine the roles of novelist and literary critic, roles which frequently tend to diverge among twentieth century writers. His books on literature—*The Territory Ahead*; *A Bill of Rites, A Bill of Wrongs, A Bill of Goods*; *About Fiction*; and *Earthly Delights, Unearthly Adornments* (1978)—are perceptive studies that reveal many of his literary origins and aims. His novels, which are in many ways extensions of his theory, testify to Morris' unwavering belief in technique as an indispensable tool of the successful writer.

Although Morris' critical comments about fiction tend to be understated and somewhat implicit, they do suggest his profound interest in a number of artistic concerns. Foremost among these concerns are the nature and role of the artist, the writer's way of handling his material, the writer's relationship to literary tradition, the value of realism as a literary approach, and the importance of technique.

The best working definition Morris provides of the artist's role is found in this statement from *The Territory Ahead*:

> Life, raw life, the kind we lead every day . . . has the curious property of not seeming real *enough*. We have a need, however illusive, for a life that is more real than life. It lies in the imagination. Fiction would seem to be the way it is processed into reality. If this were not so we should have little excuse for art. Life, raw life, would be more than satisfactory in itself. But it seems to be the nature of man to transform—himself, if possible, and then the world around him—and the technique of this transformation is what we call art.

The passage introduces two key terms in Morris' theory—"transformation" and "reality." Generally speaking, Morris uses transformation to signify the process through which unformed events, emotions, and memories—the writer's raw materials—are shaped into structured experience by the artist's imagination. The writer's role is thus to articulate experience and through such articulation build a form of reality that transcends the common plane of ordinary experience, resulting in the permanent capturing of transitory experience and feeling in the form of a work of art.

One of the reasons Morris makes such strong claims for the imagination is that he senses that the reservoir of raw material is dwindling. The workings of art, geographic expansion, and the mass media have all contributed to the exhaustion of untouched, virgin experience that fueled many early American writers. In creating material in the contemporary age, Morris senses that many American artists too often have been guilty of misplacing artistic energy. To compensate for a dwindling supply of experience, too many writers have escaped into nostalgia to supply themselves with raw material missing from their own experience. For Morris, the results of any sort of sentimental overindulgence in the past produces cliché, not art. Thus, all of his fiction represents a concerted effort to gain control over his material and to escape nostalgia by avoiding frozen and worn-out patterns of expression and behavior.

This is not to suggest that Morris completely eschews literary tradition. In his view, tradition functions to prevent disorder and the pursuit of novelty for its own sake. He has noted that an exclusive concern with newness often fails to produce the kind of art from which subsequent writers can learn. He feels that the new artist must transmute his literary inheritance through technique and imagination so that what is of value is preserved and what is exhausted is not.

Even though Morris believes that literature should be in some sense representational, he is critical of some of the contemporary by-products of the drive toward realism. To Morris, a definition of realism means more than a mere photographic rendering of the facts using the language of the vernacular. In his opinion, the successful writing of fiction requires that language be questioned, fashioned, and run through the processes of the imagination. Reality is never attained in art without being filtered through some subjective vision. As the critic G. B. Crump explains, "For Morris, the sense of life is indispensable in fiction, but it is not something that is given in the artist's materials, the automatic product of fidelity to the facts; it is achieved through his style, not through elimination of style."

Morris said in *About Fiction* that the writer's major task is to "make of this life what it failed to make of itself." To do so requires that the artist not only resist cliché, nostalgia, and vulgarity, but also that he or she stand squarely in the present and face it for what it is, a place where Morris, quoting D. H. Lawrence in *The Territory Ahead*, says there is "no perfection, no consummation, nothing finished." In such a world, Morris senses that the value of fiction is that it is perhaps the only means available for humanity to lend a sense of finish to the unfinished business of life. Morris firmly believes that a talented imagination can reveal the richness in almost any material. It is not essential that writers use a conspicuous style or parade their knowledge by making their works imitations of other novels. If a writer has talent and can realize his or her vision, the revelatory act will give fiction a sense of life and design on its own.

THE INHABITANTS

First published: 1946
Type of work: Prose with photographs

Through the combination of photographs and prose, Morris conceives an original vision of America's mythic past.

The Inhabitants, the first of Morris' volumes to combine photographs and prose, grew out of his preoccupation with the past. During the 1930's and 1940's, Morris began writing fiction using simple, compact visual cues to create "still" word pictures. After composing a number of such pictures, he concluded that he might actually photograph what he was describing in order more effectively to capture concrete detail and visible reality. What he was after was the look and feel of a specific time and place. To produce the look, he selected telling photographs from the many he had taken on his travels across the United States. For the feel, he used words. What resulted when Morris imaginatively synthesized his photographs and prose was the most experimental and innovative of Morris' four "photo-texts."

Technically, *The Inhabitants*, through its imaginative fusion of various points of view, anticipates many of the narrative devices Morris later employed in his multivoiced fictions of the 1950's and 1960's. As the critic Alan Trachtenberg points out in his 1962 essay, "The Craft of Vision," the book has a triangular structure that blends three separate strands: two narrative voices and the photographs. Each two-page spread has a monologue that announces the theme or argument of the book and occasionally meditates on the question of what an inhabitant is; a second voice—sometimes third person, sometimes first, sometimes dialogue—provides a vernacular translation that narrates a particular example of what or who it is that "inhabits." Finally, the photographs provide the visual ambience or "look" of the artifacts or land depicted. The monologue maintains the continuity of the book by relating the many individual speakers to the whole and by reminding readers of the many divergent elements, as evidenced in the second voice, that represent the United States.

Essentially, Morris uses words to add another dimension to the visual cues provided by the pictures. In *The Inhabitants*, one of his intentions was to move his audience beyond the clichés of hard times, ruin, and alienation, commonplace in the photography of the Depression, into new recognitions spawned by variform perspectives on ordinary objects, artifacts, and environments. The words help overcome that problem by revealing the nature of the object or artifact.

Beyond the reading Morris gives to the photographs, however, exists another autonomous realm. The presence of the photographs authenticates the "thing itself" as an independent entity or essence that speaks using its own voice. Morris once referred to the houses, buildings, and artifacts he photographed as "secular icons" having a "holy meaning to give out." As such, the "thing" that Morris frames in his viewfinder has a metaphysical presence that goes beyond the mundane or superficial. Thus, Morris' photographs are usually concerned with significant abstract presentations, while his words are more concerned with personal interpretations.

When the photographs are coupled with textual voices, a balanced three-dimensional image emerges that represents a harmonious blend of reality and fiction. In *The Inhabitants*, authentication of time and place rapidly fading from sight shares equal status with imaginative presentation and textual revelation. Ultimately, the photograph gives, as Morris says in *Photographs and Words*, an incomparable registry of "what is going, going, but not yet gone."

THE HUGE SEASON

First published: 1954
Type of work: Novel

Caught in the mundane present world of the 1950's, the protagonist, Peter Foley, finally faces and overcomes his obsession with the past.

The Huge Season is closely related to Morris' other novels in that it reflects one of his common themes: the hold of the past over the present. Where this book breaks fresh ground, however, is in its employment of raw material. It differs in that it is the first, and fullest, treatment that Morris gives to his experiences in college. Moreover, this is the first novel in which Morris shows a protagonist, Peter Foley, who actually escapes from the crippling forces of nostalgia and the mythic past.

In *The Huge Season*, the past is the 1920's, an artistically heroic age that produced such great writers as Ernest Hemingway, F. Scott Fitzgerald, and William Faulkner. When compared with the dull, seemingly unheroic 1950's, the past becomes magnified; in the minds of the main characters in the book—Montana Lou Baker, Jesse Proctor, Lundgren, and even Foley himself—it assumes blighting significance. All are in a sense captive to it and cannot free themselves from its compelling forces.

The central focus of the novel is one Charles Gans Lawrence, a tennis player and dormitory mate of Foley who, like Jay Gatsby in F. Scott Fitzgerald's *The Great Gatsby* (1925), has everything—money, good looks, and athletic ability. Lawrence, like Gatsby, proves to be psychologically dazzling. Exhibiting a tough, unpredictable compulsiveness, Lawrence fascinates his friends by performing audacious deeds. He first astounds them by becoming a superlative tennis player, despite the fact that he has one arm that is practically useless. Later, near the end of his sophomore year, Lawrence pulls another surprise by abruptly leaving college, apparently bored by it all, and going to Spain to become a bullfighter. Then, after being badly gored, he commits suicide, perhaps out of despair, perhaps to impress his friends, and he leaves what proves to be an indelible stamp on their imaginations.

The tension that Morris develops in the novel between past and present is filtered through the viewpoint of Foley, whose memory operates on two discreet levels. The present-day action, entitled "Foley," is a third-person narrative that follows the events of a single day in which Jesse Proctor, an old friend of Foley, had testified before the Senate Committee on Un-American Activities. Foley travels to New York City, ostensibly intending to visit Proctor and Baker. In the process, however, he spends much of his time ruminating about the effects of his twenty-three-year mental captivity, dating from May 5, 1929, when Lawrence shot himself.

The past action of the 1920's is cast in a series of episodes contained in "The Captivity" sections. Written in the first person, it represents Foley's unfinished book manuscript about Lawrence. From a functional standpoint, the historical "Captivity" chapters chronicle actual historical events, while the "Foley" sections represent an attempt to find meaning in those events. In the end, they come together when Foley realizes that his captivity has been lifelong and that he has at last escaped from the pull of the past.

What causes this recognition is hinted at in an epiphanal moment that Foley experiences near the end of the book. Summing up the heroics of his generation, Foley asks himself:

> Did they lack conviction? No. . . . What they lacked was intention. They could shoot off guns, . . . jump from upper-floor windows, . . . or take sleeping pills to quiet the bloody cries of the interior. But they would not carry this war to the enemy. That led to action, action to evil, . . . and to the temporal kingdom rather than the eternal heavenly one. That led, in short, where they had no intention of ending up. The world of men here below. The God-awful mess men had made of it.

What Foley eventually recognizes is that life enhancement requires intention, which throughout the book Morris allies with conception, or the ability to make constructive use of the past. Survival in the present requires that one face facts, be they disconcerting or no, and try to put them to positive use. By the end Foley does so, and it grants him his emancipation.

THE FIELD OF VISION

First published: 1956
Type of work: Novel

On vacation in Mexico, five characters come to imaginative terms with their lives.

The Field of Vision, like *The Huge Season* and *The Inhabitants*, reflects Morris' struggle with the past. In this book, however, he is less concerned with how one escapes the past than he is with how one confronts and conceptualizes it. One of the most sophisticated and intricate of Morris' novels, *The Field of Vision* employs multiple perspectives to capture, group, and explore scattered fragments of the lives of five Americans.

What Morris reveals through the primary voices in the novel is largely a vision of failure. Virtually all the main characters are unable or unwilling to make constructive use of the past in order to cope effectively with everyday events. McKee, for example, prides himself in his common sense and adopts a conservative response to life; however, because he is unable to see beyond the superficial, he responds to the disconcerting present by retreating into the conventionality of middle-class values. Lois, McKee's wife, is conventional as well, marrying McKee because marriage provided an accepted pattern of behavior that protected her from her subverted darker desires. The McKees share material success—a big house and money—but no love. Both have rejected sex, and Lois remains, "stiffly laced into her corset of character." Scanlon, Lois's father, sees virtually nothing in the present. During the bullfight, he spends most of his time reminiscing about a wagon train that languished from thirst as it crossed Death Valley. An eighty-seven-year-old former plainsman, he saw the turn of the century but failed to turn with it, choosing to live his life isolated in a small Nebraska town. Gordon Boyd, an influential boyhood friend of McKee who once stole Ty Cobb's pocket and was the first to kiss Lois, was something of an audacious hero in his youth. Now, however, he is unemployed, and his outlandish antics hold more entertainment value than heroic inspiration. Finally, Dr. Lehmann, a psychiatrist whom Morris employs as a commentator on the characters' lives, sports a fake German accent and is more eccentric than the odd patients he treats.

To give structure to the central perspectives, Morris cast *The Field of Vision* in terms of a spectator's reaction to a bullfight and used the circle as the unifying device. The arena, a circular sandpit, is the central focus which elicits individual responses to the experience shared by the five main characters. The present events in the novel are brief, however, and are nearly inconsequential when compared to the past to which the characters repeatedly refer. The narrative technique is circular as well, it shifts from character to character, in round-robin fashion, according to the point of view presented.

One of the keys to interpreting *The Field of Vision* is found on the flyleaf to the first edition, on which Morris said that the book grew from the belief that the "imaginative act is man himself." Such a notion is reinforced in the book's epigraph, taken from John Milton: "The mind is its own place, and in itself/ Can make a Heav'n of Hell, a Hell of Heav'n." What Morris suggests is that reality, because it is evanescent and subjective, can best be captured by the inside workings of the human mind. Thus, each individual—for better or for worse—uses the imagination to give pattern and meaning to life.

CEREMONY IN LONE TREE

First published: 1960
Type of work: Novel

Lone Tree, an abandoned Nebraska town, becomes the unlikely setting for a ceremony in honor of Tom Scanlon's ninetieth birthday.

Ceremony in Lone Tree is a continuation of the story begun in *The Field of Vision*. Once again, Morris uses many of the same characters he employed in the previous novel: Tom Scanlon, the man who lives his life in the past; McKee, the embodiment of middle-class conventionality; McKee's wife Lois, a woman encased in her inhibitions; their grandson Gordon, the "infant Davy Crocket"; and Boyd, the "self-unmade man." This time, however, the scene is different. Instead of using Mexico, Morris employs the ghost town of Lone Tree as a setting. To the five familiar faces he used in *The Field of Vision*, Morris adds Maxine Momeyer, Scanlon's second daughter, her husband Bud, and daughter Etoile, who looks like a young Lois but has none of her inhibitions. The Momeyers have a nephew named Lee Roy, who uses his car to kill two taunting classmates and who shares local headlines with Charlie Munger, a murderer who slays ten innocent victims. In addition, Morris introduces Scanlon's third daughter Edna, Edna's blustery husband Clyde, little Gordon's inarticulate older brother Calvin, Calvin's outspoken mother Eileen, a character called "Daughter" (whom Boyd picks up in a restaurant in Nevada), and an unsuccessful writer of Westerns named Jennings.

By adding to the cast of characters and changing the setting, Morris is able to refine the vision of failure he introduced in *The Field of Vision*. Although *Ceremony in Lone Tree* has a number of comic moments—such as when Bud stalks and kills "Colonel" Ewing's expensive bull pup—and shares many of the same concerns with coming to grips with the past as were voiced in *The Field of Vision*, it digs deeper into the psychic center of its characters' patterns of behavior. In *Ceremony in Lone Tree*, for example, man is portrayed as falling prey not only to nostalgia but also to dark impulses of violence and self-destruction.

In *Ceremony in Lone Tree*, Lee Roy and Charlie embody the extreme expression of such violent human impulses. By killing at random and without discretion, both express the irrational side of human nature and amplify a primitive impulse that the other characters subvert. For the McKees, Momeyers, and Ewings, this dark impulse is also the new dimension of the present and is a force to which they must awaken. Unfortunately, they do not, and choose to retreat, as in *The Field of Vision*, into the superficial.

Symbolically, Morris gives shape to this theme of destruction through the image of the atomic bomb:

The past, whether one liked it or not, was all that one actually possessed. . . . The present was that moment of exchange—when all might be lost. Why risk it? Why not sleep on the money in the bank? . . . There was this flash, then the pillar of fire . . . and the heat and the light of that moment illuminated for a fraction the flesh and bones of the present. Did these bones live? At that moment they did. The meeting point, the melting point of the past confronting the present. . . . [W]here it failed to ignite the present, it was dead.

This suggests precisely where the McKees, Momeyers, and, by implication, most Americans fail. For the most part, the past to which these characters subscribe is insubstantial and does very little to explain or illuminate uncomfortable present realities such as violence and the threat of nuclear destruction. To "live" requires constructive use of the past to combat the destructive elements of the present.

THE FORK RIVER SPACE PROJECT

First published: 1977
Type of work: Novel

Fork River, an abandoned Kansas town, becomes a site where a quasi-religious sect gathers hoping to establish contact with extra-terrestrials.

The Fork River Space Project is, unlike *Ceremony in Lone Tree* and *The Field of Vision*, a story of reconciliation and imaginative triumph. Early in his career, Morris often wrote about characters such as Foley, Proctor, or Boyd, who were at odds with society and frequently engaged their world with open hostility. In the novels written in his later years, however, Morris shows an increased affinity for characters who are at peace rather than at odds with their world. Kelcey, the narrator of *The Fork River Space Project*, is one such character, and his story of Harry Lorbeer, Lorbeer's partner Dahlberg, and their unusual search for extra-planetary life illustrates Morris' firm belief in the regenerative power of the human imagination.

The story of the novel is filtered through the perceptions of Kelcey, who hires two handy men to work on his Kansas house. Made curious by the eccentric work habits of both, Kelcey resolves to find out more about them. He discovers that one of the men, Dahlberg, is a writer of science-fiction stories. In addition, he finds that both spend their weekends in a ghost town named Fork River, where they lead a sect that believes the town to be the future site of a visit from outer space. The basis for such beliefs stems from a mysterious incident that left a huge crater in Fork River. According to legend, the event was caused by an outer-space vehicle that sucked the inhabitants of the town into the heavens. Another, more practical, theory posits that the mysterious formation was caused by a tornado. Dahlberg and Lorbeer, however, know that tornadoes never bore such scars into the earth and for that reason concede the phenomena to be extra-terrestrial. Dahlberg, in fact, writes a story, "A Hole in

Space," about the occurrence. Kelcey reads it and is impressed by its new vision of an unexplainable natural event.

What Dahlberg and Lorbeer hope to accomplish through their Sunday gatherings is to convince others that another visitation is possible. They believe, in essence, that if others believe, the mystery is more likely to repeat itself. Therefore, by presenting the facts of the case in an unconventional manner, they evolve a new and fresh perspective that they feel will reintroduce a sense of the mysterious into the event and will have the potential to expand the consciousness of the general populace.

In this incident, and a number of others throughout the book, Morris suggests some of his long-held beliefs about the nature of reality. In *Earthly Delights, Unearthly Adornments,* a book of critical commentary, he states that the American obsession with the "real" has had a depressing effect on the imagination. "In assuming we know what is real, and believing that is what we want, we have . . . measurably diminished 'reality,'" creating "more and more of what we know, and what we have," but "less of what we crave." In other words, the superficial materialism and relentless scientific fact-finding that dominate contemporary life have dried up the basic human sense of awe, mystery, and interest in the unknown. Thus, what Morris reveals through Kelcey's reaction to the Fork River Space Project is that the nature of reality is largely dependent on an imaginative construct that a number of people agree upon. For some, especially those who look for empirical facts, Dahlberg and Lorbeer would seem to be mad. For others, such as Kelcey, there is something oddly life-enhancing about the enlarged vision these two men provide. Lorbeer and Dahlberg may be eccentric and somewhat lazy, but Kelcey senses that they have found a way to make constructive use of the imagination and are able to create a durable fiction by which to live from the fragmentary facts of their quotidian existence.

The Fork River Space Project, then, is about how mystery creates the effect of wonder and gives the imagination free rein to reformulate the essential facts. "On the mind's eye, or on the balls of the eyes, or wherever it is," Kelcey remarks, "we see what we imagine, or imagine what we see." By that statement, Morris emphasizes the notion that human conceptions of reality are more like fictions than facts, that ideas form conceptions, and that facts are arranged to fit such ideas. At bottom, the mysterious is what truly moves the imagination. When everything is known, the mind simply has no avenue for free play or growth, because the "soaring imagination" has been "leashed and hooded, like a falcon."

WILL'S BOY

First published: 1981
Type of work: Autobiography

Covering the years from 1910 to 1930, Morris describes his childhood, his father, and the Midwest before the Dust Bowl.

Will's Boy, an autobiography, reworks much of the same material that went into *The Works of Love*, a book with which Morris struggled through seven drafts between 1946 and 1951; however, in this most recent reconsideration of his boyhood, Morris for the first time makes a nonfictional attempt to resurrect his past. By limiting the scope of *Will's Boy* to the years between 1910 and 1930, Morris is able to trace significant events in his life from his birth in Central City, Nebraska, through his boyhood in Schuyler and Omaha, his teen years in Chicago, and on to his eventual enrollment in Pomona College. In terms of action, Morris had a remarkable youth. His mother died when he was born, and his father, William Morris, a rambler with an eye for women, fine clothes, and money, moved from one town to another, married again, and drifted ever eastward. He dragged his son with him through a world of hotel lobbies, cafés, other women, foster parents, cars, and cross-country trips from Chicago to California and back again. Along the way, Morris showed an uncanny ability to take care of himself, finding a variety of jobs, including one at a Chicago YMCA that brought him into direct contact with street gangs and mobsters. Miraculously, he managed to make friendships, finish high school, and survive with almost no monetary or moral support from his father.

Concerning Will Morris, who is one of the central foci of the book, Morris passes subtle judgment, often relaying the pain of estrangement and conflict caused by his father's curious habits and ideas. For example, during Will's brief bachelorhood after the departure of Gertrude, his father's second wife, Morris, in a characteristic understatement, remarks that "we were almost companionable." His father rarely speaks candidly to his son, and Wright is repeatedly "farmed out" to relatives and other families. While staying with one such set of surrogate parents, the Mulligans, Morris' pride is severely injured by the fact that his father pays them either with bad checks or with nothing at all. Most of all, Wright is repelled by his father's loose ways with women and vividly recalls an uncomfortable moment when he caught him abed with a young floozy. Although Morris calls his father a "kind man," he has "scorn" for him and recalls looking forward to living on his own.

The other major foci is Morris' missing mother, who haunts his memory. Her nonpresence represents an important gap in his experience. Morris puts it this way:

> Six days after my birth my mother died. Having stated this bald fact I ponder its meaning. In the wings of my mind I hear voices . . . I see the ghosts of people without faces. . . . My life begins, and will have its ending, in this abiding chronicle of real losses and imaginary gains."

Although the loss of his mother is painful, it is also a potent stimulant to the budding writer's imagination. Though Morris cannot replace her, he recognizes that had she lived, his life would have taken a different course, perhaps filled with "more than the wings of fiction."

Such memories as Morris has of his father and mother would seem to be fit materials for a sad, somber tale rather than one about the flights of youth. Morris, however, refuses to let the negative elements obliterate the positive ones. Consistent with a trend found in his later fiction, Morris dwells on that which is life-enhancing, frequently using comic sections such as those about his stay with the Mulligans as a means to counter the sense of shame, dread, and grief that are found in his accounts of his father. The last pages of the book offer testimony to this tendency and give a sense of beginning rather than ending when they herald young Morris' arrival into adulthood with the engraving on the gates of Pomona College, "INCIPIT VITA NOVA": "Here begins a new life."

Summary

Wright Morris has been called "the least well-known and most widely appreciated" novelist in the United States today. A technical virtuoso, his unique combination of wry wit, spare rhetoric, vernacular precision, and narrative range have distinguished him as one of the most original writers of his generation.

Though Morris' writings are all deeply concerned with the ways in which the past determines human behavior, he is equally preoccupied with finding ways to function constructively in the present and the future. Because he sees the imagination as the primary force that gives shape to experience, his novels applaud those characters who find ways to use it in gaining control over their lives.

Bibliography

Bird, Roy. *Wright Morris: Memory and Imagination.* New York: Peter Lang, 1985.

Booth, Wayne. "The Two Worlds in the Fiction of Wright Morris." *Sewanee Review* 65 (1957): 375-99.

Crump, G. B. *The Novels of Wright Morris: A Critical Interpretation.* Lincoln: University of Nebraska Press, 1978.

Howard, Leon. *Wright Morris.* Minneapolis: University of Minnesota Press, 1968.

Knoll, Robert E., ed. *Conversations with Wright Morris: Critical Views and Responses.* Lincoln: University of Nebraska Press, 1977.

Madden, David. *Wright Morris.* New York: Twayne, 1964.

Trachtenberg, Alan. "The Craft of Vision." *Critique* 4 (Winter, 1961): 41-55.

Wydeven, Joseph. "Consciousness Refracted: Photography and Imagination in the Works of Wright Morris." *Midamerica* 8 (1981): 92-114.

Rodney P. Rice

TONI MORRISON

Born: Lorain, Ohio
February 18, 1931

Principal Literary Achievement

Morrison's novels develop a literary view of the black American experience that is both fabulistic and realistic.

Biography

Chloe Anthony Wofford was born in Lorain, Ohio, on February 18, 1931, the second of George and Ramah Willis Wofford's four children. As an adult, Morrison was to view her father, who had been a child in Georgia in the early part of the century, as an antiwhite racist but also as someone who encouraged excellence and impressed upon his daughter a positive self-image to help her achieve such excellence. Her mother, on the other hand, maintained an optimistic, integrationist perspective, which was nevertheless tempered by a good deal of suspicion of the violence done by whites against blacks.

Morrison was an extremely bright child who, as the only black student in her class, was already able to read in the first grade, before any of her classmates. She studied Latin in high school and graduated with honors from the Lorain Public High School in 1949. She attended Howard University for four years, where she majored in English and started to go by the nickname "Toni."

She graduated from Howard in 1953 with a B.A. in English and proceeded to graduate studies at Cornell University, where she wrote her master's thesis on Virginia Woolf and William Faulkner. She graduated with her master's in English in 1955 and began teaching at Texas Southern University that same year. In 1957, she returned to Howard as an instructor, and she married Harold Morrison, a Jamaican architect.

While a teacher at Howard, her students included Houston A. Baker, Jr., who has since established himself as one of the foremost African-American literary critics, and Stokely Carmichael, the black power leader of the 1960's. As a member of a writing group there, she wrote a short story that was eventually to develop into her first novel. In 1962, her first son, Harold Ford Morrison, was born. In 1964, she resigned her teaching post, divorced her husband, and answered an ad in *The New York Review of Books* to become a textbook editor at L. W. Singer Publishing Company, a subsidiary of Random House, a job that entailed relocating to Syracuse, New

York. In 1967, she was promoted to senior editor at Random House, where she worked especially on black fiction. In this role, she helped develop the careers of black fiction writers, including Toni Cade Bambara and Gayl Jones, as well as the writing career of the black essayist and activist Angela Davis.

It was while living in Syracuse that Morrison returned to her short story about a black girl who wanted blue eyes. At the encouragement of Alan Rancler, an editor at MacMillan and later Holt, Rinehart, and Winston, she developed it into a novel which was published by Holt in 1970 as *The Bluest Eye*. It was generally well reviewed and immediately established Morrison as a writer of great talent. It was followed in 1973 by her second novel, *Sula*, a study of an intensely individualistic black woman, Sula, and her relationships to her closest friend, Nel, and to the community of "the Bottom," from which she is an outcast. It was also well reviewed (Sarah Blackburn called it "extravagantly beautiful" in *The New York Review of Books*) and was nominated for the National Book Award.

It was probably her third novel, *Song of Solomon*, published in 1977, which established beyond any doubt that Morrison was a major American novelist. This powerful and often lyrically written novel of a middle-class black man who is coerced by circumstances into searching for his ancestral roots in slavery, won for Morrison her largest audience so far and also won the National Book Critics Circle Award. Ironically, some of the same black, female critics who had been supporters of her first two novels were initially skeptical of this third one, feeling that she had strayed from the focus in her earlier novels on the societal forces which threaten black women specifically to write a more conventional narrative about a young man growing into wisdom.

Tar Baby, her fourth novel, published in 1981, may be the one which is least often read and which has received the least critical attention. It traces the relationship between Jadine Childs, a black fashion model with a Europeanized background, and Son, a black Rastafarian. The conflict between Jadine's rather vague relationship to her African heritage and Son's more direct connection to his emerges as a major theme of the novel, one which remains to a large extent unresolved when they separate at the end of the novel.

In 1984, Morrison left Random House after twenty years to become the Albert Schweitzer Professor of the Humanities at the State University of New York at Albany. In 1985, her first play, called *Dreaming Emmett* premiered at Albany, and in 1987, her fifth novel, *Beloved*, was published by Knopf. It was widely proclaimed as her finest work to date, and many black writers and critics signed a letter of protest when *Beloved* was not awarded the National Book Award. It did, however, receive the Pulitzer Prize for fiction. In 1989, she was appointed the Robert F. Goheen Professor in the Humanities at Princeton University.

The central concerns of Toni Morrison's fiction have always been the history of physical and economic violence against black Americans, the disruption of positive black cultural traditions caused by such violence, and the strategies that are and must be employed by black Americans to try to preserve their traditions—including those strategies that backfire to some degree. Her focus has usually been primarily on the violence done to, and the cultural traditions of, black women, but her examinations of traditions and violence as they affect black men are also keenly observed and insightful. Through the power of her writing, she has succeeded in making these concerns central in American fiction, much as William Faulkner earlier made the concerns of the American South central concerns in the study of American fiction. Never one to sit on the sidelines, she also engages the same issues in public lectures and in articles that have appeared in *The New York Times Magazine, Michigan Quarterly Review,* and elsewhere. Add to this her accomplishments as an editor and influential educator, and Morrison must be ranked with W. E. B. Dubois and Langston Hughes as one of the most important and influential black writers of this century— and possibly as the most important black female writer in American history.

Analysis

The term "magical realism," often used to describe the fiction of Gabriel García Márquez, has also been applied to the fiction of Toni Morrison. Though the thematic concerns of Morrison's fiction are in most other ways very different from those of Nobel laureate Márquez, one does find in her fiction the same sense of the reality of magic, which (especially in Morrison's case) springs from a fundamental belief in the truth at the center of folklore.

The development of the use of folklore can be traced in her novels. It begins in *The Bluest Eye*, in which the sample from a child's reader which begins the novel is treated as a bit of contemporary folklore. It is an artificially constructed, white, middle-class folklore, however, which may not reveal a fundamental truth about anyone's life and which certainly does not apply to the lives of the black residents of Lorain, Ohio. Nevertheless, the main character, Pecola, is shown as having accepted the view of the world that this children's story encourages, even though it is a view which leaves no room for the realities of her life.

Sula, her second novel, incorporates many elements that feel as if they could have come from folklore, such as the light-skinned man called "Tar Baby" and the three boys that Eva Peace takes into her household. She names each one Dewey, and their identities begin to meld together. Perhaps most notably, there is the character Shadrack, who returned feeble-minded from World War I and who becomes a mysterious hermit living on the edge of the black community of Medallion (called "the Bottom"). He eventually leads many within the community to their deaths in deserted tunnels near the town. Yet though the action in *Sula* is often strange and mysterious, it is nevertheless basically realistic.

It is in *Song of Solomon* that folklore as such comes explicitly to the foreground. Not only is there a minor character who appears as a ghost, but also the premise of the novel is adapted from African-American folklore. The main character, Milkman Dead, uses a child's rhyme he overhears to uncover the secret of his own past, namely that his great-grandfather was one of the legendary men who supposedly escaped slavery by flying back to Africa. To become a complete person, Milkman not only has to make a connection to this folkloric ancestry but also must find how this ancestry can and cannot be applied to his own life.

Tar Baby explicitly continues the attempt to update and apply traditional black folklore to contemporary society and literature. The Rastafarian Son begins to perceive upper-class Jadine as a Tar Baby figure, someone who will trap him, and the last lines of the novel, describing Son running away "Lickety-split. Lickety-split," reinforce his connection to Br'er Rabbit. It is probably in *Beloved* that Morrison uses magical and folkloric elements in the most fiercely original way.

Beloved concerns itself with the plight of Sethe, an escaped slave who, facing recapture, kills her youngest daughter rather than let that daughter grow up in slavery. The novel begins several years later when Sethe and a surviving daughter, Denver, are living in the post-Civil War era in a house they believe to be haunted by this infant's ghost. Shortly after the haunting ceases, a young woman appears who introduces herself as "Beloved"—the only word on Sethe's daughter's gravestone.

When Morrison introduces folkloric and fantastic elements into her writing, she does so not to provide an element of escape but to dramatize the difficulty and necessity for black Americans of making a connection with a harsh heritage. Certainly this is the case in *Beloved*, in which the living person, Beloved, by seeming to offer Sethe and Denver a chance to re-encounter the past also begins to tie them to it and threatens to destroy their future, until events at the end seem somewhat to set them free.

Perhaps the most important theme running through all Morrison's novels is the importance of present generations making contact with the past if they are to understand the present; she herself says as much in the dedication to *Song of Solomon*: "The fathers may soar/ And the children may know their names." Authentic black folklore enables her to create that connection of knowing between generations.

THE BLUEST EYE

First published: 1970
Type of work: Novel

A young black girl who wishes to have blue eyes is raped by her father and goes insane.

Toni Morrison's first published novel, *The Bluest Eye*, is marked by much narrative experimentation and a dedication to exploring the struggles with dignity and violence that especially confront blacks. The wide-ranging narrative experimentation is something that, for the most part, her later novels would not continue; the themes with which it deals, however, were to remain important in all of her later works.

The novel begins with a brief sample story such as might be found in a typical child's reader about "Dick and Jane." This story is repeated twice, first without any punctuation, and a second time without even any spaces between the words, as if to suggest the unreasoning power that such stories have over the mind of the main character, Pecola Breedlove.

After this, the voice of the character who is also the main narrator, Claudia Mc-Teer, appears, and she very quickly summarizes the plot of the novel that follows: Pecola was raped by her father and became pregnant with a child who never grew. Claudia relates this from a child's point of view, calling the reader's attention not to the rape itself but to the marigold seeds that she and her sister, Frieda McTeer, planted at the same time, but which never grew. In this way, the shock value of this rape is removed from the narrative and the focus of the novel is shifted away from what happened to why and how it happened.

The main body of the novel is broken into four sections, entitled "Autumn," "Winter," "Summer," and "Fall." The first part of each section is narrated by Claudia and is followed by other parts, which are headed by quotations from the child's reader and are narrated from a variety of perspectives, usually in the third person. The first section begins in the autumn of 1940, in Lorain, Ohio. Shortly after Claudia and her sister Frieda recover from the flu, Pecola Breedlove comes to stay with the McTeer family temporarily because her father, Cholly Breedlove, started a fire in their rented home, landing himself in jail and putting the rest of his family out of a home. When Frieda offers Pecola a Shirley Temple mug from which to drink milk, the two girls discuss how "cu-ute" Shirley Temple is. Pecola drinks three quarts of milk in one day for the pleasure of looking at this mug. Pecola clearly idolizes Shirley Temple as the ideal girl, even though such a fair-skinned ideal leaves the dark-skinned, brown-eyed Pecola to be condemned as ugly. The reader later learns that Pecola's nightly prayer is for God to make her eyes beautiful and blue so that her family will be so impressed by them that they will never fight in front of them again. In fact, this ideal is almost a mental inheritance from Pecola's mother, Pauline Breedlove, who adopted her own standards of beauty from the silver screen—to the point of taking Pecola's name from "Peola," a light-skinned mulatto girl in the film *Imitation of Life.*

While she is still staying with the McTeer family, Pecola begins menstruating. Learning that this means she can have a baby now, she asks Claudia, "How do you get somebody to love you?" Much of the rest of the novel is a presentation of different people's ways of asking and answering that question. Pecola herself takes her question to three prostitutes; they do not answer her question, but they do make her feel welcome. Pecola also buys some Mary Jane candies so she can experience, as she eats them, what it might be like to be lovely and loved, as the girl on the candy wrapper is. These two passages between them epitomize the idea that love is something which is packaged and sold—but only in imitations.

Some of the most engrossing passages of the novel are the ones which trace the personal histories of Cholly and Pauline Breedlove. One passage that is narrated alternately by a third-person narrator and by Pauline recalls the beginning of her relationship with Cholly and the deterioration of their marriage after they moved north to Ohio. It is clear that Cholly has become increasingly harsh over the years, but she nevertheless recalls their lovemaking fondly, and this fondness is part of why she stays with him.

Cholly's story leads directly to his rape of Pecola. At the funeral of his aunt Jimmy, who reared him, he coaxes a cousin, Darlene, into having sex with him, but they are caught by a group of white men who point guns at them and tell them to keep going. This event lodges itself in Cholly's mind as an initial moment of depravity which always urges him on to other depravities. By the time he meets Pauline, the reader learns of a variety of crimes, including murder, of which he is guilty. His courting of her comes to look like only one more thing he did simply to prove that he could; his turning against her seems inevitable. His rape of Pecola is not excused, but it is seen as an extension of the early experience that forever linked violence and tenderness together for him. When, one evening while she is doing dishes, he glimpses Pecola's enormous longing for his affection, he feels that he "wanted to break her neck—but tenderly." He rapes her on the kitchen floor, then covers her with a blanket and leaves.

Pecola, pregnant, eventually takes her wish for blue eyes to Soaphead Church, a light-skinned West Indian man who supports himself as a "Reader, Advisor, and Interpreter of Dreams." He gives Pecola poison to feed to a lazy dog with the instructions that when the dog dies, she will have blue eyes. The next one sees of Pecola, she is clearly mad and is having a conversation with an imaginary friend who assures her how blue her eyes are.

The Bluest Eye ends with Claudia telling the reader that Pecola lives on as a beggar, picking through people's garbage. Claudia sees Pecola as a victim who was sacrificed by the entire community. The responsibility is not only Cholly's who, she allows, tried in his destructive way to love her. Instead, the major responsibility for Pecola's victimization lies in the society into which she was born. Speaking for the novelist, Claudia wants to indict the way society encourages people such as Pecola and Cholly to measure themselves by arbitrary standards (such as race) which deny them individual value.

SULA

First published: 1973
Type of work: Novel

An unconventional black woman becomes an outcast in a black community.

Sula is a novel about the growth, development, and destruction of a person, a friendship, and a community. At the beginning of the novel, the hill on which the black community of Medallion, Ohio, lived (called "the Bottom," because the white farmer who gave it to a freed slave in return for services told him it was the bottom of heaven) has been deserted. The narrative as a whole sets out to tell why; along the way, one meets a striking variety of characters set against a harsh world.

Sula Peace's grandmother, Eva Peace, is one of the most remarkable characters in the novel. Left by her husband with three children to care for, she drops the children off with a neighbor and leaves town, to return a year and a half later missing one foot lost in a railroad accident, but with ten thousand dollars. When Sula is still young, Eva locks Plum, her son who had returned from World War I two years earlier, in his room and sets him on fire because he has become a drug addict. This is only the first of several shocking deaths.

As a child, Sula's closest friend is Nel Wright. In a scene that demonstrates the extent to which Sula has adapted to the violence of her surroundings, she slices off the tip of her own finger with a knife in front of some white boys who have been bothering Nel, as an unspoken threat of castration. At another time, when Sula and Nel are by the side of the river, they start teasing a young boy called Chicken Little. Sula swings Chicken around until he slips from her hands and sails, giggling, into the river—from which he never emerges. This incident forms a grim link between the two friends which separates them as much as it joins them. When the reader finds out that the sole witness to this event is Shadrack, a shell-shocked war veteran who (on the third day of every year) leads a National Suicide Day, a link seems to be made between Sula and Shadrack as outsiders.

The chaotic logic of calling a hill "the Bottom" dominates the novel. The random, violent deaths that appear throughout seem an extension of this logic, the point being that the initial act of greed and viciousness with which almost valueless land was given to a black man as valuable continues to shape and control the lives of the people who live there, preventing the establishment of any healthy social order. The result is that for Sula and Nel, the Bottom is less of a community than a furnace in which their souls are shaped.

The image of the Bottom as a furnace is supported not only by the fiery death of Plum but also by the similar death of Hannah, Sula's mother. When Eva looks out a window and sees that her oldest daughter, Hannah, has set herself on fire while setting a yard fire, she leaps from her room in an attempt to smother the flames covering Hannah. Hannah bolts and runs until someone douses her flames, much too late to save her life. Later, as Eva is in the hospital with her own injuries, she realizes that Sula had watched the whole thing passively. The implication is that Sula, as an inactive witness to her mother's death, shares some blame for it; as in *The Bluest Eye*, knowledge of a situation demands action.

At the end of part 1, Nel marries Jude Greene. Part 2 begins with Sula returning to the Bottom after having attended college. She arranges to have Eva removed to a nursing home and takes up residence in her house. After re-establishing her friendship with Nel, she then destroys it by seducing Jude. Sula does not understand the extent to which things have changed since they were young and shared boyfriends; Nel does not understand the extent to which things have not changed.

After her friendship with Nel ends, Sula lives in the Bottom as a pariah. She uses and discards a string of white and black men for sexual relations, and so raises the wrath of the townspeople against her, until they come to think of her as evil. Iron-ically, Sula's "evil" presence in the town makes the parents more careful with their children, and married women more devoted to their men. Sula herself does become obsessed with one man, Albert Jacks ("Ajax"), for a while, and even fantasizes that his body is made of gold, but he goes to an air show in Dayton and leaves her.

On Sula's deathbed, Nel tries to make up with her, but they get into a fight about the past. Nel accuses Sula of not respecting anyone else's values; Sula accuses Nel of not developing any values of her own. Though Nel has come by to help, she leaves Sula to die alone. Even so, Sula dies thinking, "It didn't even hurt. Wait'll I tell Nel." Shortly after Sula's death, Shadrack leads a National Suicide Day crowd down to some abandoned tunnels; the tunnels suddenly flood, killing much of the town, in the event that effectively ends the life of the Bottom.

The final section of the novel is set twenty-five years after Sula's death, in 1965. Nel goes to visit Eva Peace, who confuses her with Sula. After leaving Eva, Nel visits Sula's grave. As she leaves the cemetery, she calls out to Sula, overcome with grief for how much she has missed her childhood friend.

While Sula is living as an outcast in the Bottom, the narrator says that she is an artist who lacks the discipline of any art to sustain her. In *Sula*, Morrison has cre-ated a novel about a character who has the ability and the need to question a mal-formed society, but who lacks the means to channel her rebellion into a constructive form. One of the formations Sula challenges is the one that sees marriage as the basic unit of society. For her, friendship with Nel is more fundamental than any relationship with a man. Twenty-five years after Sula's death, Nel realizes that friend-ship with Sula was always fundamental for her, too.

SONG OF SOLOMON

First published: 1977
Type of work: Novel

A middle-class black man growing up during a period of racial unrest un-covers his family's history.

Song of Solomon, for which Toni Morrison won the National Book Critics Circle Award, is an enormously complex novel which at the same time is her most abso-lutely clear work; it may be her most popular book.

From the first lines of the book, the novel concerns itself with the idea of black men flying, an image it gets from black folktales which said that in the days of slavery, every now and then a slave would remember how to fly and would fly back to Africa. The main character of the novel, Macon Dead III (who picks up the name Milkman because his mother, Ruth Foster Dead, nurses him until he is past the age at which a child is usually weaned.), is born the day after a black life insurance agent, Robert Smith, leaps to his death in an attempt to fly to Canada. When as a very young man Macon learns that he himself cannot fly, he loses all interest in the world.

From a young age, his closest friend is a boy who goes by the name of Guitar, who is a bit older and quicker than Milkman. It is Guitar who introduces Milkman to Milkman's own aunt, Pilate, whose name was chosen by her father at random out of the Bible (it suggests not only Pontius Pilate, but also the pilot of an airplane); she is the person who holds many of the keys to the knowledge Milkman will need to learn to fly.

Milkman's father is the son of a freed slave who was killed for his land; he grows up as a harsh, greedy man, dedicated to making money. Milkman's mother is the adored daughter of the first black doctor in the town, a man who is memorialized in the name the black population still uses for one street: Not Doctor Street. Their marriage is animated by Macon's tirades against his wife and by little else.

Milkman himself grows up spoiled. He works for his father collecting rents and has a long and ongoing affair with his cousin Hagar, Pilate's granddaughter, which he never takes seriously — not even when Hagar tries to kill him for breaking up with her. Unlike his father, who consciously shapes his own attitudes towards people after the attitudes of the white people who persecuted his family in his youth, Milkman unthinkingly adopts an attitude which allows him to use people.

When Milkman grows up, his father tells him about the feud that came between Pilate and himself as children. After their father was killed, they took refuge in a cave, where Macon assaulted and apparently killed a man carrying sacks of gold. Years later, Macon is still convinced that a sack Pilate has hanging in her living room contains that gold. Milkman and Guitar steal the sack; Milkman wants the money for himself, and Guitar wants the money for a black guerilla organization he belongs to called the Seven Days, which is dedicated to killing one white person for every black person killed by a white. When the sack proves to have nothing but rocks and bones, Milkman, Guitar, and Macon all remain convinced that Pilate did something with the money.

In part 2 of the novel, Milkman retraces Pilate's wandering as a child a half century after Macon and Pilate parted in the cave over the gold. He finds both an old woman who once sheltered the youngsters and the cave they hid in, but no gold, so he continues south to a town in Virginia called Shalimar, his grandfather's original hometown. In this way, the novel does a marvelous job of adapting a quest motif. In the process of looking for gold, Milkman in fact finds his own family's history, eventually learning (by deciphering a children's rhyme he overhears) that the town of Shalimar is named for his own great-grandfather, who supposedly flew back to Africa.

In the course of the quest, Milkman himself has become a less selfish person, and when Guitar, who has been tailing him, sees Milkman help another man load a heavy carton for shipping, he assumes that Milkman has found the gold and violated their arrangement. Thus, he begins to hunt Milkman with the intent of killing him. Milkman, however, has found his "gold" in the story of his grandfather's flight.

Having realized that Pilate's sack of bones contains her own father's remains (and not, as she thought, the remains of the white man she believed her brother had killed), Milkman flies back home to tell her, only to discover that Hagar has starved and fretted herself into a fatal fever over him. Milkman determines to care for Hagar's soul in death the way he never did in life, and returns to Virginia with Pilate to bury her father's bones on the spot from which Shalimar (also called Solomon) is supposed to have leaped. Guitar is waiting for them across a narrow ravine, however, and shoots Pilate, intending to hit Milkman.

In the last paragraph, Milkman himself leaps across the narrow ravine, to the landing below where Guitar is. It is a moment of pure inspiration that encompasses his entire history and heredity. To underscore the point, Morrison ends the novel with him in mid-air, flying toward Guitar.

Milkman's character development is triumphant, but not without troubles. As his great-grandfather's flight, which the reader is free to think of as a real, magical flight, an escape from slavery, or a suicide, caused him to abandon an entire family, so Milkman's leap at the end might be read as an impetuous act that undercuts his intentions to be more responsible to people. The reader at the end has to make a leap of faith with Milkman, not only to assume Milkman will survive this leap, but that he will be able to continue his own personal growth when he gets back home. Nevertheless, the novel's triumph is unequivocable in its vivid demonstration of how links with the past can renew and guide the present.

BELOVED

First published: 1987
Type of work: Novel

A former slave meets a young woman who may be her daughter's ghost incarnated.

Toni Morrison's novel *Beloved* is her single greatest novelistic achievement and is a tour through some of the nightmares created by slavery. When the novel begins in the post-Civil War era in 1873, Sethe, a former slave who escaped to the North while pregnant during the time of slavery, is living with her oldest daughter, Denver, in a house they both believe to be haunted by the ghost of the infant daughter Sethe killed when she was about to be recaptured (rather than let the daughter grow up in slavery). The novel is loosely based on the account of a former slave named Margaret Garner who, as an escaped slave, tried to kill all of her children when they were captured in 1850 and succeeded in killing one; the novel is also a triumph of imagination.

When Paul D, who along with Sethe was a former slave at a plantation known as Sweet Home, comes to Sethe's house on 124 Bluestone Road and quickly becomes her lover, the ghost disappears. Very shortly thereafter, however, a well-dressed young woman about the age that Sethe's daughter would have been had she lived appears on the doorstep and introduces herself as "Beloved"—which is the only word on the gravestone that Sethe placed over her dead infant.

Paul D's reappearance and Beloved's sudden appearance force Sethe to confront the past locked away in what she calls her "rememory." She tells Paul D the story of spotting Schoolteacher, the cruel master of Sweet Home, and determining to put her babies "where they'd be safe"—that is, to death. What frightens Paul D more than anything else is her continued defense of her actions years later. Paul D is also forced by his meeting with Sethe to confront his own past. When he tells her, "You got two feet, Sethe, not four," to upbraid her for her infanticide, he is accusing her of acting like an animal. The comment seems to relate also to Paul D's past and his own struggle to retain his human dignity despite having been a slave and treated as a beast of burden for much of his life.

Beloved herself is presented as childlike and self-centered, very much like the petulant ghost that had haunted the house for years. Even when the narrative goes inside her head, it is not clear to what extent she is supposed to be literally the ghost of Sethe's daughter. Stamp Paid, a local black man, suggests that she might be the young woman that was kept locked up as a sex slave in a nearby town. Her own interior dialogue seems to suggest two separate minds at work, and perhaps the explanation most consistent with everything the novel contains is that Beloved is the escaped sex slave possessed by the ghost of Sethe's dead daughter. To see this explanation as a resolution to the puzzle presented by Beloved, however, would be to miss the force of Morrison's careful ambiguity. Beloved is a ghost, and, as Denver tells Paul D toward the end, something more; she is a person and something more. That something more is the key to unlocking the past to release the future.

As events draw to a climax—as Paul D becomes Beloved's lover and then moves out, as the household on 124 Bluestone becomes more removed from the outside community, and as Beloved demands almost obsessive attention—it is Denver, the daughter Sethe gave birth to while racing to freedom, whose future seems the most to be a prisoner to the past. It is unexpectedly Denver who finds the way to unlock the future for all of them, by getting a job which takes her outside her home. By working in the community, Denver reawakens in the community a sense of responsibility for Sethe, and they come together to try to exorcise Beloved—who is fat and maybe pregnant by now—from the house.

When members of the black community are gathered around the house at 124 Bluestone, Sethe sees Mr. Bodwin, her white landlord and Denver's employer, appear on horseback looking a bit like Schoolteacher had two decades earlier when he had come for her. She tries to attack him with an ice pick but is intercepted. In the confusion, Beloved runs into the forest; later, there are reports of a madwoman having been spotted running naked. When it ends, Sethe seems finally to have given in to the despair that she had repressed for twenty years. Paul D tries to comfort her, however, and there is a strong suggestion that she is better off for being able to feel her despair.

In many ways, *Beloved* is a meditation on the ownership of human beings. Ironically, when Sethe kills her infant daughter to save her from slavery, she is committing the ultimate act of ownership—deciding that it is better for another person to die than live. She cannot help but repeat some of the sins of slavery, even in her reaction against it. The point is that slavery is so destructive that ending it is merely one step in healing the wounds it creates. Baby Suggs, Sethe's mother-in-law, who lived with Sethe for a while, seems to summarize the novel's theme early in the book when she says, "Not a house in the country ain't packed to the rafter's with some dead Negro's grief." *Beloved* is a novel about healing such grief.

Summary

All Toni Morrison's work focuses on the attempts to construct a life out of the violence and destruction of the past. She emphasizes that the true violence of the past is something that takes courage to face, and not all of her characters can face it. Faulkner said that the past is never over; "it isn't even past." In Morrison's novels, the past pursues the present, and, unless people can face it, it will overtake the present and repeat itself in its worst aspects.

Bibliography

Christian, Barbara. *Black Women Novelists*. Westport, Conn.: Greenwood Press, 1980.

McKay, Nellie, ed. *Critical Essays on Toni Morrison*. Boston: G. K. Hall, 1988.

Middleton, David L. *Toni Morrison: An Annotated Bibliography*. New York: Garland, 1987.

Morrison, Toni. "Unspeakable Things Unspoken: The Afro-American Presence in American Literature." *Michigan Quarterly Review* 28 (Winter, 1989): 1-33.

Samuels, Wilfred D., and Clenora Hudson-Weems. *Toni Morrison*. Boston: Twayne, 1990.

Willis, Susan. "Eruptions of Funk: Historicizing Toni Morrison." In *Specifying*. Madison: University of Wisconsin Press, 1987.

Thomas Cassidy

BHARATI MUKHERJEE

Born: Calcutta, India
July 27, 1940

Principal Literary Achievement
Mukherjee's novels and short stories explore the experiences of South Asian immigrants, especially women, as they try to adapt to life in North America.

Biography

Bharati Mukherjee was born in Calcutta, India, on July 27, 1940, the daughter of pharmaceutical chemist Sudhir Lal Mukherjee and his wife Bina (née Barrerjee). Mukherjee's was a comparatively wealthy Hindu Bengali Brahmin family, and during her early childhood they lived with their large extended family (numbering up to forty during wartime) in a flat in Ballygunge, a middle-class neighborhood of Calcutta. Life there was stable and somewhat insulated from the rough and tumble of Calcutta, but Mukherjee was aware of the homeless beggars roaming the streets, the funerals of freedom fighters during India's struggle for independence from British imperial rule, and the Hindu-Muslim riots at the partition of India and Pakistan. She enjoyed the affection of a loving father (who was fond of his three daughters despite his society's prevailing preference for sons), listened to the tales of her mother ("a powerful storyteller"), and feared the madness of an aunt. When Mukherjee was eight, her father sent his three daughters to school in England and Switzerland. After three years of this experiment in European education, the sisters returned to Calcutta to live in a home set up within the compound of the pharmaceutical company partly owned by their father in suburban Cossipore. From there they attended a school staffed by Irish nuns; en route to school they sometimes had to run a gauntlet of strikers and bearers of pickets. When Mukherjee was eighteen, her father lost his partnership in his company and moved to Baroda (near Bombay), where he directed research and development at a chemical complex.

In 1959, Mukherjee earned a B.A. from the University of Calcutta, followed by an M.A. in 1961 from the University of Baroda. Even as a child, Mukherjee had felt the writer's vocation, and by the age of ten she had already written an eighty-page novel—about English children in an English landscape. In 1961, Mukherjee enrolled in the Writers Workshop at the University of Iowa where she earned an M.F.A. (1963), followed by a Ph.D. in English and comparative literature in 1969.

While at Iowa, Mukherjee met and married the Canadian writer Clark Blaise, and

they have two sons. Both Mukherjee and Blaise have pursued successful careers as writers and university professors, having held appointments at several colleges, including McGill University in Montreal, Quebec, Canada; Skidmore College in upstate New York; Queens College, City University of New York; Columbia University; and University of California, Berkeley. From 1966 to 1980, Mukherjee and her husband lived in Canada and became Canadian citizens. Mukherjee experienced several incidents of Canadian-style racism, however, about which she wrote eloquently in her prize-winning essay "An Invisible Woman" (published in *Saturday Night*, March, 1981), and in 1980 she and her husband decided to emigrate to the United States. The couple are intensely interested in each other's writing and have collaborated on two nonfiction books. One, entitled *Days and Nights in Calcutta* (1977; revised, 1986), is an autobiographical account of a year spent in India during 1973-1974. The other, *The Sorrow and the Terror: The Haunting Legacy of the Air India Tragedy* (1987), is a reportorial critique of the 1985 Air India crash in which Sikh terrorists allegedly killed 329 people.

Analysis

Much of Mukherjee's fiction, like her nonfiction, has sprung from her personal background of growing up in South Asia and her experience as an Asian woman immigrant in Canada and the United States. In developing the subject of the Indian diaspora to the West, Mukherjee has acknowledged the influence and example of the distinguished writer V. S. Naipaul, himself a Trinidadian of Indian descent who lives in England. Although Mukherjee admires Naipaul's exploration of the experience of immigration, expatriation, and assimilation, or as she puts it, "unhousement," "remaining unhoused," and "rehousement," there are wide differences in their outlooks and their sympathies. Typically, Mukherjee's protagonists are immigrant women of color from the Third World trying to make their way in a technologically advanced society with a deplorable history of sexism and racism. Such characters are frequently victims of prejudice, exploitation, and violence that tend to brutalize and dehumanize them. Unlike Naipaul, whose character analysis is colder and more sardonic, Mukherjee's sympathies lie, for the greater part, with such victims. Also unlike Naipaul's unremittingly ironic stance, Mukherjee often permits her characters to recover their humanity through love, especially love between man and woman— as in her novel *Jasmine* (1989) and her stories "Orbiting" and "Buried Lives," from *The Middleman and Other Stories* (1988). Several of Mukherjee's characters are also able to empower themselves and shape their own identities, as is the case in *Jasmine* and the *Middleman* story "A Wife's Story." Mukherjee's treatment of the immigrant experience is therefore more optimistic than Naipaul's.

Though the Asian immigrant in the New World is her distinctive sphere of depiction, Mukherjee's earlier writing was greatly influenced by British authors such as Jane Austen and E. M. Forster. For example, the protagonist of her first novel, *The Tiger's Daughter* (1972), is a genteel and sensitive daughter of a wealthy Indian family—a character and a social milieu transposed into India from the mold of

Austen. The descriptive style of E. M. Forster's *A Passage to India* (1924) echoes in the opening of Mukherjee's novel: "The Catelli-Continental Hotel on Chowringhee Avenue, Calcutta, is the navel of the universe. . . . There is, of course, no escape from Calcutta. . . . Family after family moves from the provinces to its brutish center, and the center quivers a little, absorbs the bodies, digests them, and waits."

Irony is a persistent trait of Mukherjee's early work, an irony modeled consciously upon Naipaul's. This irony, expressing itself in the distance between author and protagonist, and between protagonist and her observed world, is already evident in *The Tiger's Daughter*, which records the impressions of a young and mainly passive Indian woman who has gone to America as a student, married a white American, and is returning to her native Calcutta for a holiday visit. Through the subtle interplay between the protagonist's Westernized perspective, her memories of her Asian youth, and her inactivity, Mukherjee provides an ironic critique of upper-class Indian society, whose mores and vitality are crumbling like those in Anton Chekhov's *Vishnyovy sad* (1904; *The Cherry Orchard*, 1908)—Chekhov being another of Mukherjee's most admired authors.

The texture of Mukherjee's narratives is often enriched by patterns of repeated imagery and rendered intricate by literary allusions. In *Wife* (1975), for example, a dead mouse becomes an imagistic leitmotif symbolic of violence. In *Jasmine*, the repeated image of a dead dog occurs with chilling effectiveness, while allusions to Charlotte Brontë's *Jane Eyre* (1847) form a provocative subtext to the novel.

The locales, persons, idiom, and themes of Mukherjee's later work have increasingly taken on the traits of the American grain, especially traits along the lines of Jewish American writers about immigrant life such as Abraham Cahan, Henry Roth, Isaac Bashevis Singer, and Bernard Malamud. As she stated in 1985, "The book I dream of updating is no longer *A Passage to India*—it's *Call It Sleep*," a novel published by Henry Roth in 1934. Certainly the narrative energy that infuses her later works is less genteel Anglo-Indian than raw American. For example, the beginning of the story "Angela" (in the 1985 collection *Darkness*) is a far cry from Austen: "Edith was here [in the hospital] to have her baby last November. The baby, if a girl, was supposed to be named Darlene after Mother, but Edith changed her mind at the last minute . . . while she was being shaved by the nurse." Mukherjee unfalteringly captures the idiom and cadence of her protagonist-narrator as she speaks through the throat of an Atlanta sports fan and financial consultant in "Fighting for the Rebound" (from *The Middleman*): "I'm in bed watching the Vanilla Gorilla stick it to the Abilene Christians on some really obscure cable channel when Blanquita comes through the door wearing lavender sweats, and over them a frilly see-through apron. . . . Okay, so maybe . . . she isn't a looker in the blondhair-smalltits-greatlegs way that Wendi was. Or Emilou, for that matter. But beautiful is how she makes me feel. Wendi was slow-growth. Emilou was strictly Chapter Eleven."

With her fast-paced, psychologically intriguing, and intellectually challenging narratives, Mukherjee provides valuable and moving insights into the too often buried lives and unexpressed emotions of South Asians, especially South Asian women, who are making their way in a daunting New World of high technology, unruly mores, and random violence. Mukherjee is thus carving a niche for herself and her primary subject matter, the South Asian diaspora to America, in the pluralist tradition of American letters.

WIFE

First published: 1975
Type of work: Novel

A young wife from Calcutta, India, migrates to New York City, goes insane, and kills her husband.

Wife, Mukherjee's second published novel, exemplifies the matter and manner of her early work. Unlike her first novel, *The Tiger's Daughter*, which is wholly set in India, most of *Wife* takes place in the United States. With a gentle irony that serves to alleviate and distance an otherwise pathetic protagonist, Mukherjee depicts the mental breakdown of a weak-minded young woman who cannot cope with the traumatic experience of immigration from the structured society of India to the liberated society of New York City.

The opening sentences of the novel introduce the protagonist and set the playfully ironic tone:

> Dimple Dasgupta had set her heart on marrying a neurosurgeon, but her father was looking for engineers in the matrimonial ads. . . . She fantasized about young men with mustaches, dressed in spotless white, peering into opened skulls. Marriage would bring her freedom, cocktail parties on carpeted lawns, fund-raising dinners for noble charities. Marriage would bring her love.

The literary ancestry of this narrative tone is traceable to Jane Austen, particularly to *Pride and Prejudice* (1813). The genre, a comedy of manners about marriage, is also reminiscent of Austen, though Mukherjee chooses to emphasize the woes of marriage rather than its joys (as Austen does). Also unlike Austen, Mukherjee's focus is not upon an intricate character (such as Austen's Elizabeth Bennet), but on a rather simple character.

The name of Mukherjee's protagonist, Dimple, is perhaps a measure of her simplicity (and the author's playfulness with Calcutta chic). In any case, Dimple's mind is portrayed as entirely vacant of ideas other than those associated with securing a husband. To make herself more attractive to prospective husbands, Dimple wants to lighten her wheatish complexion with creams, increase her bust by isometrics, and finish herself with a bachelor of arts degree. She fails on all three fronts. Her father does manage a match for her, however, not with a neurosurgeon but with an engineer intent upon emigrating, preferably to the United States.

Through courtship and early marriage, Mukherjee's comedy of manners continues, with complaining in-laws, unsatisfied romantic expectations, and Dimple's predictable disillusion with her groom and the married state. The comic events, however, take on a darker tinge with two incidents that indicate Dimple's naïve penchant toward violence as a quick solution to problems. One incident involves her chasing and braining a mouse. This image of violence is used as a leitmotif by Mukherjee; it stays with Dimple, and her consciousness flashes back to it several times during the course of the novel. The image also appears to be a teasing reference to the opening scene of Richard Wright's *Native Son* (1940), in which his protagonist smashes a rat with a frying pan—indeed, Dimple later in the novel asks an American friend to tell her Wright's story (though the scene is transposed from Wright's original Chicago to Harlem). The other violent episode occurs when Dimple has an unwanted pregnancy and, thinking of a baby as an impediment to immigration, induces an abortion by (ironically) skipping rope. The abortion episode connects imagistically to the mouse killing, because that animal was smashed in a pile of baby clothes and its remains are described as looking pregnant. This interweaving of imagery, theme, allusion, and characterization is illustrative of Mukherjee's complex and subtle artistry.

Soon after Dimple's abortion, the immigration papers come through for her husband, Amit Basu, and the couple depart India. Dimple's entry into the New World is occasion for Mukherjee to depict the comedy of errors of immigrés unused to new mores; the clashes of culture are initially slight and amusing, but they accrue to become a considerable shock to Dimple's fragile psychological balance.

Although Indian society had seemed overly structured and authoritarian (especially with parents controlling their children's marriages so absolutely), it had in actuality provided Dimple with clear behavioral guidelines. In the United States, by contrast, there appears to be so much freedom that Dimple loses her bearings in a seeming ocean of permissiveness. That there are American structural taboos as fastidious as Hindu ones, but which are incomprehensible to Dimple, is illustrated by her attempt to buy cheesecake from a kosher butcher. Migration to America also reduces the Indian status of her husband: No longer master of his house, he is suffered as a guest by his host and becomes just another job-seeking immigrant. Amit is consequently reduced in Dimple's eyes. Dimple is also fascinated by liberated and Americanized Indian women such as Ina Mullick, whom she finds rather incomprehensible and repellent. Mainstream American foods, too, are problematic; she forces herself to eat hamburger (beef being taboo and odious for Hindus), then vomits it up privately. Dimple feels so defeated by American life that she likes nothing better than to stay in bed all day watching television—in fact, television becomes her version of life in America.

Meanwhile, the violence of American life bombards Dimple—talk of random shootings, cautionary tales of mugging in the streets, crime statistics in the news, murder on the television soap operas. These elements, many of them amusing in isolation, add up to a substantial cultural trauma for the susceptible Dimple. Furthermore, Dimple begins an affair with a white American, while Amit becomes increasingly obtuse, antipathetic, and unmanly in her eyes. Mukherjee subtly builds up Dimple's predisposition to bloodshed by describing Amit's cutting a finger while changing a lightbulb and Dimple's accidentally wounding his hand with a paring knife when he attempts romance in the kitchen. Finally Dimple goes completely insane, and she decapitates Amit—an act that shows her perversely and grossly taking the power she had desired at the beginning of the novel by wanting marriage to a neurosurgeon.

Wife is an accomplished psychological novel about a young Asian immigrant woman who goes violently insane. Mukherjee creates with insightful deftness the psyche of a weak-minded, unhappy, and perplexed wife undergoing the shock of transition from the highly structured but protective society of India to the apparently freer but infinitely more puzzling society of the United States. The controlling irony of Mukherjee's narrative is the perfect medium for depicting this murderous but naïve woman whom the reader can understand but with whom the reader cannot fully empathize. In this novel, too, Mukherjee has defined a primary sphere of her artistic endeavor—the psychological world of the South Asian woman facing the challenge of immigration to America with its attendant traumata of culture shock, its rush of freedom, its responsibility of self definition, and its access to power.

JASMINE

First published: 1989
Type of work: Novel

While emigrating from India to the United States, a young Asian woman struggles against destiny to create her own identity and resists racial and sexual stereotypes to assert her humanity.

Soon after garnering the 1988 National Book Critics Circle Award for her second collection of short stories, entitled *The Middleman and Other Stories*, Mukherjee published her exciting and accomplished novel *Jasmine*. In fact, the novel grew out of one of the *Middleman* stories, also entitled "Jasmine," whose protagonist persisted in the author's imagination, demanding to be reincarnated or born again in a lengthier genre. *Jasmine* is a novel about survival; it is also an account of an immigrant minority woman's metamorphosis, self-invention, and self-empowerment. Inasmuch as the protagonist is a woman, the novel holds great interest for feminists. Insofar as she is an Indian, and much of the book dwells upon her experience in America, the novel adds another episode to the epic of the Asian diaspora to America.

In this tightly crafted book, which uses time shifts extensively, all the major themes and motifs are established in the opening chapter. Its first sentence begins with the phrase "Lifetimes ago," which immediately introduces the structuring theme of metamorphosis or reincarnation, and indeed, the protagonist is known by different names (signifying different identities and different lives) at different stages in the novel. The first chapter also introduces the main conflict in the novel by describing an astrologer's prophecy of Jasmine's exile and widowhood and Jasmine's violent resistance to the astrologer: It is the conflict between a humanistic-existential individualism (Jasmine's) and a cosmic-determinist worldview (the astrologer's). In resisting the astrologer, Jasmine bites her tongue and scars her own forehead, but instead of succumbing to these wounds (to be born female in her society is already to be wounded), Jasmine resolutely metamorphoses them into advantages. She imagines the wound in her forehead to be a Siva-like sage's third eye to scan invisible worlds, and the bloody tongue is an attribute of the powerful destructor goddess Kali (an image that reappears in the novel when Jasmine kills a rapist). The opening chapter then closes on two unforgettable images: As Jasmine swims wrathfully in the river, she bumps into the carcass of a drowned dog and tastes the stench of the water—both images affect her like curses then, but she is to exorcise them dramatically later in the novel.

Jasmine's native village is in the Punjab, India, where the birth of a girl is an affliction. Her mother, in fact, tries to strangle Jasmine, her fifth daughter; however, Jasmine, who was then named Jyoti, survives and grows into an intelligent girl able to obtain more than the usual amount of education. Jyoti also evinces an enjoyment of power. When electricity comes to the village, she loves the feeling of being "totally in control" as she flicks the light switch. One day she particularly "feels a buzz of power" when she smashes in the skull of a dog who attacks the village women during their morning toilet. This image of her killing the dog recalls, and in some measure indicates an overcoming of, the curse and destiny laid upon her by the astrologer. Another dead dog image will reappear in connection with a would-be lover's suicide in America.

The astrologer's prophecy of widowhood, however, comes true. Contrary to family expectation, when Jyoti is fourteen years old, she marries for love an enlightened engineering student who further educates her and renames her Jasmine. He wishes to emigrate to the United States, but before that can happen, he is blown up by a Sikh terrorist bomb. In India, the protagonist has two names, suggestive of the two conflicting cultures of the subcontinent: Jyoti is a Hindi and Hindu name, whereas Jasmine is a Persian-Arabic and Moslem name; respectively the names mean "light" and "sweetness," the two elements which English poet Matthew Arnold thought could save culture from anarchy.

Jasmine then sets out for the United States to realize her husband's immigration dream by proxy and also, like a virtuous Hindu widow, to commit *suttee* by cremating his suit (in lieu of his corpse) and immolating herself in the flames. Paradoxically, during her odyssey to achieve this, Jasmine has to sell herself unvirtuously for food and passage. When a Vietnam veteran turned smuggler rapes her and makes fun of her husband's suit, however, she strikes back and kills him instead of stabbing herself. It is noteworthy that when Jasmine kills, she first slits her own tongue; through this image Mukherjee lessens Jasmine's personal responsibility in the killing by ritualizing the act, for Mukherjee has imagistically transformed Jasmine into an aspect of the goddess Kali, whose mouth is iconically filled with blood.

In seeking virtue and death, Jasmine ironically discovers criminality and a desire to live. She is helped by a kind woman who illegally aids refugees and who renames her Jazzy, another reincarnation. Through her, Jasmine becomes an au pair, a "caregiver," to an academic couple at Columbia University; when the couple's marriage breaks up, the husband, Taylor, becomes Jasmine's lover. He nicknames her Jase, yet another reincarnation.

One day Jasmine is terrified when she recognizes a neighborhood hot-dog vendor as her husband's assassin. Leaving Taylor, she flees New York and by chance ends up in Iowa. There she becomes the common-law wife of Bud Ripplemeyer, a prominent small-town banker, and becomes known, in still another reincarnation, as Jane Ripplemeyer. Jasmine refuses to marry him for fear of her astrologer's prophecy of widowhood, and indeed Bud is shot by a distraught farmer facing foreclosure soon after he and Jasmine begin living together. Although Bud does not die, he becomes crippled. Thus Jasmine has to take increasing charge of their relationship; in sex, for example, she becomes the active partner, even deciding whether Bud should ejaculate. (This situation echoes that of Mukherjee's story "The Tenant," in which the woman sleeps with an armless man.) Thus, when Jasmine becomes pregnant, it is an event over which she is more in charge than most women, and it is an indicator of how much Jasmine is now in charge of herself and her life, of how much empowerment she has attained. More than electricity is in the hands of this erstwhile village girl.

If Mukherjee had ended her novel at this point, she would have established Jasmine largely within the archetype of woman as a powerful and supportive care-giver, very much where Charlotte Brontë ended *Jane Eyre*. Aside from Jasmine's being renamed Jane, there are at least two allusions to *Jane Eyre* in *Jasmine*, not to mention that *Jane Eyre* has a wife burnt to death, a fate Jasmine once contemplated for herself. Clearly Mukherjee's heroine is intended to look back to Brontë's, but she also looks beyond her. Mukherjee, therefore, ends her novel by endowing her protagonist not only with power but also with the freedom to exercise it. Thus Jasmine, who genuinely loves and cares for Bud, refuses to be bound to his wheelchair (as Jane Eyre is to her blinded Rochester). Instead, although she is ripely pregnant, she deserts Bud when her former lover, Taylor, tracks her down and proposes that she flee with him to find happiness in Berkeley, California. The novel's ending has provoked controversy. Some readers will criticize Jasmine's decision to leave Bud as irresponsible. Others will argue that Mukherjee is realistically pointing out that liberation has a cost, and that, furthermore, when Jasmine moves westward to a greater freedom and self-actualization, she is merely acting in the time-honored American tradition of lighting out for the territory ahead, a tradition hallowed by Horace Greeley and by Mark Twain's *The Adventures of Huckleberry Finn* (1884). Mukherjee's Jasmine has indeed come a long way—not only from the Punjab to America, but also from believing that a wife's virtue entails self-immolation to believing that a pregnant woman's happiness justifies her deserting the father of her child for the arms of a lover.

THE WORLD ACCORDING TO HSÜ

First published: 1983
Type of work: Short story

A Eurasian woman and her white Canadian husband vacation on an island off Africa while attempting to decide whether to relocate from Montreal to Toronto.

This story is to be found in Mukherjee's first collection of short fiction, entitled *Darkness* (1985). Like most of its companion stories in this collection, it records, analyzes, and dramatizes the tribulations of South Asian immigrants in North America. These *Darkness* stories are painful, often violent, and either tragic or ironic; their collective title itself seems to be an ironic inversion of the way in which the West thinks of itself as a locus of freedom, opportunity, and enlightenment in contrast to benighted Third World countries; the irony is especially mordant when one hears in Mukherjee's title echoes of Joseph Conrad's *Heart of Darkness* (1902), condemning nineteenth century European colonialism, and V. S. Naipaul's *An Area of Darkness* (1964), an Asian-denigrating travelogue about India. For Mukherjee, it appears that darkness has overtaken North America, supposedly the leading light of the Western world.

It is racism, a darkness of the mind toward the darkness of another's skin, that most benights North American life. The racism of Canada, especially, receives the brunt of Mukherjee's resentment in "The World According to Hsü." Indeed, in her introduction to these stories, Mukherjee says that during her fourteen-year sojourn in Canada, white Canadians commonly assumed that she was a prostitute, a shoplifter, or a domestic, and that Canadian society routinely made crippling assumptions about the imagined disabilities of immigrants of color.

In "The World According to Hsü," Ratna Clayton, a Eurasian woman of Indian descent, and her husband, Graeme Clayton, a white Canadian professor, are vacationing on an island nation in the Indian Ocean off the African coast. The couple is trying to decide whether to move their home from French Montreal to Anglo Toronto in order to advance the husband's career. As if in concert with their decision making, a military coup occurs on the island. The dispiriting uncertainty and irritable meanness of being uprooted and homeless, which is a major theme of this and several of Mukherjee's works, is reflected in a backdrop of seedy caravanserais, uneasy politics, and directionless supporting characters that are as expertly evoked as anything in works by Graham Greene or V. S. Naipaul.

Ratna is reluctant to move because of her experience of Toronto racists: "In Toronto, she was not a Canadian, not even Indian. She was something called, after the imported idiom of London, a Paki. And for Pakis, Toronto was hell." She also recalls a Punjabi boy's having been struck by a car with a bumper sticker that read: "Keep Canada green. Paint a Paki." Conflict, Mukherjee hints bitterly, seems to be fundamental to the world, not only conflict between races in Canada, between political ideologies in Third World nations, or between couples in marriage; the principle of conflict is also embedded in the very structure of the planet. The metaphor for this lies in the story's title, which derives from an article that Ratna's husband is reading on plate tectonics. The article is written by a scientist named Hsü and describes how continents have been formed by plates of the earth's surface smashing or grating against one another. It is a metaphor of abrasion that sums up Ratna's experience of universal racism through differing times of her life: When she was a child growing up in India, Ratna was jeered as a "white rat," and now that she is an adult in Canada, she is taunted as a "Paki."

Informed by this geological metaphor of fundamental and ubiquitous conflict, the apparently hopeful ending of the story is really ironical: "She poured herself another glass [of wine], feeling for the moment at home in that collection of Indians and Europeans babbling in English and remembered dialects. No matter where she lived, she would never feel so at home again." Initially, this last sentence may seem hopeful and comforting—Ratna feels at home. If being "at home" means feeling at ease, secure, stable, and free from conflict, however, then Ratna is only deluding herself. The fact tenaciously remains that she is an alien on that island, being regarded as a Canadian by the Third World islanders, and that she is a second-class citizen in Canada, being disregarded as a Third World person there. Furthermore, she is surrounded by babbling tourists who are without homes on that island, an island in political turmoil. Therefore, although the final sentence of the story sounds hopeful, it is in fact an ironic and despairing statement implying that Ratna will never really be "at home" anywhere.

ANGELA

First published: 1984
Type of work: Short story

A young refugee girl from Bangladesh tries to adjust to her adoptive home in Iowa.

This story is included in Mukherjee's collection *Darkness* and in *The Best American Short Stories, 1985*, edited by Gail Godwin and Shannon Ravennel.

"Angela" is not a happily ending story of a refugee successfully finding life, liberty, and happiness in the United States. Rather, it is a subtle psychological analysis of a survivor, of how survival can entail feelings of guilt and obligation, and of how survivors can be exploited by their rescuers.

The story begins with Angela, a teenage refugee from Bangladesh, at the bedside of her adoptive sister Delia Brandon in Van Buren County Hospital, Iowa. Delia is comatose after an auto accident, one which Angela survived with hardly a scratch. Naturally, Angela feels guilty that she, not Delia, has survived the accident un- scathed—Delia was the one who had instigated Angela's adoption by the Brandons. Besides, Sister Stella at the orphanage had taught Angela a Christian account of salvation, as if it were some institution of savings and loans: "The Lord saved you. Now it's your turn to do him credit." Indeed, Angela's list of indebtedness to the Almighty for letting her survive is lengthy: Surviving the death of both parents at the age of six, she also survived the political upheaval of Bangladesh, racing through "leechy paddy-fields" to avoid "the rapes, the dogs chewing dead bodies, the sol- diers." The only scars she retains are those that occurred when her nipples had been sliced off. Afterwards, Angela had found refuge in a Catholic orphanage, and even- tually she was adopted by the Brandons, a farming family in Iowa, where Angela is now a cheerleader in high school.

Angela's survival is little short of a marvel, a miracle, a holy mystery—terms which occur in Angela's first-person narrative. She would even seem to be an an- gel—or at least to be under the guardianship of one, a manifestation of God's "grace" to fallen and violent mankind. If Angela is an angel, however, she is a dark one, and not by virtue of complexion only. She says that the cook at the orphanage used to "chop wings off crows . . . so I could sew myself a sturdy pair of angel wings," and she continues, "I visualize grace as a black, tropical bat, cutting through dusk on blunt ugly wings"—this is not the usual dove of light. Through such imagery, Mukherjee makes the reader approach grace and miracle with circum- spection and irony.

The reader is also led to question how unmixed a miracle Angela's apparent good fortune may be and under what a load of obligation and guilt she is placed thereby. Clearly, she is obligated to the Brandons and feels guilty that the Almighty had visited injury on the Brandons' daughter rather than on herself during their accident. Further, it would appear that the Brandons, in turn, are obligated to a Dr. Menezies, an Indian physician who is attending to Delia and who also seems to be helping the Brandons fend off foreclosure on their farm.

Dr. Menezies, who is nearly forty years old, wants to marry Angela, but she is not attracted to him. Angela herself yearns for the self-development of going to college and the freedom of pursuing a career. Such desires would, of course, be dashed if she were to accept Dr. Menezies' marriage proposal entailing duplexes and babies. Yet marriage to Dr. Menezies would, under the circumstances, be tantamount to a dis- charging of Angela's indebtedness to the Brandons, as well as an assuagement for the guilt of having somehow undeservedly survived her accident unscathed. Exploiting Angela's sense of obligation, Dr. Menezies tries to dissuade her from going to col- lege: "I don't think you are so selfish." Mukherjee ends the story with this dilemma cxquisitely and excruciatingly imaged by Angela: As Angela falls asleep, she dreams in a sensuously ambiguous image of leeches feeding on her nippleless breasts— a richly ironic conflation of the repulsive and the medicinal, of suffering and nurtur- ing, of the appearance of grace and the reality of exploitation.

Summary

Mukherjee's short stories and novels bring unique insight and profundity to the immigration, expatriation, and assimilation of South Asians, especially South Asian women, in North America. She explores the effects of racism, sexism, violence, and human exploitation with consummate skill, measured realism, and moving drama. There is an implacable resentment of racism in her works, but there is also an implicit hope in the redeeming possibilities of love and in the positive aspects of United States society, in which individuals of color, even women of color, may realize their full humanity and empower themselves. Mukherjee's artistry is characterized by her frequent use of irony, imagistic leitmotifs that grow into meaningful symbols, literary and mythological allusions, a supple and exuberant wielding of multiple American idioms, and acute psychological penetration into a wide assortment of characters.

Bibliography

Carb, Alison B. "An Interview with Bharati Mukherjee." *Massachusetts Review* 29 (Winter, 1988): 645-654.

Desai, Anita. "Outcasts: *Darkness* by Bharati Mukherjee." *London Magazine* (December, 1985/January, 1986): 143-146.

Ispahani, Mahnaz. "A Passage from India: *Darkness* by Bharati Mukherjee." *The New Republic* 194 (April 14, 1986): 36-39.

Mukherjee, Bharati. "An Invisible Woman." *Saturday Night* 96 (March, 1981): 36-40.

_____. Interview by Geoff Hancock. *Canadian Fiction Magazine* 59 (1987): 30-44.

_____. Interview by Sybil Steinberg. *Publishers Weekly* 25 (August, 1989): 46-47.

Naipaul, V. S. "A Conversation with V. S. Naipaul." Interview by Bharati Mukherjee and Robert Boyers. *Salmagundi* 54 (Fall, 1981): 4-22.

Nazareth, Peter. "Total Vision." *Canadian Literature* 110 (Fall, 1986): 184-191.

C. L. Chua

VLADIMIR NABOKOV

Born: St. Petersburg, Russia
April 23, 1899
Died: Lausanne, Switzerland
July 2, 1977

Principal Literary Achievement

Nabokov was unique in that he became a major author in both Russian and English. He wrote stories, novels, poetry, memoirs, plays, critical essays, reviews, lectures, and translations.

Biography

Vladimir Vladimirovich Nabokov's life divides neatly into four phases, each lasting approximately twenty years. The oldest of five siblings, he was born April 10 (Old Style), 1899, to an aristocratic and wealthy family in St. Petersburg (later changed to Leningrad by the Soviets). Nabokov later insisted on the New Style birthdate of April 23, because it coincided with William Shakespeare's.

Nabokov's grandfather, Dmitri Nikolayevich, had been State Minister of Justice for two czars. His father, Vladimir Dmitrievich, a prominent liberal statesman, was married to Elena Rukavishnikova, a beautiful woman from an extremely rich family. Vladimir's parents adored their first-born child and reared him with enormous love and care. Nabokov eloquently evoked his childhood in his lyrical memoir, *Conclusive Evidence* (1951), expanded and retitled *Speak, Memory* (1966).

After the 1917 Bolshevik Revolution, life became increasingly dangerous for Nabokov's father. In 1919, the Nabokovs fled Russia. Vladimir, who had learned both French and English from governesses, enrolled in the University of Cambridge's Trinity College. Although he spent much of his time there writing poems and playing tennis, he was graduated in 1922 with first-class honors in French and Russian. Meanwhile, the other family members had settled in Berlin. Ten days after Nabokov's arrival from Cambridge, his father was assassinated on March 28 by right-wing extremist Russian expatriates who had intended their bullets for another target. Vladimir took up residence in Berlin; in 1925, he was married to Véra Slonim, an attractive, brilliant Jewish émigré, with whom his temperament and interests remained happily matched for the rest of his life.

The Nabokovs stayed in Berlin until 1937, then moved to Paris for three years. In the 1920's and 1930's Nabokov wrote nine novels, about forty stories, and consider-

able poetry. He also gave tennis and boxing lessons, composed chess problems and crossword puzzles for newspapers, and engaged in entomological research. He would become an expert on butterflies' genitalia. His most important novels during this period are commonly considered to be *Zashchita Luzhina* (1929; *The Defense*, 1964) and *Dar* (1937-1938; *The Gift*, 1963).

Nabokov's third phase started in 1940, when he escaped the Nazi menace by emigrating to the United States. After a one-term lectureship at Stanford University, he spent the next seven years as a part-time instructor at Wellesley College while also working as a lepidopterist at Harvard University's Museum of Comparative Zoology. During those years he published two novels in English, *The Real Life of Sebastian Knight* (1941) and *Bend Sinister* (1947). He also wrote a brilliant as well as eccentric study of Nikolai Gogol (1944), whose absurdist perspective deeply influenced Nabokov's writing.

From 1948 to 1959 he held a professorship at Cornell University, becoming a campus celebrity. Nabokov specialized in a course called Masters of European Fiction (in English), alternately charming and provoking his students with witty lectures, demanding examinations, and, occasionally, unfair treatment: He wanted to expel one student for disagreeing with his dismissal of Fyodor Dostoevski's literary worth.

During his summer vacations in the early 1950's, Nabokov wrote his most notorious and popular novel, *Lolita*. The book was at first refused publication by several American firms. In 1955, a Parisian English-language publisher, Olympia Press, issued the novel. By 1958, Putnam's took a chance and published it in New York, and the novel became the year's sensational seller. In 1962, *Lolita* was made into a film by Stanley Kubrick, starring James Mason as Humbert Humbert.

Nabokov's earnings from *Lolita*, which included film rights and a hefty fee for writing the screenplay, made him financially independent. In 1959, he left Cornell to travel in Europe for two years; in 1961, he established residence at an elegant hotel on the banks of Switzerland's Lake Geneva where he would enjoy fifteen more productive years. He revised his autobiography; translated his Russian long and short fiction into English, either by himself or in collaboration with his son, Dmitri; produced a four-volume translation of and commentary on Aleksandr Pushkin's novel in verse, *Evgeny Onegin* (1833; Nabokov's version, *Eugene Onegin*, 1964); and wrote several brilliant new novels, including *Pale Fire* (1962) and *Ada: Or, Ardor, A Family Chronicle* (1969). In his last years, he appeared to suffer from some form of cancer, which he declined to identify. He died in a hospital in Lausanne, Switzerland, on July 2, 1977.

Analysis

Nabokov's work has received considerable critical acclaim, and a consensus has been reached that he is at least a distinguished and arguably a great writer. He has exerted a major influence on contemporary authors such as Anthony Burgess, John Barth, Thomas Pynchon, William Gass, Tom Stoppard, Philip Roth, John Updike, and Milan Kundera. Nabokov wrote at least three masterful novels: *The Gift*, *Lolita*, and *Pale Fire*. Several of his stories, including "Vesna Fialte" ("Spring in Fialta") and "Signs and Symbols," are among the century's finest; his autobiography (*Conclusive Evidence*, published in 1951, then revised as *Speak, Memory* in 1966) rivals Marcel Proust's in the intensity and lyricism of its nostalgia.

Nabokov's work is never intentionally didactic, sociological, ideological, or psychologically oriented; he detested moralistic, message-ridden writing. While his fictive world is filled with aberrant and bizarre characters—pederasts, buffoons, cripples, and obsessives of one sort or another—they are described not as psychological types but as representatives of the overwhelming vulgarity, freakishness, and pathos that corrupt human nature imposes on the sublimity of the natural and aesthetic world. Aestheticism is Nabokov's secular religion, and his grotesques, such *Lolita*'s Humbert Humbert, *Pale Fire*'s Charles Kinbote, and *The Defense*'s Luzhin, are offenses against the sensitivity of the artistic imagination.

Nabokov's antirealism brings him firmly into the fold of Impressionism, which was inspired by the Impressionist painters Edouard Manet, Edgar Degas, and Claude Monet. Impressionistic writers employ highly selective details to stress the subjectivity of the moment's fleeting effect upon their consciousness. Neglecting accumulation of verisimilar details, they prefer to focus on memories and moods, seeking to evoke moments of ardent emotion. Nabokov's literary company includes Gustave Flaubert, Ivan Turgenev, Henry James, Joseph Conrad, Virginia Woolf, and, particularly, Proust. Nabokov's art privileges images and impressions as they flash through the limited consciousness of the observer/narrator. The protagonist may be mad or morally eccentric, however; thus, the reader must beware of empathizing too closely with the central character, who may be schizophrenic, manipulative, confused, or otherwise unreliable.

Nabokov is a difficult, enigmatic, and complex writer. He delights in playing self-consciously with the reader's credibility, considering himself a magician in command of innumerable artifices. He loves to devise absorbing, convoluted games that often baffle the unwary reader. Many of his texts are composed like daunting chess problems, with many levels of perception, structural false bottoms, and illusory plot patterns. For example, *Pale Fire*, which is apparently an exegesis of a long poem, has a chimerical confusion of identities and realities; dream fantasies constitute the fictive worlds of *Bend Sinister* and *Priglashenie na kazn'* (1938; *Invitation to a Beheading*, 1959); the Clare Quilty episode of *Lolita* parodies the conventions of melodrama; and several novels, including *Kamera obskura* (1932; *Camera Obscura*, 1936; *Laughter in the Dark*, 1938) and *The Real Life of Sebastian Knight*, mock the mannerisms of the mystery story. Nabokov's love of playing games with the reader has caused some critics to accuse him of preferring brilliantly designed surfaces to serious explorations of significant human experiences.

Nabokov's puzzle-making fun and games, however, often concerns an underlying sadness. Many of the protagonists in his novels and stories face the grim horrors of an often uncaring, senseless, sorrowful world. His persistent themes are the anguish of being unloved, the fragility of memory, and the brutishness of willfully inflicted pain. Though Nabokov practices art for the sake of art, he scorns the sadism of such artists in his fiction as *Laughter in the Dark*'s Axel Rex, *Lolita*'s Humbert Humbert and Clare Quilty, and *Ada*'s Van Veen.

Nabokov's art not only affirms a supremely talented author's precision of language, parodistic wit, and sharpness of observation but also celebrates the sanctity of life and the necessity of creative freedom. Lolita is selfish, vulgar, shallow, and materialistic, but Humbert is nevertheless guilty of having deprived her of much of her childhood. While portraying Humbert with dazzling brilliance, Nabokov denies him the moral sympathy he extends to the victim.

THE REAL LIFE OF SEBASTIAN KNIGHT

First published: 1941
Type of work: Novel

A man loses his own identity while trying to write the fictional biography of his lost brother.

The Real Life of Sebastian Knight, Nabokov's first novel in English, anticipates *Pale Fire* and *Look at the Harlequins!* (1974) in being a fictional biography of a brilliant writer who has died recently. As the reader accompanies the narrator, V., on his search for knowledge about the novelist Sebastian Knight, both reader and protagonist learn less and less about their subject, until it becomes apparent that Knight's "real life" is undiscoverable.

Nabokov parodies the formula and apparatus of the detective story. V. rushes about interviewing people who knew Sebastian, only to amass contradictory and confusing knowledge that is highly colored by his informants' self-interest. V.'s poise disintegrates as he spends many days learning less and less about his subject and following the obscure trails of Knight's correspondence. The women he interviews dupe him, and he quarrels with people whose regard for Knight is less favorable than his.

Many of the novel's stratagems resemble those of a chess game. The aptly named Knight had a mistress named Clare Bishop and a mother named Virginia—a common term for the chess queen is "virgin." V. often believes that he has become the pawn of ambiguous circumstances. Moreover, Knight's given name, Sebastian, alludes to the third century Christian martyr who was killed by arrows.

The novel also alludes to Shakespeare's comedy, *Twelfth Night* (1601-1602), which is crowded with mistaken identities and features twin brothers named Sebastian. Knight had a half brother, and the novel strongly implies that V. may be he. Knight's father was Russian, and his mother was English. Thus, V. and Knight may well be divided halves of a single identity: Nabokov.

With its involuted development and inconclusive ending, the novel contrasts the duplicity of reality with the permanence of art. Real life is an infinite maze, whose center is unreachable. The one real life is that of the writer's work. V. is on sure ground only when he analyzes Knight's writings; everything else is quicksand.

LOLITA

First published: 1955
Type of work: Novel

A pedophilic European intellectual falls in tormented love with a teenager.

Lolita, generally considered Nabokov's greatest novel, unites wildly grotesque parody, farce, and pathos with two powerful, shocking subjects: the passionate feelings of a grown man toward a pubescent girl and the complex nature of romantic love, which is not only tender and generous but also ruthless and even totalitarian.

The novel's middle-aged, middle-European narrator "writes" this book as his confession while in a prison cell awaiting trial for murder. His double-talk name, Humbert Humbert, sets the tone of punning parody that pervades the text, as various people address him as Humberg, Herbert, Humbird, Humberger, and Humbug. Humbert Humbert traces his sexual obsession for "nymphets"—girls between the ages of nine and fourteen—to a case of interrupted coitus when he was thirteen years old; he and a certain Annabel Leigh had the beginnings of their first affair forever aborted by her premature death of typhus. (The allusions to Edgar Allan Poe's poem and life number at least twenty; Nabokov refers to many other writers, including Shakespeare, John Keats, Flaubert, James Joyce, Proust, and T. S. Eliot.) After his marriage to a "life-sized" woman in Paris ends ridiculously, Humbert emigrates to the United States.

Here Humbert discovers Lolita Haze, a twelve-year-old, gum-chewing, Coke-gurgling, comic book-addicted, blatantly bratty schoolgirl. Humbert agrees to marry Charlotte, her vapid, pretentious, widowed mother, in order to be near the irresistible daughter. When Charlotte learns of his pedophilia through reading his diary, she runs distractedly out of the house and conveniently is killed by a passing car before she can publicize his perversion.

Having laid his wife to rest, the widower undertakes the clumsy comedy of seducing his stepdaughter, who, by no means sexually innocent, volunteers to show her would-be ravisher what intercourse is all about. He registers his shock:

> Suffice it to say that not a trace of modesty did I perceive in this beautiful hardly formed young girl whom modern co-education, juvenile mores, the campfire racket and so forth had utterly and hopelessly depraved. . . .
>
> My life was handled by little Lo in an energetic, matter-of-fact manner as if it were an insensate gadget unconnected with me.

"Hum" and "Lo" engage in a parody of incest—he stands legally *in loco parentis*—as they traverse the continent. They encounter a neon-lit landscape of gas stations, motels, juke boxes, billboards, coffee shops, and highways. Humbert finds Lolita coolly acquiescent to his caresses at times, peevishly self-centered at others, and capable of quickly shifting from dreamy childishness to trashy vulgarity to whining waywardness.

The couple is shadowed by a playwright, Clare Quilty ("Clearly Guilty"?) who is a peekaboo parody of the psychological double that was made famous by E. T. A. Hoffmann and Dostoevski. Both Humbert and Quilty are authors, love word puzzles, dress similarly, and are addicted to deviant sex. Quilty spirits Lolita away from Humbert, has a brief liaison with her, then discards her when she refuses to serve the boys whom he prefers to her.

Several years later, Humbert is contacted by Lolita, who desperately needs money. She is seventeen, married, plain, pale, and pregnant. In a moving episode, he discovers that he is ardently in love with her, despite her worn looks and sagging flesh. She will not return to him, but she does give him Quilty's address. Humbert then kills Quilty in a farcically protracted scene. The "editor's" preface tells the reader that Lolita died in childbirth and Humbert succumbed to cardiac arrest.

The novel works on many levels: It is a remorseless satire of middle-class, immature America and a seriocomic commentary on Continental-American cultural relations. More profoundly, it is a moving romance in the medieval tradition of courtly love, with the afflicted Humbert Humbert displaying his derangement by obsessional devotion and self-pitying masochism. He submits himself to his emotionally unattainable mistress as her slavish servant, glorying in her cruelly capricious power over him.

On a deeper level, *Lolita* is a study in the pathology of Romantic yearning for unattainable, immortal bliss. Humbert hungers for an ideal condition of supernatural, bewitching enchantment which nymphets represent—a state beyond finite space and time. His search cannot be satisfied by a flesh-and-blood adolescent: He seeks an immortal being in a never-never land, a divine faunlet. His immortal Lolita can only be realized through Nabokov's marvelous art, which manages to transform perversion into literature.

PNIN

First published: 1957
Type of work: Novel

A Russian émigré professor tries to adapt to the alien planet of the United States.

The title character of *Pnin* is a bald, myopic, middle-aged, spindly-legged professor of Russian at Waindell College, which is somewhere in New England. Timofey Pnin is a meticulous scholar who massages a multitude of details as he researches a long-standing project: A commentary on his native Russia's folklore and literature that will reflect in miniature the major events of Russian history up to the

Bolshevik Revolution. In his classes, Pnin wages Pyrrhic warfare against the English language, often digressing from his academic text to undertake mirthful excursions into his past.

Simple existence usually confounds Pnin. He manages to lose the soles of his canvas shoes in a washing machine; he fails his automobile driving test; he takes the wrong train after having carefully consulted an outdated timetable. It is not surprising that a cruel colleague, Jack Cockerell, makes a social career out of mimicking Pnin's words and gestures. Pnin is a comically inept character, whose Chaplinesque, Quixotic qualities render him essentially harmless, gentle, generous, and pathetically vulnerable.

Life has punished him. In 1925, in Paris, Pnin was married to the melodramatic and severely neurotic Liza Bogolepov, to save her from threatened suicide after an affair with another man. In 1938, Liza deserted him for a German psychiatrist, Eric Wind. When she returned a year later, he forgave her, and they reunited and took the boat together for America—only to have Wind show up on the same ship and depart with Liza after it docked in New York. When Liza reappears in Pnin's life at Waindell, Pnin again forgives her and asks her to return to him; the sole purpose of her visit, however, is to ask him to help support her son by Wind, Victor. Liza tells Pnin that she intends to forsake Wind for a poet and no longer wishes to be responsible for her son's upbringing. In spite of these humiliations, Pnin still loves Liza. He would be happy "to hold her, to keep her—just as she was—with her cruelty, with her vulgarity, with her blinding blue eyes, with her miserable poetry, with her fat feet, with her impure, dry, sordid, infantile soul." Illogically yet unconditionally, Pnin adores this histrionic, pretentious, destructively evil woman. Here Nabokov establishes one of his absolute, magical premises, akin to Luzhin's madness and Humbert's nympholepsy.

Pnin's life could easily be considered a catalog of losses: his native land and its culture; his parents; his first love, Mira Belochkin, who died in a Nazi concentration camp; his wife; and, at the novel's end, his position at Waindell. Nabokov avoids the temptation of satirizing him as the absentminded, sweet, pathetically unfortunate professor. He treats him warmly, endearingly, and respectfully. More important, he provides Pnin with several shields against defeatism and despair.

Pnin has energy, buoyancy, and a capacity for delighting in life. After Liza leaves him for what the reader hopes is the last time, he accedes to the need of a thirsty squirrel by holding down the lever of a water fountain. He is willing to wrestle with his fate even though he usually loses. After grieving for a few days over the loss of his teeth, Pnin welcomes the miracle of his dentures, which Nabokov describes as a "firm mouthful of efficient, alabastrine, humane America."

The novel's ending is open to varying interpretations. Its narrator replaces Pnin as professor of Russian and reveals that he was responsible for Liza's seduction in Paris in the 1920's. Pnin, driving a sedan overloaded with all of his possessions, spurts out of Waindell into the open road, "where there was simply no saying what miracle might happen." Pnin has no job, little money, and no set destination. Instead of being a portrait of a victim in flight, however, the book seeks to delineate an optimistic adventurer chancing his luck in the hills beyond Waindell. Possibly Nabokov meant to signify that Pnin, like Pavel Chichikov at the end of *Myortrye dushi* (1842; *Dead Souls*), was intent on creating his own fate in existential style. Thus, the most affectionately drawn and moving of Nabokov's characters will insist, as he departs his book, that harm and pain need not be the world's norm, and that the pangs of exile need not defeat a courageous sufferer.

PALE FIRE

First published: 1962
Type of work: Novel

A reader's-trap, cat-and-mouse satire involving a long poem edited and analyzed by a lunatic scholar who considers himself an exiled monarch.

Pale Fire is Nabokov's most intricate, ingenious, and controversial novel, extravagantly lauded by some of his critics and assailed as coldly concerned with only technique and gamesmanship by others.

The book begins with a brief foreword written by an academician, Dr. Charles Kinbote, who introduces a 999-line poem in heroic couplets, "Pale Fire," composed by the prominent American poet John Francis Shade, who has recently died. After the poem's text, Kinbote engages in more than two hundred pages of line-by-line interpretations. The book ends with the requisite index.

A homely man who resembles Robert Frost, Shade teaches at Wordsmith College in New Wye, Appalachia. Specializing in the poetry of Alexander Pope, Shade's masterpiece is closer to William Wordsworth's pastoral themes. (Wordsmith is a combination of two poets' names: Wordsworth and Oliver Goldsmith. The card game in Pope's spirited satire, *The Rape of the Lock* (1712) is ombre, which is the French word for shade, or shadow. In *Pale Fire*, John Shade turns out to be the trump in Kinbote's bizarre game.

Kinbote describes himself as an émigré scholar who has fled his native country of Zembla. In the index, he defines Zembla as "a distant northern land" near Russia. Pope mentions it in his *Essay on Man* (1733): "At Greenland, Zembla, or the Lord knows where." A group of islands, Novaya Zemlya, exists in the Arctic Ocean, north of Archangel. Kinbote has lived next door to John and Sybil Shade, in a house he has rented from Judge Goldsworth, of the law faculty, who is away on a sabbatical. At the time Kinbote is writing his commentary, however, he has left Appalachia and is living in a small Southwestern town. Shade has been killed by a man named Jack Grey, and Kinbote has gone into hiding to edit, with the widow's permission, the poet's manuscript for publication.

Kinbote, however, is a victim of brilliant delusions. He believes himself to be an intimate friend of Shade, although they met rarely and Sybil Shade detests him for his snooping on the family with his binoculars. In his commentary, Kinbote strongly suggests that it was he who had provided the poet with the inspiration and subject of his final work. He twists Shade's verses to suit his grandiose needs and narrates, in his interpretations, the very saga he had dinned into the bard's tolerant but indifferent ears. The reader is thus thrust into a maze of complexities: he or she must attend to Kinbote's vividly dramatic interpretation of the poem, while simultaneously surmising the far more prosaic truth obscured by Kinbote's annotations.

According to Kinbote, the poem deals with Zembla's last king, Charles the Beloved, whose reign was peaceful, progressive, and humane. Forced to flee by a Fascist revolution, Charles escaped from Zembla by motorboat and fled to the United States, where an American sympathizer who was also a trustee of Wordsmith College found him a post on the college's language faculty. In short, Kinbote is King Charles. Meanwhile, Zembla's secret police hired a killer, Jakobus Gradus, alias Jacques d'Argus or Jack Grey, to murder the royal exile. The commentary follows Gradus' journey to New Wye, where he fires at the king but mistakenly kills Shade.

The alert reader will perceive that this plot also has a false bottom. Charles the Beloved and his colorful dynastic saga are the chimeras of Kinbote's disordered mind. Kinbote is actually a harmless refugee scholar named Botkin who teaches in Wordsmith's Languages Department. Shade knew of his mania and compassionately indulged it, while the campus at large mocked and ostracized Botkin. The gunman, whose name is Jack Grey, is an escaped madman who had been sent to the state asylum for the insane by Judge Goldsworth. Thus, Goldsworth was Grey's target, not Botkin or Shade. Moreover, the paranoid politics of Zembla are transpositions of the standard academic factionalism that infests the college, which Botkin has transformed into fantasies of persecution.

The poem and novel's title stems from Act IV, Scene 3, of Shakespeare's *Timon of Athens* (1607-1608):

> The sun's a thief, and with his great attraction
> Robs the vast sea; the moon's an arrant thief,
> And her pale fire she snatches from the sun;
> The sea's a thief, whose liquid surge resolves
> The moon into salt tears.

The theme of these lines is a cosmic cycle of universal theft, with everything in nature working at a distance to borrow its light or force from something else, completely transforming what it takes.

Art, suggests Nabokov, is also part of this cycle. All reflection, including poetic representation, can be considered a theft from reality, which in turn is always plagiarizing from itself. Botkin has stolen Shade's poem and imposed his own interpretation. The division of this novel into Shade's poem and Kinbote/Botkin's fanciful commentary, however, offers a unified work of art. *Pale Fire* explores the two opposing poles of aesthetic sensibility. Shade symbolized the honest, modest, and questioning intelligence that seeks patiently to discover a meaningful design in the cosmos through art. Kinbote/Botkin personifies the obsessional side of the creative imagination, which imposes its private order on the chaos of experience and is prepared to distort or ignore any inconvenient facts obstructing its path. Kinbote/Botkin is also a successful author: His mythical kingdom is a literary achievement that entrances the reader. The visions of the craftsman and the madman thus stand in equipoise, both sharing in the title's implications. On another level, Nabokov's novel itself circles like a moon, or pale fire, around the bright flames of Shakespeare's and Pope's genius.

ADA

First published: 1969
Type of work: Novel

An affirmation of art as the enshrinement of love and victory over mortality.

Ada: Or, Ardor, A Family Chronicle is the most luxuriant, playful, difficult, allusive, ambitious, and overblown of Nabokov's novels. It is a memoir largely written by Van Veen when he is in his nineties that narrates his love for his sister Ada. As "a family chronicle," it has a hefty nineteenth-century range replete with printed genealogies, thwarted romances, duels, and a happily-ever-after ending in which the venerable Ada is finally reunited with her childhood swain, Van. The inattentive reader will, however, tread a tortuous path through the text, for Nabokov has laced it with bristling erudition, trilingual puns, ogreish conundrums, and Joycean dislocations of time and space. The work is also insistently self-conscious: Its author frequently comments on the arduous process of creating his book, sometimes implying that its readers will never understand many of its intricacies. He is undoubtedly right.

The central family plot involves two incestuous generations. The two Durmanov sisters, Aqua and Marina, are married to two first cousins, Dementiy (nicknamed Demon) Veen and Daniel (nicknamed Red) Veen. Though Demon is married to Aqua, he has an extensive liaison with Marina. He and Aqua apparently have a son, Ivan (nicknamed Van), who is actually the son of Demon and Marina. To hide the scandal, Demon and Marina take advantage of the mentally disturbed Aqua to switch baby Van for Aqua's stillborn baby. The fertile Marina is also the mother of Demon's other bastard child, Ada, as well as of another daughter, Lucinda (nicknamed Lucette), this one by Marina and her husband Red.

This genealogical maze serves as the prelude to the lifelong love between the ostensible first cousins but actual siblings, Van and Ada Veen. The affair begins in the Edenic arbors of Ardis, the family estate, when Van is fourteen and Ada is twelve. Ardis is a parody of Eden and Van and Ada parody Adam and Eve. Ardis Park is located in a half-fantastic nineteenth century United States which willfully includes films, automobiles, and a town called Lolita, Texas. The geographies of Russia and America are combined. For example, Ardis Park lies on the boundary of a Russian village called Gamlet, which is full of "kerchiefed peasant nymphs"; in Utah, a motor court preserves Tolstoy's footprints in clay. Van and Ada inhabit the superior world of Terra, while the rest of the world resides in Demonia or Antiterra, the hell of human limitations.

Van is Nabokov's sort of artist: His favorite trick as a youth is to turn the world upside down by walking on his hands, exactly as his creator composes inverted fictions. The word Ada is a palindrome; moreover, read from the middle out in either direction, it spells *da*, which is the Russian word for yes. The latter may be interpreted as an allusion to Molly Bloom's many yeses in the concluding chapter of Joyce's *Ulysses* (1922). "*Ardis*" may remind some readers of the motto *ars gratia artis* (art for the sake of art), which would be a fitting emblem both for this novel and Nabokov's entire career.

In *Ada*, the author offers his private myth of man's beginning, with Van and Ada as his primal humans. Van is *Homo poeticus*: Writing is his particular talent and poetic awareness is his especial endowment. Ada, who becomes his sometime collaborator in their later life together, has Nabokov's passion for natural history, particularly the love of flowers, trees, and butterflies. Together, Van and Ada form a privileged, imperial couple.

Unfortunately, they spend many years apart. Their parents separate them when they discover the youngsters' affair, thus playing out the Fall of Man. For years, both spend their energetic erotism in numerous amours and are enveloped in the sins of lust, jealousy, and callousness. Van almost murders two of Ada's lovers and arranges to blind a servant who tries to blackmail him and Ada with incriminating photographs. At twenty-one, Ada contracts a marriage of convenience with an American rancher, Andrey Vinelander, who dies twenty-nine years later. Ada's half-sister Lucette falls in love with Van, but he refuses to exploit her vulnerability. When Lucette despairingly drowns herself, Van and Ada are jolted into awareness of the misery and tragedy besetting the world beyond the greenness of Ardis.

Van and Ada are finally free to spend their remaining lives together when she is fifty to his fifty-two. They must now contend with the reality of their physical failings in the face of approaching death. He has become the artist-philosopher and she the botanist-biologist—all aspects of Nabokov. They discover that collaborative writing will reconcile them to time's hostility.

In part 4 of the five-part novel, Van summarizes his philosophy in an anti-Einsteinian discourse on time and space which considers past and present as linked by associated, accumulated images captured by memory. This is an arch-Proustian concept, despite Nabokov's caution to "beware . . . of the marcel wave of fashionable art; avoid the Proustian bed." The framing devices of *Ada* parallel those of *À la recherche du temps perdu* (1913-1927; *Remembrance of Things Past*, 1922-1931). At the book's end, the reader is informed that Van and Ada have composed the very text that is about to conclude and that most of this work has been a prelude to the very act of creation which the book promises (and summarizes) in its final pages.

On the penultimate page the author gives the assurance that "the story proceeds at a spanking pace." In fact, the work often saunters self-indulgently as Nabokov treats himself to myriad puns, literary asides, and jokes against jokes in a dazzlingly polyglot glitter of words. He has never been a more agile verbal acrobat. Significantly, Van and Ada delight (as did their progenitor) in playing Scrabble, using a set that was given them by Baron Klim Avidov—an anagrammatically camouflaged Vladimir Nabokov.

SPEAK, MEMORY

First published: 1966
Type of work: Autobiography

A lyrically written testament to the meaning that exile has for an acutely sensitive and responsive artist.

Speak, Memory: An Autobiography Revisited covers thirty-seven of Nabokov's first forty-one years, from August, 1903, to May, 1940. It is a considerable revision of his first partial autobiography, *Conclusive Evidence.* Most of the chapters of *Conclusive Evidence* first appeared in *The New Yorker* between 1948 and 1950, and were published as a book in 1951. In the foreword, Nabokov states that the book provides conclusive evidence of his existence. He had planned to entitle its British edition *Speak, Mnemosyne,* invoking the Greeks' goddess of memory and mother of the Muses, but the firm of Gollancz vetoed that notion. The references to memory, in whatever language, provide an apt link to Proust: Both writers employ memory as a richly sensuous medium that enables their art to vault over the abysses of time; both practice, as their core credo, the pursuit of aesthetic bliss in their treatment of such experiences as love, grief, rejection, desire, tenderness, loss, and ecstasy.

The first paragraph of *Speak, Memory* links the narrator/author to another major writer of nuance and scruple: Samuel Beckett. Nabokov recalls his fears when, as a young boy, he saw homemade motion pictures taken by his parents weeks before his birth. They featured the brand-new carriage awaiting him "with the smug, encroaching air of a coffin"—as if he had died before he had been delivered. It is no wonder that Nabokov begins the book with the somber comment, "The cradle rocks above an abyss, and common sense tells us that our existence is but a brief crack of light between two eternities of darkness." Beckett's *En Attendant Godot* (1952; *Waiting for Godot,* 1954) twice uses the same morbid metaphor: "They give birth astride of a grave, the light gleams an instant, then it's night once more."

Most of this work's fifteen chapters, however, portray a lyrically happy—hence Proustian rather than Beckettian—childhood. With his wealthy, gifted, and adoring family, the first-born Vladimir lived in a townhouse in prerevolutionary St. Petersburg and at Vyra, an idyllic, rambling country estate. For the author and his two brothers and two sisters, their existence as children was a paradisal lesson in love, order, respect, and responsibility—until the 1917 Revolution. Vladimir's mother read aloud to him in three languages, encouraged his attempts at poetry, and nourished his delight in sounds and colors.

In chapter 2, Nabokov describes his earliest aesthetic experiences: mild synesthetic hallucinations, such as hearing in colors and linking the letters of the alphabet with such textures as vulcanized rubber with the hard *g* and weathered wood with *a*. Such synesthesia has a rich literary heritage, including the work of Symbolist poets and the French novelist Joris-Karl Huysmans. Nabokov regrets that the muse of music never touched his susceptibility: "Music . . . affects me merely as an arbitrary succession of more or less irritating sounds."

In chapter 9, Nabokov magnificently renders his tall, humane, courageous, and imposing father. A former Guards officer, he was a law lecturer at the Imperial School of Jurisprudence. He was an editor for liberal newspapers, held a seat in Russia's first parliament, opposed both anti-Semitism and capital punishment, and served a three-month prison term in 1908 for having written articles assailing the czar's despotism. Vladimir Dmitrievich also knew hundreds of Russian verses, loved Charles Dickens, and "prized highly Stendhal, [Honoré de] Balzac and Zola, three detestable mediocrities from *my* point of view."

The author climaxes this chapter with an account of a duel his father almost fought against the editor of a right-wing paper that had printed a scurrilous article about him. The possibility of losing his father shocked young Vladimir into awareness of their deep affection for each other. Writing that the editor ended the affair with an abject apology, Nabokov recalls the assassination of his father that would occur ten years later, and is grateful that, back in 1912, "several lines of play in a difficult chess composition were not blended yet on the board." The image is essentially Nabokovian: Exactly as each move on a chessboard affects all subsequent moves, so his father's reprieve from an encounter with death will cause him to make moves which will finally result in his murder. In Nabokov's worldview, all events are somehow organically connected.

Speak, Memory re-creates with superlative skill not only the ethos of an idyllic upbringing but also the social upheaval of exile. Nabokov rhapsodically recounts the first creation of his poems and his first pursuits of butterflies. Best of all, he provides a poignant account of adolescent first love between him and the teenaged Tamara in 1915. He pictures "the tender, moist gleam on her lower eyelid," but is discreet about describing their sexual union: "In one particular pine grove . . . I parted the fabric of fancy, I tasted reality." They took to the woods in summer, to museums and cinemas in winter. They parted in 1916—he cannot recall the cause—only to meet by chance on a train in 1917 for a few minutes. When Tamara left him at the station, he recalls, even "today no alien marginalia can dim the purity of the pain."

In chapter 14, Nabokov deals with the spectral world of émigré society in Europe during the 1920's and 1930's. He kept himself too occupied to wallow in self-pity, and has only scorn for refugees who chronically lamented their lost wealth and estates. In *Conclusive Evidence*, Nabokov remarked that, among the younger exiled Russian writers, the only one who turned out to be a major achiever was V. Sirin. In

Speak, Memory, Sirin is no longer called a major figure—only "the loneliest and most arrogant one." The narrator devotes a page to him, citing favorable and unfavorable responses to Sirin's books, and concludes "Across the dark sky of exile, Sirin passed . . . like a meteor, and disappeared, leaving nothing much else behind him than a vague sense of uneasiness."

Readers need to know that "Sirin" was the pen name Nabokov himself assumed during this period, at first to avoid confusion with his famous father, and then as an established habit. Such deadpan self-mockery and misleading of his public is characteristic of the games he would play with increasing relish in his later fiction, particularly *Pale Fire* and *Ada*.

Summary

Vladimir Nabokov was a prodigiously gifted literary jeweler who sometimes cut deeply into human experience and at other times preferred to play clever games on its surface. At his worst, he sought to trick the reader with exotic wordplay, cultural booby traps, and exhibitionistic displays of stylistic arabesques. In his best work, such as *Lolita*; *Speak, Memory*; *Pnin*; and *Pale Fire*, however, he is a poetic fabulist and magician whose aestheticism is at the service of love, tenderness, compassion, kindness, empathy, grief, loneliness, wonder, and, above all, great art.

Bibliography

Boyd, Brian. *Vladimir Nabokov: The Russian Years*. Princeton, N.J.: Princeton University Press, 1990.

Field, Andrew. *V.N.: The Life and Art of Vladimir Nabokov*. New York: Crown, 1986.

Fowler, Douglas. *Reading Nabokov*. Ithaca, N.Y.: Cornell University Press, 1974.

Hyde, G. M. *Vladimir Nabokov: America's Russian Novelist*. London: Marion Boyars, 1977.

Maddox, Lucy. *Nabokov's Novels in English*. Athens: University of Georgia Press, 1983.

Nabokov, Vladimir. *The Annotated Lolita*, edited by Alfred Appel, Jr. New York: McGraw-Hill, 1970.

_____. *Vladimir Nabokov: Selected Letters, 1940-1977*, edited by Dmitri Nabokov and Matthew J. Bruccoli. San Diego, Ca.: Harcourt Brace Jovanovich, 1989.

Pifer, Ellen. *Nabokov and the Novel*. Cambridge, Mass.: Harvard University Press, 1980.

Toker, Leona. *Nabokov: The Mystery of Literary Structures*. Ithaca, N.Y.: Cornell University Press, 1989.

Gerhard Brand

GLORIA NAYLOR

Born: New York, New York
January 25, 1950

Principal Literary Achievement
Naylor is a distinguished black American novelist best known for representing the experiences and views of black women.

Biography

Gloria Naylor was born on January 25, 1950, in New York City, the daughter of Roosevelt Naylor, a transit worker, and Alberta McAlpin Naylor, a telephone operator. Her parents had moved from Mississippi only a few months before. The oldest of three sisters, Naylor grew up and attended schools in New York. As a young person she was shy but was an avid reader. In high school, she immersed herself in such classic British authors as Charlotte and Emily Brontë, Jane Austen, and Charles Dickens, whose influences can be seen in Naylor's own writing.

The young Naylor also felt a strong sense of religious dedication. In 1968, after graduation from high school, she began working as a missionary for the Jehovah's Witnesses, whose headquarters is in Brooklyn. She spent the next seven years as a missionary in New York, North Carolina, and Florida—travels that obviously provided materials for and influenced the settings of her novels. The strongest evidence of her early religious background might be the lingering fundamentalist outlook of her novels, wherein—for other reasons besides religion—characters are often divided into the redeemed or the damned.

In 1975, Naylor left the Jehovah's Witnesses and returned to New York City, where she worked as a hotel telephone operator while attending Brooklyn College of the City University of New York. At Brooklyn College, Naylor studied creative writing and read the book that was most influential in shaping her career, *The Bluest Eye* (1970), by black female novelist Toni Morrison. Morrison was a model for the young Naylor, inspiring her to write fiction and to focus on the realities of black women.

In 1981 Naylor received her B.A. in English from Brooklyn College, then, with a fellowship, moved on to Yale University. While at Yale, she published *The Women of Brewster Place* (1982), which in 1983 won the American Book Award for best first novel. That same year, Naylor won the Distinguished Writer Award of the Mid-Atlantic Writers Association and received her M.A. in Afro-American Studies from Yale.

Thereafter, Naylor found herself much in demand as a visiting writer and lecturer. During the summer of 1983 she was writer-in-residence at Cummington Community of the Arts in Massachusetts; during 1983-1984 she was a visiting lecturer at George Washington University; during the fall of 1985 she was a cultural exchange lecturer for the United States Information Agency in India. Naylor's second novel, *Linden Hills*, also appeared in 1985.

Further awards and invitations followed. Naylor received a National Endowment for the Arts fellowship in 1985, the Candace Award of the National Coalition of 100 Black Women in 1986, and a Guggenheim fellowship in 1988. She was a scholar-in-residence at the University of Pennsylvania in 1986, a visiting lecturer at Princeton University in 1986-1987, a visiting professor at New York University in 1986 and Boston University in 1987, Fannie Hurst Visiting Professor at Brandeis University in 1988, and a senior fellow at Cornell University's Society for the Humanities in 1988.

In 1988, Naylor also published her third novel, *Mama Day*, to even greater applause. Not all of her work was instantly successful, particularly her attempts to write television screenplays. Two screenplays written in 1984 and 1985 remained unproduced for a time, but a television miniseries of *The Women of Brewster Place*, featuring Oprah Winfrey and a host of other stars, was broadcast and was well received.

Meanwhile, Naylor expanded her literary efforts in other directions. In 1984 she became a contributing editor to *Callaloo: An Afro-American and African Journal of Arts and Letters*, and she has contributed articles to a wide range of periodicals including *Essence, People, Life, Ms., Ontario Review,* and *The Southern Review.* In 1986, she also wrote a column for *The New York Times* entitled *Hers.*

Analysis

Naylor has stated that, as a young reader, she was impressed by the lack of fiction reflecting the experiences and perspectives of black women. Besides the British classics, she read such American authors as the Southern white male writer William Faulkner. Even established black writers were almost all male and reflected a male perspective. There was a severe shortage of fiction that spoke directly to her, a black woman—the invisible woman of American literature. Naylor set out deliberately to help rectify this situation, or this injustice, by writing fiction that brought black women to the foreground.

Naylor began writing during the heyday of the women's liberation movement, which had articulated a vast body of feminist thought. Although often contradictory, feminist thinking at that time generally stressed the uniqueness of women at the same time that it called for their political equality within society and the family. More doctrinaire thinkers glorified woman as hero—a figure somehow more sensitive, loving, responsible, and courageous than the male of the species. Naylor's views on black women are permeated by these various strains of feminism.

In Naylor, however, feminism is layered onto more old-fashioned influences that work in concert with it. One set of influences is literary. From such writers as the

Brontës, Dickens, Faulkner, and Morrison, Naylor appears to have developed, underneath her surface realism, a taste for romanticism that sometimes verges on the melodramatic or Gothic.

The romantic streak comes out, for example, in many of Naylor's characters. Emotional, obsessive, and unforgiving, they are prone to extreme gestures: A single trait or event can set their whole life course or shatter relationships. As a result, the characters are somewhat one-dimensional, if not stereotypical, but they are nevertheless memorable. Notable examples are Luther Needed, who imprisons his wife and child in the basement, and the old conjure woman Mama Day.

Naylor's romanticism is also apparent in her heavy use of symbolism, which can almost make her seem to be a latter-day Nathaniel Hawthorne. As in Hawthorne, the weather usually cooperates with the mood of her story: a week of gloomy rain after the tragic climax of *The Women of Brewster Place*, bone-chilling December cold in *Linden Hills*, and a hurricane in *Mama Day*. Her novels are filled with such obviously symbolic details as an eerie howl that comes floating up the hillside or "the pinks"—imaginary blobs of pink slime—that pursue Norman Anderson in *Linden Hills* (the influence of horror films can also be noted here).

Most obvious of all is the symbolism of place: Brewster Place is a dead-end street, Linden Hills is laid out like Dante's Hell, and the barrier island in *Mama Day* recalls the magical isle of William Shakespeare's *The Tempest* (1611). Indeed, Naylor is so intent on the symbolism of her settings that she is occasionally careless about their literal accuracy. In depicting the South, for example, she has crape myrtle blooming in the spring, sugar cane growing in middle Tennessee, and interstate highways heading north years before they were actually built.

Besides literary romanticism, another influence affecting Naylor's feminism is her early religious background. In her fiction, Naylor is no longer a missionary for any religion; on the contrary, as a former insider she portrays religious hypocrites and self-righteous bigots with deadly accuracy. Rather, what is meant is that she seems to have transferred her original missionary fervor into her feminism and, in the process, retained some of the trappings of religious thought. In particular, there is a tendency in her earlier work to demonize men (black and white). In a conversation with Toni Morrison that appeared in *The Southern Review*, Naylor said that she had tried hard to avoid portraying men negatively in *The Women of Brewster Place* and thought she had succeeded. This statement is rather astounding, since practically all the men in the novel are scoundrels, except for a kindly old wino—who is killed for his troubles by a lesbian.

In *Linden Hills*, Naylor relents somewhat. Two easygoing young black men, poets, are the informal heroes, or at least sympathetic observers, of the novel (in the symbolic scheme, they play a modern-day Dante and Vergil). Luther Nedeed is a scoundrel of the old school, however; one of his black ancestors is even rumored to have "financed gunrunners to the Confederacy." Within the symbolic scheme, Luther is the devil himself, ruling over the middle-class hell of Linden Hills from its lowest, richest level.

In *Mama Day*, Naylor relents even more, offering the character George Andrews as her portrait of a good man. A gentle, understanding, hardworking engineer who loves his wife, George even comes across as a better person than most women in the book, including his wife, Cocoa. George is not a woman, however, and hence he has serious limitations deriving from his masculine propensity to approach things in a strictly rational manner—a severe kind of tunnel vision. George's failure to understand the wider worlds of nature and the supernatural inhabited by the women proves to be fatal. Over these worlds reigns old Mama Day, representing the powers that be. She is the antithesis of the demonized Luther Nedeed.

Such is the feminist gospel according to Naylor. Whether it will ultimately be limiting to her work remains to be seen, but as Naylor's varying portrayals of men indicate, her thinking has continued to develop. Naylor's abilities as a writer have progressed, as well: Her style has improved, she has tried new techniques, and with each book she has taken on a more difficult task and succeeded. It must be pointed out that Naylor's work contains much more than feminism. Her concern with serious themes is relieved by a sense of humor that presents an effective representation of black banter and repartee. She provides an intimate glimpse into black life at all levels and a daring critique of its problems. Her interest in these difficulties, while sometimes related to her feminism, at other times seems to supersede it. Outstanding among the problems that her characters face are discrimination, poverty, family breakups, and, in particular, the question of black identity.

THE WOMEN OF BREWSTER PLACE

First published: 1982
Type of work: Novel

Seven black women struggle to cope with life on a dead-end ghetto street.

Naylor began her celebration of black women's lives with *The Women of Brewster Place: A Novel in Seven Stories*. Exhibiting the varied backgrounds and experiences of seven different women, the seven stories of its subtitle can be read separately, but they are united by their setting and by characters who reappear from one story to the next. The stories also perform a kind of counterpoint to one another, with various parallels and contrasts. However varied the courses of their lives have been, the women now share a common fate: They have all arrived at the dead-end ghetto of Brewster Place, not only a racial and socioeconomic enclave but also a dumping ground for used women.

Mattie Michael, the motherly figure on the block, grew up in Tennessee and arrived on Brewster Place via repeated betrayals by the men in her life. During her youth, one weak moment in a basil patch with the sweet-talking Butch left her pregnant, for which her father brutally beat her and kicked her out. Finding refuge first with her friend Etta Mae Johnson and then in the home of another woman, Eva Turner, Mattie devoted her life to rearing and pampering her son, Basil. Basil eventually repaid her by killing a man in a tavern brawl and, after Mattie posted her house for bail, skipping town. Minus son and home, Mattie also left town and headed for Brewster Place, located in a bleak Northern city resembling Brooklyn, where Mattie feels a sense of cultural dislocation on top of her other losses.

What brings Mattie to Brewster Place specifically is a remaining personal tie there to Lucielia Louise Turner, or "Ciel," the granddaughter of Eva Turner, to whom Mattie is a mother in all but name. Mattie's presence and support are needed, since Ciel's life is devastated by her boyfriend Eugene, who is absent for long stretches and abusive when he is around. Eugene makes Ciel terminate her second pregnancy with an abortion and then indirectly causes the death of their first child, Serena. After that, Eugene is no longer welcome.

Mattie also takes in her old friend Etta Mae Johnson, a femme fatale who has lived the high life with various men around the country but whose beauty is now fading. Etta Mae has hopes of marrying a good man and settling down, and she sets her sights on a charismatic preacher. The preacher, however, turns out to be a sleazy womanizer interested only in using her for a one-night stand. It is somewhat difficult to feel sorry for Etta Mae, since she has been using men all of her life, just as it is somewhat difficult to sympathize with another of the seven women, Cora Lee. Cora Lee has loved babies from the day she was born and started having them as soon as she was able; now the number is up to seven, and assorted anonymous men continue to share her bed.

The other three women have arrived at Brewster Place more or less voluntarily. Kiswana Browne is an ardent but naïve social reformer who grew up amid the affluence of nearby Linden Hills; Brewster Place offers plenty of opportunities for her. Lorraine and Theresa are lesbian lovers who hope to find a private retreat in Brewster Place, but it is not to be. They are spied on by the old prude Sophie, who tries to stir up the street against them. The most brutal scene in the novel occurs when Lorraine is viciously raped by C. C. Baker and his alley-dwelling youth gang.

Naylor saves some of her strongest description for these young men, who "always moved in a pack" because they "needed the others continually near to verify their existence" and who, "with their black skin, ninth-grade diplomas, and fifty-word vocabularies . . . continually surnamed each other Man and clutched at their crotches, readying the equipment they deemed necessary to be summoned at any moment into Superfly heaven." The only halfway decent man in the whole novel is old Ben, the wino janitor who befriends Lorraine and is later killed by her when she becomes crazed.

Thus, Brewster Place gains its community strength from its women. Despite their clashing backgrounds, the women recognize their common fates and bond with one another. Instead of crushing them, their past and present miseries form the basis for their caring. Although victimized by society generally and by men specifically, they are able, through their black sisterhood, their community, to feel a positive sense of identity. The women rise up together in anger, love, and hope, forming a block association, throwing a block party, and—at least in Mattie's dream—tearing down the ghetto wall.

LINDEN HILLS

First published: 1985
Type of work: Novel

In suburban Linden Hills, affluent blacks make their own middle-class hell.

The other extreme of contemporary black life is shown in *Linden Hills*, set in an affluent black suburb. In contrast to Brewster Place, Linden Hills is dominated by men, most notably by undertaker Luther Nedeed. Luther's ancestors settled and laid out Linden Hills, and now Luther controls it through the Tupelo Realty Corporation and his personal influence. The suburb's name, like its allure, is deceptive: Linden Hills is actually not several hills but only part of one hillside—a large V-shaped area intersected by eight streets that curve around and down the slope. The further down the hillside one goes, the richer the residents become; in other words, the higher they climb in the socioeconomic hierarchy, the lower they sink in the moral order. Luther Nedeed's home is at the very bottom, conveniently next to the graveyard.

Naylor's symbolism seems to echo D. H. Lawrence's sentiment that America is a death society. The fact that an undertaker presides over Linden Hills throws a certain pall over the suburb, but even more unsettling is the suburb's street plan, which recalls the geography of Dante's Hell. Two young unemployed poets, Lester and Willie (corresponding to Vergil and Dante), are introduced. Under the guise of earning some Christmas money by doing odd jobs in the neighborhood, the young poets lead the reader on a guided tour of Linden Hills. The broad parallels to Dante's *Inferno* make it abundantly clear that *Linden Hills* is an allegory of the lost souls of affluent black people.

As the young poets move down the hillside, they come across varied examples of people who have sold out. One is Lester's sister Roxanne, a Wellesley College graduate who feels that black Africans in Zimbabwe are not ready to form their own nation. Other examples include Winston Alcott, a young homosexual lawyer who denies his lover David and gets married to achieve respectability; Xavier Donnell, a junior executive who fears that marrying Roxanne might hurt his chances at General Motors; Maxwell Smyth, a fellow corporate climber who confirms Xavier's decision to dump her; Chester Parker, who can hardly wait to bury his dead wife before he remarries; the Right Reverend Michael T. Hollis, a sleazy, hypocritical moral leader of Linden Hills; and Dr. Daniel Braithwaite, whose authorized twelve-volume history of Linden Hills makes no moral judgments.

The archetypal dead soul is Luther Nedeed. At the wake for Lycentia Parker, Luther voices Linden Hills's opposition to a low-income housing project planned for

Putney Wayne, a neighboring black ghetto, and proposes joining forces with the racist Wayne County Citizens Alliance in defense of property values. Luther saves his most soulless behavior for those closest to him. The horror story of how he treats his wife and child runs, in excerpts, throughout the novel. For generations, the Nedeed men have been marrying light-skinned women, but when his own wife bears a light-skinned son, Luther disowns them and locks them away in a disused basement morgue. The child starves to death, but, after reading old letters, journals, and cookbooks that document a long history of abuse heaped on Nedeed wives, Willa Prescott Nedeed makes her way back up the stairs to confront the devil himself.

Linden Hills is a powerful and sweeping indictment of black middle-class life. The broad parallels to Dante's *Inferno*, while effective for satirical and moral purposes, are somewhat forced, not allowing for enough fine-tuning. Naylor probably does not mean to condemn the black middle class as a whole or to imply that affluence is itself a problem; after all, lack of money and decent surroundings were among the problems facing the women of Brewster Place. Rather, Naylor seems to warn that affluence poses special dangers to black identity. If the price for affluence is the loss of one's soul—compromise of one's moral standards and emotional life, adoption of white values, and denial of other black people and one's own roots—then it is too high.

MAMA DAY

First published: 1988
Type of work: Novel

Mama Day reigns over the natural and spirit world of an indigenous black culture.

If *Linden Hills* strains credulity, then the main setting of *Mama Day* is even more unbelievable, if not downright mythical: Willow Springs, a Southern coastal island relatively unwashed by the tides of racism. The island is populated by the descendents of white slaveowner Bascombe Wade and his black wife Sapphira and of other slaves that he freed and deeded land to back in 1823. Since that time, the island has been plagued mainly by malaria, Union soldiers, sandy soil, two big depressions, and hurricanes. The fictitious barrier island lies off the coast of South Carolina and Georgia but is owned by no state. Willow Springs is a backwater of history where the people have been mostly left to themselves, and they have developed a black American culture strongly connected to the land, to their historical beginnings, and even to their African roots.

Willow Springs is a daring concept—an effort to imagine what black life might have been like in America if left free to develop on its own. Naylor acknowledges the concept's utopian aspects by drawing parallels between Willow Springs and the magical island in Shakespeare's *The Tempest*. Yet the conjuring that goes on in Willow Springs recalls the conjuring in *Sundiata: An Epic of Old Mali* (a translation of the thirteenth-century African epic published in 1965) and the good magic and bad magic still practiced in parts of Africa. Also very real are the closeness to the land, the recognized status of individuals within the community, the slow pace of life, and the presence of the past—things that rural Southerners, black and white, miss when they move to Northern cities.

In the novel, such a person is Ophelia "Cocoa" Day, who was born on Willow Springs and reared by her grandmother Abigail and great aunt Miranda "Mama" Day (descendants of Bascombe and Sapphira Wade). Cocoa left Willow Springs to work in New York City, but she is drawn back to the island for regular August visits. In New York, the novel's other setting, Cocoa meets George Andrews, a black engineer who was reared in an orphanage, and they eventually get married. The contrasts between the two—George gentle and straightforward, Cocoa spoiled and insecure— suggest the novel's underlying cultural clash, but this split does not become critical until George visits Willow Springs with Cocoa.

While George appreciates black life on Willow Springs, it is way beyond his urbanized, rationalistic range, particularly when a hurricane hits and when he becomes involved in a conjuring match between Mama Day and her nemesis, Ruby. Mama Day has a wealth of knowledge about herbs and various natural phenomena that she uses for the purposes of healing and aiding new life. The reader senses that much has been passed down to her from others who no longer live but whose spirits nourish the rich fabric of Willow Springs. In contrast, the evil-spirited Ruby uses the same knowledge, mixed with hoodoo, to kill anyone whom she perceives might take away her man, Junior Lee. Several women have already met terrible fates because they had contact with the philandering Junior Lee.

Unfortunately, at a party given in honor of Cocoa and George, Junior Lee follows Cocoa out to the porch and attempts to rape her, and Ruby catches him. The next day, Ruby sees Cocoa walking down the road and asks her to stop; Ruby apologizes for Junior Lee's behavior and offers to massage and braid Cocoa's hair the way she did when Cocoa was little. Right before the party, Mama Day had felt a big hurricane coming and death in the air. During the hurricane Cocoa becomes disoriented, and huge welts cover her head and face. Mama Day realizes that Ruby has poisoned Cocoa by rubbing nightshade into her head. Mama Day cuts off Cocoa's hair and works a counteracting salve into her scalp, but Cocoa is already badly poisoned.

Meanwhile, the hurricane has wreaked terrible havoc and taken out the wooden bridge between Willow Springs and the mainland. With all the boats destroyed and no telephones, George exhausts himself working to restore the bridge and get Cocoa off the island to a doctor. His efforts do not succeed, however, and, in desperation, he is forced to try Mama Day's solution. She sends him to "the other place," the island's original homeplace, to get whatever he finds behind an old brooding hen. Doubting George finds nothing, is attacked by the old hen, and dies of a weak heart.

George's doubts and weak heart represent the limits of his rationalistic outlook, his inability to participate fully in the island's culture and to comprehend Mama Day's powers. There is no doubt that those powers are real. Before George undertakes his fatal mission, Mama Day deals with Ruby by calling out three warnings, whacking each side of Ruby's house with a stick, and sprinkling a circle of silvery dust around the house. The results are two lightning strikes on Ruby's house, the second one exploding it with Ruby inside.

Summary

In her novels, Gloria Naylor surveys contemporary black American life, ranging from an urban ghetto to an affluent suburb to a pristine Southern island. While few white characters appear in her work, racism is a constant background factor, affecting the circumstances of black existence and the sense of black identity. Naylor also writes as a dedicated feminist who celebrates the lives and special powers of black women.

The male characters in Naylor's work tend either to be demonized or emasculated. Whether Naylor's doctrinaire feminism and her related tendency to write in grand, sweeping strokes will ultimately limit her development remains to be seen. Yet these same features help to account for a powerful, mythic quality in Naylor's writing.

Bibliography

Bell, Bernard W. *The Afro-American Novel and Its Tradition*. Amherst: University of Massachusetts Press, 1987.

Braxton, Joanne M., and Andrée Nicola McLaughlin, eds. *Wild Women in the Whirlwind: Afra-American Culture and the Contemporary Literary Renaissance*. New Brunswick, N.J.: Rutgers University Press, 1990.

Carby, Hazel V. *Reconstructing Womanhood: The Emergence of the Afro-American Woman Novelist*. New York: Oxford University Press, 1987.

Gates, Henry Louis, Jr. "Significant Others." *Contemporary Literature* 29 (Winter, 1988): 606-623.

Homans, Margaret. "The Woman in the Cave: Recent Feminist Fictions and the Classical Underworld." *Contemporary Literature* 29 (Fall, 1988): 369-402.

Naylor, Gloria, and Toni Morrison. "A Conversation." *The Southern Review* 21 (Summer, 1985): 567-593.

Harold Branam

ANAÏS NIN

Born: Neuilly, France
February 21, 1903
Died: Los Angeles, California
January 14, 1977

Principal Literary Achievement
Nin developed a highly imagistic idiom for expressing the creativity and sensuality of the female psyche and created a unique document of personal history.

Biography
Anaïs Nin was born near Paris on February 21, 1903, into an international, aristocratic, and cultured family. Her parents were Joaquin Nin y Castellano, a Spanish composer and pianist, and Rosa Culmell Nin, a classical singer of French and Danish descent. Their marriage was volatile and ended with Joaquin's desertion for a younger woman. In 1914, the young Anaïs, with her mother and brothers Thorvald and Joaquin, sailed from Barcelona to a new life in New York.

On this journey, Nin began keeping a diary, first as an ongoing letter to her estranged father and then as a detailed record of her experiences and feelings, a record she would maintain throughout her life. The move to America was not a happy one for her; she struggled with the language and felt unwelcome in the impersonal metropolis. An introspective, sensitive, critical, and imaginative child, she attended Catholic school in New York without enthusiasm. At the age of sixteen, after a teacher criticized her writing, she dropped out and pursued self-education in public libraries. Meanwhile, she worked as a model for artists and illustrators to augment the family income.

In the early 1920's Nin studied briefly at Columbia University and spent time with relatives in Havana, Cuba. She fell in love with a New York banker named Hugh Guiler, and the couple was married in Havana in March, 1923. Though the passion of the marriage faded within several years as Nin realized its limitations and developed her identity as a writer, it remained intact and was, in an unconventional way, successful. Guiler, under the name of Ian Hugo, later provided illustrations for his wife's novels. Nin rarely talked about him, however, and all references to him were edited out of her diary before its first publication in 1966.

Shortly after their marriage, Guiler was transferred to Paris. For Nin it was a return home. In 1924, she saw her father for the first time in a decade and con-

fronted their complex relationship. She continued her self-education and writing, pursued a brief career as a Spanish dancer, and developed many lasting and influential friendships. A teacher named Hélène Boussinescq introduced her to modern writers; she and her cousin Eduardo Sánchez shared a fascination with psychological pioneers Sigmund Freud and Carl Jung and novelists D. H. Lawrence and Marcel Proust. Her friendship with American novelist John Erskine developed into a passionate and near-suicidal obsession.

Nin's continuous writing led to her first book, *D. H. Lawrence: An Unprofessional Study*, published in Paris in 1932. Financial difficulties following the stock market crash of 1929 led Nin to relocate to a small house in the suburb of Louveciennes, where she entertained a steady stream of visiting artists and intellectuals. She became intimate with the emerging American writer Henry Miller and his wife June, and she strongly encouraged Miller's first novel, *Tropic of Cancer* (1934). Miller exposed her to his underground milieu of gangsters, addicts, and prostitutes. Her interest in the human psyche led her into psychoanalysis, first with the noted French analyst René Allendy and then with Otto Rank, a controversial disciple of Freud. Other intimates included French theatrical innovator Antonin Artaud, Peruvian musician and revolutionary Gonzalo More, and the young British author Lawrence Durrell. Throughout her life, both in Paris and in the United States, Nin's social sphere included bright and fascinating contemporary figures; in addition to her mother and brothers, these people became her family, and she shared their aspirations and struggles.

In 1934, Nin gave birth to a stillborn child, a traumatic experience which led to deeper spiritual and emotional introspection. Later that year, she accepted an invitation to assist Rank in New York and begin a career as a psychoanalyst. She soon became disenchanted with both New York and her promising practice and returned to writing and Paris, where she lived in a houseboat on the Seine and began looking for a publisher for her prose poem *House of Incest*. Finding a publisher proved difficult, however, because her writing was considered too surrealistic and visionary. Nin, Miller and others in the "Villa Seurat circle" initiated Siana Editions to ensure publication of avant-garde works such as *House of Incest* (1936). In 1939, she published the novella *Winter of Artifice*, which focused on a woman's reunion with her estranged but idolized father.

With the arrival of a new decade, the imminent war in Europe drove Nin and Guiler back to New York, where publishers were equally apprehensive. She thus purchased a secondhand, foot-operated printing press and published limited editions of her works from her Greenwich Village apartment. With the publication in 1944 of *Under a Glass Bell*, a volume of short stories, Nin finally received critical attention. Praise from such noted reviewers as Edmund Wilson validated her literary standing in the eyes of both mainstream readers and established publishers. There followed in succession *Ladders to Fire* (1946), *Children of the Albatross* (1947), *The Four-Chambered Heart* (1950), *A Spy in the House of Love* (1954), *Solar Barque* (1958), and *Seduction of the Minotaur* (1961). With the last two titles considered together, the five novels appeared as a "continuous novel" in 1959 under the title *Cities of the Interior.*

During this period, Nin traveled across America by car, journeyed throughout Mexico, and settled in Los Angeles. Her diary was now a multivolume compilation reflecting a half century of living, and many of Nin's friends urged her to publish it. During the 1950's Nin had become determined to destroy it, but she ultimately sat down to the task of editing. The first volume appeared in 1966, with publication completed in ten more volumes over two decades. *The Diary of Anaïs Nin* was an instant literary sensation and made Nin an international celebrity.

Nin received numerous honors and awards, including her 1974 election to the National Institute of Arts and Letters. She traveled widely—to Asia, North Africa, and the South Pacific—and lectured frequently. She also continued writing, and her publications included *Collages* (1964), *The Novel of the Future* (1968), and *In Favor of the Sensitive Man and Other Essays* (1976). The threat of cancer led to Nin's effective retirement in 1974, and the disease finally took her life on January 14, 1977, in her home in Los Angeles. According to her wishes, her ashes were scattered over the Pacific Ocean. Later that year, the publication of *Delta of Venus* and *Little Birds*, two volumes of short erotic fiction written for a private patron during the 1940's, placed her for the first time on best-seller lists.

Analysis

Anaïs Nin's life and writings span and reflect a good part of the twentieth century. Her work as a whole is less broad in terms of style and technique than it is deep; she was very concerned with certain themes and issues and explored them with imagination and rigor through her writing.

A central question for Nin was the role of women in modern society and their relationships to men and to one another. Nin wrote from an insistently feminine perspective—not out of a precious or meek femininity but rather from a keen awareness of women's psychic and social dependence on and involvement in a male-dominated culture and their continual struggle for identity and independence as women. Through the heroines appearing and reappearing in her stories and novels—Stella, Djuna, Lillian, and Sabina—Nin applied careful and sensitive introspection to women and their modes of artistic, spiritual, emotional, and sensual expression and their roles as daughters, lovers, and autonomous individuals. These explorations mirrored and expanded upon specific issues in Nin's own life, as an abandoned daughter, an ambivalent wife, and a woman writer putting forth a unique, and uniquely feminine, voice into an overwhelmingly male literary tradition.

She did, however, know that tradition well. Through her personal studies, she had read and appreciated many of its greatest writers, both in French—François Rabelais, Gustave Flaubert, and Victor Hugo—and in English—Ralph Waldo Emerson, Edgar Allan Poe, and Alfred, Lord Tennyson. Her true literary mentors were Marcel Proust and D. H. Lawrence. Though French was Nin's first language, she used it only in her early diaries; upon her arrival in New York, she vigorously applied herself to mastering English and never left it once she had succeeded. Her narrative voice remains truly international; her stories, like her life, are set primarily in New York and Paris milieus of artists, polyglots, and expatriates, where national identities fade and universal human qualities come into focus.

Unlike many writers in the European literary tradition, Nin eschewed conventional notions of plot, language, characterization, and style and responded rather to development in other artistic disciplines. Whereas she basically distrusted words because of their ability to obfuscate or lie, she loved and had an inherent faith in music and art. Her musical family certainly influenced her, and her experiences with commercial art, professional dance, and artists and sculptors such as André Breton, Salvador Dali, and Yanko Varda acquainted her with the principles of surrealism and reinforced her faith in the power of sensually evocative images. Her writing is infused with such images, as well as with the rhythms and suggestions of both jazz and classical music.

An equally strong influence was Nin's involvement with the practice of psychoanalysis. As both a subject and an analyst working with articulate and strong-minded theoreticians in the growing discipline, Nin developed a keen and untiring sensitivity to the details and dynamics of human behavior. The careful scrutiny she attained through introspection applied equally well to observation of others. In terms of her writing, "character" is not a static or fixed entity, but a reflection of the constant flux of life. Her characters, while being distinct individuals, exhibit a multiplicity of personality: They are mutable, they embody contradictions, and they are capable of dramatic transformations which nevertheless sustain their inherent integrity. Nin knew the theater and had performed in both films and dances; she recognized the potential in any individual to act, to become, and to wear costumes and masks, intentionally or not, that create unique patterns of behavior. The sequencing and spontaneous alteration of such patterns ultimately determine personality and character.

In a corresponding manner, Nin was never concerned with linear plot, logical ordering, or precise chronology. Rather than painstakingly structure her stories and novels, she would determine the starting premises of a work—the possibilities of characterization, the themes, the recurring motifs or images—and then improvise, determining many of the plot specifics as she progressed. As a result, readers expecting a conventionally composed story will be disappointed, for the movement that Nin achieves is less from a beginning to an end than from a surface to a center, or from an interior seed to an expansive truth. One of her favorite dicta, taken from the psychoanalyst Carl Jung, was "proceed from the dream outward."

As both analyst and writer, Nin was fascinated with dreams. She often used her own dreams as a source of ideas and images for her writing. Dreams seemed to her a tunnel into the inner world of emotion, which is the world that she sought above all to portray. Adapting the principles of Emersonian Transcendentalism as well as the stream-of-consciousness and interior monologue techniques of novelists James Joyce and Virginia Woolf to her own sensibility and vision, Nin focused on a psychological reality only tangentially related to appearances and surfaces. In her works, the phenomenological world is little more than dressing on the true reality of emotion and soul. Fact is subjugated to feeling, and sensory experience is less important in itself than for the images and perceptions it suggests in the complex labyrinth of personality.

Nin ultimately left the practice of psychoanalysis to devote her full energies to writing. As the volume of her work attests, writing was a deeply felt need. It helped her to articulate and capture the fleeting past as well as to formulate decisions and attitudes for the future. Through the steady practice of writing, at first spontaneously and intuitively, she naturally arrived at the elements of craft—the criteria by which artistic decisions are made. Her journey as a writer was from first- to third-person narrative, from introspection to outward vision, from obscurity to fame, and from innocence and insecurity to wisdom and courage.

For years, even after her literary stature and widespread recognition were established, Nin's writing was often criticized as murky, meaningless, solipsistic, neurotic, and inaccessible. Readers often lack the patience and imagination—that is, the ability to formulate and respond to images—that her writing requires. Yet millions of readers, especially women and adolescents, have found a personal truth in the psychological reality that Nin depicts. People and relationships were crucial to her, and she strove to create a unique connection with every individual she encountered; "I would like to meet the whole world at once," she wrote. The same individual connection is the goal of her writing.

HOUSE OF INCEST

First published: 1936
Type of work: Novel

In a dreamlike and mutable landscape of haunting images, a struggle occurs to liberate the self from the tyranny of neurosis and narcissism.

House of Incest was Nin's first published work of fiction. Though she was thirty-three years old when it was published and had been writing continuously for two decades, it exhibits the youthfulness of a first work in both its indulgence and its freedom. Nin called *House of Incest* a "prose poem" rather than a novel and, referring to a work by the French poet Arthur Rimbaud, "a woman's *Season in Hell*." She also took inspiration from Octave Mirbeau's 1898 painting *Le Jardin des supplices* (*The Garden of Tortures*). The seven sections of *House of Incest*, each headed with a figure or glyph of distantly suggested astrological or mythological significance, can be seen as the seven days of creation, seven heavens, or seven hells. Rather than a story, this prose poem is a series of images and parables united by thematic patterns.

Written in the first-person voice in a highly poetic and imagistic idiom, *House of Incest* relates the inner experiences and sensations of a woman, or perhaps several women, in the House of Incest. Given Nin's views of the multiplicity of personality, resolving the single or multiple nature of the protagonist is less relevant than the nature of the various interactions described. The narrative begins with the protagonist's description of her birth, experienced as an emergence from a primordial sea. It goes on to depict two dramatic situations: an obsessive lesbian relationship involving the dependent narrator and her dismissive lover, named Sabina, and the narrator Jeanne's guilt-ridden incestuous pursuit of and flight from her brother. The narrator then encounters cryptic figures and herself becomes a dancer deprived of her arms even as she achieves, in the closing paragraphs, harmony with her world and hope for freedom.

The house of incest itself is a metaphor for the human body and psyche as they are trapped in self-obsession. In the section dealing with Jeanne and incest, the house is described as worn, static, and rotting. Nin is portraying the meaninglessness of a life without a true regard for or appreciation of others. Just as the lesbian relationship becomes compulsive, draining, and destructive, so the incestuous passion is not a true love of other but a love of self as perceived or manifested in the blood relation. Though the situations portrayed are unconventional, Nin is not making moral judgments on them as such; rather, she uses the homosexual and incestuous passions to express the emptiness of love derived from narcissistic impulses.

The language of *House of Incest* is characterized by unrestrained lyricism and emotional exuberance. The images Nin employs combine natural, material, and corporal elements to striking effect, such as "[f]ishes made of velvet, of organdie with lace fangs." Evocations of violence—acid, scissors, serpents, and storms—are set against those of vitality—the sea, eggs, and orgasms. The text is richly filled with allusions drawn from the fields of metallurgy, alchemy, astronomy, geography, and biology. Nin utilized poetic techniques of sound—alliteration, rhythm, and repetition—to create musical values in the piece:

> The steel necklace on her throat flashed like summer lightning and the sound of steel was like the clashing of swords. . . . Le pas d'acier. . . . The steel of New York's skeleton buried in granite, buried standing up. Le pas d'acier . . . notes hammered on the steel-stringed guitars of the gypsies, on the steel arms of chairs dulled with her breath; steel mail curtains falling like the flail of hail, steel bars and steel barrage cracking. Her necklace thrown around the world's neck, unmeltable.

The suggestion of real contexts, places, and languages; the juxtaposition of mineral reality with breath and emotion; and the nervelike tautness of a guitar string all exemplify the many elements that recur and undergo transformations of meaning through the course of the prose poem.

In the preface to the piece and at various points throughout are references to the book itself. Often set apart or emphasized with block letters, these references become an object of meaning within the narrative. The book in the reader's hands is alternately the truth as the narrator can tell it and the narrator's place of refuge from the weight of truth. How the book reflects the characters and how they are reflections of one another become central to the issue of telling the simple truth or evading oneself and others with lies. Thus, when the armless dancer turns "towards daylight" at the end, *House of Incest* concludes with a suggestion that truth is emerging from the darkness within.

A SPY IN THE HOUSE OF LOVE

First published: 1954
Type of work: Novel

A woman explores the multiplicity of her personality through a series of erotic and emotional adventures with a variety of men.

A Spy in the House of Love is the fourth installment in Nin's "continuous novel" entitled *Cities of the Interior.* The latter unites six shorter individual works and focuses on three women—Djuna, Lillian, and Sabina—and the men in their lives. The novels are not necessarily sequential but are connected by a network of characters, settings, imagery, and language. Thus, they do not need to be read in any particular order and, though certain information and echoes may be missed, each volume stands as a complete work independent of the others.

A Spy in the House of Love focuses on Sabina, a fiery actress who is only partially content in her marriage to an attentive but dull husband, Alan, and yearns for erotic and spiritual stimulation. While performing in an amateurish production of *Cinderella* in Provincetown, on Massachusetts' Cape Cod, she is seduced by a romantically visualized Austrian singer named Philip. At a jazz club in New York, she indulges in an affair with Mambo, an exotic and sensuous drummer. In a Long Island beach town, a grounded British pilot named John captivates her imagination with his dark, angry intensity. She becomes a nurturing mother figure for Donald, a lively young jester. She also encounters Jay, a perceptive artist and her former lover in Paris. During and between these "multiple peregrinations of love," she returns to the comfort of her marital home and Alan's trusting paternal love.

A controlling image for the novel is taken from Marcel Duchamp's Dadaist painting *Nude Descending a Staircase, No. 2* (1912), which presents a fractured image of a woman's multiple outlines. Nin's portrait of Sabina is equally fractured, for each of the selves that she becomes or discovers with her different lovers is a valid though incomplete expression of her identity. As an actress skilled with vocal, physical, cosmetic, and behavioral transformations, her various identities are accentuated. Nin's portrait is not one of perversity or psychosis, however; Sabina illustrates the multiplicity of personality that Nin perceived in herself and in all individuals who actively respond to their environment.

Sabina's journey through the novel tracks the continuous manifestation and aggravation of the inner tension she feels between her need for peace, stability, and intimacy and her desire for freedom, motion, and anonymity. Such is the mutability of her nature that each interaction or encounter stimulates a pronounced and often opposite response. Sabina is a restless soul; her congress with Philip or John fulfills her fantasies while simultaneously heightening her need to return to Alan. Yet Sabina is repeatedly unable to take the meaningful essence from each encounter; her longing and dissatisfaction are not relieved by passionate, imaginative sexual liaisons. Even as she pursues adventure, she is haunted by guilt and tantalized by the possibility of discovery. As her struggle approaches climactic proportions, it is only in a final chance encounter with her wise and sensitive friend Djuna that Sabina directly confronts the essential turmoil of her life and begins to find remedy and rescue.

Nin gives Sabina's inner turmoil concrete expression through the device of the "lie detector"—a mysterious man who appears to Sabina in the opening paragraph, follows her through her adventures, and ultimately receives her confession and pronounces psychic judgment upon her. The lie detector is not a real or imagined character so much as another manifestation of Sabina's personality, the one which holds the key to achieving a harmonious sense of identity.

A Spy in the House of Love exhibits Nin's characteristic use of imagery to depict psychological reality, including imagery of voyages, excavations, labyrinths, prisons, fire, and bodies of water. In addition, specific objects take on metaphorical significance, such as the black cape that symbolizes Sabina's distrust and hostility. A recurrent motif involving modes of transportation—the grounded aviator and his bicycle, the sailboat in which Philip seduces Sabina, the Parisian elevator in which she and Jay impulsively made love years before—signify Sabina's restlessness and recklessness, as do the descriptions of her random and incessant gesturing. In the various encounters of the novel, Nin has carefully detailed gesture and behavior to convey the precise dynamics of human interaction.

Finally, music is another device used throughout the novel. In addition to the jazz played in Mambo's club, compositions by Richard Wagner, Igor Stravinsky, Ludwig van Beethoven, and Claude Debussy are heard by characters within the narrative. Donald even alludes to Stravinsky when he calls Sabina his "Firebird." The music combines with the evocative language and imagery to give texture and sensuality to this account of a passionate woman's search for freedom and meaning.

THE DIARY OF ANAÏS NIN

First published: 1966-1986
Type of work: Diary

Nin's lifelong diary documents the details of her fascinating life and stands as a unique accomplishment in English and in women's literature.

Anaïs Nin began keeping a diary on July 25, 1914, as an ongoing letter to her father that she hoped would someday bring him back to the family. Sixty years later, in the summer of 1974, Nin concluded her diary while enjoying the exotic landscape and culture of Bali. During those six decades, her personal journal of daily life and experience grew to 150 volumes, or some fifteen thousand typewritten pages. It is unquestionably her masterpiece, both as a literary work and as a social document of the artistic life of the twentieth century.

The diary reflects Nin's creative attitude toward existence and the connection she perceived between life and literature. She viewed life as an adventure, or as a story that the individual freely and imaginatively creates and narrates to herself. The Diary eventually developed a persona, becoming a friend, a confidant, and a place to go for escape or succor, or at times even an enemy, an agent of deceit, and a threatening obsession. Whatever her feelings were at the moment, Nin came to her diary for uninhibited introspection and absolute truthfulness; even when the truth of her feelings or aspirations were not to be reckoned, her earnestness was unflagging.

On one level, the diary is a record of Nin's external life. She faithfully detailed the specifics of her daily movements, including her adjustment to New York, her adolescence, her courtship and marriage, her explorations into sensuality and sexuality, her activities as an aspiring writer and psychoanalyst, her travels between Europe and America, the homes she occupied, the people with whom she associated, the publication of her books, her movements in later life, and the rewards and difficulties of celebrity and wealth. Her skills as a writer are evident in the descriptions of her life's settings and the sketches of her friends and colleagues. Many prominent individuals are sharply drawn, including Henry Miller, his wife June, Lawrence Durrell, Gonzalo More, Eduardo Sánchez, Otto Rank, John Erskine, and others.

On another level, Nin's diary, like her fiction, delves into psychological reality. In her diary, she recorded sensations and emotions, including her ambivalent feelings toward her father, her internal struggles with her conflicting roles as wife and artist, her search for a sense of identity amid frequent relocation and alienation, the frustrations of literary rejection, and her soul-searching deliberations and anxieties over publication of the diary itself. Multiplicity of personality, a theme prevalent in the fiction, is reflected in the apparent contradictions and reinterpretations found throughout the successive volumes of the Diary. Nin's rigorous honesty communicates the constant changeability and unpredictability of her life. "It is my thousand years of womanhood I am recording," she wrote in 1966, "a thousand women."

Through the course of the volumes in which the *Diary* has been published, from *Linotte: The Early Diary of Anaïs Nin, 1914-1920* (1978) to *The Diary of Anais Nin: 1966-1974* (1980), several general developments can be seen. Nin began as a shy, sensitive, and uncertain child and grew into an enlightened, wise, and mature woman. The earlier volumes are characterized by deep introspection, while in the later years Nin wrote more about other people and the world she observed. By the 1970's, Nin came to her diary much less regularly, and it took on the qualities of a scrapbook. Aware from the beginning of the need to make artistic choices, Nin gradually developed her form and craft as she progressed. Her diary was also at times a literary playground, as with her 1928 "diary within a diary" of the imagination-inspired fantasy character "Imagy." She gave names to individual volumes, from "The Childhood Diary," "Diary of a Fiancée," and "Diary of a Wife," to the more expressive "John," "The House," "The Woman Who Died," "Disintegration," and the last books, "The Book of Pain" and "The Book of Music."

The titles, the experiments, and her habits of greeting and signing off each entry give evidence of conscious artistry during the actual composition. In the 1960's, the decision to publish the diary led to a second, more formal editing process. Respect for the privacy of individuals mentioned in the diary and the final shape of the published version—originally it was to be condensed into a single volume—become issues. As a result of those concerns, certain individuals or questionable sections were edited out, decisions were made about how to divide the entirety into volumes, and parts were altered for purposes of consistency and flow. The process of preparing the diary for publication was a natural final stage in the evolution of Nin's artistry, for it further refined her editing skills and made public what was probably the most important private relationship of her life. As she wrote in the spring of 1972, what began as a dialogue with the self had "become a correspondence with the world."

Throughout the transitions of her life and the development of her writing, both so vividly documented in the diary, Nin's generosity and optimism shone. As she approached the end of her life, she chose to end its monumental journal with entries written under the spell of Bali rather than lead her readers through the devastation of cancer. In a brief excerpt from "The Book of Music," included as an epilogue to the diary, Nin meditated on death:

> Yes, music indicates another place, a better place. . . . One should think of this place joyfully. Then if it follows death, it is a beautiful place. A lovely thing to look forward to—a promised land. So I shall die in music, into music, with music.

Summary

"I believe one writes because one has to create a world in which one can live," Anaïs Nin wrote in 1954, responding by letter to a reader's question. "I had to create a world of my own, like a climate, a country, an atmosphere in which I could breathe, reign, and re-create myself when destroyed by living." More than most writers, Nin's work and life were intricately interwoven; through her novels and diary, she created a world ideally suited to her unique sensibility and filled with imagination and insight that speak to generations of readers.

Bibliography

Cutting, Rose Marie. *Anaïs Nin: A Reference Guide*. Boston: G. K. Hall, 1978.

Evans, Oliver. *Anaïs Nin*. Carbondale: Southern Illinois University Press, 1968.

Franklin, Benjamin, V, and Duane Schneider. *Anaïs Nin: An Introduction*. Athens: Ohio University Press, 1979.

Hinz, Evelyn J. *The Mirror and the Garden: Realism and Reality in the Writings of Anaïs Nin*. Columbus: Ohio State University Press, 1971.

Knapp, Bettina L. *Anaïs Nin*. New York: Frederick Ungar, 1978.

Nin, Anaïs. *A Woman Speaks: The Lectures, Seminars and Interviews of Anaïs Nin*, edited by Evelyn J. Hinz. Chicago: Swallow Press, 1975.

Scholar, Nancy. *Anaïs Nin*. Boston: Twayne, 1984.

Snyder, Robert. *Anaïs Nin Observed: From a Film Portrait of a Woman as Artist*. Chicago: Swallow Press, 1976.

Spencer, Sharon. *The Writings of Anaïs Nin*. New York: Harcourt Brace Jovanovich, 1977.

Barry Mann

FRANK NORRIS

Born: Chicago, Illinois
March 5, 1870
Died: San Francisco, California
October 25, 1902

Principal Literary Achievement

One of America's leading naturalistic writers, Norris was also a Romantic moralist whose acclaimed novels depicted human failings while attesting a belief in nature's ultimate benevolence toward humankind.

Biography

Benjamin Franklin Norris, Jr., was born in Chicago, Illinois, on March 5, 1870, the first of five children born to Gertrude Doggett Norris and Benjamin Franklin Norris, Sr., the wealthy owner of a wholesale jewelry business. Only two boys besides Frank survived infancy; Lester was born in 1878 (and died in 1887), and Charles was born in 1881. Because of Frank, Sr.'s, health problems, the Norrises moved to Oakland, California, in 1882 and the following year settled in San Francisco.

After attending a preparatory school and Boys' High School, neither of which suited his limited interest in schooling, Frank was enrolled in the San Francisco Art Association, where he studied painting. Although he studied art in London and Paris, his interest in painting soon waned, and after two years he returned home.

During this time, however, he had begun to write. His first article, "Clothes of Steel," was published in the *San Francisco Chronicle* shortly after his return in 1889. The following year, he entered the University of California at Berkeley as a limited-status student. By this time, Norris knew precisely what career would suit him: College was preparatory to becoming a professional writer. It was at Berkeley that Norris first read the naturalistic works of French novelist Émile Zola that greatly influenced his own developing literary philosophy.

While Norris was attending college, his parents filed for divorce. His father soon remarried; Frank, Charles, and their mother moved to Massachusetts, where Frank studied creative writing at Harvard University for one year. It was during this period that he began writing *McTeague* (1899) and *Vandover and the Brute* (1914).

When Norris left Harvard, he traveled and wrote sketches in South Africa, but he was forced to return to San Francisco when his involvement in the political aspects of the Boer War resulted in his expulsion from the country. It was a disheartening

event, but it resulted in a unique opportunity: In San Francisco, he became an assistant editor on a weekly publication, the *Wave*. The magazine published several of his short stories and serialized his first novel, a pirate story entitled *Moran of the Lady Letty* (1898). In spite of the poor quality of this work, it caught the attention of the editor of *McClure's Magazine* in New York, who offered Norris a position.

As a writer for *McClure's Magazine*, Norris met William Dean Howells, who would become his greatest supporter, and was sent to Cuba to cover the Spanish-American War. It was during this assignment that he met Stephen Crane, Richard Harding Davis—who would become his literary competitors—and Frederic Remington, the artist. The trip was a painful experience all around for Norris. Reared in a luxurious and sheltered atmosphere, he found the realities of war horrifying; moreover, the magazine decided not to publish his stories.

In San Francisco once again, Norris found success both personally and professionally. His relationship with Jeannette Black, who encouraged his work and appreciated the realistic character of his fiction, led to their marriage on January 12, 1900. They returned east and lived first in the elite residential area of New York's Washington Square and then settled into their own home in Roselle, New Jersey. Additionally, both *McTeague* and *Blix* were published in 1899, and he began his research in California for his next project, *The Octopus* (1901).

Norris knew that the graphic realism and naturalistic philosophy of *McTeague* would be controversial, but he was able to withstand the ensuing literary scandal in large part because of the publication by the influential William Dean Howells of a supportive analytical essay on the novel that compared Norris to Zola and Charles Dickens. Several New York critics praised Norris' novel, but many critics deemed it repulsive, unhealthy, and sordid, reflecting the genteel attitudes at the end of the nineteenth century. One review is representative of the offense that many readers felt upon reading the novel:

> Mr. Norris has written pages for which there is absolutely no excuse, and his needless sins against good taste and delicacy are fatal spots upon his work. *McTeague* undoubtedly will be widely read . . . but we pray that a kind fate may bring it only to those of vigorous mind and, shall we say it, strong stomach.

Norris, however, was already deeply involved in the research for his next project, a projected trilogy that would follow the growth, production, and distribution of wheat.

As Norris prepared to write the first novel of the trilogy, he moved from *McClure's Magazine* to a position of a reader for Doubleday, Page, and Company, a new publishing company. This position was meant to afford Norris a reasonable income and time for his writing, but he also found himself embroiled in a major literary controversy. For the past several years, Norris had been developing and reshaping a literary philosophy that embraced naturalism but retained the transcendental belief in human potential. When, as a reader, he read a manuscript by Theodore Dreiser entitled *Sister Carrie* (1900), he recognized not only a kindred spirit but also an extraordinary novel. Upon his recommendation, Dreiser's novel was accepted for publication.

Although the publisher later sought unsuccessfully to negate Dreiser's contract, Norris continued to support the publication of what has come to be known as one of America's major naturalistic works of fiction.

The Octopus (1901) was the most successful novel of Norris' career; when it appeared he was already living in Chicago and collecting materials for the second novel of the trilogy. Although he and his wife were joyful over the birth of a daughter, Jeannette, Jr., on February 9, 1902, he had become dissatisfied with industrialized urban settings while writing *The Pit* (1903) and decided that he and his family would prosper by moving back to San Francisco before they began a world cruise aboard a tramp steamer to gather materials for the final novel in the trilogy, which was to be entitled *The Wolf*.

Norris was at the prime of his career: His previous novel had sold more than thirty thousand copies, he was publishing short stories again, and he was drafting ideas for another trilogy, on the Battle of Gettysburg. While Jeannette was recovering from an operation for appendicitis, however, Norris became ill. For whatever reasons, he ignored his discomforts, and he died on October 25, 1902, from peritonitis that developed from a perforated appendix. He was thirty-two years old.

Analysis

Once deemed the "father of American naturalism," Norris is better understood as an author who delved into a variety of literary modes as a means of blending his naturalistic recognition of human failings and the potential emergence of a brute self with his romantic belief in the capacity of love to reform people into becoming their better selves.

What Norris sought to capture in his novels was a record of modern life. While he recognized literature as a marketable item (like any other commodity), he also believed that it had the capacity to express the life of the people. This should not necessarily be taken as a call for democratization of American life, however; Norris' fiction is rife with the elitist and racist attitudes that shaped late-nineteenth century American culture. What Norris meant by this assertion was that the people have a right not to be deluded by illusionary views of life that relate only the heroic and self-sacrificing elements of human nature. What he deemed a "right to truth" meant that history as well as emotions must be truthfully rendered, depicted as they are and not as people would like them to be. This demands that the writer responsibly and objectively confront the society in which he or she lives.

The purpose behind every novel and the responsibilities that its author embraced in the act of writing were of great interest to Norris. His desire to define the moral responsibilities of an author grew in large part out of changes that were occurring in publishing trends at the turn of the century. Because of a significant increase in the number of Americans who had benefited from some form of education and thus had the capacity to consume a large quantity of printed matter, inexpensive and "easy reading" works were being published in record numbers. The authors of these works, however, often had little concern for the quality of information that they delivered.

Against such an influx of irresponsible publications, Norris suggested certain criteria for writers of novels. In essays such as "The Novel with a Purpose" (1902) and "The Responsibilities of the Novelist" (1902), Norris asserted that while lesser novelists simply told a story, the works by writers with higher artistic yearnings would entail a study of human motivations and representative human characteristics.

This required the novelist to draw fictional characters from his or her observations of actual people and to realize that the purpose of the highest form of novel was to reform (while maintaining a keen eye for aesthetics and the action of the story), to bring the reader to a moral rather than a popular conclusion. Since readers will believe whatever is rendered with skill, that places upon the author a tremendous responsibility to act with the greatest awareness and sincerity.

There was an on-going debate at the turn of the century over the need for someone to produce the Great American Novel. In this respect, Norris' belief in evolutionary processes was brought to bear upon the issue. The United States had not yet sufficiently developed a nationalistic spirit, he asserted, and such a spirit was required before any nation could produce a national epic. Like other realistic authors of the period, including Rebecca Harding Davis, Hamlin Garland, and Sarah Orne Jewett, Norris believed that a writer should present the essential factors of a particular region of the country. Only after the accumulation of these particular studies could the United States hope to develop its own great novel.

Norris' own shifting alliance between realism (which he defined as fiction devoted to the subject of typical life) and romanticism (fiction that focused upon the exceptional rather than the normal) suggests his own lifelong struggle to find a literary means of expressing his fears for and beliefs in the capacity of human beings to shape their lives. If he ultimately failed to synthesize these elements, it is a failure representative of that modern life which he sought to record.

Norris' early fiction was often sentimental and romantic. His first long publication was a romantic poem entitled *Yvernelle: A Tale of Feudal France* (1891) that reflected his fascination with medieval themes and was highly moralistic in tone. Although the poem was a work of his apprenticeship years, the attention to romantic moralism remained long after the settings of his fiction moved from medieval to modern times. Years later, Norris still asserted that "preparations of effect" were the central feature of "fiction mechanics." The difference between the hack writer and the great writer was the subtlety with which they rendered those preparations.

As Norris matured as a writer, his naturalistic philosophy developed into a belief that human beings are always destined to fail against the indifference and power of natural forces, of nature itself. In *The Octopus*, he expressed these ideas most clearly:

> Men were nothings, mere animalcules, mere ephemerides that fluttered and fell and were forgotten between dawn and dusk. . . . Men were naught, death was naught, life was naught; FORCE only existed—FORCE that brought men into the world, FORCE that crowded them out of it to make way for the succeeding generation, FORCE that made the wheat grow, FORCE that garnered it from the soil to give place to the succeeding crop.

Most prevalent in Norris' large category of forces that controlled human beings were those of heredity and environment.

Yet this evolutionary process as it related to human beings was not envisioned by Norris as a debilitating feature of human development but rather as the capacity for humankind to evolve into the perfect species. Thus, if in describing human failings, Norris depicted the force of sexual desire as one of the most overpowering facets of human nature, one that often devolved into a bestial, self-serving lust for gratification, he also acknowledged the regenerative capacity of the human spirit.

A year before his death, Norris published a short essay on "The True Reward of the Novelist" (1901). The reward could not be defined in terms of popularity or sales; it came from the knowledge that the author had told his audience the truth as he knew it. Such honesty and realism did not preclude romance, Norris asserted:

> The difficult thing is to get at the life immediately around you, the very life in which you move. No romance in it? No romance in *you*, poor fool. As much romance on Michigan Avenue as there is realism in King Arthur's court. It is as you choose to see it.

That recognition, then, becomes the ultimate responsibility of the novelist.

McTEAGUE

First published: 1899
Type of work: Novel

In late nineteenth century San Francisco, a community is completely disrupted when temptations and greed bring out the brute nature of its inhabitants.

Norris had begun writing *McTeague* while a student at Harvard, but by the time of its publication seven years later, in 1899, the influence of French and Russian naturalism was well-recognized in American literary communities. Yet no native novelist had yet created quite so grim and unyielding a representation as Norris did in this, his first major novel. *McTeague* is deeply indebted to the works of the French naturalist, Émile Zola, whose naturalistic-romantic vision of the complex nature of human relationships and the compelling forces which led men and women into destructive behavior patterns reflected and encouraged Norris' own beliefs. Although Norris would continue to incorporate the techniques of naturalism into his fiction, *McTeague* stands as his purest experiment in the genre.

As Norris would later counsel in his essays on fiction, he focused in this novel on one area in one region of the country: Polk Street in San Francisco. More specifically, the novel follows a particular period of time in the life of "Mac" McTeague, a dentist on Polk Street. McTeague's initial mood of melancholy and nostalgia for the country life of his youth reflects the sense of loss that has come with the prosperity of urban existence.

Like all naturalists, Norris did not assert that environment alone could be blamed for the present condition of man's slow evolution, and it is the brute strength of McTeague that is most striking. This beastlike nature, which Norris believed was a hereditary feature of all men, lies beneath the surface of McTeague's lumbering presence. When circumstances threaten to reveal that he had never received proper certification as a dentist, the façade of his personality is uncovered and the uncontrollable brute self emerges.

Although Norris believed that there had been no great American women novelists and that this phenomenon was attributable to the fact that women led sheltered lives which did not allow them to study "real" life, he did not limit his depiction of the brute self to men. If McTeague's base nature is rooted in masculine strength, his wife Trina's innate baseness is depicted in her greed.

When Trina wins five thousand dollars in a lottery, her sweet nature is replaced by an obsession with the money she receives. It is this greed that comes to pervade the novel, as McTeague, his friend Marcus Schouler, and minor characters Maria Macapa and the Polish Jew, Mr. Zerkow, are immediately changed by the intrusion of money—or the lust for it—into their lives. Norris satirically renders this facet of human nature through the grotesquely enormous gold tooth that McTeague hangs outside his place of business. The day that McTeague removes the tooth from its crate, he sets in motion the "trap" (the naturalistic symbol of the forces that propel human beings toward their fate) that will result in his death.

As the various characters become more and more enamored of money, they devolve into violent, animalistic creatures. McTeague, like his father, begins to drink excessively, and his lustful nature soon rages out of control. Trina's affection for her husband is replaced by her own lust—for constant contact with the coins themselves. Marcus, who had unwittingly given the winning lottery ticket to Trina in hopes of luring her away from McTeague, is enraged at his loss. Once simply an inept and untrained dog surgeon, he becomes doglike himself in his brutish anger, and in the final scene of the novel, both he and McTeague have devolved to such a stage that they crawl on all fours in the arid desert landscape.

Norris firmly believed that the naturalist, like any other author, was necessarily a moralist, and in the violent deaths of McTeague, Trina, Marcus, Maria, and Zerkow, he renders the punishment that he believed such greed demands. There are two other characters in the novel who are often overlooked but who, in fact, extend Norris' moralistic depiction of modern life: Old Grannis and Miss Baker. The pathetic romance of the two elderly people, as they carry on a vicarious courtship without speaking or meeting, represents the isolation and fear that dominates modern urbanized society. Unlike the other main characters in the novel, they do survive, but their tragic failure to engage in any meaningful human exchange is Norris' ironic prophecy for American life: They are old, they are separated physically and spiritually, and when they die with no offspring, they will take with them any hope for the future of the Polk Street community.

Through such depictions, *McTeague* remains not only a classic text in American naturalism but also a record of Norris' concern for the future of the novel and for the future of American society itself.

THE OCTOPUS

First published: 1901
Type of work: Novel

Against the fertile landscape of nineteenth century California's wheat fields, the men who grow the wheat must confront the ruthless railroad barons.

Subtitled "A Story of California," *The Octopus* was the first novel in a projected trilogy that Norris envisioned as an epic study of the cultivating, processing, and distribution of wheat; the wheat would move from the Western fields to Chicago's marketplace to the starving peoples of Europe. In the United States, the Populist party had been formed in 1891 as a collective Western movement by farmers and labor against the rise of political "machines" and trust organizations that threatened the farmers' livelihood. The party's demise, which would occur around 1904, was already foreshadowed at the time Norris was completing the novel. Several American authors, from Rebecca Harding Davis to Thorstein Veblen, had recognized the dangers inherent in these contrived economic shifts and made political trusts the center of their literature. Although Norris had no direct involvement in the Populist movement, his novel stands securely among the major social protest novels of the turn of the century.

No other novel by Norris so clearly combines his naturalistic and romantic philosophies. *The Octopus* is a study in natural versus unnatural forces: the wheat versus the railroad and its representatives, nature's boundaries versus the steel tentacles of the railroad's artificial boundaries, the unnatural "Other" force of rape (literal and metaphoric) that destroys the natural force of love.

Combining his beliefs about the appropriate scope of an American novel (to depict the realities of a particular region) and the sense of alienation in contemporary society, Norris creates as his protagonist an artist, the poet Presley, who spends a summer in the San Joaquin Valley, where he tries to find a purpose for his poetry. The narrative structure of the novel coincides with Presley's indecisiveness about whether a realistic or romantic vision is the most truthful art form and reflects Norris' own waffling opinions.

Through Presley's eyes, however, the reader discovers the intricate processes of growing wheat and the tenacious hold that the railroad conglomerate has on the fate of the farmers. Without a decent price and reasonable travel schedules, the farmers' crops can be destroyed more readily by the trust's false manipulations of the market than by the indifference of natural weather conditions. The demise of all of the major characters among the farmers represents Norris' insistent belief that no one can withstand the power of irresistible forces.

In the community of the San Joaquin wheat growers, Norris discovered a setting that allowed him to study with scientific precision human interactions in everyday circumstances and in moments of crisis. If this community represents those who love the land and respect its fertile power, it is also symbolic of the fact that no region is exempt from the brute nature of human beings. This dark side of human nature is openly depicted in the railroad people, from the corporate leaders to their pawn, Shelgrim. As in *McTeague*, Norris also continues his study of how temptation can lead even the best of people into false actions. Thus Magnus Derrick, the leader of the community, becomes the railroad's dupe while his son extends this betrayal to open association with the enemy.

The rape of Angèle becomes a metaphor for the rape of the entire community by an intrusive "Other." The railroad is a known perpetrator, but its ability to pervade the community before inhabitants were aware of its presence and brute nature is symbolized in the mysteriousness surrounding Angèle's rape and death. Her lover Vanamee's obsession with discovering the truth parallels Presley's obsessive artistic quest. That both remain thwarted in their goals at the novel's end reflects Norris' belief in the dangerously elusive nature of truth itself; however, through the efforts of each character he also reveals the worthiness of that quest.

Vanamee's mystic experiences can hardly be termed naturalistic or realistic, but they embrace Norris' belief in a moral purpose. The shepherd's sense of loss at the death of Angèle is the beginning of a philosophic journey which culminates in his belief that, although individuals cannot withstand irresistible forces, the good will ultimately prevail. This is a dramatic turn toward the romantic for Norris.

This philosophy prevails at the end of the novel through the characters of Presley, Vanamee, and Hilma Tree. Hilma's natural sensuousness represents a human correlation with the fertility of the land, and it is her love that converts Annixter from a vulgar, brute man into a loving and nurturing human being. If Annixter's slaughter, like Angèle's, depicts the indifferent nature of force, the survival of Hilma Tree embraces Vanamee's—and Norris'—belief in the prevailing nature of good over evil. If the railroad won in California, other forces would prevail on a wider, epic scale because *"the WHEAT remained. Untouched, unassailable, undefiled, that mighty world force, that nourisher of nations."* As the final line of the novel reflects, "all things surely, inevitably, resistlessly work together for good." It was as true for philosophic and literary battles as it was for the battle of the wheatfields.

THE PIT
First published: 1903
Type of work: Novel

The enticement of "cornering" the supply of wheat in the Chicago futures market leads to the financial and moral decline of a wealthy speculator at the turn of the century.

The Pit was the second novel in Norris' proposed trilogy of "The Epic of the Wheat." In this "Story of Chicago," Norris moves from the production of wheat to its distribution on world markets, from the natural countryside of California to the artificial terrain of futures speculation. Continuing his portrayal of the effects of temptation and greed, Norris also depicts the hereditary decline evident in the space of only one generation—from the moral elder generation that made their money through honest labor to their degenerate offspring who labor only after money and the power it bestows.

The Pit was Norris' most successful novel in terms of sales and initial reception; this may have been aided in part by its publication so soon after his sudden death, but it was also a novel that spoke directly to the times. Every major American naturalist, from Stephen Crane to Jack London and from Rebecca Harding Davis to Edith Wharton, acknowledged through their fiction that speculation—gambling on the future—had become an ironic indicator not only of economic but of social "progress" in the country.

Norris' plot of Curtis Jadwin's fascinating and ruthless efforts to corner the Chicago wheat market was based on an actual event in 1897, when Joseph Leiter attempted the same feat. In fictionalizing the story, however, Norris reflected upon the cultural implications of such daring maneuvers. He was interested not only in the consequences of illegal market manipulations but also in the facets of human nature that would lead someone to commit such an act. In Curtis Jadwin, one discovers a man whose life is so financially secure (but without direction, without goals for achievement) that it is the adventure of such an endeavor that becomes its greatest appeal.

Norris had predicted in *The Octopus* that the wheat would always prevail as a natural force; in *The Pit*, he demonstrates that power against all calculations of human reason when an unexpected bumper crop thwarts Jadwin's illegal designs.

Against this background, Norris also studied another cultural current of the turn of the century: the rise of the New Woman. Suffragist and women's rights movements had flourished to greater or lesser degrees for most of the nineteenth century. At the end of the century, women had finally made several initial inroads into the public arena. The New Woman—self-liberated, intelligent, and outspoken—was juxtaposed against the True Woman, the domestic and dominated self-sacrificing "angel of the house." These issues had dominated women authors' writings for decades, and *The Pit* represents Norris' first major engagement with these issues.

Laura Dearborn had been reared in New England, the breeding ground of the culturally imposed True Womanhood. To escape these oppressive attitudes, she moved to Chicago. Although she had several suitors, Laura's attraction to Curtis was his potential life of wealth and luxury, and she agreed to marry him. Thus she traps herself through greed, in spite of her liberating endeavors. When Curtis becomes involved in his market schemes, she seeks solace in flirtations with the artist Sheldon Corthell. Such a love affair is the stuff from which popular novels were made, and Norris specifically suggests, as he had in his nonfiction, the falseness of such novels' representations of love and romance.

In depicting Laura's affair with Corthell and her attempt at arousing her husband's interest once again with a dance of seduction, Norris acknowledges the reality of women's sexual needs. Ironically, however, Norris cannot complete this depiction of a New Woman. When her husband's business fails, Laura returns to woman's self-sacrificing role and accepts the "duties" of marriage. Norris asserts this is the achievement of love over self-love, but he thereby negates the process of a woman's movement toward liberation by seeing self-love as a negative force that must be overcome.

The Pit seems to conclude with a sentimentalized vision of the poorer, but now happy, couple and of their rejection of the debilitating urban lifestyle. As they almost literally ride off into the sunset, Laura looks back at the city landscape, seeing

> the tall gray office buildings, the murk of rain, the haze of light in the heavens, and raised against it, the pile of the Board of Trade building, black, monolithic, crouching on its foundations like a monstrous sphinx with blind eyes, silent, grave—crouching there without a soul, without a sign of life, under the night and the drifting veil of rain.

Thus Norris seemingly leaves the reader with the demise of evil and the prevailing spirit of goodness—"light in the heavens."

This reading, however, would ignore the irony of Norris' conclusion: Jadwin intends to move west and go into the railroad business. The consequences of this, as depicted in *The Octopus*, are ominous for the entire country. If Jadwin had been defeated by the natural force of the wheat, he is about to attempt to control his defeator through manipulation of the steel tentacles of the railroad.

Since Norris died before he could begin the third novel of the series, this conclusion leaves the battle between the wheat and the machine, unintentionally but appropriately, without resolution.

Summary

Frank Norris was not consistent in his literary philosophies, sometimes advocating realism, sometimes romanticism; if he blended literary techniques, however, it was because he recognized that those techniques were vehicles for expression and not truths in themselves. He created graphic and dramatically powerful novels that addressed the issues of his day and have continued to speak to contemporary debates on human nature and social progress.

For a young man who died just as he was maturing as a writer, he left a surprisingly large body of work, which influenced writers who followed him and has retained its place in American literature's exploration of regional realism.

Bibliography

Conder, John J. *Naturalism in American Fiction: The Classic Phase.* Lexington: University of Kentucky Press, 1981.

French, Warren. *Frank Norris.* New York: Twayne, 1962.

Graham, Don, ed. *Critical Essays on Frank Norris.* Boston: G. K. Hall, 1980.

_____. *The Fiction of Frank Norris: The Aesthetic Context.* Columbia: University of Missouri Press, 1978.

Hochman, Barbara. *The Art of Frank Norris, Storyteller.* Columbia: University of Missouri Press, 1988.

Howard, June. *Form and History in American Literary Naturalism.* Chapel Hill: University of North Carolina Press, 1985.

Marchand, Ernest LeRoy. *Frank Norris: A Study.* Stanford, Calif.: Stanford University Press, 1942.

Pizer, Donald, ed. *The Literary Criticism of Frank Norris.* Austin: University of Texas Press, 1964.

Walcutt, Charles Child. *American Literary Naturalism: A Divided Stream.* Reprint. Westport, Conn.: Greenwood Press, 1973.

Walker, Franklin. *Frank Norris: A Biography.* Garden City, N.Y.: Doubleday, Doran, 1932.

Sharon M. Harris

JOYCE CAROL OATES

Born: Lockport, New York
June 16, 1938

Principal Literary Achievement

Recognized as a talented novelist and master of the short story, Oates has prolifically and passionately depicted the personal dislocation and troubled national identity of twentieth century America.

Biography

Joyce Carol Oates was born on June 16, 1938, in Lockport, New York, a small city on the Erie Barge Canal near Buffalo, to Fredric James and Caroline (Bush) Oates. Her father was a tool and die designer, and Oates's childhood was spent in a rural town, where she attended a one-room schoolhouse. From earliest memory she wanted to be an author. As a small child she drew pictures to tell stories; later she wrote them out, sometimes producing handwritten books of up to two hundred pages with carefully designed covers.

Her childhood was simple and happy, and she developed a closeness to her parents that flourished in her adult years. A brother, Fredric, Jr., was born in 1943, and a sister, Lynn Ann, in 1956; by that year Oates herself had been graduated from Williamsville Central High School, where she had written for the school newspaper, and was entering Syracuse University under a New York State Regents Scholarship, the first in her family to attend college. During her freshman year, a tachycardiac seizure during a basketball game profoundly affected her view of life by bringing her face to face with her mortality. She continued writing stories, and in 1959 she was selected cowinner of the *Mademoiselle* college fiction award for "In the Old World." An excellent student, she was elected to Phi Beta Kappa and was graduated in 1960 at the top of her class.

She received a Knapp Fellowship to pursue graduate work at the University of Wisconsin, where she met a Ph.D. candidate named Raymond Joseph Smith. She and Smith were married on January 23, 1961, and later that year she received her M.A. in English. Smith and Oates moved to Texas, where he taught in Beaumont and she began doctoral work at Rice University in Houston; however, with one of her stories appearing on the honor roll of Martha Foley's *Best American Short Stories*, Oates soon decided to devote herself to her own writing.

Her first collection of stories, *By the North Gate*, appeared in 1963, followed a

year later by her first novel, *With Shuddering Fall*, which, like many of her stories, depicted passionate individuals and violent situations. In 1967, *A Garden of Earthly Delights* appeared as the first novel in a thematic trilogy exploring the American obsession with money. It was followed by *Expensive People* (1968) and *them* (1969), the latter earning the 1970 National Book Award.

Oates taught at the University of Detroit from 1961 to 1967, when she and Smith accepted teaching positions at the University of Windsor in Ontario, Canada. A prolific author, Oates continued publishing stories in such periodicals as *Literary Review, Prairie Schooner,* and *Cosmopolitan,* and she produced a steady flow of books, including the novels *Wonderland* (1971), *Do with Me What You Will* (1973), *The Assassins: A Book of Hours* (1975), *Childwold* (1976), *Son of the Morning* (1978), and *Angel of Light* (1981); the story collections *Upon the Sweeping Flood* (1966), *The Wheel of Love and Other Stories* (1970), *Where Are You Going, Where Have You Been?* (1971), *The Goddess and Other Women* (1974), *The Seduction and Other Stories* (1975), *Night-Side* (1977), and *A Sentimental Education: Stories* (1980); and volumes of poetry entitled *Anonymous Sins and Other Poems* (1969), *Angel Fire* (1973) and *Women Whose Lives Are Food, Men Whose Lives are Money* (1978). Various other writings—essays, plays, and reviews—add to the unusual breadth of her oeuvre.

In 1978, Oates moved to New Jersey to become the Roger S. Berlind Distinguished Professor of Creative Writing at Princeton University. From their home, she and Smith edited *The Ontario Review* and ran a small publishing company associated with the literary magazine. As her body of work grew, so did its formal and thematic diversity. *Bellefleur* (1980), *A Bloodsmoor Romance* (1982), and *Mysteries of Winterthurn* (1984) are experimental ventures into the genres, respectively, of the family chronicle, the romance, and the Gothic mystery. After the experimental trilogy, her work turned more toward a modern naturalism. In the 1980's, her output included the novels *Solstice* (1985), *You Must Remember This* (1987), and *American Appetites* (1989), and the collections *Raven's Wing* (1986) and *The Assignation* (1988).

Oates's many honors include several O. Henry Awards for her short stories, Guggenheim and Rosenthal fellowships, and election to the American Academy and Institute of Arts and Letters. She has traveled and lectured widely, and in December of 1987 was among a group of American artists, writers, and intellectuals invited to greet the Soviet President Mikhail Gorbachev at the Soviet Embassy in Washington, D.C. Her extensive expression as a writer, thinker, and teacher have ensured Oates's role as a respected and vigorous participant in America's intellectual and literary life from the 1960's onward.

Analysis

In a literary tradition populated by many figures known for a single play or a handful of painstakingly wrought novels, Joyce Carol Oates is notable, first, for her consistently prodigious output. Hundreds of stories and poems, printed and anthologized in a wide variety of publications, and dozens of novels, novellas, plays, essays, prefaces, and reviews have come from her pen, with an equally wide variety of settings, themes, genres, and styles. This productivity has even been a source of some criticism, inspiring suspicions that Oates works too fast and carelessly, that she lacks the basic self-censorship necessary to a writer. Oates, unaffected by criticism, has never slowed her pace. While some of her novels seem more felt than planned, and some of her stories inevitably overlap, Oates is a writer whose meanings can be appreciated cumulatively and whose craft and imagination are beyond question.

A more serious criticism is that her writing, especially in the 1960's and 1970's, is too violent, too dark, too obsessed with blood and death. (In 1981, in an essay in *The New York Times Book Review* entitled "Why Is Your Writing So Violent?" Oates branded such criticism blatantly sexist and asserted the female novelist's right to depict nature as she sees it.) A typical Oates novel may feature mass murder, rape, suicide, arson, an automobile accident, or an autopsy, portrayed with detachment and graphic detail. Such violence is less a literal portrayal of the author's experience of life (though her great grandfather committed suicide in a rage after trying to kill his wife, Oates's own life has been relatively sedate) than an expression of the violence she sees beneath the surface of American life.

One of Oates's primary concerns is the shape of American identity in the twentieth century. Her novels often trace the lives of prototypical Americans and can be seen as paradigms of their collective history. Very aware of her parents' experiences through the 1930's, Oates often places the Depression at the beginning, chronologically if not narratively, of the stories she tells, for that is the source of much of the history of the 1960's, 1970's, and 1980's. (In *Bellefleur*, she goes further back to trace all of American history through a single family chronicle.) Many of her works are set in an imaginary Eden County modeled on the familiar Erie and Niagara counties of western New York. As the name suggests, Eden County is a mythical Paradise where Oates depicts the American loss of innocence.

Oates documents, and at times seems to prophesy, this loss of innocence through a pattern reflecting the national heritage. This historical paradigm involves derivation from a strong familial tradition, be it the migrant workers of *A Garden of Earthly Delights* or the patricians of *The Assassins: A Book of Hours*; dislocation, often violent and senseless, from that home or tradition; the search for parent figures; the lack of fixed identity; acceptance of the American Dream, with all of its materialistic manifestations; emergence from poverty and anonymity; the obsession that arrives with single-minded pursuits; and the vacuity and transparency of contemporary American modes of being and communicating.

This paradigm is not inviolate, nor does it inform all Oates's work. One of her most noted novels, *them*, is drawn quite faithfully from the life experience of a woman Oates knew while teaching in Detroit, and *Marya: A Life* (1986) is based to an extent on her mother's and her own early lives. Conversely, the stories in *Marriages and Infidelities* (1972) are modeled on (and even named for) earlier stories by acknowledged masters, such as James Joyce's "The Dead" (1914) and Franz Kafka's *Die Verwandlung* (1915; "The Metamorphosis," 1936), and their appreciation can depend on familiarity with—indeed, "marriage" to—their predecessors. A number of her works, including the satirical collection *The Hungry Ghosts: Seven Allusive Comedies* (1974), are set in academic institutions not unlike Oates's own universities of Windsor and Princeton.

Whatever the setting and the model for dramatic movement, certain themes are central. Oates is fascinated with the multiple facets of individual personality, and her characters often undergo dramatic upheavals and transformations (which are larger metaphorical expressions of the violence of modern life). They are constantly questioning who and where they are, constantly feeling detached from their bodies and their immediate experiences of the world. Nothing is certain or fixed. In such a whirlwind, emotion and sensation are all one can really know and trust; having a name; as the fundamental unit of identity, becomes of paramount importance.

Many of Oates's novels and stories, therefore, based in the emotional reality of a character, have a surrealistic quality. Oates is fascinated with dreams; not only do her characters relate theirs, but also the lines between perception, imagination, and dream or nightmare often become hazy. Because objective reality is unavailable, people become trapped within their own personalities, and connections between them are often tenuous and false. Many of the short stories, such as "The Census-Taker" (1963), "Queen of the Night" (1979), and "The Seasons" (1985), focus on jarring and unsuccessful encounters or relationships between very disparate personalities.

Generally, Oates's style is controlled and detached; her narrative voices do not cater to the reader but demand that the reader make necessary connections and assumptions. Her works are sometimes challenging puzzles that require careful attention. She is a skilled technician who uses precise and explicit language and portrays personality through detailed sketching of both interior and exterior reality. Not surprisingly, the imagery Oates employs is often violent: exposed flesh, broken glass, explosions, floods, fire. All these elements—the detachment, the ambiguity, the detail, the imagery—combine to create an uncertain world where reality is constantly reconceived and re-imagined through the window of perception, and truth—historical, subjective, and psychic—is ever-changing.

A GARDEN OF EARTHLY DELIGHTS

First published: 1967
Type of work: Novel

A woman's quest to escape her impoverished past bequeaths to her son a world full of power but empty of meaning and identity.

A Garden of Earthly Delights is a novel that portrays the American economic system and the ills suffered both by those who fail and by those who succeed in it. Oates tells the story of Clara, from the day of her birth among migrant laborers to her waning years watching television in a nursing home, and the men—father, lovers, son—that define her life experience.

The title is taken from a dramatic triptych by the fifteenth century Dutch painter Hieronymus Bosch. The three panels of the original "Garden of Earthly Delights" illustrate Eve's creation in paradise, the debauchery of her descendants, and mankind's punishment in hell, and Oates's novel mirrors this structure in its three sections. The first, entitled "Carleton," focuses on a bitter migrant laborer named Carleton Walpole as he takes his growing family from state to state, struggling to control his rage and maintain his lost sense of dignity. Clara, the third and favorite of his five children, learns to look beyond the distress and misery of their migrant existence and eventually runs off with a virtual stranger to find a better life.

The second section, "Lowry," follows Clara through adolescence. The stranger, an enigmatic drifter named Lowry, sets her up in a small Southern town, but he is involved in shady activities and soon disappears, spurning her obsessive love and unknowingly leaving her pregnant. Clara, a survivor, has attracted the attentions of a wealthy landowner, Curt Revere; she becomes his mistress, leads him to believe he is the father of her child, accepts his boundless generosity, and, with the death of his ailing wife, becomes the second Mrs. Revere.

Now established in comfort and wealth, having achieved a perfect vision of the American Dream, Clara consolidates her power. The third section of the novel, "Swan," focuses on Clara's son Steven (whom she calls Swan) and the pressures he feels growing up an outsider among someone else's wealth, destined to inherit it, but unable to make sense of his destiny or to fulfill his mother's exaggerated expectations for him.

Within this structure, the narrative moves chronologically but with a greatly modulated pace. Oates relates individual scenes or periods in the lives of her characters with slow and careful accuracy and feeling, and then shifts the action months or years ahead, establishing the passage of time casually with age or year references. Such shifts highlight the suddenness of the events and changes that have occurred. This irregular flow serves to emphasize, as if microscopically, certain telling moments or encounters. Carleton's rage explodes during an arm-wrestling match and he kills his best friend, an event that Clara recalls throughout her life. A jaunt into a nearby town where Clara impulsively steals a flag, her first night with Lowry, and her decision to run away are vividly portrayed and establish the fearlessness and pride that will bring tragedy in later life. A pivotal encounter comes at the end of the second section when, after years of silence, Lowry shows up at Clara's house to reclaim her: She does not love Revere, and she feels a flood of emotion at the sight of Lowry, but her resolution to accumulate power at any cost is too firm, and she sends her former lover—and her only hope for true happiness—away forever.

Swan, however, only three years old at the time, is affected by Lowry—by some deep instinct of his own paternity—and the knowledge of that ominous visitor stays with him. Swan is not at home with Revere and his rightful sons, for Swan's true identity has been sacrificed to Clara's lust for power. Though she acts with his future supremacy in mind, she cannot understand his psychic needs, and, in the novel's ultimate violent act, he refuses the power she has achieved for him and renders the struggles of her life meaningless.

Clara's is a very American story, for her ascent and accomplishments reach a point of diminishing returns, but she refuses to relent. Set against a subtly drawn backdrop of national events from the 1920's through the 1960's—the Depression, the renewal of industrial prosperity, the transformation of race relations and erosion of class structures in the South—Clara's story takes on wider repercussions as an American fable, with implicit commentary on the misguided motives and empty values of American political and materialistic ethics.

WONDERLAND

First published: 1971
Type of work: Novel

A young man undergoes a series of transformations as he comes to maturity and strives for identity in a dreamlike American landscape.

Wonderland bears certain rough similarities to *A Garden of Earthly Delights*: It follows three generations of a family through stages of rage, searching, and emptiness; it offers critical comment on the lust for knowledge and power; it spans a particular period of American political and economic history; it moves irregularly, with sudden shifts and changes; and it, too, draws on another work of art as a model. *Wonderland*, is, however, stylistically much less naturalistic, its commentary more satirical, and its concern for the issues of dislocation and identity more fully focused on a single central character, Jesse.

As the title suggests, Oates used Lewis Carroll's *Alice's Adventures in Wonderland* (1865) as a thematic source for her novel. Like Alice, Jesse bursts into new worlds and must deal with characters that verge on caricatures and that parallel the Mad Hatter, Cheshire Cat, and others. Oates has taken Carroll's thematic framework and applied it sharply and imaginatively to the American scene.

The novel begins abruptly: Fourteen-year-old Jesse Harte returns home one day to find his family murdered by his crazed father. Jesse escapes through a window (like Alice's "looking glass") and is orphaned by his father's suicide. Emotionally numbed, Jesse embarks on a passive search for replacements—for a father figure, for a home, for a viable belief system, for a name that is truly his. He lives first with his silent, bitter grandfather (taking the surname Vogel), then with uncomprehending cousins, then in an orphanage.

Book 1 of the novel is entitled "Variations on an American Hymn," and most of it details Jesse's life with the Pedersens, his adoptive family of virtual freaks. The father is a dogmatic morphine-addicted doctor/mystic, the mother an obsequious alcoholic, the son a blithering piano virtuoso, the daughter an angry mathematical genius. The Pedersens are all grotesquely obese, and with them Jesse expands accordingly. He takes their name and their ways but never gives himself completely to the doctor's maniacal egoism; in the end, after helping Mrs. Pedersen in an aborted attempt to escape, Jesse is disowned, dislocated, and, again, nameless.

He goes to college at the University of Michigan to study medicine and, an excellent student, falls under the tutelage of Drs. Cady and Perrault and an errant scientist and poet named T. W. Monk (whose poem "Wonderland" provides the epigraph to Oates's novel). Each of the men expresses a distinct and limited worldview—empiricism, behaviorism, nihilism—which Jesse adopts to a point but is unable to accept fully or embody.

He becomes a brilliant surgeon, marries Cady's daughter Helene, and fathers two daughters, but the marriage is unfulfilling and Jesse becomes inexplicably obsessed with a woman he encounters at a chance moment in the emergency room—Reva Denk, whose name suggests "think/dream." Book 2, entitled "The Finite Passing of an Infinite Passion," ends with Jesse's impulsive decision to begin a new life with Reva, and, once she agrees, his equally impulsive decision to return at once to Helene.

Book 3, "Dreaming America," alternates between Jesse's search for his runaway daughter Shelly and her angry, enigmatic letters home declaring insistently that his pursuits—of knowledge, of love, of wealth, of metaphysical supremacy—have ruined her life. Her letters contain veiled hints, and when Jesse finally locates her among a community of draft dodgers in Toronto, the novel ends on a reservedly optimistic note.

Throughout *Wonderland*, Oates's language and imagery are palpable and graphic. Certain scenes are striking: Hilda Pedersen gluttonously devouring chocolates during a mathematical competition; Helene's obsession with her own reproductive capacities turning to panic during a gynecological examination; a man, who turns out to be Reva's lover, arriving at Jesse's hospital self-mutilated; later, Jesse symbolically mutilating himself with a rusty razor before abandoning Reva. Such scenes reinforce the thematic presence of science and medicine as means of knowing and experiencing life. There are recurrent perceptions of living organisms as reduced to their simplest form, protoplasm, and as beings that emerge from and consume other beings. The concept of "homeostasis"—the natural tendency toward balance—which Dr. Pedersen asks Jesse to explain one evening at the dinner table, provides a standard for the desirable pattern of functioning that Jesse, not to mention the gallery of characters that surround him, cannot achieve.

Wonderland—which is also the name of the new shopping mall where the dissatisfied Helene meets her lover—is an Oatesian world of unnatural proportions where, like the Pedersens' obesity, ideas, emotions, and aspirations are often ridiculously reduced or magnified. The portraits Oates creates are exaggerated, narcissistic, and often very comical.

The only exception is Jesse, who lacks an inherent personality and becomes a reflection or embodiment of the people and ideas around him. Thus, the other characters take on the dimensions of allegory: They become emotional or philosophical options for him to review and try, but his movement through and experience of them, like his movement from name to name and home to home, leaves him at the novel's end only barely less innocent and passive than he was at its start. Ultimately, his search for identity and longing for a sense of solidity in his existence are the only reliable facts of his life.

THE ASSASSINS: A BOOK OF HOURS

First published: 1975
Type of work: Novel

After the supposed assassination of a prominent political figure, his brothers and widow struggle to find meaning in their lives.

The Assassins: A Book of Hours is perhaps Oates's darkest and most pessimistic novel. It takes its subtitle from a canonical book that ends with the Office of the Dead, and it is concerned with characters mourning or obsessed with death.

The four characters central to the novel are Andrew Petrie, a former senator from New York and outspoken political observer, his brothers Hugh and Stephen, and his widow Yvonne. Andrew himself is dead and appears only through memory or flashback; Hugh, Yvonne, and Stephen provide the viewpoints for the three parts of the novel, which are accordingly named for them.

"Hugh" begins enigmatically, and only later does it become evident that his diffuse and convoluted first-person narrative takes place within his conscious mind as he lies inexpressive and paralyzed in a hospital bed. Hugh is a bitter and sardonic political cartoonist who has devoted his life to hating and lampooning all that his successful older brother represents. His character—greedy, impotent, hypochondriac, alcoholic—is expressed through his obsessive rantings as he recounts his experience during the year following Andrew's death. Without Andrew, Hugh's life lacks the pivot on which it had turned. Consumed with a desire to discover his brother's assassins and convinced that Yvonne holds the key, he embarks on a maniacal pursuit of her and ends up a professional and romantic failure—even failing in his dramatically staged but essentially comic attempt at suicide.

Yvonne, the object of Hugh's deluded affections, is left completely isolated by her husband's death. Assisting the police, she draws up a list of Andrew's potential enemies, but the list is really an emblem of her own paranoia, for she views all others as her personal enemies and recedes further into her own private world. Having immersed herself completely in Andrew's intellectual life and their marriage, she strives after his death to continue his work, but that also soon loses meaning. She engages in casual affairs with various men connected with Andrew, but she is both frigid and incapable of bringing her lovers pleasure. Part 2, "Yvonne," ends with a violent scenario of Yvonne's own death at the hands of ax-wielding assassins.

"Stephen" focuses on the youngest Petrie brother, who experienced a religious awakening as a teenager, dissociated himself completely from his family and its wealth, and has been living in a religious retreat. His last meeting with Andrew was a fiery one, and Andrew's death now challenges the peace Stephen has found by forcing him to acknowledge himself as a Petrie. In attending the funeral, in meeting with Hugh in New York and Yvonne in Albany, the firmness of his Jesuit foundation begins to disintegrate, and he finds himself deprived of his sense of God, and with it his sense of himself. He becomes an aimless and ever-accommodating drifter.

The three parts of the novel treat the same events, encounters, and revelations through three disparate perceptions; together they suggest an objective account of events and define the limitations of the individual personalities. The novel abounds in carefully wrought detail and corroboration, and it is populated with a world of other characters: the Petries' father, a ruthless judge now in retirement; their sister Doris, a plump suburban busybody; their cousin Pamela, a superficial society woman; their cousin Harvey, Andrew's cutthroat rival; Andrew's sensuous first wife Willa and brilliant son Michael; Hugh's psychoanalysts, Drs. Wynand and Swann; and the mysterious Raschke, a political activist from both Yvonne's and Stephen's pasts.

There is an element of mystery throughout *The Assassins*, for Hugh's desire to locate Andrew's assassins renders all the characters suspect and creates expectations that the murder will be solved at the end of the novel. The title and the mystery are misleading, however, for Oates's "assassins" are the characters themselves, who, through their obsessions and limited vision, unwittingly murder themselves and one another. It is even intimated that Andrew's death, on which so much depends, was not an assassination at all, but a carefully disguised suicide.

The Assassins is a challenging novel, for Oates demands that the reader join together the disparate elements of the story. Though the three sections are expressed through three different temperaments, they all have a staccato, nearly stream-of-consciousness flow which can blend memory, conjecture, dream, imagination, and physical reality into a single stratum of experience. Thus, certain issues are unclear: Hugh's condition at the outset, the circumstances of Andrew's death, and whether Yvonne's brutal murder is real or imagined.

Such questions fade beneath the psychic weight of the novel. Philosophically, the novel shows the influence of the American philosopher William James, whose *The Varieties of Religious Experience* (1902) may have suggested a thematic model. James was concerned with the tyranny of pluralism and the inability of individuals to connect. *The Assassins* portrays three philosophical approaches—Hugh reduces all to two dimensions, ridiculing it; Yvonne reduces all to reason, sterilizing it; and Stephen reduces all to God, subsuming it in mystery—and all the approaches fail, leaving the characters trapped within their own egos. They deny necessary aspects of reality, thereby denying the possibility of love, and effectively assassinate any real life that exists within.

SOLSTICE

First published: 1985
Type of work: Novel

A friendship between two women, a newly divorced young schoolteacher and a flamboyant and somewhat celebrated painter, develops to an intensity that threatens their lives.

During the early part of her career, Oates was viewed as a female writer on the periphery of the women's movement; in the 1980's, her writing began to focus more frequently on stories and characters with particularly feminine or feminist concerns. *Solstice*, like *Marya: A Life* which followed it, exemplifies this development, portraying the relationship between two women in a small Pennsylvania town.

Monica Jensen, recently divorced and attempting to start a new life in the wake of her failed marriage, has relocated from New York City and accepted a teaching assignment at the local boys' academy. Sheila Trask, older and more worldly, is a successful artist, the widow of a famous sculptor; she lives alone and detached from the community in a fine old country house. The novel, which is told from Monica's viewpoint, is divided into four sections that reflect four stages in her development.

The first, entitled, "The Scar," details Monica's adjustment to country life, her first casual encounters with Sheila, and her growing attraction to the other's lively personality. Sheila is the stronger of the two, and Monica, in emotional recovery, is timid, hesitant, and flattered to accept Sheila's friendly attention.

As they become acquainted, their friendship becomes the foundation of their social lives. "The Mirror-Ghoul," the second section, shows the process by which the women come to know each other's strengths and weaknesses, to provide necessary support, to reflect one another. On Sheila's urging, they begin frequenting local taverns and bowling alleys, pretending to be lively country divorcées; this activity delights Sheila but leads to adventures and moral considerations that discomfort and frighten Monica. Eventually, Sheila becomes demanding and burdensome to Monica; Monica withdraws. Sheila's work suffers, and she drinks and takes pills; by Christmas, mere months after their first meeting, their confrontations crescendo and plummet into silence. Sheila disappears; Monica assumes she has gone globe-trotting to Paris or Morocco.

Part 3 is "Holiday," a period of separation. Monica returns to her family in Indiana for the New Year holiday and mourns the passing of her golden adolescence. Returning from vacation, she is keenly aware of Sheila's absence. She begins dating an attorney but without feeling any passion; she becomes more involved with her work and students; she misses Sheila but tries not to think of her.

Then Sheila returns, and with her the relationship, the obsessive behavior, and the manipulation. Monica can identify the effect that Sheila is having on her, but she cannot stop it. She allows herself to become indispensable to Sheila's life, including the running of the house and the arrangement of an upcoming exhibition. She neglects her own work at school, then her health as well, until she is ultimately relieved of her teaching responsibilities. Their friendship is now consuming and debilitating: The women lose the ability to console or support each other, move in and out of illness, and behave with veiled malice or open spite. In the end, Monica's health deteriorates so dramatically that Sheila finds her helpless and rushes her to the hospital, where she very possibly may die.

The title of this last section, "Labyrinth," is taken from a painting Sheila is doing of the mythical Ariadne and her arduous journey out of the maze of the Minotaur's palace. The novel is itself Monica's account of her similar journey, and the narrative twists and turns with labyrinthine complexity. It is also, as the title suggests, about a sort of solstice—the passing of two distinct and very different bodies in a close, rare, and distorting conjunction.

Solstice is episodic; it creates portraits of Monica, Sheila, and their interaction through occasional moments, diverse comments, and unconnected impressions. It is more straightforward and naturalistic than much of Oates's writing, yet its apparent simplicity is misleading, for beneath the daily texture of the relationship portrayed, even at its most intense moments, is a deeper reality of repressed emotion and personality. Monica, seeking an easy escape from a painful past—including an abortion to which she rarely refers—and Sheila, using sham joy and passion to avoid facing her art, her fear, and her loneliness, both refuse to confront the deeper truths of their lives. Their emotional dishonesty renders their friendship futile and brings them, by the novel's inconclusive end, to the brink of utter tragedy.

IN THE REGION OF ICE

First published: 1965
Type of work: Short story

A nun's encounter with a brilliant but disturbed young man illustrates her emotional isolation and spiritual sterility.

"In the Region of Ice," first published in *The Atlantic Monthly* and later in the collection *The Wheel of Love and Other Stories*, won the O. Henry first prize in short fiction for 1967. It shares with other of Oates's early works, including the novel *Son of the Morning* (1978) and the story "Shame" (1968), a religious protagonist and a concern for spiritual issues. Sister Irene teaches Shakespeare at a small Catholic university. For all practical purposes, she lives "in the region of ice"—a region void of feeling and passion. She is perfectly comfortable in front of a class lecturing on literature, but otherwise she is timid and essentially incapable of developing meaningful human contact.

Into her insulated existence comes Allen Weinstein, a brilliant but emotionally disturbed Jewish student. Having failed to cope successfully in his own discipline, history, and obsessed with the reality of ideas, he sits in on Irene's class and, unlike the other students, challenges and engages her. Eventually he dominates the class, inspiring the hatred of his classmates but awakening intellectual and emotional life in the professor herself.

The story is narrated through Irene's viewpoint, and Oates carefully charts the emotional journey she travels in response to Allen's erratic and striking behavior. Inexplicably, Irene finds herself anticipating Allen's presence and feeling hurt at his absence; her emotional life becomes dependent on his behavior, moods, and ideas. Their relationship, through her perception, is like a dance of intellectual passion and spiritual magnetism.

Then Allen stops coming to class. After a prolonged absence, he contacts Irene from a sanatorium with a veiled plea for help: quoting Claudio in Shakespeare's *Measure for Measure*, he begs her to communicate his passion to his father. As Irene goes to the Weinstein home to do Allen's bidding, she feels a religious awakening, a sense of her Christianity and the true meaning of sacrifice, but her heroism quickly fades and she allows herself to be bullied by Allen's hateful, exasperated, unsympathetic father.

Later, released from the sanatorium and desperate to leave the country, Allen comes to Irene for emotional and financial support, but she painfully and inarticulately denies him. Now, as throughout their unusual relationship, she is equally aware of his desire to establish a meaningful communion and of her own inability to oblige. She is simply terrified of being connected to another human being. While Allen is clearly on the edge of sanity, Irene's situation is more pathetic, for she is knowingly trapped within the trivial limits of her own selfhood. Even the inevitable news of Allen's suicide provokes only a longing for feeling, but no true emotional response.

Like "Where Are You Going, Where Have You Been?" (1966), "In the Region of Ice" details the effects of a male intruder into the life of a female protagonist. Here, the emotional power of the story lies in the lack of response, in the utter sterility that remains invulnerable against great passion and anguish. Oates depicts in Sister Irene the very human discrepancy between the ideals of the mind and the limits of the individual will in real life. The "Ice" of the title goes beyond the cold clarity of academia and the chosen celibacy of the nun's habit to describe the irony of an emotionally frigid human being taking refuge in a frail travesty of spiritual and humanitarian fullness.

IN THE AUTUMN OF THE YEAR

First published: 1978
Type of work: Short story

A successful poet is forced by her former lover's son to reexamine the only passionate romance of her life.

"In the Autumn of the Year," which is included in the collection *A Sentimental Education*, received an O. Henry Award in 1979, a year after its first publication in *The Bennington Review*. Like many of Oates's stories, it tells of a single but important encounter between a man and a woman from different backgrounds and with different attitudes.

The protagonist, Eleanor Gerhardt, is a Pulitzer Prize-winning poet, an articulate spinster suggestive of the nineteenth century American poet Emily Dickinson, who has come to a small New England college to accept an award. Her host for the visit is Benjamin Höller, a man she knew as a boy in Boston, because at the time she was his father's mistress. Eleanor, now sixty-three years old, lives life with a sense of its near-completion. She lives in the past and no longer considers herself an active, feeling woman. Never married, her passion for Edwin Höller and the dramatic dissolution of their relationship form a memory that she sustains, though she has not seen him in decades and he is now dead. Upon meeting Benjamin and throughout her visit in his midst, her consciousness shifts back and forth from the uneventful present to the tumultuous and deeply felt past.

Then, in a casual meeting after the ceremony, Benjamin and Eleanor start discussing his father, to Eleanor's surprise, he expresses accumulated anger and hatred. As he openly confronts her with his father's cruelty, her own insensitivity, the cheapness of their affair, and their responsibility for the emotional misery of his childhood, her sentimental vision of the past is shattered. She tries impulsively to protest her innocence, but she is shocked and left essentially speechless. Benjamin offers her the love letters and suicide threats that she sent to Edwin upon their separation, but she cannot face them and denies their authenticity. In the end, alone, she tosses the unopened letters in the fire, as if so doing will alleviate her guilt and folly.

Oates uses balance to create powerful emotional dynamics. The juxtaposition of immediate experience and memory communicates the temporal and emotional dislocation with which Eleanor perceives her existence in the "autumn" of her life. Her detached contemplation of seemingly imminent death and the subsequent disposition of her worldly goods contrasts sharply with the suicidal desperation she recalls enduring when Edwin deserted her. The device of remembering a distant past in which she imagined a distant future—now arrived—reinforces the swirling sense of her life.

The second half of the story comes suddenly and unexpectedly, and Benjamin's brutal honesty plays against the complacent politeness of their earlier encounters. Unbeknown to Eleanor, he provides a missing piece to the puzzle of her life. Without the delusions by which her past drained her present of meaning, she is forced to face the past honestly and recognizing its mixed qualities, to let go of it. Through this encounter, she can begin to take responsibility for her continued existence and for the long-repressed reality of herself as a woman who is still very much alive and capable of deep feeling.

RAVEN'S WING

First published: 1985
Type of work: Short story

A husband's fascination with a wounded racehorse imperceptibly reinvigorates his marriage with warmth and understanding.

"Raven's Wing," a story in the volume of the same title, first appeared in *Esquire* and was included in *The Best American Short Stories, 1985*. It is a brief story, told with simplicity and subtlety and without the violence and passion of much of Oates's other work, presenting a slice-of-life view of a rather ordinary marriage.

Billy is thirty-two years old and has been married to his twenty-four-year-old second wife Linda for barely a year. Though Linda is five months pregnant, Billy feels little passion for or interest in her, and he treats her with indifference and condescension. Linda, in turn, to stimulate his attention, baits, teases, and spites him. Their conversations are empty and end in noncommittal bickering.

Billy, who likes racing and gambling, becomes fascinated with a two-million-dollar racehorse named Raven's Wing after it is crippled during a race. Linda cannot understand Billy's fascination with the horse's sheer size and value—he tells her that she lacks the adequate "frame of reference." He resourcefully finds a way to visit Raven's Wing in Pennsylvania, where it is recovering from major surgery, and, eye to eye with it, feels a sense of connection, an implicit mixture of awe, sympathy, and trust.

The story ends a short time later in two brief scenes. Billy gives Linda a pair of delicate earrings and finds excitement in watching her put them on. Weeks later, as he talks on the telephone, Linda comes to him warmly, holding out a few strands of coarse black hair, and presses close against him.

In "Raven's Wing," rather than stating Billy's true feelings, of which he himself is only hazily aware, Oates suggests them through the details of external reality. Billy's boredom with his home life is contrasted by his unexpected fascination with the racehorse. When he has "the vague idea" that Linda is pregnant with "another man's baby," and when he has sudden violent impulses toward her, he is responding less to her character or behavior than to his own inner discontent. In reality, it is his own "frame of reference" that is inadequate.

Oates's story is about perception—about how things appear differently through the blurring lens of familiarity and routine. At one point, Billy remembers seeing a beautiful woman on the street; only after a moment did he realize that it was Linda, unusually dressed up and very sexy. At another point, Linda, seeking to engage him, says that if men had to have the babies they probably would not do it; Billy barely hears her, just as he does not appreciate how full his own life truly is, if he would only recognize it.

It is the encounter with Raven's Wing that helps him to see. His fascination with the crippled creature betrays an unconscious awareness of the crippled state of his own psyche. Billy's astonishment at the size, beauty, and value of the prize animal implicitly compares with the insensitivity of his attitude toward Linda. Similarly, the millions of dollars spent to save the horse for stud purposes humble Billy and bring home the reality of Linda's pregnancy, of the very human power they share to love, to support, and to create.

The end of the story suggests, through the gift of the earrings, a more comfortable intimacy and Billy's heightened awareness of Linda, indicating that the nature of their relationship has undergone a slight but very important shift. The black hairs that Linda holds, which are never explicitly identified, are a good luck souvenir from the mane of Raven's Wing.

Summary

The novels and stories of Joyce Carol Oates offer a plethora of subjects, styles, themes, and philosophical concerns; given their wide publication and anthologization, they have reached an unusually large audience. Throughout Oates's work is a concern not only to articulate her perception of personal and social conditions but also to imaginatively delve into the depths of meaning she finds there. By dreaming and re-imagining America, she invites her readers to explore the true nature of the world around them.

Bibliography

Allen, Mary. *The Necessary Blankness: Women in Major American Fiction of the Sixties*. Urbana: University of Illinois Press, 1976.

Creighton, Joanne V. *Joyce Carol Oates*. Boston: G. K. Hall, 1979.

Friedman, Ellen G. *Joyce Carol Oates*. New York: Frederick Ungar, 1980.

Grant, Mary Kathryn. *The Tragic Vision of Joyce Carol Oates*. Durham, N.C.: Duke University Press, 1978.

Kazin, Alfred. *Bright Book of Life: American Novelists and Storytellers from Hemingway to Mailer*. Boston: Little, Brown, 1973.

Oates, Joyce Carol. *The Edge of Impossibility: Tragic Forms in Literature*. New York: Vanguard Press, 1972.

_____. *New Heaven, New Earth: The Visionary Experience in Literature*. New York: Vanguard Press, 1974.

Wagner, Linda, ed. *Critical Essays on Joyce Carol Oates*. Boston: G. K. Hall, 1979.

Waller, G. F. *Dreaming America: Obsession and Transcendence in the Fiction of Joyce Carol Oates*. Baton Rouge: Louisiana State University Press, 1979.

Barry Mann

FLANNERY O'CONNOR

Born: Savannah, Georgia
March 25, 1925
Died: Milledgeville, Georgia
August 3, 1964

Principal Literary Achievement

In her stories and two short novels, O'Connor combined religious themes from her Roman Catholic vision with comically realistic characters from the rural protestant South to create a fiction that is simultaneously serious and comic.

Biography

Mary Flannery O'Connor was born in Savannah, Georgia, on March 25, 1925, the only child of Edward Flannery and Regina Cline O'Connor. Both her parents were Roman Catholics from active Catholic families, a religious heritage that had a deep effect on her thinking and writing. As a child, she attended parochial school and early developed an interest in domestic birds and poultry. In her later writings she recalled that, when she was five, a newsreel company came to film her pet bantam, which could walk both forward and backward. Years later, in a high school home economics class, she responded to an assignment to make a child's garment by creating a white pique coat for a pet chicken. Also during her early years, O'Connor began to develop a talent for drawing and cartooning, an interest which remained with her through her life.

In 1938, her father was diagnosed as having disseminated lupus, a progressive disease in which the body forms antibodies to its own tissues. With that, the family moved from Savannah to Milledgeville, where Regina O'Connor's father had been mayor. Edward O'Connor died in February of 1941, and Flannery remained in Milledgeville for most of the rest of her life, with time away only during her brief period of healthy adulthood between 1945 and 1950.

In 1942, O'Connor entered Georgia State College for Women (it is now Women's College of Georgia) in Milledgeville. She was graduated with an A.B. degree in English and social sciences in 1945. During her college years, her interests were divided between fiction writing and cartooning. She did both, along with editing, for college publications. After her graduation, she decided to attend the Writers' Workshop at the University of Iowa, where she had been awarded a fellowship on the basis of some of her stories, which one of her teachers had submitted to the work-

shop. It was about this time that she began to drop "Mary" and to use "Flannery" alone as a writing name.

The Writers' Workshop, founded by Paul Engle, was the most prestigious program of its kind when O'Connor was a student there, and she learned much from the experience. One biographer, Harold Fickett, records her willingness to accept criticism from the workshop and her willingness to rewrite work in accord with her teachers' suggestions. This sort of docility probably did not come easily to O'Connor, who was a person of strong convictions and a willingness to stand up for them. During her time at Iowa, she began to publish stories; her first publication was "The Geranium" in *Accent* in 1946. That story was one of the six stories of her thesis collection for the M.F.A. degree, which she received in 1947. She stayed on at Iowa for an additional year, teaching and writing the beginnings of her first novel, *Wise Blood* (1952). Her start on that book earned her the Rinehart-Iowa Prize for a first novel.

O'Connor spent much of 1948 at Yaddo, an artists' colony at Saratoga Springs, New York, where she continued to work on *Wise Blood* and where she formed some literary friendships, particularly with the poet Robert Lowell, who introduced her to Robert Giroux (he later published her work). Through him she made the lifelong friendship of poet and teacher Robert Fitzgerald and his wife Sally. They too were Catholic, and when O'Connor decided to leave Yaddo, after a short stay in New York, she arranged to board with the Fitzgerald family at their home in Ridgefield, Connecticut. O'Connor found that a happy time during which, as Harold Fickett records, after Mass, she spent her mornings writing, her afternoons writing letters (including a daily letter to her mother), and her evenings with the Fitzgeralds.

At Christmas, 1950, on the train home to Milledgeville, O'Connor suffered her first attack of lupus. The drug ACTH finally brought the disease under control, but it was a serious attack and her recovery was slow. She was very weak and debilitated for months. Her slow recovery led her to give up her plans to return to the North; for the rest of her life she lived with her mother, Regina, on her dairy farm, Andalusia, near Milledgeville. Her relationship with Regina is reflected in many of her letters, which convey the pair's deep affection and her mother's selfless care-giving, as well as the inevitable stresses which accompanied their living together. For the most part, O'Connor's references to those stresses are indirect and offered with the ironic humor (sometimes in a mock backwoods style) which suggests that even when O'Connor was irritated with her mother's occasional insensitivity to her literary work, she was always certain of her mother's devotion to her and always returned that love while expressing it in her own style. (She once gave her mother a donkey for Mother's Day, saying it was the gift for a mother who had everything.)

Through much of the rest of her life, O'Connor followed a standard routine of writing in the morning, riding into Milledgeville for lunch, reading, painting, and caring for her large flock of peafowl and other birds in the afternoons and evenings. After about 1955, she had to use aluminum crutches because the ACTH had weakened her bones so that they would not support her weight. Nevertheless, as her literary reputation increased, she accepted as many lecture invitations as she was able. Some of her addresses have been published as *Mystery and Manners* (1969).

Only once did O'Connor travel abroad, in 1958, when her mother persuaded her to travel to Lourdes, France, in the hope of a miraculous cure for her lupus. The trip was an arduous one, and O'Connor undertook it mostly to please her mother. After the trip, she wrote to a friend, "Now for the rest of my life I can forget about going to Europe, having went." Her mother's dreamed-of cure did not occur.

During her years at Andalusia, O'Connor wrote and published a collection of short stories, *A Good Man Is Hard to Find* (1955), and a second novel, *The Violent Bear It Away* (1960). At her death, she had just completed a second collection of stories, published posthumously as *Everything That Rises Must Converge* (1965). She also carried on a voluminous correspondence with other writers, publishers, friends, and readers, some of which is collected in *The Habit of Being: Selected Letters of Flannery O'Connor* (1979), edited by her friend Sally Fitzgerald. Her letters testify to her lively sense of humor (often self-deprecating) and to her interest in the opinions, reading habits, and spiritual states of the people she loved.

In 1964, O'Connor had surgery for the removal of a fibroid tumor. The surgery was successful, but it reactivated her lupus, and her condition deteriorated as she fought to finish her second collection of stories. She died in Milledgeville on August 3, 1964, at the age of thirty-nine.

Analysis

Flannery O'Connor always saw herself as writing from an explicitly Christian point of view; indeed, given her convictions, that was the only way she could consider writing. She saw her religion as liberation and considered it a vocation in much the way one might be called to the priesthood. At the same time, she resented the sentimental expectations which people frequently hold toward what they might call "religious" fiction—maudlin stories about deathbed conversions and inspirational saints' lives. O'Connor undermined those expectations by her use of humor; she avoided pious characters and conventionally "churchy" settings. Instead, she drew her characters and settings from the rural South she knew so well. Those characters were sometimes labeled "grotesques" by critics and scholars, but she rejected the term, feeling that it originated with writers who understood the South as little as they understood Christianity, a condition of ignorance she intended to remedy. She understood that she was writing to a secular world, and she intended to instruct it in the Christian understanding of grace and redemption as the elements most central to human life. At the same time, O'Connor recognized the dangers of becoming a sermonizer instead of an artist (she talked about that issue in some of her addresses), although the satiric humor in her style, the violence in her plots, and her strange characters made it unlikely that she would fall into that difficulty.

O'Connor's themes return to the issue of grace and redemption again and again. In her first novel, *Wise Blood*, the story's central character, Hazel Motes, begins as a man who is determined to escape the compelling image of Jesus which haunts him.

In an effort to avoid the call to preach, he becomes a sort of "anti-preacher," preaching the "church of Christ without Christ" on street corners. This is a church, he says, in which there was no fall from grace and consequently is no need for redemption, a church for which Jesus was an ordinary human being and nothing more. O'Connor implies that Hazel's view of the world is shared by most people, but Hazel can no more escape his call than could Jonah (to whom O'Connor compares him). At last, events drive him to recognize that his ideas about his church's "new Jesus" (a mummy stolen from a museum) are as worthless as the mummy itself. He loses the car which represented all his high expectations for a life without grace ("Nobody with a good car needs to be justified," Hazel had claimed) and finds himself stripped down to nothing but the insistent vision of Jesus, which leads him to self-mortification and death. His death, however, is an affirmation of grace, as O'Connor is careful to make clear in imagery which suggests that in his death Hazel is returning to Bethlehem.

O'Connor's other novel, *The Violent Bear It Away* (1960), has a similar major theme. Its central character is Francis Marion Tarwater, a boy who, like Hazel Motes, is attempting to escape a calling. It was announced to him by his uncle, a backwoods bootlegger and preacher, who tells him that God's first task for him will be to baptize his retarded cousin, Bishop, the son of his uncle's promiscuous sister (now dead) and her earnest, sociologist/teacher husband, Rayber, who is committed to a life without any vestiges of what he considers to be the illusions and superstitions offered by religion. When old Tarwater dies, his nephew responds to his call much the same way Hazel Motes did; he works hard to escape it, but after a few weeks in the city he succumbs to the power of that call, and he baptizes Bishop while drowning him at the same time. Hitchhiking home to the country, Tarwater is drugged and raped by a satanic stranger; when at last he returns to consciousness, he is somehow galvanized into action. At the end of the novel, he is setting out to return to the city in his new role as prophet. What both Hazel and Tarwater have experienced is the lacerating effect of God's grace, a grace which, O'Connor implies, is far removed from its syrupy portrayal in popular hymns. Instead, it seems to have more in common with the terrifying experiences of Old Testament prophets, for whom it is manifested as God's relentless insistence on bestowing mercy as he chooses.

O'Connor's short stories reveal similar thematic material. In "A Good Man Is Hard to Find" (1955), one sees a foolish and self-centered old woman who comes to a moment of grace just as she ceases mouthing platitudes to a mass murderer who is going to kill her seconds later. In "Revelation" (1965), smug, self-satisfied Ruby Turpin has a vision that teaches her what she never before understood—that the last shall be first in heaven and that her material well-being is not necessarily a mark of divine favor. Similarly, in "The River" (1955), the little boy simply accepts the preacher's assertion that baptism in the river leads to the kingdom of Christ. It also leads to his death by drowning, but, as O'Connor shows from the rest of the characters, he has paradoxically died into life, while people such as his worldly parents are caught in a sort of living death.

Violence is often an element in O'Connor's stories; in fact, she once said that her own faith made her conscious of the constant presence of death in the world, and her illness must have had the same effect. That probably explains the large number of deaths in her stories, and it may also account for the strong sense of danger in many of them. In "Good Country People" (1955), for example, Hulga's wooden leg is stolen by a dishonest Bible salesman. In "Revelation," mentioned above, Mrs. Turpin is attacked in the doctor's office by a girl who has suddenly gone mad.

Events and characters such as these are the source of the charge that O'Connor's characters are grotesques. The word seems to imply that they are too exaggerated to belong in realistic fiction. Early critics, especially, had a difficult time understanding what O'Connor intended, and they often believed that characters such as Tarwater and Hazel Motes were simply insane or too out of touch with modern values (which the critics themselves, O'Connor felt, too often embodied) to be taken seriously. O'Connor's comments about her own work, however, make clear that she was quite serious about them. Her backwoods preachers, she believed, came closer to understanding the human condition in relationship to God than any number of psychologists, teachers, and sociologists, none of whom ever appear very flatteringly in her fiction.

Another way of looking at the issue of the grotesque in O'Connor's work, however, may lend more weight to the charge. Her novels and stories are peopled almost entirely with characters who are the result of O'Connor's satiric view of the world. They are often funny, but they are almost always unpleasant. Enoch Emery in *Wise Blood* is an excellent example of this kind of characterizing. Almost everything about him is simultaneously funny and terrible. His ignorance is responsible for much of his grotesque response to the world. He hates and fears the zoo animals he guards; he never knows how ludicrous he looks to others, and so he imagines that the ugly cook at the snack shop is in love with him and that no one knows he hides in the bushes to watch the women at the swimming pool. His only real hero is Gonga the Gorilla from films. It is characteristic of O'Connor's work that even Enoch Emery's father, who never appears in the novel at all, is another example of ugliness and brutality. On his return from the penitentiary, Enoch's father gave him a gag gift: a can that appeared to contain peanut brittle but, when opened, released a steel spring that popped out and broke Enoch's two front teeth.

Again and again O'Connor offers comic but extremely unflattering pictures of the people who inhabit her characters' worlds. In "Revelation," for example, all the people in the doctor's office are grimly funny reminders of the varieties of human ugliness—Mrs. Turpin, who offends the reader with smugness and bigotry; Mary Grace, the mad girl who goes to college but who makes her ugliness even worse by making faces at Mrs. Turpin; the "white trash" family that sits immobile in poverty, ignorance, and dirt. Even Mrs. Turpin's husband Claud, a man she really loves, is revealed by his racist jokes to be as corrupt as everyone else in the story. Unremitting human ugliness is a source of much of O'Connor's humor. She is able to present the dirty, the disfigured, the stupid as also funny and recognizable as inhabitants of the real world we live in. Since they are almost the only inhabitants of O'Connor's fictional world, they probably justify the term "grotesque."

Another characteristic of O'Connor's style that concerns her characters is her use of southern dialects, especially those associated with poor whites. In her earlier stories, she often indicated some of their quality with spelling. In *Wise Blood*, for example, the phrase "worse than having them" is spelled "worsen havinum." O'Connor reduced the number of such dialect indicators in her later work, but she always took joy in the sounds and sometimes the flamboyance of Southern speech. "THE PROPHET I RAISE UP OUT OF THIS BOY WILL BURN YOUR EYES CLEAN," old Tarwater writes to his worldly nephew. In "A Good Man Is Hard to Find," the Misfit quotes his father speaking about him: "It's some that can live their whole life out without asking about it and it's others has to know why it is, and this boy is one of the latters."

One last issue about O'Connor's characters deserves mention, and that concerns race. O'Connor's stories almost all contain black characters—not surprisingly, since all but one are set in the South. O'Connor wrote much of her work in the period just before the first nationwide attention to civil rights, so it may seem curious that she never addressed that issue directly in her fiction. Some scholars have made an effort to find evidences of her sympathy for the growing Civil Rights movement in her work, but such evidence is very slight, if it exists at all. O'Connor herself implied that Southern blacks and whites inhabited worlds that were so different that a white writer could never really expect to understand the black world. Still, her black characters seem no less attractive than her white ones (none of them is very sympathetic anyway), and the racist comments in her stories come from characters who are themselves racists and would be likely to say such things (a good example is the doctor's office conversations in "Revelation").

In contrast to her basically satiric view of human characters, O'Connor's physical descriptions of people and landscapes are often serious, dramatic, and weighted with symbolism. References to eyes and their color and to the various colors and qualities of the sky are numerous in almost every story. The sky and particularly the sun often seem intended to evoke images of God and Christ looking down on the world. The sun is an ancient symbol for Christ, and O'Connor's descriptions make clear that the references are intentional. Another frequent symbol in O'Connor's work is the use of birds to suggest the Holy Spirit or even, in the case of peacocks, Christ himself. Other animals sometimes appear as well, particularly pigs and monkeys, which often seem intended to suggest the bestial nature of fallen humanity, intelligent but debased and corrupt (the pigs in "Revelation" and Gonga in *Wise Blood* are good examples).

Like many writers, O'Connor often gave symbolic or evocative names to her characters, and they are often worth considering in that light. Mary Grace in "Revelation," for example, is certainly an agent of divine grace in that story. Hazel ("Haze") Motes's name seems to draw one's attention to his cloudy or hazy vision, reminding the reader of the biblical injunction not to try to take the mote or speck from another's eye until one has removed the beam from one's own. Tarwater, the protagonist of *The Violent Bear It Away*, simply has the name of an old folk remedy.

O'Connor's literary reputation has risen steadily since her death. Modern readers are increasingly likely to see her serious intentions while relishing her humor. Her debt to Nathaniel Hawthorne has long been noted, but some scholars had begun to notice, too, her debt to Mark Twain—the former for his concern for moral issues, the latter for his comic view. It is on that combination of qualities that O'Connor's reputation rests.

WISE BLOOD

First published: 1952
Type of work: Novel

A backwoods preacher attempts to escape his call but at last gives in to a sort of martyrdom.

Wise Blood was O'Connor's first novel; she began work on it while she was still in the Iowa Writers' Workshop. It embodies most of her major themes, and it contains some of her best comedy. It is flawed, however, by her difficulties in pulling the two parts of the plot together. The Enoch Emery story is never fully integrated into the Hazel Motes story. O'Connor also had difficulties clarifying the issues about Motes's past that have turned him into what she called a "Christian *malgre lui*," a Christian in spite of himself.

The novel opens on a train as Hazel Motes leaves the Army. He is the grandson of a backwoods preacher, but he finds the image of a Jesus who insists on claiming the human recipients of his mercy to be unbearably disturbing; he has resisted inheriting his grandfather's role, that of preaching from the hood of a car to listeners on a small-town square. Hazel has long decided that he wants to avoid that Jesus, first by trying to avoid sin and later by asserting that Jesus is nothing more than a trick. Even on the train, however, O'Connor makes clear that Hazel's cheap blue suit—brand-new, with the price tag ($11.98) still attached—and his black hat look exactly like the traditional garb of the preacher he refuses to be. Nevertheless, Hazel startles his worldly fellow passengers by suddenly claiming that if they are saved he would not want to be. Like many such comments in O'Connor's work, this carries an ironic weight, for it is quite clear that salvation is the last thing the ladies in the dining car desire.

When Hazel arrives in the city of Taulkinham, he heads for the house of a prostitute, Leora Watts, as the next step in asserting that sin is an irrelevant issue in his life. Significantly, however, both the cab driver and Leora herself identify Hazel as a preacher, an identification he violently rejects. Soon Hazel sees a street preacher, Asa Hawks, who claims to have blinded himself as a demonstration of faith, although early in the novel the reader learns that his blindness is a sham. Hazel is both drawn to and repelled by Hawks and his adolescent daughter Sabbath Lily. Gradually it comes to Hazel that seducing Hawks's daughter would make a dramatic assertion of sin's irrelevance.

In the course of seeking Hawks's house, Hazel meets Enoch Emery. Enoch is eager to tell Hazel—or anyone—his story, about how his father gave him to a welfare woman who sent him off to the Rodemill Boys' Bible Academy and from whom he later escaped. Now he works for the city as a zoo guard. Desperately lonely and not very smart, Enoch ignores Hazel's rebuffs and follows him like a puppy, offering to help him find where Hawks lives. Like Hawks, Enoch senses Hazel's intense concern with Jesus. Hawks, in fact, says that some preacher has left his mark on Haze, but Hazel insists that he believes in nothing at all.

To prove his point, Hazel sets about buying a car, an ancient, rat-colored Essex, for which he pays forty dollars. The car seems to be Hazel's vision of American materialism ("Nobody with a good car needs to be justified," he says), but significantly he uses it exactly as his grandfather had used his Ford, as a platform to preach from. His one attempt to use the car in a "traditional" American way, for a date with Sabbath Lily, turns out to be a travesty. It is notable that the first thing Hazel does with his car is to stop in the middle of the highway to read a "Jesus Saves" sign.

Meanwhile, Enoch Emery is acting out his own sort of religion. Enoch claims to have "wise blood," which tells him what to do, and in fact he acts mostly from instinct. He insists that Hazel meet him at the park where he works, and after an elaborate set of ritual activities that include going through the zoo to ridicule the animals, Enoch leads Hazel to the city museum. Enoch finds it a place of enormous mystery because its name is carved Roman-style on the front, MVSEVM, creating a word that Enoch is unable to pronounce—like Yahweh, the unutterable name of God in the Old Testament. Inside the museum, Enoch shows Hazel the tiny, mummified man which has captured his imagination, but Hazel is unimpressed.

Hazel has rented a room in the house where Hawks and his daughter live, begun his plan to seduce Sabbath Lily (a plan he executes with a remarkable lack of finesse), and started a sort of church, the Church of Christ Without Christ, to dramatize his rejection of faith. Hazel's preaching is met with public indifference; however, after a few nights, he gains a disciple in the form of a former radio preacher, Onnie Jay Holy (his real name is Hoover Shoats), who shows no understanding of Hazel's message but is certain that money can be made from it if they "keep it sweet." He cannot understand why Hazel is unwilling to collect money from his audience. When Hazel runs him off, Holy threatens to run Hazel out of business.

Holy attempts to make good on that threat with a rival preacher whom he calls the True Prophet, a man who preaches the Holy Church of Christ Without Christ directly across the street from Hazel's post. The two are dressed exactly alike. Hazel's only comment is ambiguous: "If you don't hunt it down and kill it, it'll kill you." When Hazel returns to his room, he is met by Sabbath Lily, who tells him that Hawks has abandoned her, presumably because Hazel discovered his fraudulent blindness. She moves in with Hazel.

On the heels of these events, Enoch Emery re-enters the plot. Listening to his wise blood, Enoch has undergone what can only be described as purification rituals, cleaning his room and fasting to prepare for stealing what he believes to be the "new jesus" of Hazel's church—the mummy from the city museum. He delivers the mummy to Sabbath Lily, who is supposed to keep it for Hazel. Enoch then disappears from the novel in a dramatic way: He steals Gonga's gorilla suit from the actor who impersonates the monster and travels to the country. We see him last, stripped of his human clothing and identity, standing in his gorilla suit in the countryside, happy at last.

Returning to Sabbath Lily, Hazel finds her holding the mummy. O'Connor takes pains to make the scene look like a parody of a Madonna and Holy Child, an effect which is heightened by Hazel's blurred vision; he is wearing his mother's old reading glasses, the ones she used to read the Bible. Infuriated by the sight, he seizes the mummy and bangs it against the wall, releasing the sawdust inside it; like Hazel's perception of Jesus, it is empty and worthless. On that note Sabbath Lily leaves him, saying that she always knew that he wanted nothing but Jesus anyway.

Hazel hunts down the True Prophet, Solace Layfield, follows him home, and prepares to run over him with the Essex. O'Connor's imagery makes clear that in some sense it is himself that Hazel is killing, perhaps especially his fraudulent self. Unlike the True Prophet, Hazel's deception is his insistence that no redemption exists, that Jesus is nothing but trickery. For that reason it is significant that Layfield dies after making a confession of his sins and calling on Jesus. In an ironic reversal of Hazel, Layfield's preaching was false, but his life finally recognized the truth.

Hazel now has only one thing left—the Essex. In it, he sets out to find new preaching territory, but he is stopped by a policeman who discovers that he has no driver's license. Casually, callously, the policeman pushes the Essex off a cliff. "Them that don't have a car don't need a license," he says, unknowingly echoing Hazel's comments about justification." Hazel has now been stripped of all the trappings of his faithless life—his church, his sexual attachment, and his car. He has come to the dark night which opens his eyes and—with the same sort of irony that Oedipus' life fulfilled—having seen the truth, Hazel blinds himself.

The rest of the novel is told from the point of view of Mrs. Flood, his scheming and dishonest landlady. The idea of self-mortification as a penance is completely foreign to her; she never understands why Hazel has blinded himself or why he cares nothing about his social security check or why he might feel a need to punish himself. Hazel says only that he has done these things "to pay." Gradually Mrs. Flood becomes less interested in stealing from Hazel and more interested in understanding him. She is especially fascinated by his ruined eyes, which somehow remind her of the light of the star on Christmas cards. After Hazel has wandered away from home, sick and blind, he is found in a ditch by two policemen who casually, meaninglessly, beat him to death. They return the body to Mrs. Flood, who is moved by the sight to think of that retreating point of light which O'Connor has already described. The implications are that Hazel has been reborn in the ditch where he died, that he is moving back to Bethlehem, called by the truly wise blood of Christ, and perhaps that even the venal Mrs. Flood has begun a similar journey.

THE VIOLENT BEAR IT AWAY

First published: 1960
Type of work: Novel

A young man tries to escape his late uncle's directive to baptize his cousin but finds the spiritual legacy unavoidable.

The Violent Bear It Away shares many qualities with *Wise Blood*. Francis Marion Tarwater is much like Hazel Motes in his efforts to escape what seems to be a divine call, and like Hazel he at last must give in to God's imperative. This novel is more tightly unified than *Wise Blood*; although it lacks some of *Wise Blood*'s humor, it also lacks its loose ends.

Francis Marion Tarwater (named for the Swamp Fox, the Revolutionary War hero) has been reared in the woods by his great uncle Mason, a bootlegger and prophet. Mason has assured young Tarwater that he will inherit his great uncle's call and that after Mason's death, the young man's first task will be to baptize Bishop, his retarded cousin and son of Tarwater's schoolteacher nephew, Rayber, who was himself the son of Tarwater's sister. When Rayber was seven, old Tarwater had kidnapped him, taking him to the backwoods and baptizing him, though he kept him only a few days. Years later, old Tarwater had kidnapped Francis Marion, the son of Rayber's promiscuous sister; this time he managed to keep the child. He has reared him to be a prophet who will carry on his own tradition by rescuing young Bishop from his father's godless life.

Young Tarwater has doubts about his calling, however, from the very beginning of the novel, and when his great uncle dies, he quickly rejects his first task, which is to bury the old man according to his carefully rehearsed plans. Instead, the boy (he is fourteen) gets drunk, and, rather than digging the decent grave his uncle expected, Tarwater burns down the cabin with, as he supposes, his uncle's body in it. Only much later does he learn that a neighboring black man, shocked at the boy's faithlessness, buried the old man while the boy was unconscious.

In this early section of the novel, O'Connor introduces a character called "the stranger," who is actually a voice in young Tarwater's head. Tarwater and the stranger have a series of dialogues in which it becomes clear that the stranger represents a version of the kind of rationalism that Rayber displays—perhaps an even more cynical kind, since it actually rejects the old man's religion, while Rayber mostly ignores it.

Having disposed of his great uncle, Tarwater decides to go to the city to see Rayber, whom he saw once years before. Once at Rayber's house, Tarwater discovers that his cousin intends to reverse the kidnapping. Just as the old man once tried to save Rayber, Rayber now intends to save Tarwater from what he can see only as religious mania. In his sterile academic way, he believes that Tarwater and his uncles are mere relics from a superstitious past. Old Tarwater himself had once stayed for a while at Rayber's house, hoping to get access to his soul, but he gave up in horror and disgust when he realized that Rayber had made him the subject of an article in an academic journal.

Young Tarwater's feelings about Rayber are ambivalent. On the one hand, he has nothing but contempt for his passionless cousin, who seems trapped in his own rationalistic view of the world. He also finds his young cousin Bishop (an interesting name for the child of an atheist) to be repellent even while the child seems drawn to him. On the other hand, despite the whisperings of the stranger, it is clear that Tarwater feels his call as surely as Hazel Motes felt his. Rayber recognizes that nearly every time Tarwater and Bishop are near water, Tarwater considers performing the baptism. In fact, Rayber tries to defuse the issue by offering to allow Tarwater to do the baptism in an attempt to make the sacrament meaningless, but Tarwater will have none of it.

Wandering the city at night in an effort to escape Rayber's constant talk, Tarwater gazes for a long time in a bakery window. Later he spends a long time at a revival, listening to a child evangelist who seems to be talking to Rayber himself, peering into the hall from a window. In fact, Tarwater is wrestling with his uncle's promise to turn him into a prophet who will burn Rayber's eyes clean, a calling he wishes to reject as completely as he rejects Bishop. Ironically, Rayber, the rational man, has also tried to reject his son by attempting to drown him, an attempt that failed when he lost his nerve. At Lake Cherokee, on a fishing trip organized by Rayber, Tarwater both baptizes and drowns Bishop.

From this point on in the novel, O'Connor emphasizes Tarwater's hunger; it is a hunger nothing can fill. He vomits up the hot dogs he ate at the lake. Hitchhiking home, he accepts a sandwich from a truck driver but cannot eat it; his mind rejects food even while his body cries for it.

This hunger is part of the novel's central metaphor. Eyes and vision dominated *Wise Blood* (they are important here, too), but in *The Violent Bear It Away* the central image is the "bread of life," to which Tarwater refers again and again. The bread of life is a New Testament metaphor for Jesus and is the central image of the sacrament of communion. That seems to be the bread Tarwater was gazing at in the bakery; that is the bread he concluded he did not hunger for when his great uncle preached to him. When Tarwater first sees Bishop, however, he has a sudden vision of "his own stricken image of himself, trudging into the distance in the bleeding stinking mad shadow of Jesus, until at least he received his reward, a broken fish, a multiplied loaf."

Tarwater's hunger is spiritual, and it cannot be filled by the drugged liquor in the satanic stranger's flask that Tarwater drinks on his ride home, even though he exclaims that it tastes better than the bread of life. That evil stranger takes the unconscious Tarwater to the deep woods and rapes him. When he regains consciousness,

Tarwater knows what has happened and somehow recognizes that the event is like Jonah's being swallowed by the fish; it is God's directing him into prophecy. He returns home and has a vision of old Tarwater's feasting on the miraculous loaves and fishes. Suddenly he understands the source of his hunger and starts out for the city to begin his career of prophecy.

Aside from bread, fish fill the other part of the novel's metaphoric structure. They appear not only in Tarwater's vision but also in almost every mention of old Tarwater's eyes. It is even on a fishing trip that Bishop is baptized, a baptism which O'Connor means the reader to take seriously even though Tarwater has not yet accepted his calling, for the power of the sacrament exists outside the failings of the one celebrating it. The novel's conclusion suggests that now Tarwater will turn his attention to Rayber and the rest of the city.

A GOOD MAN IS HARD TO FIND

First published: 1955
Type of work: Short story

A smug old woman is jolted out of her complacency by a confrontation with a mass murderer.

"A Good Man Is Hard to Find" is one of O'Connor's most frequently anthologized short stories, and it makes an excellent illustration of her ability to combine grotesque humor with serious thematic material.

The story opens as a family prepares to go on vacation in Florida. The story focuses immediately on the grandmother, who wants to visit relatives in east Tennessee and who uses the escape of the Misfit, a murderer, from prison to try to persuade her son, Bailey, to change his mind. He refuses. The two children, John Wesley and June Star, are quickly characterized as smart-alecks who nevertheless understand their grandmother and her motives very well. When the family sets out, the grandmother is resigned to making the best of things. She is first to get into the car, and has even, secretly, brought along her cat. As she rides along, her conversation is conventional, self-centered, and shallow.

When the family stops for lunch at a barbeque stand, their conversation again turns to the Misfit, and the adults agree that people are simply not as nice as they used to be. Later, back in the car, the grandmother persuades Bailey to take a road which she imagines (wrongly, as it turns out) will lead by an old mansion. Suddenly the cat escapes its basket and jumps on Bailey's neck, and the car runs into the ditch. As the family assesses its injuries, a man who is obviously the Misfit drives up with his armed henchmen. The grandmother immediately feels that she recognizes him as someone she has known all her life, and she tells him that she knows who he is.

Methodically, the henchmen lead first Bailey and then the mother and children off to be shot in the woods while the Misfit begins to talk about himself and his life of crime. He blames his career on Jesus, who, he says, threw everything "off balance" by raising the dead. Because the Misfit cannot be sure that the miracle really occurred, he cannot know how to think about it. If Jesus really raised the dead, the Misfit says, the only logical response would be to drop everything and follow him. If he did not, then life is meaningless and only crime makes sense: "No pleasure but in meanness."

The grandmother is terrified; she knows that she, too, will be shot. Yet she knows something more, and suddenly she stops her empty prayers and meaningless assertions that the Misfit is a "good man," and she utters perhaps the truest words of her life in telling him that he is one of her own children. At that the Misfit shoots her, but he says that she would have been a good woman if someone had been there to shoot her every minute of her life. O'Connor intends the reader to take the Misfit's comments seriously (he is the most serious-minded character in the story, after all) and notice that the grandmother in her moment of receiving grace has recognized that she and the Misfit (and presumably all the rest of humanity) are related as children of God. She is left in death smiling up at God's sky.

THE ARTIFICIAL NIGGER

First published: 1955
Type of work: Short story

Old Mr. Head and his grandson overcome their estrangement in a reconciliation brought on by a plaster statue.

In "The Artificial Nigger," Old Mr. Head and his ten-year-old grandson Nelson live in a state of subdued tension in which each works to outdo the other, and their planned trip to Atlanta (they live in rural Georgia) has made this competition worse. Even though Nelson has never been to the city, he is cockily sure that he will enjoy it.

Gradually the reader understands that Mr. Head is thoroughly uncertain of his own ability to manage the city, and he uses the sight of the city's blacks (a race Nelson has never seen) as a sort of weapon over Nelson, a threat of something foreign that he may find frightening but with which his grandfather can claim, not quite accurately, to be familiar. Nelson is unimpressed with his grandfather's talk.

When they arrive in the city, Mr. Head is frightened by Nelson's immediate delight in it and by his refusal to be intimidated by the unfamiliar. After walking for a while, they become lost and, at the same time, realize that they have also lost their lunch bag. Nelson takes things into his own hands and asks directions from a black woman to whom he feels drawn, but Mr. Head's resentment grows. At last, while Nelson naps at the curbside, Mr. Head finds a way to retaliate and hides from the boy.

When Nelson wakens, he thinks he has been abandoned and races into the street, knocking down an old woman. That is when Mr. Head commits his worst sin and denies knowing Nelson at all. His grandson is deeply wounded and refuses all of his grandfather's subsequent attempts to make peace. Mr. Head feels certain that this is a divine judgment on him. They walk on in separate misery, getting ever more lost, until Mr. Head cries out to a passing stranger, "Oh Gawd I'm Lost!" The two are rescued with directions to the train station. It is the sight of a plaster lawn statue of a black man (or child, the statue being too battered to be easily identified) that really reconciles the pair. The statue's pictured misery seem to be a monument to the black man's victory, a portrayal which moves both Mr. Head and his grandson. The notion that in a city which already has so many blacks someone should feel the necessity to make an artificial one strikes them both as mysterious and somehow powerful. Reunited, they travel home peacefully, having miraculously escaped the consequences of their anger.

GOOD COUNTRY PEOPLE

First published: 1955
Type of work: Short story

Hulga's negative view of the world is challenged by the even greater nihilism of a dishonest Bible salesman who steals her wooden leg.

In "Good Country People," Mrs. Hopewell's perennial optimism is balanced by what seems to be her daughter Joy's self-chosen misery. It is characteristic of Joy's attitude that she has changed her name to Hulga, evidently because it is the ugliest name she can think of. If that way, her name matches her faded sweatshirt, her scowl, and her wooden leg (she lost her leg in a hunting accident long ago). While her mother is frustrated by her daughter's bad temper, she is equally frustrated by her daughter's Ph.D. in philosophy, a degree which makes her unable easily to identify her daughter's achievement to others. She worries that Hulga never seems to enjoy anything, not even young men.

That makes her concerned when Hulga, an atheist who refuses to let her mother keep a Bible in the parlor, confronts Manley Pointer, a fresh-faced and earnest Bible salesman who wins Mrs. Hopewell's trusting heart with his brave stories of childhood hardships and religious devotion. Partly as a joke, Hulga agrees to meet Pointer on a picnic. The falsity of their relationship is marked by the thirty-two-year-old Hulga telling Pointer that she is seventeen, while he calls her both brave and sweet. It has occurred to Hulga that she might be able to seduce Pointer.

At the picnic it becomes clear that Pointer has similar ideas and that, in fact, he is far more cynical than Hulga. His hollow Bible contains playing cards, whiskey, and condoms. He is hardly one of the "good country people" of the title. Perhaps that cynicism is what wins enough of Hulga's confidence that she lets him see her wooden leg and even remove it from her, although she feels helpless without it. That is when Pointer announces that he collects things such as glass eyes and wooden legs, marks of his own complete nihilism. "I been believing in nothing ever since I was born!" he exclaims. Hulga is left in the hayloft to think about the real meaning of unbelief.

REVELATION

First published: 1965
Type of work: Short story

A smug, self-satisfied woman wakens to new values when she is attacked in a doctor's office and then experiences a vision.

"Revelation" opens in a doctor's waiting room where Ruby Turpin is waiting with her husband Claud. As she often does, Mrs. Turpin passes the time by categorizing the other waiting-room inhabitants by class—"white trash," middle class (like her), and so forth. This is the segretated South, so there are no blacks here, but Mrs. Turpin is happy to judge them, too.

She identifies a pleasant-looking woman as one of her own class, and they begin an idle conversation that centers first on their possessions and eventually on their disapproval of Civil Rights demonstrators. They conclude that it would be a good idea to send all blacks back to Africa. During this conversation the other woman's daughter, Mary Grace, an obese college student with severe acne, has been making faces directly at Mrs. Turpin. At last she cracks entirely, throws her book (*Human Development*) at her, and then physically attacks her. When Mary Grace has been subdued, Mrs. Turpin begins to think that the girl has a message for her, and when she moves closer, Mary Grace calls her a wart hog and tells her to go back to hell where she came from.

Later, at home, Mrs. Turpin is deeply shaken by the message. At last, while hosing down the hogs, she questions God about why he sent her such a message when there was plenty of "trash" in the room to receive it. His answer comes in the form of a vision of people marching to heaven, a procession led by all the people she has most held in contempt. The vision fades, and Mrs. Turpin returns to the house in the midst of a cricket chorus of hallelujahs. Critics have disagreed about the meaning of the end of this story, but Mrs. Turpin's serious acceptance of the violent message of grace and the imagery of the ending seem to suggest that her vision was a gift of mercy that has clarified her vision of the world, its people, and her possessions.

Summary

Serious fiction with religious themes has never been common in American literature, and perhaps that explains part of why O'Connor has frequently been misunderstood. When one views her work in the context of her Catholic orthodoxy, however, its focus becomes clear. The fact that most of her characters are evangelical Protestants simply reflects her use of the population around her to inhabit her stories. Her intense concern with divine grace and redemption as the central facts of human life does not preclude her use of humor to communicate her ideas about that concern and her distrust of the secular rationalism that she believed pervades most of American life.

Bibliography

Baumbach, Jonathan. *The Landscape of Nightmare: Studies in the Contemporary American Novel*. New York: New York University Press, 1965.

Fickett, Harold, and Douglas R. Gilbert. *Flannery O'Connor: Images of Grace*. Grand Rapids, Mich.: Wm. B. Eerdmans, 1986.

Friedman, Melvin J., and Beverly Lyon Clark, eds. *Critical Essays on Flannery O'Connor*. Boston: G. K. Hall, 1985.

Friedman, Melvin J., and Lewis A. Lawson, eds. *The Added Dimension*. New York: Fordham University Press, 1966.

Stephens, Martha. *The Question of Flannery O'Connor*. Baton Rouge: Louisiana State University Press, 1973.

Walters, Dorothy. *Flannery O'Connor*. New York: Twayne, 1973.

Ann Davison Garbett

JOHN O'HARA

Born: Pottsville, Pennsylvania
January 31, 1905
Died: Princeton, New Jersey
April 11, 1970

Principal Literary Achievement

O'Hara was one of the foremost realists of the twentieth century; his huge body of work is marked by its incisive examination of social behavior and richness of detail.

Biography

John Henry O'Hara was born in Pottsville, Pennsylvania, on January 31, 1905, the son of Patrick Henry O'Hara, a well-known doctor, and Katherine Elizabeth Delaney O'Hara. He was the eldest of eight children in a Catholic family. O'Hara attended Fordham Preparatory School and the Keystone State Normal School, and he was graduated from Niagara Preparatory School in 1924, after which he worked at odd jobs—a great variety of them—before finally settling into journalism. He had passed the required examinations to enroll at Yale University, but his father's death precluded his attending college.

O'Hara first worked as a reporter for two newspapers in Pennsylvania, then for three in New York. His journalistic experience was as varied as his previous work had been: He covered sports, news, politics, and religion. He served as film critic on the *Morning Telegraph*, football editor at *The New Yorker*, and editor-in-chief of the Pittsburgh *Bulletin-Index*. He was employed by *Time* magazine and would eventually write columns for the Trenton *Times-Advertiser*, *Collier's*, *Newsweek*, and *Holiday*. Some sources list Franey Delaney as an O'Hara pseudonym because he once wrote a radio column under that name. After the publication of his first novel, *Appointment in Samarra* (1934), he became a writer for motion pictures, working in turn for four of the largest studios in Hollywood.

Appointment in Samarra was such an extraordinarily successful first novel that O'Hara was immediately considered a major American writer. He went on to publish seventeen novels, eleven volumes of short stories, plays, essays, and sketches. Of his more than three hundred short stories, many first appeared in *The New Yorker*.

Most of O'Hara's novels were best-sellers, and a number were adapted as motion pictures. Among the most popular novels, in terms of both sales and critical recep-

tion were *Butterfield 8* (1935), *Ten North Frederick* (1955), and *From the Terrace* (1958). For *Ten North Frederick*, O'Hara received the National Book Award in 1956. It became a successful film, as did both *From the Terrace* and *Butterfield 8*. Major film stars—such as Gary Cooper, Paul Newman, and Elizabeth Taylor—were cast in adaptations of O'Hara novels. Among his collections of short stories are *The Doctor's Son and Other Stories*, (1935), *Pipe Night* (1945), *Hellbox* (1947), *Assembly* (1961), *The Cape Cod Lighter* (1962), *The Horse Knows the Way* (1964), *Waiting for Winter* (1966), and *Good Samaritan and Other Stories* (1974). He also published collections of his essays and newspaper articles. He adapted some of his sketches about nightclubs and their habitués, first published in 1940, into a successful musical comedy, *Pal Joey* (1940), later a motion picture starring Frank Sinatra. O'Hara frequented nightclubs himself, once taking an apartment close to his favorite, "21," in New York City. In 1964, the American Academy of Arts and Letters presented O'Hara with the Gold Medal Award of Merit.

In 1931, O'Hara was married to Helen Ritchie Petit, from whom he was divorced in 1933. On December 3, 1937, he was married to Belle Mulford Wylie, who died in January, 1954. His only child, Wylie Delaney, was the issue of his second marriage. His third marriage was to Katherine Barnes Bryan on January 31, 1955. O'Hara was a blond, blunt-featured man, often described as tough and cynical. He was independent and impatient by nature—he was expelled from his first two schools, and he abandoned the Roman Catholicism in which he had been reared. When O'Hara left Pottsville in 1927 to seek work first in Montana, later in Chicago, and still later in New York and Hollywood, his travels and the many jobs he briefly held—steward on a boat, steel mill worker, soda jerk, guard at an amusement park, gas meter reader, press agent for Warner Brothers, even actor in one scene of a 1936 film—gave him rich material and a wealth of details for the realistic fiction he would write.

He affected no interest in his reputation with the critics, and he laid no claims to being a great artist. Rather, he characterized himself as an honest and ordinary person who was a professional. He said that he knew what the "ordinary guy" liked and how to write it. Disparaged by some critics during the first half of his career as a writer of merely popular fiction, he was accused during the last half of his career of being old-fashioned and irrelevant. His answer to all criticism, favorable and unfavorable, was more stories. He once told an interviewer that he would like to fill the world up with his books. Although critics have generally argued that he is at his best in the short story genre, he is probably remembered most for his many best-selling novels. O'Hara died at his home in Princeton, New Jersey, on April 11, 1970.

Analysis

Critical opinion of O'Hara's work has long been divided. His receipt of the National Book Award in 1956 and the Gold Medal Award of Merit from the American Academy of Arts and Letters in 1964 indicates that the literary establishment considered him an important writer. The academic community, however, has largely ignored him. He is seldom found in the anthologies used on college campuses. One reason for this neglect, and the most obvious one, is that O'Hara's fiction gives the professor little to discuss in a literature class. O'Hara avoids figurative language and rhetorical richness. His style was permanently influenced by his newspaper training. He is very traditional in his narrative technique, eschewing all trends toward experimentation with chronology, point of view, or dialogue.

Perhaps it is this spareness of style which led the eminent American critic Edmund Wilson to comment that O'Hara's long works always seemed like first drafts of what might eventually have become nice little novels (Wilson did, though, praise O'Hara highly as a short story writer). Another adverse criticism often leveled against the novels is that they lack a moral center. The argument is that the narrative voice is so detached, so like the ideally objective journalist, that it is unclear how the author feels about his characters. O'Hara's fictional world is a very dangerous place; his characters are never secure. Their lives may be blighted at any moment by financial reversals, social missteps, even violent death. As is true in life (but often unsatisfying in fiction), what happens to the characters may have little to do with their behavior. As is also often true in real life, some characters appear to have no good reason for being in the story. They seem to result more from the protagonist's randomness of experience than from any necessity of the plot.

It has also been observed that O'Hara is America's foremost out-of-date novelist. As this argument goes, he took little note of the immense changes wrought by World War II and the nuclear age, continuing to write the same kind of stories he had written throughout the 1930's. In fact, say these critics, O'Hara continued to retell the same story in endless variety right up until his death. A substantial body of opinion holds that *Appointment in Samarra* is O'Hara's best novel. As a rule, novelists do not welcome being told that their first novel is their best, since the implication is that they have shown no improvement in all the work that followed. Perhaps this is why O'Hara stated that *Appointment in Samarra* was his second favorite novel.

On the credit side of the critical ledger, O'Hara has been called one of the finest social commentators in American literature. He has been favorably compared to Honoré de Balzac, Anthony Trollope, and William Faulkner—authors who take a society, or some segment of a society, and examine it from every possible angle in one work after another. O'Hara is especially effective in revealing the workings of class in a society that gives lip service to its democratic character. Since Americans are uncomfortable with the idea of a class structure, O'Hara seems to say, they disguise their class consciousness and make snobbery even more cruel.

O'Hara's ear for dialogue is almost unfailing. He also has the ability to characterize quickly and deftly with a snatch of dialogue or a few well chosen details. O'Hara is justly famed for his accuracy of observation; his characters do not merely climb into a car, they climb into a particular make and model of car. A man is not merely wearing a blue suit, he is wearing a blue suit of a certain shade, made from a specific material, and cut in a particular style. Someone once made the point in this way: When O'Hara introduced into a story the schedule for trains running between two Eastern cities, the contemporary commuter could have relied upon O'Hara's schedule every bit as much as upon the one issued by the railroad. O'Hara, the old newsman, always did his research and would not allow himself to be caught in a discrepancy or an anachronism. It has been argued that the myriad details sometimes overwhelm the story, that O'Hara's fiction is in danger of becoming more artifact than art. It is probably true that his books will serve future generations as valuable social histories of the first half of the twentieth century.

O'Hara revealed that he wrote very fast and revised little. He attributed this tendency to his early work as a rewrite man, when he was constantly getting pieces to rework just before deadline. The English novelist John Braine, who admired O'Hara very much, observes, of *Appointment in Samarra* particularly, that this rapid writing may account for the brisk pace and the energy of the narrative. He also praises O'Hara for not making judgments in his fiction, asserting that the proper role of the fiction writer is observer, not judge.

APPOINTMENT IN SAMARRA

First published: 1934
Type of work: Novel

The pointless life of a young country clubber drives him to destruction.

Appointment in Samarra was O'Hara's first published novel. For a 1953 Modern Library edition of the book, O'Hara wrote a foreword recounting how he had composed it. He wrote it over the period from September, 1933, to March, 1934, in a small hotel room in New York City. He worked five nights a week—he had developed a preference for nighttime writing during his early years in newspaper work. After completing the first twenty-five thousand words, O'Hara submitted the manuscript to Harcourt, Brace & Company. Alfred Harcourt was impressed with what he read and subsequently gave the young author a subsidy of fifty dollars a week until the novel was finished.

O'Hara credits Dorothy Parker with giving him, indirectly, the title of the novel. He had been using "The Infernal Grove" as a working title until the day Parker showed him a copy of W. Somerset Maugham's play *Sheppy* (1933). It contained Maugham's rendering of the Samarra legend: A servant meets Death, in the form of a woman, in the marketplace at Baghdad. He imagines that she makes a threatening gesture. Terrified, he borrows his master's horse and flees to Samarra. Death later tells the master that she was startled rather than threatening when she came upon the servant in the marketplace: She was surprised to see him in Baghdad, for she had an appointment to meet him that night in Samarra. O'Hara believed that *Appointment in Samarra* was the perfect title for the story of his doomed protagonist, Julian English. Parker disapproved of the title, as did O'Hara's editor and publisher, but he stubbornly insisted upon it and, in the end, had his way.

The setting is Gibbsville, Pennsylvania, in 1930. Many of O'Hara's stories would be set in Gibbsville, which was no doubt modeled upon his own hometown of Pottsville. He uses Gibbsville as a study of American society in microcosm and is, therefore, often compared to Honoré de Balzac and William Faulkner. In fact, he referred to Gibbsville on at least one occasion as his version of Faulkner's Yoknapatawpha County.

Julian English is thirty years of age. He sells automobiles, and he and his wife, Caroline, are well accepted in Gibbsville society. The Great Depression has just begun, and F. Scott Fitzgerald's world of the roaring twenties has come to its apocalyptic end. For this reason, and because of certain stylistic similarities, O'Hara has been called Fitzgerald's successor as a chronicler of American society. The novel is also reminiscent of Sinclair Lewis in its depiction of small-town businessmen— their shallowness, superficiality, and class consciousness. Some critics see the influence of Ernest Hemingway as well in the taut construction and spare language of the novel. In the foreword to the 1953 edition, O'Hara acknowledges his debt to Fitzgerald and Lewis but says that, unlike the case with his early short stories, he sees no Hemingway influence in *Appointment in Samarra*.

Very much like a Fitzgerald hero, Julian English drinks too much. He is subject to compulsions which threaten his marriage, his financial well-being, and his social status. He is not a stupid man. He has some insight into his self-destructive nature, but he lacks the values that might save him from himself. He can see his life only in terms of money and social standing. It is not farfetched to compare Julian's story to a Greek tragedy. In his own mind, he lives under a curse: His paternal grandfather committed suicide after embezzling a considerable amount of money. Julian's father, a successful and straitlaced surgeon, fears that the character flaw has been passed down to his son. Also as in a Greek tragedy, the novel recounts the final catastrophic events in a situation which has been building for many years.

Over several days at Christmastime, 1930, Julian suffers a series of social disasters. Harry Reilly is a rich acquaintance of Julian and Caroline who is constantly attempting to overcome his Irish-Catholic background and ascend Gibbsville's social ladder. The previous summer, he lent Julian twenty thousand dollars when Julian's Cadillac agency was in straitened circumstances. He now believes—or so Julian believes—that this gives him the right to make advances toward Caroline. At a Christmas party at the country club, Julian has again drunk too much. He snaps and throws a drink in Reilly's face; Reilly is given a black eye by a big piece of ice. On the way home, Julian and Caroline have a terrible quarrel.

On Christmas Day, Julian falls out with another benefactor. Ed Charney is the local bootlegger. He has been a good customer and has helped Julian's agency sell cars to other bootleggers. Charney owns a roadhouse called the Stage Coach, where his mistress, Helene Holman, sings. Hung over, unhappy, and drinking again, Julian goes to the Stage Coach. He dances with Helene and eventually leaves with her but passes out in the backseat of a car. Charney is furious, as is Caroline. The next day, she and Julian quarrel on the street. She cancels the big party they were to have given that evening. She leaves him, determined to end their four-year-old marriage. Julian has lost his wife, has alienated the man who holds the mortgage on his agency and has a strong influence over potential Irish-Catholic customers, and has angered his powerful bootlegger.

Julian tries to work but cannot. He goes to his club for lunch in a foul mood. He ends up in an altercation with some elderly lawyers from another table. He hits one of them in the mouth and knocks out his false teeth. He goes home, where later he experiences his final fiasco. A society reporter calls at his door, wanting a story about the canceled party. Julian invites her in and begins drinking again. He makes a futile and humiliating attempt to seduce her. After her departure, he closes himself up in the garage and starts the engine of his car, keeping his appointment in Samarra. In the final pages of the book, others discuss Julian's death but have apparently learned nothing from it.

O'Hara is rightly labeled a literary realist, but the heavily deterministic nature of this novel causes it to be classified as naturalistic. Although the author concentrates primarily on the rich and the upper-middle class of Gibbsville, other strata of society are represented by Ed Charney, Helene Holman, and Al Grecco, Charney's ex-convict handyman. O'Hara wrote that *Appointment in Samarra* was his second-favorite novel; he did not reveal which he ranked ahead of it.

FROM THE TERRACE

First published: 1958
Type of work: Novel

This long novel charts the protagonist's rise to a position of power and status and his subsequent fall.

From the Terrace is representative of O'Hara's later novels. The narrative covers a period from the protagonist's birth in 1897 to the postwar 1940's. *From the Terrace* is much longer than O'Hara's first novel and presents power struggles at the highest levels of business and government against a background of sexual intrigue and violent death. Thus, it provided excellent material for a motion picture and eventually became a successful vehicle for the actor Paul Newman.

Some similarities between *From the Terrace* and *Appointment in Samarra* are discernible. Raymond Alfred Eaton, called Alfred, is, like Julian English, born into the upper economic and social stratum of a small Pennsylvania town, Port Johnson. Alfred's father, Samuel Eaton, owns the local steel mill. Like Julian English, Alfred Eaton is deeply suspicious of himself, largely because of an occurrence during his boyhood over which he had no control. His elder brother, William, was the favorite son and was destined to succeed his father as the first citizen of Port Johnson until he died of meningitis at fourteen. Alfred's father can never bring himself to show his surviving son the same attention he lavished upon William. Two later events reinforce Alfred's sense of himself as a sort of jinx to others. He quarrels with his first love, sixteen-year-old Victoria Dockwiler, forbidding her to go riding in a borrowed Stutz Bearcat. She defies him and is killed in a car crash. Alfred then begins an affair with a family friend, Norma Budd, seven years older than he. Norma is later the victim of a married lover, who kills first her and then himself. Although it is irrational for Alfred to think that he corrupted Norma, he feels vaguely responsible for her death.

Alfred attends Princeton University until the United States enters World War I. He serves with distinction as a naval officer and does not return to Princeton after the war. He also chooses to decline his father's tepid offer of a job at the mill. Instead, he and Lex Thornton, a friend from Princeton, start an aircraft company together. Alfred meets eighteen-year-old Mary St. John at a party, and here begins the sort of sexual triangle typically found in O'Hara's later novels.

Mary is engaged to Jim Roper, a pre-medical student. Alfred is strongly attracted to Mary, more sexually than romantically, and he succeeds in winning her away from Roper. Their marriage in the spring of 1920 corresponds exactly with the death of Alfred's father. The marriage is not a happy one. Mary has never completely broken her ties with Roper, and Alfred will later learn that his wife has resumed her relationship with her former fiancé. Mary's adultery is especially sordid because Roper, who has become a psychiatrist, is also a declared homosexual who introduces her to a variety of deviant sexual practices. Meanwhile, Alfred has happened upon a young boy who has fallen through the ice into a pond. Alfred saves the child from drowning, thus earning the gratitude of the boy's grandfather, James MacHardie. MacHardie is a rich and powerful Wall Street banker. He offers Alfred a job in New York, and the protagonist decides to leave his struggling company and take it. Alfred is an immediate success in banking, but he soon learns that he has relinquished his freedom of action. The image of MacHardie and Company is not to be tarnished by the divorce of any of its executives.

On a business trip back to Pennsylvania, Alfred meets and falls in love with Natalie Benziger. She becomes his mistress, but only after having suffered through a failed marriage of her own. Alfred's and Mary's adulterous marriage of convenience continues for more than twenty years but is finally destroyed by the dislocations of World War II. Alfred takes a leave from MacHardie and Company to become an assistant secretary of the Navy in Washington, D.C. Mary's behavior becomes even more outrageous, and the couple's elder son, Rowland, is killed while in training as a naval aviator. Alfred feels compelled to resign his government post because of the questionable practices of some of his former business associates. In his absence, Alfred's enemies have forced him out of the company. Foremost among these enemies is Creighton Duffy, a prominent lawyer, who is James MacHardie's son-in-law and the father of the boy whose life Alfred saved. The Eatons are finally divorced.

Like Julian English in the earlier novel, Alfred Eaton is destined to fall. His neglected boyhood taught him to rely upon himself, and the resulting independence and individuality accounted for his early success; however, it failed to teach him how to connect with and cultivate others. He won the girl, Mary, but earned the undying enmity of his rival. He saved the boy, Sandy Duffy, but in later years neither Sandy nor his father like the man to whom they owe so much. Creighton Duffy has been waiting for the right moment to bring Alfred down. As the novel ends, Alfred is recovering from an illness brought on by the travails of his public and private life. He is unable to find another position, having cut himself off from the business and government arenas in which he previously thrived. He is financially secure, but he is not yet fifty and is restive at the prospect of a future of enforced idleness. He is now married to Natalie, but even their happiness is marred by her loss of the child she was carrying. Natalie is thirty-eight and is unlikely to conceive again.

Other members of the large cast of characters are Jack Tom Smith, a Texas oilman and Alfred's temporary ally, and Tom Rothermel, a union organizer (O'Hara often balances his privileged protagonist with a working-class character). As usual in O'Hara's fiction, the physical details are flawless. The clothing, architecture, technology, and language of the novel's succeeding decades are authentic down to the minutest point.

CHRISTMAS POEM

First published: 1964
Type of work: Short story

A young man, home from college for Christmas vacation, has dinner with his family and spends an evening with friends.

O'Hara is an acclaimed master of the short story genre. His numerous short stories of the 1930's and 1940's were, as a rule, very short. In the 1950's and 1960's, they were longer and less numerous (he did, however, still average more than one short story per month during the last ten years of his life). "Christmas Poem" is one of the later, longer stories. It was first published on December 19, 1964, in *The New Yorker.*

Billy Warden has just arrived home from Darmouth College for the Christmas vacation. The setting is Gibbsville, Pennsylvania, during some period earlier than the time of publication. No dates are given, but one character drives a new Marmon (not a Dort, his girlfriend insists), Billy orders a lemon phosphate at the drugstore soda fountain, and there is a discussion of getting a couple of pints of whiskey on credit, a suggestion of the Prohibition era. The Stage Coach Inn, featured so prominently in *Appointment in Samarra*, is mentioned in passing, though now spelled "Stagecoach." For the first six pages, the story is almost exclusively dialogue as the Warden family chats at the dinner table. Clearly, Billy is loved and valued by his parents and his older sister, Barbara (Bobby). For the period between Christmas and New Year's Eve, he has been invited for skiing and a house party at Montrose, above

Scranton. The hostess will be Henrietta (Henny) Cooper, who comes from a very wealthy family. Billy excuses himself, although he really enjoys being with his family, and goes downtown in search of his friends.

Billy spends an aimless evening. He fails to get a date with Irma Hipple, a young woman nicknamed "the Nipple" and rumored to go "all the way," even though none of the local boys has actually made the trip. He loses the ten dollars his father gave him in a crap game and his loose change in a game of pool. He hopes to pick up a girl when the cinema lets out, but no appropriate target appears. A familiar O'Hara motif is introduced when Teddy Choate asserts the superiority of his family's Yale University connections over Billy's matriculation at Dartmouth and, in turn, Billy lords it over Andy Phillips, a student at State. When Billy returns home, he has had a long distance call from the Scranton operator, suggesting that perhaps his relationship with Henny Cooper is more than casual. He also finds his father writing a Christmas poem to his mother. Mr. Warden has written such a poem every Christmas for twenty-six years, but Billy has learned of the practice only tonight. He goes to bed wondering if Henny's father has ever written a poem to her mother.

The reader is reminded of the opening chapter of *Appointment in Samarra*. That novel begins not with the desperately unhappy Julian English, but with one of his salesmen, Luther L. Fliegler. Julian's crumbling marriage stands in stark contrast to the stable, happy relationship of Luther and his wife, Irma. A critic has remarked that going to Hell in style is O'Hara's one and only theme. The reader wonders if Billy Warden will forsake the loving environment of his home and family for a world of house parties and skiing excursions among the rich—and concludes that probably he will.

GOOD SAMARITAN

First published: 1968
Type of work: Short story

After hosting a lunch, a woman is driven by a friend to the sheriff's station to get her husband, who has been missing for two days.

"Good Samaritan" first appeared in *The Saturday Evening Post* for November 30, 1968. As the story begins, Mary Wood is hosting twenty people for a buffet lunch. Her party may be associated with a golf tournament that is being held that weekend. The setting is not identified specifically, but it is an affluent community of suburban or summer homes in the present day. When the Reeds—George and Carrie—arrive, they ask where Willoughby Wood is. Mary confides to them that her husband has been missing for two days, but she tells the other guests that he has been suddenly called away to Washington. Since it is Sunday, Mary's story is unconvincing. Only one of her guests, however, is sufficiently interested in the whereabouts of Willoughby Wood to challenge her. After all the other guests have left, Agatha Surtees, a "notorious stayer," attempts to intrude herself into the private conversation Mary has been waiting to have with the Reeds. Mary practically expels Agatha with physical force, and the latter goes huffing off to her hired limousine. Agatha's age is given as fifty-two, Willoughby's as fifty-nine, so the reader infers that the other characters are in their fifties as well.

Mary receives a call from Lieutenant Hackenschmidt of the sheriff's patrol. Willoughby has been found wandering aimlessly in East Quantuck, unshaven, disheveled, and without money, watch, or identification. When picked up, he was not intoxicated—he appeared to have suffered some sort of nervous breakdown. The Reeds set out to take Mary to the substation where her husband is being held, but it is soon decided that George will drop Carrie off at their home. As George and Mary drive on alone, the reader is furnished with much exposition.

Willoughby Wood quit working about ten years earlier when he inherited his father's money, and the Woods' marriage has been in a precipitous decline ever since that time. Willoughby is estranged from their daughter, Marietta, because he insists that her husband and the father of her two children is a homosexual. Years before, George and Mary were romantically involved to some unspecified degree, and Mary proposes that they become lovers now. George is receptive to the idea, but he tells her that he already has a mistress in Detroit. Mary also confesses, for the first time, to a sexual indiscretion with another member of their set only a week before serving as a bridesmaid in his wedding.

At the sheriff's substation, Lieutenant Hackenschmidt is very deferential to George, whom he recognizes as the president of the hospital. Hackenschmidt believes that Willoughby has been "rolled," although he bears no bruises or other signs of having been attacked. Another possibility, suggested though never stated, is that the missing identification and personal possessions represent Willoughby's temporary rejection of his identity. Willoughby is released, but on the way home he becomes offensive toward his wife almost immediately. He is obsessed with the idea that Mary had an affair while visiting Marietta in California (in fact, she did), and he begins to accuse her again. George, the contemporary good samaritan, becomes exasperated and puts Willoughby out of the car a half a mile from home. Mary declines to join her husband on the side of the road, and the story ends. The narrative is carried forward almost exclusively by means of dialogue.

THE JOURNEY TO MOUNT CLEMENS

First published: 1974
Type of work: Short story

On a drive through the snow, squabbling erupts between two members of an electric company engineering crew.

"The Journey to Mount Clemens" was written in 1966 or earlier, but *The Saturday Evening Post* did not accept it for publication until 1974. It was reprinted that same year in *Good Samaritan and Other Stories.* "The Journey to Mount Clemens" is narrated in the first person and contains a number of autobiographical elements. The time period of the story is never stated outright, but all the details point to the 1920's. The narrator is eighteen years old, is Catholic, has just been expelled from prep school, and has recently acquired a job through the influence of his physician father. Despite not having an engineering degree, he is working with an engineering crew from an electric power corporation. All the preceding biographical details apply to the young John O'Hara as much as to his narrator. Further, the narrator is more or less an objective observer, not the protagonist.

The scene is eastern Pennsylvania in winter. The narrator's crew is making a tour of power plants, putting a valuation on the entire physical property of each. They have just finished their work at plant number 4 and are having their last supper at Dugan's Hotel before heading to their next assignment, a new substation at Mount Clemens. Carmichael, the chief of their party, has driven them relentlessly during the two weeks at number 4, and the men dislike him heartily. He wants to end the tour quickly so that he can return to the main office in New York, then join a dam-building project in the Sudan. No one in the crew dares to challenge the austere Carmichael except King, a man who has worked all over the world for the company and who once was Carmichael's superior. The narrator observes that the company has gotten everything out of King that he had to give and has shunted him off to finish his career in a minor job. The narrator speculates that Carmichael will eventually suffer the same fate. When the conversation turns to Carmichael's upcoming trip to North Africa, he and King have words.

It has been snowing heavily for two hours. The crew starts the hazardous twenty-eight-mile trip to Mount Clemens in two cars. Carmichael, King, and Thompson go first in the Paige; the narrator and Edmund follow in the Studebaker. The company has furnished drivers—Carney for the Paige and Ed Stone (Stoney) for the Studebaker. The journey is slow, uncomfortable, and dangerous. Either of the cars may stall, leaving its passengers stranded in below-zero weather, or, worse still, may plunge three or four hundred feet down into the timber. As in other O'Hara stories, the working-class characters (here, Carney and Stoney) are less interesting than their economic and social superiors but are also more stable, clear-headed, and dependable. The drivers handle their automobiles admirably in the snow, and, when the bickering between King and Carmichael erupts into fisticuffs, with the former giving the latter a bloody nose, "Sergeant" Carney is the man who restores order. He sends King back to ride the rest of the way in the Studebaker. Amid Edmunds' repeated assertions that King has finally ruined himself with the company, King wraps a blanket about himself and goes to sleep. When the little caravan finally reaches Mount Clemens, Edmunds tries to rouse King but discovers that he is dead.

Again, O'Hara has traced the decline of the once powerful (or rich or prominent) to its ultimate conclusion. King's regal name adds an ironic touch to the story.

Summary

John O'Hara has been likened to F. Scott Fitzgerald for interpreting the America of the 1930's through fiction as Fitzgerald had the America of the 1920's. He has been likened to Ernest Hemingway in the cleanness and spareness of his style. He has been likened to the great naturalistic writers because of his trapped, doomed characters. The implication of the several comparisons is that he reminds the reader of these writers but fails to reach their level of achievement. What can be said with certainty is that he was a master craftsman, a prolific creator of works which have demonstrably pleased the reading public for many years.

Bibliography

Carson, Edward Russell. *The Fiction of John O'Hara*. Pittsburgh: University of Pittsburgh Press, 1961.

Grebstein, Sheldon Norman. *John O'Hara*. New York: Twayne, 1966.

Kazin, Alfred. *On Native Grounds*. Garden City, N.Y.: Anchor Books, 1956.

Long, Robert E. *John O'Hara*. New York: Frederick Ungar, 1983.

Shannon, William V. *The American Irish*. New York: Macmillan, 1963.

Walcutt, Charles Child. *John O'Hara*. Minneapolis: University of Minnesota Press, 1969.

Patrick Adcock

MAGILL'S
SURVEY
OF
AMERICAN
LITERATURE

GLOSSARY

Absurdism: A philosophical attitude underlining the alienation that humans experience in what absurdists see as a universe devoid of meaning; literature of the absurd often purposely lacks logic, coherence, and intelligibility.

Act: One of the major divisions of a play or opera; the typical number of acts in a play ranges from one to four.

Agrarianism: A movement of the 1920's and 1930's in which John Crowe Ransom, Allen Tate, Robert Penn Warren, and other Southern writers championed the agrarian society of their region against the industrialized society of the North.

Allegory: A literary mode in which a second level of meaning (wherein characters, events, and settings represent abstractions) is encoded within the narrative.

Alliteration: The repetition of consonant sounds focused at the beginning of syllables, as in: "Large *m*annered *m*otions of his *m*ythy *m*ind."

Allusion: A reference to a historical event or to another literary text that adds dimension or meaning to a literary work.

Alter ego: A character's other self—sometimes a double, sometimes another side of the character's personality, sometimes a dear and constant companion.

Ambiguity: The capacity of language to sustain multiple meanings; ambiguity can add to both the richness and the concentration of literary language.

Angst: A pervasive feeling of anxiety and depression, often associated with the moral and spiritual uncertainties of the twentieth century.

Antagonist: The major character or force in opposition to the protagonist or hero.

Antihero: A fictional figure who tries to define himself and to establish his own codes, or a protagonist who simply lacks traditional heroic qualities.

Apostrophe: A poetic device in which the speaker addresses either someone not physically present or something not physically capable of hearing the words addressed.

Aside: A short passage generally spoken by one dramatic character in an undertone, or directed to the audience, so as not to be heard by the other characters onstage.

Assonance: A term for the association of words with identical vowel sounds but different consonants; "stars," "arms," and "park," for example, all contain identical "a" (and "ar") sounds.

Atmosphere: The general mood or tone of a work; it is often associated with setting, but can also be established by action or dialogue.

Autobiography: A form of nonfiction writing in which the author narrates events of his or her own life.

Avant-garde: A term describing works intended to expand the conventions of a genre through the experimental treatment of form and/or content.

Bardic voice: A passionate poetic voice modeled after that of a bard, or tribal poet/singer, who composed lyric or epic poetry to honor a chief or recite tribal history.

Bildungsroman: Sometimes called the "novel of education," the *Bildungsroman* focuses on the growth of a young protagonist who is learning about the world and finding his place in life; typical examples are James Joyce's *A Portrait of the Artist as a Young Man* (1916) and Thomas Wolfe's *Look Homeward, Angel* (1929).

Biography: Nonfiction that details the events of a particular individual's life.

Black humor: A general term of modern origin that refers to a form of "sick humor" that is intended to produce laughter out of the morbid and the taboo.

Blank verse: Lines of unrhymed iambic pentameter; it is a poetic form that allows much flexibility, and it has been used since the Elizabethan era.

Caesura: A pause or break in a poem; it is most commonly indicated by a punctuation mark such as a comma, dash, semicolon, or period.

Canon: A generally accepted list of literary works; it may refer to works by a single author or works in a genre. The literary canon often refers to the texts that are thought to belong on university reading lists.

Catharsis: A term from Aristotle's *Poetics* referring to the purgation of the spectators' emotions of pity and fear as aroused by the actions of the tragic hero.

Character: A personage appearing in any literary or dramatic work.

Chorus: An individual or group sometimes used in drama to comment on the action; the chorus was used extensively in classical Greek drama.

Classicism: A literary stance or value system consciously based on classical Greek and Roman literature; it generally denotes a cluster of values including formal discipline, restrained expression, reverence for tradition, and an objective rather than a subjective orientation.

Climax: The moment in a work of fiction or drama at which the action reaches its highest intensity and is resolved.

Comedy: A lighter form of drama that aims chiefly to amuse and that ends happily; comedic forms range from physical (slapstick) humor to subtle intellectual humor.

Comedy of manners: A type of drama which treats humorously, and often satirically, the behavior within an artificial, highly sophisticated society.

Comic relief: A humorous incident or scene in an otherwise serious or tragic work intended to release the reader's or audience's tensions through laughter without detracting from the serious material.

Conceit: One type of metaphor, the conceit is used for comparisons which are highly intellectualized. When T. S. Eliot, for example, says that winding streets are like a tedious argument of insidious intent, there is no clear connection between the two, so the reader must apply abstract logic to fill in the missing links.

Confessional poetry: Autobiographical poetry in which personal revelation provides a basis for the intellectual or theoretical study of moral, religious, or aesthetic concerns.

Conflation: The fusion of variant readings of a text into a composite whole.

Conflict: The struggle that develops as a result of the opposition between the protagonist and another person, the natural world, society, or some force within the self.

GLOSSARY

Connotation: A type of meaning that depends on the associative meanings of a word beyond its formal definition. (*See also* Denotation.)

Conventions: All those devices of stylization, compression, and selection that constitute the necessary differences between art and life.

Counterplot: A secondary action coincident with the major action of a fictional or dramatic work. The counterplot is generally a reflection on or variation of the main action and is strongly integrated into the whole of the work.

Couplet: Any two succeeding lines of poetry that rhyme.

Cubism: In literature, a style of poetry, such as that of E. E. Cummings and Archibald MacLeish, which first fragments an experience, then rearranges its elements into some new artistic entity.

Dactyl: A metrical foot in which a stressed syllable is followed by two unstressed syllables; an example of a dactyllic line is "After the pangs of a desperate lover."

Deconstruction: An extremely influential contemporary school of criticism based on the works of the French philosopher Jacques Derrida. Deconstruction treats literary works as unconscious reflections of the myths of Western culture; the primary myth is that there is a meaningful world which language signifies or represents. The Deconstructionist critic is often concerned with showing how a literary text tacitly subverts the very assumptions or myths on which it ostensibly rests.

Denotation: The explicit, formal definition of a word, exclusive of its implications and emotional associations. (*See also* Connotation.)

Denouement: Originally French, this word literally means "unknotting" or "untying" and is another term for the catastrophe or resolution of a dramatic action, the solution or clarification of a plot.

Detective story: In the so-called "classic" detective story, the focus is on a crime solved by a detective through interpretation of evidence and clever reasoning. Many modern practitioners of the genre, however, have deemphasized the puzzle-like qualities, stressing instead characterization, theme, and other elements of mainstream fiction.

Determinism: The belief that a person's actions are essentially determined by biological and environmental factors, with free will playing a negligible role. (*See also* Naturalism.)

Deus ex machina: Latin, meaning "god out of a machine." In the Greek theater, it referred to the use of a god lowered by means of a mechanism onto the stage to untangle the plot or save the hero. It has come to signify any artificial device for the easy resolution of dramatic difficulties.

Dialogue: Speech exchanged between characters or even, in a looser sense, the thoughts of a single character.

Dime novel: A type of inexpensive book very popular in the late nineteenth century that told a formulaic tale of war, adventure, or romance.

Domestic tragedy: A serious and usually realistic play with lower-class or middle-class characters and milieu, typically dealing with personal or domestic concerns.

Donnée: From the French verb meaning "to give," the term refers to the premise or the given set of circumstances from which the plot will proceed.

Drama: Any work designed to be represented on a stage by actors. More specifically, the term has come to signify a play of a serious nature and intent which may end either happily (comedy) or unhappily (tragedy).

Dramatic irony: A form of irony that most typically occurs when the spoken lines of a character are perceived by the audience to have a double meaning or when the audience knows more about a situation than the character knows.

Dramatic monologue: A poem in which the narrator addresses a silent persona whose presence greatly influences what the narrator tells the reader.

Dramatis personae: The characters in a play; often it refers to a printed list defining the characters and their relationships.

Dramaturgy: The composition of plays; the term is occasionally used to refer to the performance or acting of plays.

Dream vision: A poem presented as a dream in which the poet-dreamer envisions people and events that frequently have allegorical overtones.

Dualism: A theory that the universe is explicable in terms of two basic, conflicting entities, such as good and evil, mind and matter, or the physical and the spiritual.

Elegy: The elegy and pastoral elegy are distinguishable by their subject matter, not their form. The elegy is usually a long, rhymed, strophic poem whose subject is meditation upon death or a lamentable theme; the pastoral elegy uses a pastoral scene to sing of death or love.

Elizabethan: Of or referring to the reign of Queen Elizabeth I of England, lasting from 1558 to 1603, a period of important artistic achievements; William Shakespeare was an Elizabethan playwright.

End-stop: When a punctuated pause occurs at the end of a line of poetry, the line is said to be end-stopped.

Enjambment: When a line of poetry is not end-stopped and instead carries over to the next line, the line is said to be enjambed.

Epic: This term usually refers to a long narrative poem which presents the exploits of a central figure of high position; it is also used to designate a long novel that has the style or structure usually associated with an epic.

Epilogue: A closing section or speech at the end of a play or other literary work that makes some reflection on the preceding action.

Episodic narrative: A work that is held together primarily by a loose connection of self-sufficient episodes. Picaresque novels often have an episodic structure.

Epithalamion: A bridal song or poem, a genre deriving from the poets of antiquity.

Essay: A nonfiction work, usually short, that analyzes or interprets a particular subject or idea; it is often written from a personal point of view.

Existentialism: A philosophical and literary term for a group of attitudes surrounding the idea that existence precedes essence; according to Jean-Paul Sartre, "man is nothing else but what he makes himself." Existential literature exhibits an awareness of the absurdity of the universe and is preoccupied with the single ethical choice that determines the meaning of a person's existence.

Expressionism: A movement in the arts, especially in German painting, dominant in the decade following World War I; external reality is consciously distorted in order to portray the world as it is "viewed emotionally."

Fabulation: The act of lying to invent or tell a fable, sometimes used to designate the fable itself.

Fantastic: The fantastic has been defined as a genre that lies between the "uncanny" and the "marvelous." All three genres embody the familiar world but present an event that cannot be explained by the laws of the familiar world.

Farce: A play that evokes laughter through such low-comedy devices as physical humor, rough wit, and ridiculous and improbable situations and characters.

First person: A point of view in which the narrator of a story or poem addresses the reader directly, often using the pronoun "I," thereby allowing the reader direct access to the narrator's thoughts.

Flashback: A scene in a fictional or dramatic work depicting events that occurred at an earlier time.

Foot: A rhythmic unit of poetry consisting of two or three syllables grouped together; the most common foot in English is the iamb, composed of one unstressed syllable attached to one stressed syllable.

Foreshadowing: A device used to create suspense or dramatic irony by indicating through suggestion what will take place in the future.

Formalism: A school of literary criticism which particularly emphasizes the form of the work of art—that is, the type or genre to which it belongs.

Frame story: A story that provides a framework for another story (or stories) told within it.

Free verse: A poem that does not conform to such traditional conventions as meter or rhyme, and that does not establish any pattern within itself, is said to be a "free verse" poem.

Genre: A type or category of literature, such as tragedy, novel, memoir, poem, or essay; a genre has a particular set of conventions and expectations.

Genre fiction: Categories of popular fiction such as the mystery, the romance, and the Western; although the term can be used in a neutral sense, "genre fiction" is often used dismissively to refer to fiction in which the writer is bound by more or less rigid conventions.

Gothic novel: A form of fiction developed in the eighteenth century that focuses on horror and the supernatural.

Grotesque: Characterized by a breakup of the everyday world by mysterious forces, the form differs from fantasy in that the reader is not sure whether to react with humor or with horror.

Half rhyme. *See* Slant rhyme.

Hamartia. *See* Tragic flaw.

Harlem Renaissance: A flowering of black American writing, in all literary genres, in the 1930's and 1940's.

Hero/Heroine: The most important character in a drama or other literary work. Popularly, the term has come to refer to a character who possesses extraordinary prowess or virtue, but as a technical term it simply indicates the central participant in a dramatic action. (*See also* Protagonist.)

Heroic couplet: A pair of rhyming iambic pentameter lines traditionally used in epic poetry; a heroic couplet often serves as a self-contained witticism or pithy observation.

Historical novel: A novel that depicts past events, usually public in nature, and that features real as well as fictional people; the relationship between fiction and history in the form varies greatly depending on the author.

Hubris: Excessive pride, the characteristic in tragic heroes such as Oedipus, Doctor Faustus, and Macbeth that leads them to transgress moral codes or ignore warnings. (*See also* Tragic flaw.)

Humanism: A man-centered rather than god-centered view of the universe that usually stresses reason, restraint, and human values; in the Renaissance, humanism devoted itself to the revival of the life, thought, language, and literature of ancient Greece and Rome.

Hyperbole: The use of gross exaggeration for rhetorical effect, based upon the assumption that the reader will not respond to the exaggeration literally.

Iamb: The basic metric foot of the English language, the iamb associates one unstressed syllable with one stressed syllable. The line "So long as men can breathe or eyes can see" is composed of five iambs (a form called iambic pentameter).

Imagery: The simulation of sensory perception through figurative language; imagery can be controlled to create emotional or intellectual effects.

Imagism: A school of poetry prominent in Great Britain and North America between 1909 and 1918. The objectives of Imagism were accurate description, objective presentation, concentration and economy, new rhythms, freedom of choice in subject matter, and suggestion rather than explanation.

Interior monologue: The speech of a character designed to introduce the reader directly to the character's internal life; it differs from other monologues in that it attempts to reproduce thought before logical organization is imposed upon it.

Irony: An effect that occurs when a writer's or a character's real meaning is different from (and frequently opposite to) his or her apparent meaning. (*See also* Dramatic irony.)

Jazz Age: The 1920's, a period of prosperity, sweeping social change, frequent excess, and youthful rebellion, for which F. Scott Fitzgerald is the acknowledged spokesman.

Künstlerroman: An apprenticeship novel in which the protagonist, a young artist, faces the conflicts of growing up and coming to understand the purpose of his life and art.

Leitmotif: The repetition in a work of literature of a word, phrase, or image which serves to establish the tone or otherwise unify the piece.

Line: A rhythmical unit within a poem between the foot and the poem's larger structural units; the words or feet in a line are usually in a single row.

Lyric poetry: Poetry that is generally short, adaptable to metrical variation, and personal in theme; it may explore deeply personal feelings about life.

Magical realism: Imaginary or fantastic scenes and occurrences presented in a meticulously realistic style.

Melodrama: A play in which characters are clearly either virtuous or evil and are pitted against one another in suspenseful, often sensational situations.

Memoir: A piece of autobiographical writing which emphasizes important events in which the author has participated and prominent people whom the author has known.

Metafiction: Fiction that manifests a reflexive tendency and shows a consciousness of itself as an artificial creation; such terms as "postmodernist fiction," "antifiction," and "surfiction" also refer to this type of fiction.

Metaphor: A figure of speech in which two different things are identified with each other, as in the T. S. Eliot line, "The whole earth is our hospital"; the term is also widely used to identify many kinds of analogies.

Metaphysical poetry: A type of poetry that stresses the intellectual over the emotional; it is marked by irony, paradox, and striking comparisons of dissimilar things, the latter frequently being farfetched to the point of eccentricity.

Meter: The rhythmic pattern of language when it is formed into lines of poetry; when the rhythm of language is organized and regulated so as to affect the meaning and emotional response to the words, the rhythm has been refined into meter.

Mise-en-scène: The staging of a drama, including scenery, costumes, movable furniture (properties), and, by extension, the positions (blocking) and gestures of the actors.

Mock-heroic style: A form of burlesque in which a trivial subject is absurdly elevated through use of the meter, diction, and familiar devices of the epic poem.

Modernism: An international movement in the arts which began in the early years of the twentieth century; modernism in general was characterized by its international idiom, by its interest in cultures distant in space or time, by its emphasis on formal experimentation, and by its sense of dislocation and radical change.

Monologue: An extended speech by one character in a drama. If the character is alone onstage, unheard by other characters, the monologue is more specifically referred to as a soliloquy.

Musical comedy: A theatrical form mingling song, dance, and spoken dialogue which was developed in the United States in the twentieth century; it was derived from vaudeville and operetta.

Myth: Anonymous traditional stories dealing with basic human concepts and fundamentally opposing principles; a myth is often constructed as a story that tells of supposedly historical events.

Narrator: The character who recounts the story in a work of fiction.

Naturalism: The application of the principles of scientific determinism to fiction. Although it usually refers more to the choice of subject matter than to technical conventions, conventions associated with the movement center on the author's attempt to be precise and objective in description and detail, regardless of whether the events described are sordid or shocking. (*See also* Determinism.)

Neoclassicism: The type of classicism that dominated English literature from the Restoration to the late eighteenth century. Modeling itself on the literature of ancient Greece and Rome, neoclassicism exalts the virtues of proportion, unity, harmony, grace, decorum, taste, manners, and restraint; it values realism and reason.

New Criticism: A reaction against the "old criticism" that either saw art as self-expression, applied extrinsic criteria of morality and value, or gave credence to the professed intentions of the author. The New Criticism regards a work of art as an autonomous object, a self-contained universe. It holds that a close reading of literary texts will reveal their meanings and the complexities of their verbal texture as well as the oppositions and tensions balanced in the text.

New journalism: Writing that largely abandons the traditional objectivity of journalism in order to express the subjective response of the observer.

Nonfiction novel: A novel such as Truman Capote's *In Cold Blood*, which, though taking actual people and events as its subject matter, uses fictional techniques to develop the narrative.

Novel: A long fictional form that is generally concerned with individual characterization and with presenting a social world and a detailed environment.

Novel of ideas: A novel in which the characters, plot, and dialogue serve to develop some controlling idea or to present the clash of ideas.

Novel of manners: The classic example of the form might be the novels of Jane Austen, wherein the customs and conventions of a social group of a particular time and place are realistically, and often satirically, portrayed.

Novella, novelle, nouvelle, novelette: These terms usually refer to that form of fiction which is said to be longer than a short story and shorter than a novel; "novella" is the term usually used to refer to American works in this genre.

Ode: A lyric poem that treats a unified subject with elevated emotion and seriousness of purpose, usually ending with a satisfactory resolution.

Old Criticism: Criticism predating the New Criticism and bringing extrinsic criteria to bear on the analysis of literature as authorial self-expression (Romanticism), critical self-expression (Impressionism), or work that is dependent upon moral or ethical absolutes (new humanism).

Omniscient narration: A godlike point of view from which the narrator sees all and knows everything there is to know about the story and its characters.

One-act play: A short, unified dramatic work, the one-act play is usually quite limited in number of characters and scene changes; the action often revolves around a single incident or event.

Opera: A complex combination of various art forms, opera is a form of dramatic entertainment consisting of a play set to music.

Original Sin: A concept of the innate depravity of man's nature resulting from Adam's sin and fall from grace.

Paradox: A statement that initially seems to be illogical or self-contradictory yet eventually proves to embody a complex truth.

Parataxis: The placing of clauses or phrases in a series without the use of coordinating or subordinating terms.

Pathos: The quality in a character that evokes pity or sorrow from the observer.

Pentameter: A line of poetry consisting of five recognizable rhythmic units called feet.

Picaresque novel: A form of fiction that involves a central rogue figure, or picaro, who usually tells his own story. The plot structure is normally episodic, and the episodes usually focus on how the picaro lives by his wits.

Plot: The sequence of the occurrence of events in a dramatic action. A plot may be unified around a single action, but it may also consist of a series of disconnected incidents; it is then referred to as "episodic."

Poem: A unified composition that uses the rhythms and sounds of language, as well as devices such as metaphor, to communicate emotions and experiences to the reader or hearer.

Point of view: The perspective from which a story is presented to the reader. In simplest terms, it refers to whether narration is first-person (directly addressed to the reader as if told by one involved in the narrative) or third-person (usually a more objective, distanced perspective).

Postmodernism: The term is loosely applied to various artistic movements which have followed so-called high modernism, represented by such giants as James Joyce and Pablo Picasso. The term is frequently applied to the works of writers (such as Thomas Pynchon and John Barth) who exhibit a self-conscious awareness of their predecessors as well as a reflexive treatment of fictional form.

Prose poem: A type of poem, usually less than a page in length, that appears on the page like prose; there is great stylistic and thematic variety within the genre.

Protagonist: Originally, in the Greek drama, the "first actor," who played the leading role. The term has come to signify the most important character in a drama or story. It is not unusual for there to be more than one protagonist in a work. (*See also* Hero/Heroine.)

Psychoanalytic theory: A tremendously influential theory of the unconscious developed by Sigmund Freud, it divides the human psyche into three components— the id, the ego, and the superego. In this theory, the psyche represses instinctual and sexual desires, and channels (sublimates) those desires into socially acceptable behavior.

Psychological novel: A form of fiction in which character, especially the inner life of characters, is the primary focus. The form has characterized much of the work of James Joyce, Virginia Woolf, and William Faulkner.

Psychological realism: A type of realism that tries to reproduce the complex psychological motivations behind human behavior; writers in the late nineteenth and early twentieth centuries were particularly influenced by Sigmund Freud's theories. (*See also* Psychoanalytic theory.)

Pun: A pun occurs when words which have similar pronunciations have entirely different meanings; a pun can establish a connection between two meanings or contexts that the reader would not ordinarily make. The result may be a striking connection or simply a humorously accidental connection.

Quatrain: Any four-line stanza is a quatrain; other than the couplet, the quatrain is the most common type of stanza.

Rationalism: A system of thought which seeks truth through the exercise of reason rather than by means of emotional response or revelation.

Realism: A literary technique in which the primary convention is to render an illusion of fidelity to external reality. Realism is often identified as the primary method of the novel form; the realist movement in the late nineteenth century coincided with the full development of the novel form.

Regional novel: Any novel in which the character of a given geographical region plays a decisive role; the Southern United States, for example, has fostered a strong regional tradition.

Representationalism: An approach to drama that seeks to create the illusion of reality onstage through realistic characters, situations, and settings.

Revue: A theatrical production, typically consisting of sketches, song, and dance, which often comments satirically upon personalities and events of the day; generally there is no plot involved.

Rhyme: A full rhyme comprises two or more words that have the same vowel sound and that end with the same consonant sound: "Hat" and "cat" is a full rhyme, as is "laughter" and "after." Rhyme is also used more broadly as a term for any correspondence in sound between syllables in poetry. (*See also* Slant rhyme.)

Rhyme scheme: Poems which establish a pattern of rhyme have a "rhyme scheme," designated by lowercase letters; the rhyme scheme of ottava rima, for example, is abababcc. Traditional stanza forms are categorized by their rhyme scheme and base meter.

GLOSSARY

Roman à clef: A fiction wherein actual persons, often celebrities of some sort, are thinly disguised.

Romance: The romance usually differs from the novel form in that the focus is on symbolic events and representational characters rather than on "as-if-real" characters and events. Character is often highly stylized, serving as a function of the plot.

Romantic comedy: A play in which love is the central motive of the dramatic action. The term often refers to plays of the Elizabethan period, such as William Shakespeare's *As You Like It* and *A Midsummer Night's Dream*, but it has also been applied to any modern work that contains similar features.

Romanticism: A widespread cultural movement in the late-eighteenth and early-nineteenth centuries, Romanticism is frequently contrasted with classicism. The term generally suggests primitivism, an interest in folklore, a reverence for nature, a fascination with the demoniac and the macabre, and an assertion of the preeminence of the imagination.

Satire: Satire employs the comedic devices of wit, irony, and exaggeration to expose and condemn human folly, vice, and stupidity.

Scene: In drama, a division of action within an act (some plays are divided only into scenes instead of acts). Sometimes scene division indicates a change of setting or locale; sometimes it simply indicates the entrances and exits of characters.

Science fiction: Fiction in which real or imagined scientific developments or certain givens (such as physical laws, psychological principles, or social conditions) form the basis of an imaginative projection, frequently into the future.

Sentimental novel: A form of fiction popular in the eighteenth century in which emotionalism and optimism are the primary characteristics. The best-known examples are Samuel Richardson's *Pamela* (1740-1741) and Oliver Goldsmith's *The Vicar of Wakefield* (1766).

Sentimentalism: A term used to describe any emotional response that is excessive and disproportionate to its impetus or occasion. It also refers to the eighteenth century idea that human beings are essentially benevolent, devoid of Original Sin and basic depravity.

Setting: The time and place in which the action of a literary work happens. The term also applies to the physical elements of a theatrical production, such as scenery and properties.

Short story: A concise work of fiction, shorter than a novella, that is usually more concerned with mood, effect, or a single event than with plot or extensive characterization.

Simile: Loosely defined, a simile is a type of metaphor which signals a comparison by the use of the words "like" or "as." Shakespeare's line, "My mistress' eyes are nothing like the sun," establishes a comparison between the woman's eyes and the sun, and is a simile.

Slant rhyme: A slant rhyme, or half rhyme, occurs when words with identical consonants but different vowel sounds are associated; "fall" and "well," and "table" and "bauble" are slant rhymes.

Slapstick: Low comedy in which physical action (such as a kick in the rear, tripping, and knocking over people or objects) evokes laughter.

Social realism: A type of realism in which the social and economic conditions in which characters live figure prominently in their situations, actions, and outlooks.

Soliloquy: An extended speech delivered by a character alone onstage, unheard by other characters. Soliloquy is a form of monologue, and it typically reveals the intimate thoughts and emotions of the speaker.

Sonnet: A traditional poetic form that is almost always composed of fourteen lines of rhymed iambic pentameter; a turning point usually divides the poem into two parts, with the first part presenting a situation and the second part reflecting on it.

Southern Gothic: A term applied to the scenes of decay, incest, madness, and violence often found in the fiction of William Faulkner, Erskine Caldwell, and other Southern writers.

Speaker: The voice which speaks the words of a poem—sometimes a fictional character in an invented situation, sometimes the author speaking directly to the reader, sometimes the author speaking from behind the disguise of a persona.

Stanza: When lines of poetry are meant to be taken as a unit, and the unit recurs throughout the poem, that unit is called a stanza; a four-line unit is one common stanza.

Stream of consciousness: The depiction of the thought processes of a character, insofar as this is possible, without any mediating structures. The metaphor of consciousness as a "stream" suggests a rush of thoughts and images governed by free association rather than by strictly rational development; the term is often used loosely as a synonym for interior monologue.

Stress: When more emphasis is placed on one syllable in a line of poetry than on another syllable, that syllable is said to be stressed.

Subplot: A secondary action coincident with the main action of a fictional or dramatic work. A subplot may be a reflection upon the main action, but it may also be largely unrelated. (*See also* Counterplot.)

Surrealism: An approach to literature and art that startlingly combines seemingly incompatible elements; surrealist writing usually has a bizarre, dreamlike, or nightmarish quality.

Symbol: A literary symbol is an image that stands for something else; it may evoke a cluster of meanings rather than a single specific meaning.

Symbolism: A literary movement encompassing the work of a group of French writers in the latter half of the nineteenth century, a group that included Charles Baudelaire, Stéphane Mallarmé, and Paul Verlaine. According to Symbolism, there is a mystical correspondence between the natural and spiritual worlds.

Syntax: A linguistic term used to describe the study of the ways in which words are arranged sequentially to produce grammatical units such as phrases, clauses, and sentences.

Tableau: A silent, stationary grouping of performers in a theatrical performance.

Terza rima: A rhyming three-line stanza form in which the middle line of one stanza rhymes with the first line of the following stanza.

Tetrameter: A line of poetry consisting of four recognizable rhythmic units called feet.

Theater of the absurd: The general name given to plays that express a basic belief that life is illogical, irrational, formless, and contradictory and that man is without meaning or purpose. This perspective often leads to the abandonment of traditional theatrical forms and coherent dialogue.

Theme: Loosely defined as what a literary work means. The theme of W. B. Yeats's poem "Sailing to Byzantium," for example, might be interpreted as the failure of man's attempt to isolate himself within the world of art.

Thespian: Another term for an actor; also, of or relating to the theater. The word derives from Thespis, by tradition the first actor of the Greek theater.

Third person: Third-person narration is related from a point of view more distant from the story than first-person narration; the narrator is not an identifiable "I" persona. A third-person point of view may be limited or omniscient ("all-knowing").

Three unities. *See* Unities.

Tone: Tone usually refers to the dominant mood of a work. (*See also* Atmosphere.)

Tragedy: A form of drama that is serious in action and intent and that involves disastrous events and death; classical Greek drama observed specific guidelines for tragedy, but the term is now sometimes applied to a range of dramatic or fictional situations.

Tragic flaw: Also known as hamartia, it is the weakness or error in judgment in a tragic hero or protagonist that causes the character's downfall; it may proceed from ignorance or a moral fault. Excessive pride (hubris) is one traditional tragic flaw.

Travel literature: Writing which emphasizes the author's subjective response to places visited, especially faraway, exotic, and culturally different locales.

Trimeter: A line of poetry consisting of three recognizable rhythmic units called feet.

Trochee: One of the most common feet in English poetry, the trochee associates one stressed syllable with one unstressed syllable, as in the line, "Double, double, toil and trouble."

Unities: A set of rules for proper dramatic construction formulated by European Renaissance drama critics and derived from classical Greek concepts: A play should have no scenes or subplots irrelevant to the central action, should not cover a period of more than twenty-four hours, and should not occur in more than one place.

Verisimilitude: The attempt to have the readers of a literary work believe that it conforms to reality rather than to its own laws.

Verse: A generic term for poetry; verse also refers in a narrower sense to poetry that is humorous or merely superficial, as in "greeting-card verse."

Verse paragraph: A division within a poem that is created by logic or syntax rather than by form; verse paragraphs are important for determining the movement of a poem and the logical association between ideas.

Victorian novel: Although the Victorian period extended from 1837 to 1901, the term "Victorian novel" does not include works from the later decades of Queen Victoria's reign. The term loosely refers to the sprawling works of novelists such as Charles Dickens and William Makepeace Thackeray, which are characterized by a broad social canvas.

Villanelle: The villanelle is a French verse form assimilated by English prosody. It is usually composed of nineteen lines divided into five tercets and a quatrain, rhyming aba, bba, aba, aba, abaa.

Well-made play: A type of play constructed according to a nineteenth century French formula; the plot often revolves around a secret (revealed at the end) known only to some of the characters. Misunderstanding, suspense, and coincidence are among the devices used.

Western novel: The Western novel is defined by a relatively predictable combination of conventions and recurring themes. These predictable elements, familiar from television and film Westerns, differentiate the Western from historical novels and other works which may be set in the Old West.

Worldview: Frequently rendered as the German *weltanschauung*, it is a comprehensive set of beliefs or assumptions by means of which one interprets what goes on in the world.

LIST OF AUTHORS

LIST OF AUTHORS